Accountancy

Fifth Edition

Wm. Harrison
FCIB, Cert.Ed.

NORTHWICK PUBLISHERS

Published by
Northwick Publishers,
14 Bevere Close, Worcester, WR3 7QH.
Telephone (0905) 56876/56529

Printed and bound by Ebenezer Baylis & Son Ltd.,
The Trinity Press, London Road, Worcester, WR5 2JH.

British Library Cataloguing in Publication Data
Harrison, William
  Accountancy
  5th ed.
  1. Great Britain. Banking. Accounting
  I. Title II. Series
  657.833300941

ISBN 0-907135-59-5

PERSONAL COURSE FOR BANKERS

ACCOUNTANCY
Fifth Edition

Wm. Harrison, F.C.I.B., Cert.Ed.

Foreword

This text has been written *specifically* for the student who is preparing to take The Chartered Institute of Bankers examination in Accountancy at the Associateship (Stage 2) level and no consideration has been given to the requirements of any other examining body. However, the content will be of benefit to any other students who are studying the subject of Accountancy for various examining bodies.

I have made the task of study as easy as possible by presenting the topics in the simplest possible manner and my main aim throughout the book has been to enable the student to *understand* what is happening rather than to attempt to memorise procedures. This is based on my firm belief that if the student *understands*, he or she will not forget.

The banking student will find that the book covers all of the requirements of the Chartered Institute of Bankers examination with each lesson providing appropriate exercises and full model answers incorporating explanatory notes on the more tricky parts of the answer. Extra exercises (marked 'EX') accompany each lesson and full model answers to these, with explanatory notes, are in a separate 'Extra Solutions' booklet.

With the exception of a few early exercises, all questions have been taken from past Bankers' examination papers.

Some of the early lessons in this book are intended to revise and consolidate important concepts, the understanding of which I consider to be critical in preparation for this examination. For example, a full understanding of what actually happens and why it happens when shares are redeemed (dealt with in the early lessons) provides a very sound 'platform' from which the student can jump into more advanced topics with confidence and understanding. Do not therefore be tempted to skip over the first lessons in this book - they are there for very good reasons!

Most students will have heard of 'The Wilkinson Report ' which drafted recommendations of change over the whole structure of Stage Two Banking Diploma examinations. The subsequent approved changes come into effect from the May 1991 examinations.

Fortunately, for the accountancy student the changes are not too severe - the requirements in certain areas have been reduced but there is now an additional requirement for the student to answer a compulsory question on the interpretation of accounts. This requirement is not really new as the syllabus many years ago had an identical requirement for which earlier editions of this book catered. It is *not* a difficult area of study, which most students initially believe it to be, *provided* that the rest of the syllabus has been studied conscientiously. That is why this topic of interpretation is dealt with last! Have no fears!

You are in possession of the book which has produced 'success slips' to many thousands students throughout the world over the past twelve years - use it well and you will join them!

This book was first published in 1978 and was the first Accountancy book written specifically for banking students - it has remained the most popular and effective since then.

Grateful acknowledgement is due to The Chartered Institute of Bankers for kindly granting permission to use past examination questions in this book.

I should like to record my gratitude to David Cox of Worcester Technical College and Bernard Kay of Oldham College of Technology for their help and advice in the writing of this new edition.

Also to Rosemary and Bill Slyfield for their skilful typesetting of the new text in record time.

William Harrison, F.C.I.B., Cert. Ed

July 1990

CONTENTS

Statements of Standard Accounting Practice (S.S.A.P.s) appear at the end of the Lessons, unless their content is incorporated within the relevant Lesson.

LESSON 1

INTRODUCTION AND REVISION OF PRINCIPLES

Introduction

In preparing for your Associateship Accountancy examination you are building up your knowledge and abilities on the foundation laid in your Stage 1 studies. If this foundation is weak you could have problems and I must stress the importance of thoroughly revising some of the basic principles of accounting before moving on to specific topics in the Associateship syllabus. Many questions in the examination paper can be answered easily by applying very basic principles, so do not be tempted to skip over this topic of revision.

If you feel that you *are* weak in basic accounts and therefore at a disadvantage to start with, you will find my 'Foundation Series - Financial Accounting' book to be a very useful revision aid (obtainable from Northwick Publishers).

Revision of Principles

First of all let us consider the balance sheet of a business. What is it? It is nothing more than a statement (NOT an account) showing a list of that business's assets - i.e. things *owned* with a value - and a list of its liabilities - i.e. things *owed* by the business. Obviously, the total value of the assets must be the same as the total liabilities - i.e. the balance sheet must balance - because *someone* has provided those assets and therefore the business owes that amount to that (those) persons. In a well managed business the bulk of the assets will have been provided by the owners of the business (i.e. the trader, the partners or the shareholders) and therefore the main liability of the business will be to the owners - i.e. 'Capital'.

Let us look at a simple example and build it up so as to bring in some more principles:

Day 1

The owners of a new business, which we will call 'Enterprise Ltd', start it off by providing £10,000 cash, part of which is immediately used to buy machinery, £8,000, and office furniture, £800. At this point Enterprise's balance sheet will look like this :-

Balance Sheet of Enterprise Ltd as at Day 1

	£		£
Liabilities		Assets	
Capital	10,000	Machinery	8,000
		Office Furniture	800
		Cash	1,200
	10,000		10,000

NOTE :   Enterprise Ltd owns £10,000 of assets and owes £10,000 to the owners, who have provided the money for all of the assets.

1

Day 2

Stock is purchased on *credit*, £2,000, and a long-term loan is obtained from Financiers Ltd, £3,000.

Balance Sheet as at Day 2

Liabilities	£	Assets	£
Capital	10,000	Machinery	8,000
Financiers Ltd	3,000	Office furniture	800
Trade Creditors	2,000	Stock	2,000
		Cash (increased by loan)	4,200
	15,000		15,000

NOTE: Enterprise Ltd now owns £15,000 of assets and owes various amounts to the various people who have provided the money for the assets. The amount owed to the owners (capital) has not changed because they have not contributed any more money to the business *themselves*.

Day 3

£1,500 of stock is sold *on credit* for £2,000 (i.e. £500 profit is made *by the business*).

Balance Sheet as at Day 3

Liabilities	£	Assets	£
Capital	10,000	Machinery	8,000
Plus Profit	500	Office Furniture	800
	10,500	Stock	500
Financiers Ltd	3,000	Debtors	2,000
Trade Creditors	2,000	Cash	4,200
	15,500		15,500

NOTE: The profit of £500, made by the business has increased the value of the assets owned by the business, but as this profit belongs to the owners the liability of the business to the owners is correspondingly increased.

Most important, you must observe that *all* the liabilities listed are represented by *something* on the assets side of the balance sheet - e.g. the £10,500 is represented (or backed up) by:

Machinery (all of it)	£8,000
Office furniture (all of it)	800
Debtors (part of them)	500
Cash (part of it)	1,200
	£10,500

The £3,000 is represented by :

Cash (part of it)	£3,000

The £2,000 is represented by :

Debtors (part of them)	£1,500
Stock (all of it)	500
	£2,000

Such little exercises as these are not necessary, nor are they practicable in a business dealing with many transactions, but I have shown them to illustrate the fact that *any item* on the liabilities side of a balance sheet will *always* be represented by some asset, or a combination of assets, but it will never be so easy to pinpoint the exact assets which represent that liability, as I have done, nor will it be necessary. The really important things to note with regard to the assets are :

and

(a)   the total,

(b)   the amount of assets which are easily convertible into cash, i.e. liquid assets such as stock, debtors and bank, etc.

Why, we will see in a moment.

Day 4

Purchased £5,000 stock on credit and sold this for £8,000 cash.
Also purchased premises for £12,000 cash.

Balance Sheet as at Day 4

Liabilities	£	Assets	£
Capital	10,000	Premises	12,000
Plus profit made	500	Machinery	8,000
Plus new profits	3,000	Office furniture	800
	13,500		20,800
Financiers Ltd.	3,000	Stock	500
Trade Creditors	7,000	Debtors	2,000
Cash			200
	23,500		23,500

NOTE :   New profits earned by the business, increase what is owing to the owners. Now, it is obvious that as profits are made, either cash or debtors must be increased by the amount of profit made, and it should therefore be possible for the owners to draw their profits from the business at any time - in other words there should always be enough cash (or debtors who will soon be converted to cash) to pay out profits to the owners. In this example, the £3,000 profit *did* increase cash but it was immediately withdrawn to purchase the premises. There is not now sufficient cash (or debtors) to pay the owners their full entitlement of profits (i.e. £3,500 to date). *The profits shown on the liabilities side of the balance sheet are represented by assets but these are not ready realizable assets.* They are 'tied up' in the business.

Let us assume that the owners agree to leave *all* of the profits in the business. As we have already seen, they have not much option in the absence of overdraft facilities at the company's bank. The profit item on the liabilities side is now regarded as a RESERVE - i.e. undistributed profits. The basic idea of a reserve is that some profits are left in the business every year (i.e. not distributed to the owners) so creating an ever-growing reserve of profits to meet some future need. For example, if the owners agree to leave £1,000 of profits in the business every year for 10 years, then at the end of this period the business will be holding in *reserve* £10,000 of undistributed profits. We know that any profit increases cash/debtors and therefore we would expect this business to now have £10,000 more cash/debtors than it would have had if no reserve had been created. This accumulated money could now be used to pay the owners an extra big dividend (i.e. distribute past undistributed profits) or to pay off debenture holders (people who have lent money to the business on a long term basis) or to pay off Redeemable Shares or to pay taxes, etc.

If, however, some of the extra cash that has been made over the years has been used to buy any fixed assets then our £10,000 in reserve will not be represented wholly by cash - part of the reserve will be 'tied up'.

Look at this balance sheet :

	£		£
Capital	10,000	Fixed assets	39,000
Reserve (i.e. profits not distributed)	30,000	Current assets	4,000
Current liabilities	3,000		
	43,000		43,000

NOTE :   What a build-up of profits! The only trouble is that most of these have been tied up in fixed assets as soon as they have been earned and the company is desperately short of current assets (i.e. assets which will soon turn into cash, such as stock and debtors). This kind of business will soon be knocking on the bank door for an overdraft. Also, what hope have the owners got of receiving, in cash, some of their past retained profits - unless of course the fixed assets are sold!

Let us look back at our balance sheets covering days 1 - 4 . If a business prepared balance sheets daily, like this, there would be no need to keep ledger accounts. But would this be practicable? Even the smallest business would have so many transactions each day that it would be an impossible task to work out at the end of a day, which assets or liabilities had increased or decreased, and by how much, and it would be even harder to work out 'today's ' profit! We keep ledger accounts therefore, so that we can record *movements* in the value of an asset or liability, and provided these are kept up to date we can draw up a balance sheet at any time we want to (say at the year end) by looking at the balances on the respective accounts. Convention is that we record an *asset as a debit balance*, and a liability therefore, as a credit balance. If we want to record an increase in an asset (e.g. cash, or furniture received) we must therefore *debit* the respective asset account in order to increase the debit balance which represents the asset. From this, the following should be obvious :

Entry on account	
Decrease in an asset	credit
Increase in a liability	credit
Decrease in a liability	debit

The only thing we need to remember therefore is that an ASSET is a DEBIT BALANCE. In preparing our balance sheet we now go along to the ledger, and any account which has finished up with a debit balance is shown as an asset - the accounts with credit balances are shown as liabilities.

How do we keep a record of profits? We only need to work out our profit at, say, the year end - in which case we must keep records (by using ledger accounts) during the year, of the following:

> purchases as they are made,
> sales as they are made,
> overhead expenses as they are incurred,
> miscellaneous gains as they are made.

All we now have to do is to look at these accounts at the year end, and we have all the information we need to work out the profit for the year. These accounts are closed off by transferring the balances to the Trading or Profit and Loss Accounts. Note - any *part* of these balances which does not relate to the year in question (e.g. rates prepaid, owing, etc.) is not transferred to the Profit and Loss Account but is carried down as a balance on the account and shown on the balance sheet.

4

The final accounts may look like this :

1st Year of Trading
Trading and Profit and Loss Account for year -

	£		£
Opening Stock	5,000	Sales	60,000
Purchases	30,000		
	35,000		
Less Closing Stock	3,000		
	32,000		
Gross Profit	28,000		
	60,000		60,000
Various expenses		Gross Profit	28,000
(shown separately)	16,000		
Depreciation	2,000		
Net profit	10,000		
	28,000		28,000

The business has made £10,000 profit and to show what happens to this profit we must add another section to the Profit and Loss Account which is the Profit and Loss 'Appropriation Account' (the account which shows how the profit is appropriated).

The net profit is carried down to this section (i.e.. to the credit side) and how it is used up is shown on the debit side, e.g. :

Appropriation Account

	£		£
		Balance B/d	7,000
Dividends proposed	6,000	Net profit b/fwd	10,000
Balance c/d	11,000		
	17,000		17,000
		Balance b/d	11,000

NOTE :   The double entry to the debit for 'proposed dividend' will be completed by a credit to a 'dividends proposed account' and this credit balance will have to be shown on the balance sheet as a current liability. This account will remain open until the dividend is actually paid (when cash is credited and the dividend proposed account is debited so closing the account).

In the above example only £6,000 of the available £10,000 of profit has been used up and the unused (retained) £4,000 of profits has been added to the retained (unused) profits of previous years (the £7,000 accumulation brought down from the previous year). The total, £11,000 will be left on Appropriation Account as a balance, and as it is a *credit* balance it will appear as a liability on the balance sheet (i.e. it is *owed* by the company to its shareholders). It is of course, a reserve.

Usually, companies like to have different reserve accounts for different purposes, so instead of showing £11,000 on *one* reserve account, we can appropriate this over several reserve accounts, e.g. :

Appropriation Account

	£		£
		Balance b/d	7,000
Dividends proposed	6,000	Net profit b/d	10,000
Transfer to General Reserve	2,000		
Transfer to Reserve for			
Redemption of Debentures	1,000		
Balance c/d	8,000		
	17,000		17,000
		Balance b.d	8,000

We now have the £11,000 reserve spread over three different reserves :

(i)	Credit balance on General Reserve	£2,000
(ii)	Credit balance on Reserve for Debentures	1,000
(iii)	Credit balance on Profit and Loss account	8,000
		£11,000

When we are preparing *next* year's balance sheet we must remember that there are already balances on these accounts and that we are simply *adding* to them.

The above example of a Profit and Loss Account could be shown in vertical format which is how companies normally show them, viz :

Trading and Profit and Loss Account for year 19-

	£	£
Sales (Turnover)		60,000
Less Stock at say, 1 Jan	5,000	
Purchases	30,000	
Stock at, say, 31 Dec.	(3,000)	
Cost of Goods Sold		32,000
Gross Profit		28,000
Less Various expenses	16,000	
Depreciation	2,000	18,000
Net Profit		10,000
Add Balance of retained profits at 1 Jan		7,000
		17,000
Less Dividends Proposed	6,000	
Transfer to General Reserve	2,000	
Transfer to Debenture		
Redemption Reserve	1,000	9,000
Retained profits at 31 December		8,000

All the reserves we have looked at so far are reserves of *trading* profits which the shareholders have agreed to leave in the business over the years. There is no reason why these reserves should not be drawn on in some future year in order to pay a dividend - unless of course as we saw earlier, the cash from profits has been tied up in fixed assets. Such reserves as these are called REVENUE RESERVES. Another kind of reserve is a CAPITAL RESERVE and this is one which represents retained *non-trading* profits - e.g. a profit on the sale of a fixed asset, or on the sale of shares at a premium, (i.e. share premium reserve) or profit which appears as a result of revaluing premises in the books, or any other kind of profit which is not earned through *normal trading*.

Please note at this point that the Companies Act 1985 defines distributable profits as 'accumulated realised profits, not yet distributed. e.g. P & L Account/General Reserve balances), MINUS realised losses'.

Before leaving Reserves, I must say how very important it is for you to appreciate just what they are. They are *Retained Profits* - profits being left in the company - but they *do* belong to the owners (the shareholders) and that is why they are shown on the balance sheet as a liability of the company to the shareholders. As they represent profits earned by the company there must be a corresponding asset somewhere which has increased in value as a result of the profit. In the case of a revaluation of premises, the asset 'Premises' has increased in value and this is matched by a Revaluation Reserve (a Capital Reserve) on the other side of the balance sheet. In the case of trading profits the debtors or cash have increased and this is matched by a corresponding increase in the Profit and Loss account balance (a Revenue Reserve) on the other side of the balance sheet - any payment of dividends will of course reduce cash *and* the balance on the Profit and Loss account - trading profits left in the business will be represented by cash (or debtors for the time being) and a corresponding increased Profit and Loss account balance - but bear in mind that this cash may then be used to buy fixed assets in which case the increased Profit and Loss account balance is then represented by, not cash, but a fixed asset. *All* reserves have a corresponding asset *somewhere*, but this asset is not necessarily in liquid form. Do not forget this!

Before leaving this topic I must draw attention to a most important item, and that is 'depreciation'. Turn back to the Trading and Profit and Loss Account we have just been examining. We know that profit increased cash, or at least current assets which are all 'near cash'. How much has cash, etc. been increased during the year by profits being earned? - £10,000. Let us analyse this. Cash was increased by the amount of gross profit, £28,000 but then £16,000 of it had to be *paid out* to meet expenses like rates, wages, light and heat, etc., etc. so that left only £12,000 as clear profit. Depreciation of £2,000 *did not involve any cash going out*, so cash has been increased, through profits, by £12,000.

Depreciation is nothing more than a book-keeping entry - i.e. debit P & L a/c and credit Provision for Depreciation a/c - or a 'non-cash debit'. Why show it at all? Because the depreciation entry in the P & L a/c has the effect of reducing the *figure* of net profit (in our example from £12,000 to £10,000) and therefore the amount that is likely to be drawn out in cash by the owners. Cash is therefore conserved in the business which might otherwise have left the business. For example, let us assume that the shareholders always draw by way of dividends all of the net profit shown in the Profit and Loss account, viz:

	(a) £	(b) £		(a) £	(b) £
Various expenses	3,000	3,000	Gross profit	8,000	8,000
Depreciation		1,000			
Net profit c/d	5,000	4,000			
	8,000	8,000		8,000	8,000

In example (a) the shareholders would take £5,000 cash from the business.

In example (b) they would take only £4,000 cash, and the business has therefore retained £1,000 cash which, but for the book-keeping entry for depreciation, would have left the business.

If this is done every year for the next ten years the business will have saved a total of £10,000 cash which can then be used to replace the worn-out asset, if we ignore inflation. The chances are, however, that the cash saved has been used for some other purpose in the meantime, and so at the end of the life of the fixed asset concerned there may not be ready cash available to replace the asset. If the company is concerned about keeping the cash

7

saved each year in a liquid form then it could invest the £1,000 each year before anyone has a chance to spend it, so that when the time comes to replace the worn-out asset, it is only necessary to realise the investment. When a company does this it is setting up what is called a *Sinking Fund* and this is advisable when the company's main concern is to accumulate, over the years, sufficient cash to *replace* the asset. It is probable however, that the company's concern is simply to *recoup* the cash originally paid out for the asset in which case it will not be anxious to retain each year's 'savings' in a liquid form.

Therefore, whenever you are considering how much cash has been created through the making of profits do not just look at the net profit figure - add to this the amount of any non-cash debits which may appear in the P & L a/c such as depreciation - e.g. in example (b) above, add back the £1,000 figure for depreciation to the net profit figure of £4,000, making £5,000 in all. An understanding of this is very important.

Finally, let me draw your attention to the following example showing the general set-out of a company balance sheet, in conventional form :

Balance Sheet of XYZ Co. Ltd as at 31 December, 19-

	£	£		£	£	£
1) Authorised Share Capital			Fixed Assets (5)			
10,000 6^1/$_2$% Preference Shares			Freehold Premises at cost	18,000		
of £1 each		10,000	Less Provision for deprn.	2,000		16,000
60,000 Ordinary Shares of						
£1 each		60,000	Machinery at cost 18,000			
		70,000	Less provision for deprn.	1,000		17,000
Issued Share Capital			Fixtures, etc. at cost	8,000		
4,000 6^1/$_2$% Preference Shares of			Less provision for deprn.	500		7,500
£1 each (fully paid)		4,000	Trade investments at cost			5,000
2) 40,000 Ordinary Shares of						45,500
£1 each (75p called)		30,000	Current Assets			
		34,000	Stock		3,200	
3) Capital Reserves		5,000	Debtors	2,000		
4) Revenue Reserves		3,000	Less provision for			
		42,000	bad debts	900	1,100	
			Cash at Bank		1,500	
			Cash in Hand		300	6,100
Long Term Liabilities						
8% Debenture Stock		5,000				
Current Liabilities						
Trade Creditors	1,600					
Proposed dividend	3,000	4,600				
		51,600				51,600

(1)   Also referred to as 'Nominal' or 'Registered' Capital - this section is a *note* only.
(2)   Note - Calls in arrears are deducted, whilst calls in advance are added to this figure.
(3)   Share Premium and Revaluation Reserve are two important kinds of Capital Reserve.
(4)   The balance of Profit and Loss Appropriation account is included in this figure.
(5)   Goodwill, Patents, Trade Marks, usually head the list.

NOTE : TOTALS of fixed assets, current assets and liabilities and shareholders' capital, are available *at a glance*.

Now, the same company balance sheet in vertical format - the way such a balance sheet would be presented in practice. *The 1985 Companies Act will however allow either format to be used.*

Balance Sheet of XYZ Co. Ltd as at 31 December, 19-

		£	£
<u>Authorised Share Capital</u>			
10,000 $6^1/_2$% Preference Shares of £1 each			10,000
60,000 Ordinary Shares of £1 each			<u>60,000</u>
			70,000

Capital Employed

		£	£
<u>Issued Share Capital</u>			
4,000 $6^1/_2$% Preference Shares of £1 each (fully paid			4,000
40,000 Ordinary Shares of £1 each (75p called)			<u>30,000</u>
			34,000
Capital Reserves		5,000	
Revenue Reserves		<u>3,000</u>	<u>8,000</u>
			42,000
<u>Long Term Liabilities</u>			
8% Debenture Stock			<u>5,000</u>
			47,000

Utilisation (Employment) of Capital

		£	£
<u>Fixed Assets</u>			
Freehold Premises at cost		18,000	
Less : Provision for depreciation		<u>2,000</u>	16,000
Machinery at cost		18,000	
Less :provision for depreciation		<u>1,000</u>	17,000
Fixtures etc at cost		8,000	
Less : provision for depreciation		<u>500</u>	7,500
Trade Investments at cost			<u>5,000</u>
			45,500

	£	£	
<u>Current Assets</u>			
Stock		3,200	
Debtors	2,000		
Less : provision for bad debts	<u>900</u>	1,100	
Cash at Bank		1,500	
Cash in Hand		<u>300</u>	
		6,100	
<u>Less Current Liabilities</u>			
Trade Creditors	1,600		
Proposed Dividends	<u>3,000</u>	<u>4,600</u>	<u>1,500</u>
			47,000

You must be very familiar with the above presentations of balance sheets. Remember that, although *not* insisted upon by the Companies Act 1985, the usual presentation of a company balance sheet is in the vertical format.

MANUFACTURING ACCOUNTS

Many of you will have covered this area in your previous studies but I have included the topic for the benefit of those who have not or who wish to revise.

We are now looking at the person who makes finished goods for re-sale from various raw materials. Obviously when he has made the goods, he is going to sell them, perhaps to a wholesaler or direct to the retailer, so he will still need a trading account. The *only* difference will be that he is not *purchasing* goods to sell - he is *manufacturing* goods to sell. Therefore, in place of 'purchases' in his trading account he will show instead *the cost to him* of manufacturing those finished goods, and the difference between this figure and his sales figure (allowing of course for unsold stocks) will be his gross profit, e.g.

Trading and Profit and Loss Account of a Manufacturer

DR	£	CR	£
Stock of Finished Goods	6,000	Sales	30,000
Cost of Manufacture of goods	20,000		
	26,000		
Less Closing Stock of Finished Goods	4,000		
Cost of Goods Sold	22,000		
Gross Profit c/d	8,000		
	30,000		30,000
(Profit and Loss account dealt with as usual)		Gross Profit b/d	8,000

Presumably his cost of manufacture is less than he would have to pay if he bought the goods in a finished state from another manufacturer - if not, he is wasting his time!

How does he calculate the cost of manufacture of the finished units? He prepares at the year end a '*Manufacturing Account*' to immediately precede his 'Trading Account', and this manufacturing account simply shows his manufacturing costs ('stored up' in nominal accounts throughout the year), the final total being brought down to his Trading Account as 'Cost of Manufacture'. Before we look closer at this account, what manufacturing expenses will he incur? The main expenses of any manufacturing are materials and labour (together known as 'prime cost'). Other manufacturing expenses are power, factory light heat and rates, depreciation of machinery, etc, etc - any expense connected directly to the *factory* (not the warehouse or office).

The total of these expenses will eventually be transferred to the debit side of trading account (see above), but as the trading account is only concerned with the cost of manufacture of *finished* goods (which can be sold), an adjustment will have to be made in the manufacturing account for goods which are in between the raw material stage and the finished goods stage - i.e. partly finished goods or *work-in-progress*.

Let us study an actual manufacturing account and see how each item 'fits in' :

Manufacturing Account for year ended —

DR	£		£	CR
Opening stock of Raw Materials	4,000	Cost of Manufacture of		
Purchases of Raw Materials	28,000	Finished Goods c/d		
Carriage inwards on Raw Materials	500	to Trading Account	55,000	
	32,500			
Less Closing Stock of Raw Materials	2,500			
Raw Materials Used	30,000			
Manufacturing Wages	14,000			
PRIME COST	44,000			

Manufacturing Account (continued)

DR	£	£	CR
B/fwd	44,000	55,000	
Indirect Costs			
Power	1,500		
Light and Heat	1,000		
Rent and Rates	1,250		
Depreciation of Machinery	750		
Indirect labour	6,000		
	———		
Cost of Manufacture of Finished and			
Unfinished Goods	54,500		
Opening Stocks of Work-in-Progress	2,000		
	———		
	56,500		
Less Closing stocks of Work-in-Progress	1,500		
	———	———	
Cost of Manufacture of Finished Goods	55,000	55,000	

NOTE; All the costs of manufacture are on the debit side of the account - the double-entry (i.e. the credits) to these will be in the nominal accounts described, as their totals are transferred at year end to manufacturing account. The same principle exactly as with the expenses in the P & L account. The total costs of manufacture of *finished goods* is transferred from the manufacturing account (credit entry to 'clear it ') to the debit side of trading account in the place where 'purchases' would normally appear.

The figure for 'raw materials used' (£30,000) represents the raw materials in hand at the start of the year, *plus* the purchases of raw materials during the year, *less* those which haven't been used at the end of the year - i.e. those *used*. Carriage inwards on purchases of raw materials is, of course, an additional cost of purchases.

The manufacturing wages are those wages *directly* connected with the production process, and these, together with the materials used make up the *main* cost of production - i.e. the *prime* cost.

The 'indirect costs' need no explanation, except perhaps the indirect labour cost of £6,000. This represents the labour costs of those people not *directly* connected with the actual production process - e.g. foremen, messengers, cleaners, maintenance engineers, 'general' help, etc.

The sub-total of £54,500 is the cost of *all* production in the period - the making of finished units (ready for sale) *and* the making of partly finished units (not yet ready for sale). The trading account is only concerned with *finished* goods, and this account compares the cost of such goods with the selling price, to produce a gross profit figure. There is therefore no point in transferring £54,500 to trading account, because part of this figure represents goods which are not yet ready for selling and which must therefore remain in the factory. Hence the final adjustment for these partly-finished goods in the manufacturing account. Having added the opening stock of work-in-progress and deducted the closing stocks, (the normal procedure for any stocks, which you are already familiar with) we are left with a figure of £55,000 representing the cost of manufacture of *finished goods only*. This can now be transferred to Trading Account.

Try to think of the final accounts of a manufacturer as follows:

Manufacturing, Trading and Profit & Loss Account for year ending —

(i) Manufacturing Account - i.e. 'The Factory'

	£			£
Opening Stock of Raw Materials	x	Cost of Manufacture of Finished Goods c/d to		
Purchases of Raw Mat.	x	Trading Account		x
	X̄			
Less Closing Stock of Raw Materials	x			
Raw Materials Consumed	X̄			
Manufacturing Wages	x			
PRIME COST	X̄			
Indirect costs	x			
	X̄			
Opening Stock of Work-in-Progress	x			
	X̄			
Less Closing Stock of Work-in-Progress	x			
	X̄			X̲

(ii) Trading Account - i.e. 'The Warehouse'

	£			£
Opening Stock of Finished Goods	x	Sales		x
Cost of Manufacture b/d	x			
	X̄			
Less Closing Stock of Finished Goods	x			
Cost of Goods Sold	X̄			
Gross Profit c/d	x			
	X̲			X̲

(iii) Profit & Loss Account - i.e. 'The Office'

	£			£
Various Expenses including depreciation of office furniture, etc.	x	Gross Profit b/d		x
		Various Gains		x
Net Profit	x			
	X̲			X̲

NOTE : The finished goods, produced in the factory, are then transferred to the warehouse for selling. The goods have left the factory, and if not sold will remain in the warehouse (i.e. Trading Account) until they *are* sold.

If you are ever unsure as to *where* to place an expense then think 'is it an expense of manufacture, or is it an expense which would be incurred whether the owner was a manufacturer or not?' If the former, debit Manufacturing Account; if the latter, debit profit and loss account. For example, bank charges, advertising, office salaries, etc., are incurred by traders *and* manufacturers - they are not expenses *peculiar* to manufacturers only -

therefore they are a P & L account expense. Depreciation of a factory asset is charged to manufacturing account whilst depreciation of an office asset is charged to P & L account.

Obviously, the balance sheet of a manufacturer will be the same as a normal trader. The only difference will be that the manufacturer will show under the heading of 'current assets', *three* types of stock rather than one - i.e. stock of raw materials, stock of work-in-progress, and stock of finished goods. Everything else will be the same.

STATEMENTS OF STANDARD ACCOUNTING PRACTICE

These statements of accounting standards lay down guidelines for procedures and concepts which have the approval of all the major professional accounting bodies. Practising accountants are expected to observe the standards laid down and any significant departures from these standards should be disclosed in the accounts and explained.

As an addition to S.S.A.P.s (Statements of Standard Accounting Practice) the Accounting Standards Committee (ASC) has now stated :

i)   That Standards (S.S.A.P's requirements) need not now be applied to items where the effect is judged *to be immaterial* (i.e. of no real consequence).

ii)   That a new type of publication, 'Statements of Recommended Practice' (S.O.R.P.s) will be issued. These statements are *not* mandatory but they do indicate the accounting professions *preferred* methods of treatment.

We are going to see more of these, and whilst the standards (S.S.A.P.s) must be observed the new S.O.R.P.s could cover situations not covered effectively by mandatory standards.

S.S.A.P. 2

ACCOUNTING POLICIES

This statement is concerned with the proper understanding of financial information through presentation of accounts according to accepted practice. When 'reading' accounts and other financial statements one should be aware of the main assumptions on which they are based. Four basic concepts are generally accepted :

(i)   *The 'Going Concern' concept* - i.e. acceptance that the business in question will continue to trade for the foreseeable future - i.e. we don't expect it to 'pack in' in the near future!

(ii)   *The 'Accruals' concept* - i.e. that expenses and gains for the financial period under review will be shown in the profit and loss account whether or not they have actually been paid or received. This is the application of the 'rule' mentioned earlier in the book that profit and loss account is debited not with what has been paid, but with what should have been paid in the period - profit and loss account is credited with what should have been received in the period.

(iii)   *The 'Prudence' concept* - i.e. profits are never anticipated in the accounts; they only appear as profits when they actually happen. Expected losses however are estimated and shown in the accounts.

(iv)   *The 'Consistency' concept* - i.e. there is consistency in the treatment of items from one year to another. For example, whatever method of depreciation or stock valuation is adopted this method should be then used consistently from period to period.

NOTE : If accounts are prepared on different assumptions than those shown above, then this fact must be revealed by way of note in the accounts. Otherwise it will be *assumed* that the above four concepts are being observed.

EXERCISE 1.1

Indicate with a tick where the following items should appear :

			P & L a/c proper	P & L Appropriation a/c
e.g.		Rent and Rates	√	
Item	1)	Proposed Dividends		
	2)	Salaries		
	3)	Transfers to specific Reserves		
	4)	Directors' Fees		
	5)	Writing off goodwill and Patents		
	6)	Debenture Interest		
	7)	Directors' Fees based on profits		
	8)	Increase or decrease in Provision for Bad Debts		
	9)	Depreciation		

EXERCISE 1.2

The following trial balance was extracted from the books of Lingford Ltd. as at 31 December 19-9 :

	£	£
Share capital		120,000
Share premium		25,000
Freehold land and buildings at cost	87,000	
Motor vans at cost	40,000	
Provision for depreciation on motor vans at 1 January, 19-9		14,800
Purchases	129,938	
Sales		179,422
Rent and rates	2,500	
General expenses	5,842	
Wages	19,876	
Bad debts	542	
Provision for doubtful debts at 1 January 19-9		684
Directors' salaries	16,000	
Debtors and creditors	16,941	11,171
Stock in trade at 1 January 19-9	28,572	
Bank balance	24,921	
Profit and loss account as at 1 January 19-9		21,055
	372,132	372,132

You are given the following additional information:

(i)   The authorised and issued share capital is 120,000 shares of £1 each all of which are issued and fully paid;

(ii)   wages due but unpaid at 31 December 19-9 amounted to £264;

(iii)   the provision for doubtful debts is to be increased by £102;

(iv)   stock-in-trade at 31 December 19-9, was £38,292;

(v)   rent and rates amounting to £300 were paid in advance at 31 December 19-9;

(vi)   depreciation on motor vans is to be charged at the rate of 20 per cent. per annum on cost;

(vii)   it is proposed to pay a dividend of £5,000 for the year 19-9.

Required :

A trading and profit and loss account for the year 19-9, and a balance sheet as at 31 December 19-9. Prepare both in vertical format.

EXERCISE 1.3

Show each of the two balance sheets below in vertical format.

Balance Sheets as at 31 December

	19-0 £	19-1 £		19-0 £	19-1 £
Issued Share Capital	56,000	56,000	Freehold premises (at cost or valuation)	64,000	86,000
Capital reserve arising on property revaluation	-	22,000	Equipment (cost less depreciation)	24,000	28,320
Retained profits	10,000	19,000			
10% Mortgage (repayable 19-9)	32,000	32,000	Stock	12,500	19,680
Trade creditors	8,000	9,800	Debtors	7,500	3,900
Bank overdraft	2,000		Bank		900
	£108,000	£138,800		£108,000	£138,800

EXERCISE 1.4

From the following Balance Sheets reconstruct the Profit and Loss Appropriation Account as it would have appeared on 31 December, 19-0. Ignore depreciation.

	31 Dec 19-9 £	31 Dec 19-0 £		31 Dec 19-9 £	31 Dec 19-0 £
Share Capital	15,000	18,000	Goodwill	5,000	4,500
Share Premium	–	300	Premises at cost	12,000	9,000
Capital Reserve (re-sale of premises)	–	1,000	Fixtures at cost	2,500	2,500
General Reserve	4,000	5,000	Current Assets	3,900	12,800
P & L Appropriation a/c	1,800	1,600			
	20,800	25,900			
Creditors	1,600	1,600			
Proposed Dividend	1,000	1,300			
	23,400	28,800		23,400	28,800

EXERCISE 1.5

X & Co. Ltd has a nominal capital of £60,000 being divided into 40,000 Ordinary Shares of £1 each and 20,000 5% Preference Shares of £1 each. All shares had been issued, the Ordinary Shares being fully paid, and the Preference being 75p called.

In addition to the balances arising from the above, there were the following balances in the ledger on 31 December, 19-0.

	£
Debtors	11,000
Rent received	800
Creditors	4,100
Calls in advance (Preference Shares)	200
Advertising	600
Bad debts	800
Provision for bad debts	900
Purchases	57,000
Sales	78,000
Stock (1 January, 19-0)	6,000
Bank (DR balance)	23,360
Rates	480

Salaries	7,400	
Insurance	200	
5% Debentures	8,000	
General Reserve	5,000	
Premises	45,000	
Machinery (cost)	4,000	
Fixtures and Fittings (cost)	4,000	
P & L account (1 January, 19-0)CR.	5,840	
Provision for depreciation : Fixtures and Fittings	2,000	

NOTES

(1) Depreciate Fixtures and Fittings at 10% of cost
(2) Depreciate machinery by 20% of cost
(3) Bad debts provision to be increased to £1,200 ✓
(4) Debenture interest due (12 months)
(5) £200 is due to the Company, for rent owing at 31 December, 19-0
(6) £50 insurance is paid in respect of 19-1
(7) Stock at 31 December, 19-0 is £12,000 ✓
(8) Provision to be made for a dividend of 20% on ordinary shares
(9) Preference dividend for year to be provided for
(10) Transfer £5,000 to General Reserve

From the above, prepare Trading and Profit and Loss Account for the year ending 31 December, 19-0, and a balance sheet as at that date.

EXERCISE 1.6 EX

The XYZ Co. Ltd. has an authorised capital of 50,000 ordinary shares of £1 each and 10,000 6% preference shares of £1 each. At 31 December, 19-6, the following trial balance was extracted from the company's ledger :

	£	£
Ordinary Share Capital		50,000
6% Preference Share Capital		8,000
Plant and machinery (cost) ✓	24,000	
Motor Vehicles (cost) ✓	6,000	
Creditors		17,870
Debtors	34,980	
Bank	35,585	
5% Debentures (issued in 19-1)		9,000
Stock (1 January 19-6) ✓	5,200	
General Expenses	11,020	
Sales ✓		232,834
Bad Debts	2,400	
Debenture interest	225	
Purchases	165,214	
Discounts Received		640
Salaries	24,210	
Insurance	300	
Provision for Depreciation -		
Plant and Machinery		6,000
Motor Vehicles		1,200
Directors' Fees	17,000	
Interim Preference Dividend	240	
Profit and Loss a/c (1 January 19-6)		300
Provision for bad debts (1 January, 19-6)		530
	326,374	326,374

The following information is provided :

(a) Insurance, amounting to £60 was paid in advance at 31 December, 19-6
(b) Depreciation on fixed assets is at the rate of 20 per cent. per annum calculated on cost. ∕
(c) The provision for bad debts is to be increased to £1,000
(d) Stock at 31 December, 19-6 is valued at £8,247 ✓
(e) The directors propose to pay an ordinary dividend of 10 per cent. to the ordinary shareholders and to pay the remaining dividend due to the preference shareholders.

Required :

A trading and profit and loss account for the year 19-6 and a balance sheet as at 31 December, 19-6, *both prepared in vertical format. Ignore taxation.*

EXERCISE 1.7 EX

From the information given below relating to the Opex Manufacturing Co. Ltd for the year ended 31 December, 19-6, prepare appropriate final accounts for the year 19-6 and a balance sheet at 31 December, 19-6.

	£
Issued Share Capital	130,000
6% Debentures	30,000
Debtors	14,700
Creditors	9,100
Fuel and power for factory	6,227
Furniture and Fittings (cost)	10,000
General Reserve	18,000
Interest on Debentures	900
Investments	16,000
Investment Income	1,600
Provision for depreciation - furniture & fittings	4,000
Provision for depreciation - Machinery and Plant	24,000
Bank charges and interest	1,400
Bank balance	5,459
Machinery and Plant (cost)	80,000
Office expenses	4,820
Manufacturing Wages	27,210
Profit and Loss Account balance 31 December 19-5	6,250 (CR)
Rates and Insurance	3,915
Land and Buildings	120,000
Salaries	9,137
Purchases of Raw Materials	49,250
Sales	138,700
Stocks at 1 January, 19-6 :	
Raw Materials	12,600
Work in progress	2,850
Finished goods	8,100
Stocks at 31 December 19-6 :	
Raw Materials	11,200
Work in progress	1,300
Finished goods	9,900

NOTES:

(1) Depreciation of furniture and fittings and machinery and plant is calculated at 10% p.a. on cost value.
(2) Transfer £4,000 to General Reserve.
(3) At 31 December, 19-6 rates are paid in advance, £200.
(4) Provide for a final dividend of 10%.
(5) Prepare in either horizontal or vertical format. (Ideally, practice both!)

Gurnery Ltd was incorporated on 1 January 1986 with an authorised share capital of £1,000,000 divided into ordinary shares of £1 each. On the same date 400,000 shares were issued at par for cash. Long term prospects are excellent, but profits are expected to fluctuate due to changes in trading conditions. The estimated profits (loss) and planned dividend per share for each of the next six years are as follows :

	Profits (Loss) £ 000s	Dividend pence
1986	110	15
1987	20	16
1988	95	17
1989	30	18
1990	200	19
1991	(20)	20

The dividend to be paid each year is the lower of the planned payment for the year and the maximum legal distribution.

The directors plan to finance a modest rate of expansion over the next six years out of retained profit and, for this reason, they have decided to capitalise the balance of undistributed profits at the end of 1991.

Required :

(a)   Calculate the planned dividend payment for each of the years 1986-91.

(b)   For each of the years 1986-91 prepare a statement showing the profit available for distribution, the amount of distribution and the amount of retained profits carried forward. You should give effect to any legal restrictions on the amount of dividend payable in the year in question. You should explain the treatment you adopt.

(c)   Indicate the amount of the capitalisation issue on 31 December 1991.

NOTE   Ignore taxation

SOLUTIONS

SOLUTION 1.1

Item		P & L a/c Proper	P & L Appropriation a/c	
1.	Proposed Dividends		√	
2.	Salaries	√		
3.	Transfers to Specific Reserves		√	
4.	Directors' Fees	√		
5.	Writing off Goodwill and Patents	√	√	(immediate write-off)
6.	Debenture Interest	√		
7.	Directors' Fees based on profits		√	
8.	Increase or decrease in Provision for Bad Debts	√		
9.	Depreciation	√		

NOTE :

Item 6 must be paid whether profits are made or not - it is not dependent on profits being made and is therefore a charge against, rather than an appropriation of, profits.

SOLUTION 1.2

Trading and Profit & Loss Account
for year ended 31 December 19-9

		£	£
Sales (Turnover)			179,422
Less	Stock at 1 January	28,572	
	Purchases	129,938	
	Stock at 31 December	(38,292)	
Cost of Goods sold			120,218
GROSS PROFIT			59,204
Less	Depreciation - Vans	8,000	
	Rent and Rates	2,200	
	General Expenses	5,842	
	Wages	20,140	
	Bad Debts	542	
	Provision for Doubtful Debts	102	
	Directors' Salaries	16,000	52,826
NET PROFIT			6,378
Add	Balance of retained profits at 1 January 19-9		21,055
			27,433
Less	Proposed Dividends		5,000
Balance of Retained Profits at 31 December 19-9			22,433

19

Balance Sheet as at 31 December 19-9

Capital Employed

	£	£	£
Authorised and Issued Share Capital			
120,000 Shares of £1 each			120,000
Share Premium			25,000
Retained Profits			22,433
			167,433

Employment of Capital

	£	£	£
Fixed Assets			
Freehold Land and Buildings (cost)			87,000
Motor Vans (cost)		40,000	
Less Depreciation		22,800	17,200
			104,200
Current Assets			
Stock		38,292	
Debtors (net)		16,155	
Bank		24,921	
Prepayments		300	
		79,668	
Less Current Liabilities			
Creditors	11,171		
Wages due	264		
Proposed Dividend	5,000	16,435	63,233
			167,433

SOLUTION 1.3

Balance Sheet as at 31 December 19-0

a)

	£	£	£
Capital Employed			
Issued Share Capital			56,000
Retained Profits			10,000
			66,000
10% Mortgage 19-4			32,000
			98,000
Represented by			
Fixed Assets			
Freehold Premises at cost			64,000
Equipment at cost less depreciation			24,000
			88,000
Current Assets			
Stock		12,500	
Debtors		7,500	
		20,000	
Less Current Liabilities			
Trade Creditors	8,000		
Bank Overdraft	2,000	10,000	10,000
			98,000

Balance Sheet as at 31 December 19-1

b)

Capital Employed	£	£
Issued Share Capital		56,000
Revaluation Reserve		22,000
Retained Profits		19,000
		97,000
10% Mortgage 19-4		32,000
		129,000

Utilisation of Capital

<u>Fixed Assets</u>

Freehold Premises at valuation		86,000
Equipment at cost less depreciation		28,320
		114,320

<u>Current Assets</u>	£	
Stock	19,680	
Debtors	3,900	
Bank	900	
	24,480	

<u>Less</u> Current Liabilities		
Trade Creditors	9,800	14,680
		129,000

SOLUTION 1.4

Appropriation Account

	£		£	
Transfer to General Reserve	1,000	Balance b/fwd	1,800	(2,800)*
Proposed dividend	1,300	Net profit b/d	2,600	
Written off goodwill	500			
Balance c/d	1,600			
(To Capital Reserve (£1,000)*	4,400		4,400	

NOTES : The non-trading profits made during 19-0 were £300 (premium) from a new issue of shares and £1,000 on the sale of some premises. (Cost £3,000 - sold for £4,000). These were capital profits (as distinct from trading profits) and do not therefore appear anywhere in the Profit and Loss Account which is only concerned with trading, and therefore distributable, profits.

 * In practice, however, extraordinary items such as the profit on sale of premises would appear in the profit and loss account before being transferred to a capital reserve. This point will be dealt with fully later on.

SOLUTION 1.5

Trading and Profit & Loss Account
for the year ended 31 December 19-0

	£		£
Stock (1 January)	6,000	Sales	78,000
Purchases	57,000		
	63,000		
Less stock (31 December)	12,000		
	51,000		
Gross Profit c/d	27,000		
	78,000		78,000

Advertising	600	Gross profit b/d	27,000
Bad debts	800	Rent received	1,000
Provision for bad debts (increase)	300		
Rates	480		
Salaries	7,400		
Insurance	150		
Debenture interest	400		
Provision for depreciation :			
Fixtures and Fittings	400		
Machinery	800		
Net Profit c/d	16,670		
	28,000		28,000
General reserve	5,000	Balance b/fwd	5,840
Proposed Ordinary Dividend	8,000	Net Profit b/d	16,670
Preference Dividend	750		
Balance c/d	8,760		
	22,510		22,510
		Balance b/d	8,760

Balance Sheet as at 31 December 19-0

	£		£	£
Authorised Share Capital		Fixed Assets		
40,000 Ordinary Shares of £1 each	40,000	Premises (cost)		45,000
20,000 5% Preference Shares of £1 each	20,000	Machinery (cost)	4,000	
	60,000	Less provision for deprn.	800	3,200
		Fixtures and fittings (cost)	4,000	
Issued Share Capital		Less provision for deprn.	2,400	1,600
40,000 Ordinary Shares of £1 -				49,800
fully paid	40,000			
20,000 5% Preference Shares of £1		Current Assets		
(75p called)	15,000	Stock		12,000
Add calls in advance	200	Debtors	11,000	
	55,200	Less provision	1,200	9,800
General Reserve	10,000	Bank		23,360
Profit and Loss a/c	8,760	Rent due		200
	73,960	Insurance prepaid		50
5% Debentures	8,000			
Current Liabilities				
Creditors	4,100			
Debenture Interest due	400			
Proposed Ordinary Dividend	8,000			
Preference Dividend	750			
	95,210			95,210

LESSON 2

RECONSTRUCTIONS OF COMPANY CAPITAL

Reconstruction of a company's capital can take many forms. New shares may be issued or may be redeemed - the nominal value of the shares may be reduced in value - an amalgamation or takeover of another organisation may take place.

We will look at the effect of all these happenings starting with new issues of shares by way of a bonus issue.

Look at this balance sheet of a company which has been established since 1950 :

Balance Sheet

	£		£
Share Capital		Fixed Assets	22,000
5,000 Ordinary Shares of £1	5,000	Current Assets	5,000
Reserves (including Profit & Loss)	20,000		
	25,000		
Current Liabilities	2,000		
	27,000		27,000

This company presumably started off in 1950 in issuing 5,000 shares, and over the years profits have been left in the company by the shareholders until there is now £20,000 of undistributed profits held in reserve. Whether these reserves have been built up through prudent management or because the company has never has sufficient liquid resources to pay a good dividend is not known!

It is obvious however, that the reserves are now out of all proportion to the issued capital. For example, what hope is there of the shareholders claiming most to these undistributed profits from the past, as an extra dividend? Very little, for the reason that most of them are now represented by fixed assets - in other words 'tied up'. As you will see from the balance sheet, working capital (i.e. current assets less current liabilities) only amounts to £3,000 and therefore, to pay out a bumper dividend in cash is just not possible.

Would it not be reasonable then to suggest that, as the reserves are being used *permanently* in the business - in the same way that share capital is - they should be regarded as permanent capital, rather than as undistributed profits capable of being distributed? In other words should the reserves or part of them anyway, be capitalised - i.e. 'frozen' for permanent use? To do this the company could convert the reserves into Issued Share Capital by utilising them to issue BONUS SHARES. In our example the shareholders would be given 4 bonus shares of £1 each for every £1 share they hold. As there are 5,000 shares held at the moment this would involve the giving away of 20,000 (4 x 5,000) bonus shares which would use up the whole balance on reserve. The procedure in issuing bonus shares simply involves a transfer from Reserve Account to Share Capital Account and the new balance sheet would look like this :

Balance Sheet

	£		£
Share Capital			
25,000 Ordinary Shares of £1	25,000	Fixed Assets	22,000
Current Liabilities	2,000	Current Assets	5,000
	27,000		27,000

The balance sheet now shows a much more realistic position and the company will not be in the embarrassing position of having to explain why the shareholders cannot have extra dividends out of retained past profits. The company has acknowledged that the reserves are just as tied up as the issued share capital is.

After such a reconstruction of the company's capital the shareholders would be in just the same position as they were in before the reconstruction. Before the bonus issue, one share was worth £5 (i.e. value of business £25,000 divided by the number of shares, 5,000) Now 5 shares (i.e the original share, plus the 4 bonus shares) are worth £5. An alternative to the issue of bonus shares of £1 each would have been for the company to change the nominal value of the shares from £1 to £5. The final balance sheet would then have shown '5,000 Ordinary Shares of £5 each - £25,000' the increase in share capital being due to the decrease of the Reserves, as before (i.e. the capitalisation of reserves).

The important thing to remember about bonus shares is that their issue does *not* affect cash at all - no cash comes into the company - it is achieved by book entries only (i.e. Dr. P & L Appropriation account, or general reserve or, in fact, any reserve whether it be a revenue or capital reserve - Cr. Share Capital account).

Bonus issues are sometimes referred to as 'scrip issues' or 'capitalisation issues'. In making such an issue the company must ensure that the resultant increased issued share capital is still within its permitted Authorised capital. As indicated above, the shareholders do not really benefit by a bonus issue; they simply finish up with more shares which are worth the same in total. In practice however, with many quoted companies a bonus issue does often cause an increase in the *market* value of the shares. One of the reasons for this is that the reduced market price of each share (because there are now more of them) makes them more marketable.

Rights Issues.

This is where a company offers new shares to existing shareholders at a favourable price. The purpose of such an issue is to raise finance and therefore, unlike bonus shares, cash *is* increased. The reason for offering such shares to existing shareholders rather than to the public at large is to protect their interests by allowing them to maintain their percentage holding in the company. The other reason is to save the considerable expense of offering shares to the general public.

Let us now look at another company whose capital is in need of reconstruction in a different way.

Balance Sheet

	£		£
Share Capital			
25,000 Ordinary Shares of £1	25,000	Fixed Assets at cost	11,000
Less Profit and Loss a/c	10,000	Current Assets	
	15,000	Stock	4,000
Current Liabilities		Debtors	3,000
Bank	1,000		
Creditors	2,000		
	18,000		18,000

Current profits : £1,000 per year

In our first balance sheet we had a situation where the permanent capital (i.e. share capital) of the company was backed up, or supported, by too many assets and we therefore increased the permanent capital by capitalising some reserves, thereby putting everything into perspective.

In our second example however, we have a balance sheet which shows the opposite picture - there are insufficient assets supporting the share capital! Let us look at this - issued share capital is £25,000 - the net assets of the company amount to £15,000 (fixed and current assets less current liabilities) - the debit balance on Profit and Loss account has been caused by an accumulation of losses over the years and therefore capital has been lost. The company is no longer worth the nominal amount put into it by the shareholders; the nominal value of the shares (£1) is no longer realistic - they are not worth £1.

To make matters worse it is clear from the balance sheet that depreciation of fixed assets has not been allowed for at any time, nor has a provision for bad debts been created. Presumably the reason for this has been to keep the past losses as low as possible. If provisions for depreciation and bad debts had been allowed for, the debit balance on Profit and Loss account would have been much bigger, You will note that the company is now making profits of £1,000 per year which means that in 10 years time the debit balance on Profit and Loss account will have been wiped off, *provided* the shareholders do not take any of the £1,000 profit each year as a dividend. In other words, the shareholders must be willing to leave all profits in the business for at least 10 years - they are not going to like that!

Obviously the share capital must be brought into line with the true value of the assets and a realistic picture must be obtained. Suppose that we reduced the nominal value of the shares to 50p - this would be nearer their true value and it would release half of the liability of share capital, £12,500, which could then be used to clear off the debit balance on Profit and Loss account and still leave enough to create a provision for depreciation and for bad debts. The journal entries to do all this must be visualised to appreciate fully what is happening.

Journal Entries

	Dr. £	Cr. £
Ordinary Share Capital	12,500	
To Profit and Loss account		10,000
To Provision for depreciation		2,350
To Provision for bad debts		150
(say, 5% of debtors)	12,500	12,500

After entering up the accounts from the journal the new balances would give us a balance sheet like this :

Balance Sheet

	£		£	
Issued Share Capital				
25,000 Ordinary Shares of 50p	12,500	Fixed Assets at cost	11,000	
		Less Provision for depreciation	2,350	
			8,650	
Profit and Loss account	-	Current Assets		
Bank	1,000	Stock	4,000	
		Debtors less provision		
Creditors	2,000	for bad debts	2,850	
	15,500		15,500	

This is now a reasonable looking balance sheet, in that the nominal value of the shares is in line with the value of the business - and, most important, assets are being shown at a truer valuation in that fixed assets are reduced by depreciation and debtors by a provision for doubtful debts. Also as far as the shareholders are concerned they have a clear Profit and Loss account which is waiting to receive the first year's profits of £1,000, out of which they can take a small dividend and leave a balance in the account as a reserve (NOTE : A CREDIT BALANCE!) This account can then gradually be built up as more profits are made. On the whole then the shareholders benefit from this reconstruction of capital and the halving of the nominal value of their shares is nothing more than an acknowledgement of the true worth of the shares.

It must be pointed out that schemes of reconstruction as outlined above must only be done subject to the powers conferred by the company's memorandum and articles of association - e.g. any increase in share capital must not exceed the *authorised* share capital. Also, a company may not reduce its share capital without the consent of the Court.

A company which has not been doing too well but is now 'getting on its feet' again and starting to make profits, may want to start off with a 'clean sheet' and to do this it may well adopt a reconstruction scheme such as we have just looked at, or it may decide to start again as a new company with a different or amended name. In this case, the shares issued by the new company would be given to the shareholders in exchange for their shares in the old company. This swap of shares would of course have to be made fairly attractive to the shareholders to get them to agree to it. Similarly, any debenture holders in the old company would have their debentures exchanged for a new issue of debentures by the new company. In fact, it is possible that the old shareholders will be offered debentures in exchange for their shares, in which case they cease to be owners of the company. As debentures carry a fixed rate of interest though, payment of which is not dependent on profits being made, it may well be that the shareholders would welcome a change of status to that of a secured creditor, especially if dividends from their shares in the past have been very poor ones - also, their security position would be better as debenture holders always rank in priority to shareholders for repayment of capital in the event of liquidation.

In such a reconstruction of a company the terms of exchange of shares for shares, debentures for debentures or debentures for shares will be such that the old shareholder or debenture holders gain in some way by the exchange. All the old shares and debentures will of course cease to exist as the old company ceases to exist.

How many shares/debentures the shareholders/debenture holders will receive in exchange for their shares/debentures is just a matter of careful calculation and we do not therefore need to dwell on this topic any longer, except to practice on the following exercises.

EXERCISE 2.1

Downe & Co. has been experiencing trading difficulties for some years and the directors decide, on 31 December, 19-7, to adopt a scheme of reconstruction. At this date the balance sheet showed the following position :

Balance Sheet (before reconstruction)

	£			£
Authorised & Issued Share Capital				
100,000 $6^1/_2$% Preference Shares of £1	100,000	Fixed Assets		
125,000 Ordinary Shares of £1	125,000	Goodwill		27,000
	225,000	Plant, etc. (cost)	240,000	
Share Premium Account	15,000	Less depreciation	100,000	140,000
	240,000	Current Assets		
Less : Profit & Loss account	50,500	Stock		37,500
	189,500	Debtors (less provision)		43,000
Current Liabilities				
Bank	20,000			
Creditors	38,000			
	247,500			247,500

The Court agreed to the following scheme :
    (i)   The Preference Shares to be reduced by £0.25 per share
    (ii)   The Ordinary Shares to be reduced by £0.50 per share
    (iii)   The goodwill is to be written off and also the debit balance on Profit & Loss account

(iv)   The provision for depreciation of Plant is to be increased by £10,000
(v)   The Share Premium Account is to be utilised in giving ordinary bonus shares of £0.50 each to the Preference Shareholders in lieu of the arrears of dividends which have built up in past years.

You are required to show the balance sheet as it would appear AFTER this reconstruction.

EXERCISE 2.2

Form Ltd made substantial losses in the early years of its existence, but has recently returned to profitability. The company's balance sheet at 31 August, 19-8 showed :

	£ 000		£ 000
Ordinary Shares of £1	150	Net Assets	215
7% Preference Shares of £1	50		
	200		
Less : Profit & Loss a/c balance	25		
	175		
6% Debentures	40		
	215		215

The company is considering a scheme of reconstruction under the Companies Act along the following lines:

(i)   The reconstructed company will be named Reform Ltd.
(ii)   It is expected that Reform Ltd will pay a total annual dividend of £10,000 on its ordinary shares after meeting interest payments considered below.
(iii)   In exchange for every 100 7% preference shares in Form Ltd there will be issued :
        £20 of 5% debenture stock in Reform Ltd and a number of £1 ordinary shares in Reform Ltd.
        The number of ordinary shares will be so determined that the expected annual income (debenture interest and ordinary share dividends) receivable by former preference shareholders will be the same as that due annually from their preference shares in Form Ltd.
(iv)   In exchange for every £100 6% debentures in Form Ltd there will be issued :
        £80 of 5% debenture stock in Reform Ltd and a number of £1 ordinary shares in Reform Ltd.
        The number of ordinary shares will be so determined that the expected annual income (debenture interest and ordinary share dividends) receivable by former 6% debenture holders will be equivalent to 7% per annum on their former debenture holdings in Form Ltd.
(v)   The issued ordinary share capital of Reform Ltd will consist of 125,000 £1 shares. After the issue of ordinary shares indicated above, the balance of the 125,000 shares will be issued on a pro rata basis in exchange for the ordinary shares of Form Ltd.

Ignore taxation and any arrears or accruals of dividends or interest.

Required :
        A table completed in the manner shown below, indicating the holdings of ordinary shares and debentures in Reform Ltd if the proposed reconstruction is adopted.

<u>Holdings in Reform Ltd</u>

	£1 Ordinary Shares	5% Debentures
Form Ltd :		
Ordinary Shareholders		
Preference Shareholders		
Debenture Holders		

Oils Ltd deals in vegetable oils. The Company recently suffered from a substantial fraud in which the company's stocks of oil were privately sold by certain employees. Consequently the company has been forced to propose a scheme of reconstruction which will reduce its financial commitments.

The company's current balance sheet is shown below :

	£		£
Issued Share Capital			
£1 Ordinary Shares	60,000	Net Assets	150,000
8% Cumulative Preference Shares	40,000		
	100,000		
Less accumulated losses	50,000		
	50,000		
10% Debenture stock	100,000		
	150,000		150,000

Before its recent difficulties the company consistently earned about £30,000 per year before paying interest on debenture stock.

The reconstructed company, Oils (1988) Ltd, would issue securities to existing participators in Oils Ltd as follows:

1. The existing debenture stockholders would receive £50 of 12% debenture stock plus 24 ordinary shares in Oils (1988) Ltd in exchange for every £100 of 10% debenture stock currently held.

2. The existing preference shareholders would receive £10 of 12% debenture stock plus 6 £1 ordinary shares in Oils (1988) Ltd in exchange for every 40 preference shares currently held.

3. The existing ordinary shareholders would receive one £1 ordinary share in Oils (1988) Ltd in exchange for every two ordinary shares currently held.

Required :

(a) Calculations for each class of the existing participators in Oils Ltd, showing the total amount of earnings (before debenture interest) which Oils (1988) Ltd would have to achieve for the relevant participators to obtain the same income before and after the reconstruction. Calculate for each class independently and assume that all earnings are distributed.

Present the results of your calculations in a table, as follows :

Total earnings (before interest) of Oils (1988) Ltd
required to maintain income.

Participation in Oils Ltd :

Debenture Stock £_____

Preference Shares £_____

Ordinary Shares £_____

(b) Comment on whether you consider the scheme to be equitable between the different classes of participators.

NOTE: Ignore taxation and any arrears of dividends or interest.

Sutherland Ltd is a private company. Three quarters of the issued share capital is held by the directors or members of their families. The company's draft balance sheet as at the end of 19-5 was as follows :

Balance Sheet at 31 December 19-5

	£	£
Fixed Assets		
Intangible assets :Development costs		85,000
Goodwill		60,000
Tangible assets : Land and buildings		270,000
Plant and machinery		326,000
		741,000
Current Assets		
Stocks	426,000	
Debtors	531,000	
	957,000	
Creditors falling due within one year		
Creditors	393,000	
Bank loans and overdrafts	687,000	
	1,080,000	
Net current liabilities		(123,000)
Total assets *less* current liabilities		618,000
Capital and Reserves		
Called up share capital (800,000 shares of £1 each)		800,000
Share premium account		50,000
Profit and loss account		(232,000)
		618,000

Bank loans and overdrafts consist of a 10% loan of £400,000 repayable in 19-6 carrying a fixed charge on the company's land and buildings, and an unsecured overdraft of £287,000.

The demand for the company's products fell drastically in recent years owing to the import of high quality and cheaper products from south-east Asia. The development costs appearing in the balance sheet above relate to a new product which has been perfected to a marketable stage, and for which there is believed to be a strong demand. The costs have been properly capitalised in accordance with the provisions of SSAP13. The company is in urgent need of capital to meet existing liabilities and the necessary new investment in plant and working capital.

A scheme for financial reorganisation has been drawn up for the consideration of shareholders and creditors. The terms are as follows :

(i)   The shares of £1 each are to be written down to 20p per share and subsequently every five shares of 20p each are to be consolidated into one fully paid share of £1.

(ii)   The existing shareholders are to subscribe for a rights issue of two new £1 ordinary shares, at par, for every share held after the proposed reduction and consolidation.

(iii)   A major supplier agrees to exchange a debt of £180,000, included in creditors, for 180,000 ordinary shares of £1 each fully paid.

(iv)   In full satisfaction of the £687,000 owing, the bank agrees to accept an immediate payment of £87,000 and to consolidate the balance of £600,000 into a loan, carrying interest of 13% per annum, repayable in five equal annual instalments commencing 31 December 19-7. The loan is to be secured by a fixed charge on the land and buildings and a floating charge on the company's remaining assets.

(v)   The credit balance on share premium account and debit balances on the profit and loss account and goodwill, considered valueless, are to be written off.

(vi)   The assets listed below are to be restated at the following amounts :

29

	£
Plant and machinery	125,000
Stock	210,000
Debtors	500,000
Land and buildings	320,000

A group of dissatisfied shareholders plan to oppose the scheme on the following grounds : 'We have to bear the whole burden of the reorganisation whereas the bank loses nothing'.

The company has received a cash offer of £1,120,000 for its fixed and current assets.

Required :

(a)   The revised balance sheet of Sutherland Ltd at 1 January 19-6 giving effect to the proposed scheme for reorganizing the company.

(b)   A report for the group of dissatisfied shareholders explaining whether they should accept or oppose the scheme.

(c)   A report for the bank explaining the matters to be taken into account in deciding whether it would be better to support the scheme or press for immediate liquidation of the company

NOTE:

Assume you are making the calculations and writing the reports on 1 January 19-6 and that no other changes occur.

SOLUTIONS

SOLUTION 2.1

Balance Sheet

	£			£
<u>Authorised and Issued Share Capital</u>		<u>Fixed Assets</u>		
100,000 6½% Preference Shares of		Plant, etc. (cost)	240,000	
75p each	75,000	Less depreciation	<u>110,000</u>	
155,000 Ordinary Shares of 50p each	<u>77,500</u>			130,000
	152,500			
<u>Current Liabilities</u>		<u>Current Assets</u>		
Bank Overdraft	20,000	Stock	37,500	
Creditors	<u>38,000</u>	Debtors	<u>43,000</u>	
	210,500		210,500	

NOTE: In this question the Share Premium account (a capital reserve) was utilised to give bonus shares, whereas in the examples used in the lesson, it was a revenue reserve which was used to make a bonus issue. Both capital and revenue reserves may be used and the only difference is the reason for the bonus issue. For example, as we have already seen, a revenue reserve may be capitalised, (a) because the reserve is now represented by permanent assets and (b) to stop shareholders demanding a distribution of past profits at a time when liquid assets are not available. The reason for using a Capital Reserve to make a bonus issue obviously cannot be either (a) or (b). Do you agree? In this exercise the reason was to compensate the Preference Shareholders for past dividends not paid.

SOLUTION 2.2

<u>Holdings in Reform Ltd.</u>

	£1 Ordinary shares	5% Debenture stock
Form Ltd :		
Ordinary Shareholders	<u>72,500</u>	NIL
Preference Shareholders	<u>37,500</u>	£10,000
Debenture Holders	<u>15,000</u>	£32,000

Workings   (and explanations of workings)

Step 1

Total Ordinary Shares to be issued by Reform Ltd = £125,000.
Total dividend on Ordinary Shares to be paid by Reform Ltd = £10,000.

(The information so far is taken straight from the question)

£10,000 dividend on £125,000 capital = *8%*

Step 2

Form's Preference Shareholders will receive in exchange for their shares £20 of 5% Debentures for every 100 Preference shares - therefore they will receive 500 x £20 = *£10,000 5% Debentures*, PLUS enough shares to make their total income the same as they received from Form Ltd. How much *did* they receive? - 7% of £50,000 = £3,500.

Receipts from their new debentures will = £500 (5% of £10,000). Therefore, receipts from the ordinary shares have got to = *£3,000* to make a total of *£3,500*. At 8% dividend (see Step 1) they must therefore receive *37,500 ordinary shares of £1* to get a £3,000 dividend.

31

We now have the answer to what holdings in Reform Ltd the Preference shareholders of Form Ltd will have - i.e. 37,500 ordinary shares and £10,000 of debenture stock.

Step 3

The Debenture holders of Form Ltd are to receive for every £100 of debentures held :

£80 of 5% Debentures in Reform Ltd
Plus? ordinary shares in Reform Ltd
They will therefore receive <u>£32,000 of 5% Debentures</u> (400 x £80) which will bring in a yearly income of £1,600 (5% of £32,000).

Now the question says that the TOTAL yearly income must be equivalent to 7% p.a. on their former holdings (i.e. 7% of £40,000) which = £2,800

As they will only receive £1,600 from their new debentures they must receive another £1,200 from their ordinary shares, to make their total yearly income £2,800. How many ordinary shares would they have to have to make a £1,200 dividend when the rate of dividend is 8%?

Calculation :

8% = £8 dividend for every £100 of shares.
How many £8s are there in £1,200? - 150
Therefore, 150 x £100 = No. of £1 shares held,
= <u>15,000 shares of £1 each.</u>

We now know what the Debenture holders of Form Ltd will receive in exchange for their debentures - i.e. 15,000 shares and £32,000 of 5% Debentures in Reform Ltd.

Step 4

The ordinary shareholders of Form Ltd are to receive in exchange for their shares, the *remaining* ordinary shares which have yet to be issued by Reform Ltd. How many *have* been issued?

To Form's Preference Shareholders	37,500	(see Step 2)
To Form's Debenture holders	<u>15,000</u>	(see Step 3)
Total issued	<u>52,500</u>	

This leaves another 72,500 shares to be issued to make a total issued capital of £125,000 (as per the question) - so the ordinary shareholders of Form Ltd receive *72,500 new ordinary £1 shares* and *NO debentures.*

LESSON 3

AMALGAMATIONS AND TAKEOVERS

Businesses can amalgamate in a variety of ways, e.g.

(a)   A sole trader may be taken over by a partnership
(b)   A partnership may be taken over by a limited company
(c)   A limited company may be taken over by another limited company
(d)   A new company may be formed to take over one or more existing companies

With (a) and (b) the business being taken over is simply absorbed into the other business, which means that the assets and liabilities of both businesses are combined (i.e. added together). If the purchaser acquires £5,000 of new assets from the business being taken over, then the purchaser's net assets are obviously increased by £5,000 and immediately decreased by the £5,000 cash which has to be paid as the purchase price. In the (b) type of amalgamation, the purchaser is a limited company and may settle the purchase price partly by a payment in cash and partly by an issue of its own shares or debentures.

EXAMPLES

Balance Sheet of Business A. Limited

	£		£
Issued Share Capital (£1 shares)	20,000	Fixed Assets	16,000
Current Liabilities	7,000	Current Assets	11,000
	27,000		27,000

Balance Sheet of Business B. (Sole Trader)

	£		£
Capital	5,000	Fixed Assets	4,000
Current Liabilities	1,000	Current Assets	2,000
	6,000		6,000

SITUATION (1)   A. Ltd is to take over B's assets and liabilities at balance sheet values for £5,000, payment to be made in cash.

SITUATION (2)   A. Ltd is to take over B's assets at its *own valuation* of £3,000 for fixed assets and £1,500 for current assets. Current liabilities of B. are agreed at the balance sheet figure. Purchase price, £3,500 to be made : £500 in cash, the balance by the issue of £1 shares in A. Ltd, at par.

SITUATION (3)   A. Ltd is to take over B's assets and liabilities at balance sheet values. Purchase price agreed at £6,000 - payment to be made £1,000 in cash and the balance by the issue of an appropriate number of £1 shares at a premium of 25%.

We will look at these three different situations in turn, and in doing this we will understand some important basic principles which can be used to solve more complicated questions later on.

NOTE: In each situation the business of B. CEASES TO EXIST.

SITUATION (1)

A. Ltd agrees with the balance sheet values of B's assets and liabilities, and after acquiring the business of B., the balance sheet of A. Ltd will appear like this.

	£		£
Issued Share Capital (£1 shares)	20,000	Fixed Assets (£16,000 + £4,000)	20,000
Current Liabilities		Current Assets	8,000
(£7,000 plus £1,000)	8,000	(£11,000 plus £2,000 less £5,000	
		paid in cash)	
	28,000		28,000

NOTE: Issued share capital is unchanged because no new shares have been issued by A. Ltd, payment for B. having been made entirely in cash. All that has happened is that A. Ltd has given out £5,000 in cash and received in return £5,000 of new assets which once belonged to B.

If you are now asking yourself what has happened to the £5,000 described in B's balance sheet as 'Capital' or, if you are saying 'Why hasn't the £5,000 'Capital' of B. been incorporated into A's balance sheet?' - then you have not fully understood Lesson 1. Go back to it!

The £5,000 'Capital' of B. has been incorporated into A's balance sheet in the following way :

	£
B's Fixed Assets	4,000
B's Current Assets	2,000
	6,000
Less B's Current Liabilities	1,000
Net value of B. (i.e. Capital)	5,000

SITUATION (2)

In this example A. Ltd does not agree with the balance sheet values of B. and as far as A. Ltd is concerned, it is only taking over the assets at the values it agrees with.

After acquiring B. the balance sheet of A. Ltd will appear thus :

	£		£
Issued Share Capital (£1 shares)	23,000	Fixed Assets	
Current Liabilities		(£6,000 plus £3,000)	19,000
(£7,000 plus £1,000)	8,000	Current Assets	
		£11,000 plus £1,500 less £500	
		paid in cash)	12,000
	31,000		31,000

NOTE: £4,500 of assets and £1,000 of liabilities are acquired by A Ltd, in other words, £3,500 of net assets - and the agreed purchase price for these is the same figure. The payment of this purchase price has caused two things to happen to A Ltd.

(1)   Its assets have been depleted by £500 (cash).
(2)   Its liabilities have been increased by £3,000 (Issue of 3,000 £1 shares at £1 each, i.e. at par).

        In return, of course, A Ltd's net assets have increased by £3,500 due to the taking over of B's assets and liabilities.

34

SITUATION (3)

A. Ltd has agreed with the balance sheet values shown by B. and is therefore to acquire £6,000 of assets and £1,000 of liabilities, (i.e. £5,000 of net assets), but it is being asked to pay £6,000 for them!

What is A. getting for this extra £1,000 it is being asked to pay? It is acquiring the goodwill of B - in other words the reputation and custom of B. - A. Ltd is being asked to pay £1,000 for an intangible type of asset, goodwill! So - in return for the £6,000 to be paid A. Ltd acquires the following :

	£
Fixed assets of B.	4,000
Plus Goodwill (regarded as a fixed asset) of B	1,000
Plus current assets of B.	2,000
	7,000
Less current liabilities of B.	1,000
	6,000

These increases in A. Ltd's assets and liabilities will be incorporated into its balance sheet.

Payment now has to be made and this is to be partly in cash and partly in shares - as in situation 2. Obviously then, A's cash will be reduced (by £1,000) and its issued share capital will be increased by the shares issued. In this example however, unlike the last, A. Ltd considers its shares to be worth 25% more than the nominal value of £1 - i.e. worth £1.25. Therefore in order to satisfy the rest of the purchase price (£5,000) it need only issue 4,000 shares (4,000 x £1.25 = £5,000). The Issued Share Capital of A. will therefore increase by £4,000 (nominal value) and a Capital Reserve will be created for the other £1,000. The name of this Capital Reserve will be 'Share Premium Account' as this is what it represents. To clarify this let us look at the balance sheet of A. Ltd as it will appear after the take-over.

Balance Sheet of A. Ltd

	£		£
Issued Share Capital (£1 shares)	24,000	Fixed Assets (including goodwill)	21,000
Share Premium Account	1,000	Current Assets	12,000
Current Liabilities	8,000		
	33,000		33,000

Comparing this with the balance sheet before A. took over B., it is clear that A. has issued a further 4,000 shares of £1 nominal value - it has also made a profit of £1,000 which is being held in Reserve, as the profit is not from normal trading and is NOT therefore available for distribution to shareholders as dividends. It is, despite this, an amount which is owed by the company to its shareholders which explains why it must appear as a liability. Remember that *all* profits made by a business belong to the owners.

Current assets of £12,000. This is the combination of A. and B's current assets (£2,000 plus £11,000) less the £1,000 cash paid as part of the purchase price.

In the amalgamation we have just been looking at, the businesses being taken over were NOT limited companies and on being taken over they ceased to exist in their own right, their assets and liabilities being incorporated into the purchaser's business.

The (c) or (d) type of amalgamation - i.e. a limited company taking over another limited company or a new limited company taking over one or more existing limited companies, would be treated in exactly the same way as those we have already looked at, *provided the company being taken over ceases to exist after the takeover.* In other words, if the assets and liabilities are to be taken over by the purchasing company and incorporated into its own assets and liabilities, then the company being taken over will cease to exist once it has given up its assets and liabilities to the purchasing company.

An example of this would be to look back at our last examples of A. Ltd taking over B. and read it as A. Ltd taking over B. *Ltd.* The procedure is not affected at all.

However, a limited company often 'takes over' another limited company by purchasing sufficient shares in it to gain complete *control* of it. For example, if you had sufficient money and you were given the opportunity to buy 51% of the issued shares of a company, then you would be in complete control of the company as the major shareholder. Whatever you said would over-rule what the other shareholders had to say. In the same way that an individual may gain control in this way, why shouldn't a company (say A. Ltd) gain control of another company (say B. Ltd) by purchasing enough of its shares. B. Ltd would continue to exist as before but now with fewer shareholders including one major shareholder.

In return for the purchase price paid for the shares, A. Ltd would acquire NOT assets and liabilities which once belonged to B. Ltd, but an 'Investment' which would appear on the assets side of A's balance sheet. The position would be that A. Ltd had bought an Investment (being shares in B. Ltd), and from this investment A. Ltd would expect to receive dividends as would any shareholder.

Payment for acquiring control in this way would of course be made in cash and/or shares and debentures as with the other kind of takeover already discussed. The persons who receive the cash/shares/debentures are, of course, the old shareholders of B. Ltd who have been induced to sell their holdings.

EXAMPLES

Balance Sheet of A. Ltd.

	£		£
Issued Share Capital (£1 shares)	20,000	Fixed Assets	18,000
Profit and Loss Account	2,000	Current Assets	8,000
	22,000		
Current Liabilities	4,000		
	26,000		26,000

Balance Sheet of B. Ltd

	£		£
Issued Share Capital (£1 shares)	6,000	Fixed Assets	5,000
Profit and Loss Account	1,000	Current Assets	4,000
	7,000		
Current Liabilities	2,000		
	9,000		9,000

A. Ltd takes control of B. Ltd by purchasing 4,000 £1 shares of B. Ltd at a cost of £5,000. The purchase price is to be settled by a cash payment of £1,000 and an issue by A. Ltd of an appropriate number of its own £1 shares at a premium of 25%.

Balance Sheets of A. Ltd and B. Ltd
after the take-over

A. Ltd	£		£
Issued Share Capital (£1 shares)	23,200	Fixed Assets	18,000
Share Premium Account	800	Investment - Shares in B. at cost	5,000
Profit and Loss Account	2,000	Current Assets	7,000
	26,000		
Current Liabilities	4,000		
	30,000		30,000

B. Ltd	£		£
Issued Share Capital (£1 shares)	6,000	Fixed Assets	5,000
Profit and Loss Account	1,000	Current Assets	4,000
	7,000		
Current Liabilities	2,000		
	9,000		9,000

NOTE : *Re A. Ltd.* Fixed assets *are not affected* - i.e. none are acquired. Current assets are reduced by the cash paid out, £1,000, as part of the purchase price for the shares in B. Ltd. Share capital goes up by the nominal amount of the shares issued in part payment and the 'profit' (25% premium) is held in reserve on Share Premium a/c.

A. Ltd has therefore acquired and Investment (an asset) for £5,000 in return for which it has increased its liabilities by £4,000 (share capital and share premium) and decreased its assets by £1,000 (cash). There is no question of goodwill arising in this kind of takeover. A. is simply buying an investment which is shown AT COST on A's Balance Sheet. Whether or not the true value of the investment is the same as its cost does not concern us. A. Ltd is now the Holding Company of B. Ltd.

Re B. Ltd. On the face of it nothing has happened to B. Ltd. Its assets and liabilities are unchanged. The company continues to trade as before, i.e. it still exists. All that has happened, as stated before, is that the make-up of B's shareholders is now different. There is one major shareholder who may dictate on policy, etc. The register of shareholders will therefore be amended so that future dividends will be paid to the right persons. B. Ltd is now a Subsidiary Company of A. Ltd.

Summary

Amalgamations or takeovers can be broken down into two main types :

(i)   Where the purchaser buys and *takes possession* of the assets and liabilities of another business so incorporating them into its own assets and liabilities. The purchaser may have to pay something for the Goodwill of the business it is buying. The business which is being taken over ceases to exist.

(ii)   Where the purchaser buys sufficient shares to give it a controlling interest in the company. The purchaser does not acquire any assets or liabilities of that company, but instead acquires the asset Investment. The business which is being taken over continues as though nothing had happened.

Most large takeovers are of type (ii). When a company (A) makes a takeover bid for control of another company (B) it has to persuade the present shareholders of that company (B) to sell their shares and it does this by offering attractive substitutes for their shares - e.g. 2 or more shares in (A) in exchange for every share in (B), etc.

Dividends received by Holding Company

A Holding Company will receive annual dividends from its subsidiary and at the year end these will be credited to the Holding Company's Profit and Loss account as a gain, and will therefore, increase the distributable profits for its own shareholders (i.e. dividends received will increase the net profit which is to be carried down to the Appropriation Account). You may be wondering why the shareholders of the Holding Company are allowed to receive this part of profits (which are not trading profits) as dividends. The reason is that the dividends received from the subsidiary become *normal* profits to the Holding Company in the same way that Rents Received are regarded as normal, and therefore available for distribution.

Such dividends are however, only available for distribution by the Holding Company if they are dividends which come from profits earned *since* the Holding Company acquired control of the subsidiary. Any payment of dividends by the subsidiary which come out of profits earned *before* the Holding Company acquired control, must be treated as being a refund of part of the purchase money paid for the shares.

Summary

Dividends received by Holding Company are out of profits earned by the subsidiary company.

EITHER (a) since the takeover,

OR (b) before the takeover.

IF (a) Available for distribution to Holding Company's Shareholders (Cr. Profit and Loss account)

IF (b) Not available for distribution (Cr. Investment account, thereby reducing the cost of the investment)

EXERCISE 3.1

Halstead Ltd was incorporated on 1 January, 19-7 with an authorised capital of 16,000 shares of £1 each. 10,000 of these shares were issued at par and fully paid up on 1 January, 19-7. A profit of £4,448 was made during 19-7. At 31 December, 19-7 the company's fixed assets were £8,000, stock amounted to £4,261, debtors to £3,847, balance at bank (before undertaking the transactions with Bardfield mentioned below), was £2,624 and its creditors were £4,284.

On 1 January, 19-8 Halstead took over the assets and assumed responsibility for the liabilities of Bardfield Ltd at an agreed price of £7,500, which was satisfied by the issue of 6,000 shares of £1 each at a premium of £0.25. per share. The shares were issued and Bardfields overdraft was paid off on 1 January, 19-8. The assets were taken into the books of Halstead at the figures at which they appeared in the balance sheet of Bardfield dated 31 December, 19-7 as follows :

	£	£		£	£
Share Capital		4,000	Fixed Assets		4,000
Profit and Loss account		2,160			
		6,160	Stock	2,816	
Creditors	1,481		Debtors	891	3,707
Bank overdraft	66	1,547			
		7,707			7,707

Required : The balance sheet of Halstead Ltd on 1 January, 19-8 immediately after the completion of the purchase of Bardfield's assets. Ignore depreciation.

38

EXERCISE 3.2

Summarised balance sheets of Mortice Ltd and Tenon Ltd at 21 April, 19-1 were :

	Mortice Ltd	Tenon Ltd
	£	£
Issued Share Capital (£1 ordinary shares)	20,000	40,000
Profit and loss account	48,000	32,000
Current Liabilities	22,000	18,000
	90,000	90,000
Property and equipment (at cost less depn.)	50,000	57,000
Current Assets	40,000	33,000
	90,000	90,000

On 22 April, 19-1 the two companies are to be amalgamated to form a new company, Joint Ltd, which will take over all assets and liabilities of Mortice Ltd and Tenon Ltd at that date.

Shares and debenture stock will be issued by Joint Ltd as consideration, on the basis shown below:

1. To shareholders in Mortice Ltd :
   Three £1 ordinary shares in Joint Ltd for each share held in Mortice Ltd, and £75 of 10% Debenture Stock for every 100 shares held in Mortice Ltd.

2. To shareholders in Tenon Ltd :
   Three £1 ordinary shares in Joint Ltd for every two shares held in Tenon Ltd and £100 of 10% Debenture Stock for every 100 shares held in Tenon Ltd.

Property and equipment, current assets and current liabilities acquired by Joint Ltd will appear in that company's books at the values at which they appear in the balance sheets of Mortice Ltd and Tenon Ltd. Shareholders have made the following criticisms of the proposed scheme for amalgamation :

(i) Mortice's profit and loss account balance indicates that it will contribute three-fifths of the profits of the amalgamated company; therefore, Mortice's shareholders should receive three-fifths of the capital to be issued by Joint.

(ii) Tenon has twice as many issued shares as Mortice; therefore, Tenon's shareholders should receive two-thirds of the capital to be issued by Joint

(iii) Mortice and Tenon contribute capital plus reserves (profit and loss account) to the amalgamated company in the proportion 68:72; therefore, capital of Joint should be allocated to the shareholders of Mortice and Tenon in that proportion.

Required :

(a) Balance Sheet of Joint Ltd at 22 April, 19-1 after the proposed amalgamation has taken place.

(b) Your views (with brief reasons) on whether you agree or disagree with each of the three criticisms made by shareholders.

SOLUTIONS

Solution 3.1

Halstead Limited
Balance Sheet as at 1 January, 19-8

	£		£	£
Authorised and Issued Share Capital		Fixed Assets (including		
16,000 shares at £1 each (fully paid)	16,000	Goodwill £1,340)		13,340
Share premium	1,500	Stock in Trade	7,077	
	17,500	Debtors	4,738	
Profit and Loss account	4,448	Balance at Bank	2,558	
	21,948			14,373
Creditors	5,765			
	27,713			27,713

NOTE :	Value of acquired	=	£6,160	
	Cost of acquisition	=	£7,500	
	Therefore:	=	£1,340	was paid for goodwill

Solution 3.2

Balance Sheet of Joint Ltd

	£		£
Share Capital (£1 shares)	120,000	Goodwill *	35,000
(60,000 to Mortice/60,000 to Tenon)			
10% Debenture Stock	55,000	Property, etc.	107,000
(15,000 to Mortice/40,000 to Tenon)			
Current liabilities	40,000	Current Assets	73,000
	215,000		215,000

* Purchase Price = £175,000 - Net Assets acquired amount to £140,000 - therefore Goodwill of £35,000 is paid for.

VIEWS: (i) The difference in Profit and Loss account balances does not mean a difference in profits *earned* . One company may pay out more dividends than the other.

(ii) Nominal values should not be compared - e.g. Tenon's shares (on a balance sheet basis) are worth £1.80 each whilst Mortice's are worth £3.40 each!

(iii) What are the *current* values of the assets making up the capital and reserves? The amounts shown in the balance sheets are not a good basis for comparing: see (i) above also.

LESSON 4

REDEMPTION AND PURCHASE OF SHARES

REDEMPTION OF DEBENTURES

Redemption of Redeemable Shares

Look at this simple balance sheet :

	£		£
Share Capital			
10,000 Ordinary Shares of £1	10,000	Fixed Assets	17,500
4,000 Preference Shares of £1	4,000	Stock and debtors	2,500
	14,000	Bank	4,500
Profit and Loss account	5,000		
	19,000		
Debentures (secured)	2,000		
Creditors	3,500		
	24,500		24,500

Suppose now, that you were one of the creditors. Your main interest in this balance sheet would be to see that there were sufficient assets to pay the money owing to you. How secure is your debt? In the event of the company going into liquidation, the debts of the company would be paid in the following order of priority :

      1st -   Debenture Holders
      2nd - Creditors (i.e. YOU!)
      3rd - Shareholders

The company has £24,500 of assets, so allowing for the £2,000 due to debenture holders, this leaves £22,500 out of which the creditors want £3,500, so leaving £19,000 for the shareholders. Everybody appears to be free from worry! But, suppose the fixed assets did not realise their balance sheet value, or suppose the debtors turned out to be bad debts or some of the stock was obsolete - suppose that the total assets realised only £15,000. After paying the debentures off, that only leaves £13,000 to settle total debts of £22,500 (£19,000 to shareholders and £3,500 to creditors). Who goes without? The shareholders of course! In fact, you (as a creditor) don't mind if the assets realise up to £19,000 less than the balance sheet value, because the shareholders will bear this, not you!

In other words the shareholders' capital is your 'cushion' of security for repayment. This capital represents the assets which the shareholders have put into the business, and it is their capital which is lost first. As a creditor then, you feel secure whilst that 'cushion' is there. But what if the company suddenly started to pay away part of your 'cushion' by using up the balance of undistributed profits on the Profit and Loss account to pay dividends? Well you must accept that it would be possible for up to £5,000 of your security to be lost in this way but you would normally expect this to soon be replaced again by new profits. Anyway, your security is worth without question, at least £14,000 (the amount of issued capital) - *unless* the company decided to buy back some of its shares! Then you *would* be alarmed. And because of this the Companies Act specifically states that a company may *not* redeem any shares it has issued. This is an important protection for creditors, for without it a dishonest company on seeing itself heading for liquidation, might decide to pay off the shareholders whilst funds were still available, and by the time the company was wound up the creditors would only have the remaining 'crumbs' to pick up. Because of the protection of the Act it is the shareholders who must be left with the 'crumbs'.

However, it was realised many years ago that many companies were often in need of *temporary* capital and were not too happy about issuing shares which could not be redeemed when the need for additional capital had passed. To cater for this situation therefore, an early Companies Act permits companies to issue Redeemable Preference Shares - i.e. shares which can be redeemed by the company at a later date. Now the 1985 Companies Act permits companies to issue Redeemable Ordinary Shares as well. Whichever type of redeemable share is issued by the company there are conditions to be satisfied when the time for redemption arrives, so that the creditors' security is not affected by the redemption. When the shares are paid off, the amount so paid must *immediately* be replaced by a NEW issue of shares. In this way the creditors will retain their full protection, because any cash going out of the company to pay off the shareholders is immediately replaced from the new issue of shares. An alternative procedure to this is allowed by the Act, and this is for the company, instead of issuing new shares to replace the old ones, to *capitalise* some of the distributable profits (i.e. the balance on Profit and Loss account or General Reserve) - in other words to 'freeze' some of the distributable profits and make sure that they can never be distributed to shareholders. This is done by taking part of the Profit and Loss account balance (or General Reserve) and transferring it to a Capital Reserve account (which you will remember, cannot be used to pay dividends). The Act insists that this be called a CAPITAL REDEMPTION RESERVE. How does this protect the creditors you might be asking - cash isn't coming into the company as with a new issue of shares - all that has happened is a book-keeping entry, transferring part of one account to another one. The answer is, that the company has not received any cash but has ensured that a certain amount of its existing cash balance will never be paid out to shareholders, and has therefore *conserved* cash which might otherwise have been paid out. Remember what I said earlier about the creditor having to accept that the balance on Profit and Loss account is not permanent security to him as it may be withdrawn from the business at any time in cash. If, however, some of that balance is taken away and put into a permanent form (i.e. in a Capital Redemption Reserve) then, providing that the amount transferred to this Reserve is the same as the amount of shares being repaid (and not being covered by a new issue) the creditor is in exactly the same position of security as before.

Using the following Balance Sheet let us look at some examples :

Balance Sheet

	£		£
Ordinary Shares	30,000	Fixed Assets	32,000
Redeemable Preference Shares	5,000	Stock,etc.	2,000
	35,000	Cash	10,000
Profit and Loss account	5,000		
	40,000		
Creditors	4,000		
	44,000		44,000

NOTE: The creditors have solid security of assets worth £35,000.

EXAMPLE 1

The Preference Shares are redeemed and an equivalent amount of ordinary shares are issued. How does our balance sheet change?

(Important Note : Look at the foregoing balance sheet and then try to see a mental picture of the changes which take place - this is an excellent exercise in grasping accountancy).

Point (i)   Cash remains the same (i.e. £5,000 goes out to Preference Shareholders and £5,000 comes in from the new ordinary shares).

Point (ii)   Share capital is reduced by £5,000 but immediately replaced by new shares.

42

Point (iii)   The creditors still have solid security of £35,000, as before.

EXAMPLE 2

The preference shares are redeemed but no new shares are issued. How does the balance sheet change?

Point (i)   Cash goes down by £5,000

Point (ii)   £5,000 of the Profit and Loss account balance is capitalised (i.e. taken from the Profit and Loss account and moved to a Capital Redemption Reserve where it can't be 'got at'). There is now no danger that the shareholders will exercise their rights and take the remaining £5,000 of cash to pay themselves a dividend.

Point (iii)   The creditors have solid security of £35,000 of assets (as before) which, in the event of winding up would be used to meet their claims first, and the shareholders have no way of reducing these available assets.

EXAMPLE 3

The preference shares are redeemed partly from the proceeds of 3,000 new ordinary shares of £1 each and partly out of profits. What happens to the balance sheet?

Point (i)   Cash goes down by £2,000

Point (ii)   £2,000 of distributable profits (i.e. Profit and Loss account) are capitalised by transferring them to a Capital Redemption Reserve.

After this last example the balance sheet would appear thus:

Balance Sheet

	£		£
Ordinary Shares	33,000	Fixed Assets	32,000
Capital Redemption Reserve	2,000	Stock, etc.	2,000
	35,000	Cash	8,000
Profit and Loss account	3,000		
	38,000		
Creditors	4,000		
	42,000		42,000

To summarise :

If a company reduces its permanent capital by repaying redeemable shares, then the resulting 'gap' in the capital must be filled by:

      (a)   a new issue of shares,

OR   (b)   capitalisation of distributable profits (e.g. any REVENUE reserve),

OR   (c)   a combination of (a) and (b).

Redemption of shares at a premium (i.e. a £1 share redeemed at £1.50), or an issue of new shares at a premium, does not complicate the issue one little bit. For the purpose of calculating how much to take to the Capital Redemption Reserve ignore ALL premiums. In finally dealing with the premiums it is just a matter of crediting the premiums received to a share premium account and taking any premiums necessary for repayment of the preference shares out of either the existing share premium account (if any) or out of any revenue reserve. In the latter case you would simply be diverting profits (which might be used to pay dividends) to some other use, whilst in the former case you would be utilising share premium instead. However, the 1985 Companies Act laid down certain conditions regarding the use of Share Premium Accounts. These are that the premium to be paid on redemption of the shares can only come out of Share Premium Account if the shares to be redeemed were *originally* issued at a premium. Whatever that premium amounted to is also the maximum amount which can come out of share premium account to cover the premium on redemption. The rest must come out of normal *revenue* reserves. Therefore, the premium paid on redemption reduces cash and reduces Share Premium Account and/or Revenue Reserves. Where there is NO new issue of shares involved (i.e. the redemption is wholly out of profits) then NO premium payable on redemption can come out of the share premium account. In other words, anything coming out of share premium account should always be 'covered' by incoming cash from a new issue.

A COMPANY PURCHASING ITS OWN SHARES

The 1985 Companies Act allows a company to buy its own shares provided that the shares are then cancelled and not held by the company as an investment.

If a company therefore decides to buy its own shares (in the same way that an individual would buy shares in a company - i.e. in the case of quoted shares, through a stockbroker) the effect is just the same as if the company had redeemed some of its shares - i.e. paid them off! Think about this - the outcome of the transactions are identical. Cash goes out to either, a) holders of redeemable shares which are going to cease to exist any more or, b) to holders of current shares who are going to transfer ownership to the company at which point the position will be as though such shares had never been issued.

The resultant 'gap' in the company's capital must be filled in exactly the same way as detailed earlier in the Lesson in connection with redeemable shares - i.e. by either a new issue of shares or by the capitalisation of revenue reserves to a Capital Redemption Reserve (or a combination of both procedures).

Therefore, any question you may get on 'purchase by a company of its own shares' can be treated in the accounts as though redeemable shares were being redeemed. Easy!

One extra point to be noted though is the fact that *Private Limited Companies* are allowed by the 1985 Act to use *capital* reserves in order to help create a Capital Redemption Reserve *if necessary*. For example, if a private company is purchasing its own shares and is not covering the *whole* purchase by an equivalent (in amount) new issue of shares, then the amount of undistributed profits (i.e. reserves) which have to be transferred to the Capital Redemption Reserve (to fill the 'gap') are not restricted to Revenue Reserves - Capital Reserves *can* be used *but only if absolutely necessary*.

EXAMPLE

Balance Sheet of Private Ltd Co.

	£		£
Share Capital (£1)	100,000	Cash	50,000
Revaluation Reserve	30,000	Other Assets	100,000
Revenue Reserves	20,000		
	150,000		150,000

The company decides to purchase 40,000 of its own shares, at par. To finance this the company issues 10,000 £1 shares at par for cash.

Balance Sheet Afterwards

	£		£
Share Capital	70,000	Cash	20,000
Capital Redemption Reserve	30,000	Other Assets	100,000
Revaluation Reserve	20,000		
Revenue Reserves	-		
	__120,000__		__120,000__

NOTE - the 'gap' created by the purchase is £40,000 - £10,000 of this is 'filled' by the issue of 10,000 new shares, so leaving a 'gap' of £30,000 to be filled by a capital redemption reserve. As there are only £20,000 of revenue reserves available to capitalise, then *because it is a private company,* capital can be used to cover the shortfall (i.e. £10,000 can be taken from Revaluation Reserve to help create the necessary Capital Redemption Reserve). Public Companies would not be allowed to do this - in the above example it would be necessary for a *public* company to issue a minimum of 10,000 shares to finance the purchase.

If a private company has insufficient reserves to create the necessary Capital Redemption Reserve, then the 'shortfall' can be ignored in effect and a smaller Capital Redemption Reserve (than would be normal) created. The company would then be utilising a capital reserve (Capital Redemption Reserve) out of necessity.

EXAMPLE

Balance Sheet of a Private Ltd Co.

	£		£
Share Capital (£1)	200,000	Cash	120,000
Revenue Reserves	__80,000__	Other Assets	__160,000__
	280,000		280,000

The company purchases 100,000 of its own £1 shares at par. No new issue of shares is to be made.

NOTE - in normal circumstances the company would need to capitalise reserves of £100,000 to a Capital Redemption Reserve. However, in view of the 1985 Act this private company can utilise the capital reserve (Capital Redemption Reserve) to cover the shortfall of £20,000 and show a Capital Redemption Reserve of only £80,000 - viz:

Balance Sheet

	£		£
Share Capital (£1)	100,000	Cash	20,000
Revenue Reserves	-	Other Assets	160,000
Capital Redemption Reserve	__80,000__		
	180,000		180,000

In this case the 'gap' of £100,000 which has been created has *not* been completely filled (to the detriment of the creditors!) but the 1985 Act says that capital *can* be used to cover purchase of own shares *in the case of a private limited company.* In this example, £20,000 of capital has been used. Who are we to argue?

REDEMPTION OF DEBENTURES

The owners of a company are its shareholders - the people who have put *permanent* capital into the company by buying its shares. As owners, they have a say in how the company is to be run by voting on varied issues at meetings of shareholders. They can never expect to get their money back from the company (unless they hold redeemable shares or unless the company goes into liquidation) but they can always sell their shares to someone else through the Stock Market. Any profits made by the company belong to them and these are regularly shared out by paying the shareholders *dividends*. Any profits which are not to be distributed as dividends are held in reserve as we have already seen (e.g. as a Profit and Loss account or General Reserve balance).

If a company requires more *permanent* capital it will issue some new shares - i.e. invite the public to buy a share in the business or to increase their existing share in the business.

Quite often though, a company is in need of temporary capital only - capital which is only required for a limited period of time. The obvious answer is for the company to borrow money and this can be done in a variety of ways. A bank or finance company may lend the required amount or the company may ask the general public to lend money - the company does this by the process of offering for sale DEBENTURES which are acknowledgements (in the form of a certificate) of money received on loan. Persons buying these debentures are simply lending money to the company. As with all loans they will be repaid at some future date (compare with shares) and in the meantime the lender (debenture holder) will receive interest at a fixed rate on the loan he has made to the company. This interest is payable *whether profits are made by the company or not*, and this is why the expense 'debenture interest' is always charged to the Profit and Loss account proper and not to the appropriation account. With shares you will remember, payment of dividends is entirely dependent on profits being made and such payments are therefore *appropriations* of profit.

When anyone lends money they usually wish the loan to be secured in some way, and loans to a company in the form of debentures are usually secured on certain assets of the company (e.g. the premises) which means that should the company be unable to repay the debenture holders on the due date, then the premises would have to be sold to pay off the debenture holders. Debentures so secured are called Mortgage Debentures and most debentures are of this kind.

Mortgage Debenture holders are then in a fairly safe position. Not only will they receive their interest, whether profits are being made by the company or not, but if things start going wrong within the company their debts will always be safe whilst the assets which secure the debentures are still standing!

Repayment of the debentures is a very straightforward business - there are no legal aspects for the company to consider as with redeemable shares, because in redeeming debentures the company is not reducing the permanent capital of the company which the creditors rely on - it is simply paying off a special kind of creditor. A creditor is expected to be aware of the fact that debentures will, at some time in the future, be repaid by the company and no businesslike creditor would ever rely on the amount of assets provided by money obtained from debenture holders.

Procedure then, on repayment of debentures? Credit bank with the money leaving the company and debit Debentures account, so reducing this liability, and that is that! As you will appreciate though, this will make quite a 'hole' in the bank account, as debentures are not usually in small amounts, and, if at the same time the shareholders are due for a large slice of profits in the form of dividends, the two payments will together make a real mess of the bank balance! Therefore, at the time debentures are repaid, it is the practice of companies to divert some of the profits available to shareholders (e.g. on appropriation account) into a special Reserve Account thus reducing the amount of profit which is available for payment of dividends and therefore reducing the amount of cash which the company will have to pay out in dividends. The cash thereby 'saved' can be used to repay the debenture holders.

EXERCISE 4.1

Balance Sheet of Plastico Ltd

	£		£
Issued Share Capital		Fixed Assets	20,000
5,000 5% Redeemable Preference Shares of £1	5,000		
15,000 Ordinary Shares of £1	15,000	Current Assets	
	20,000	Stock	2,000
General Reserve	3,000	Debtors	2,000
Profit and Loss account	6,000	Bank	6,000
	29,000		
Creditors, etc.	1,000		
	30,000		30,000

The Preference Shares are redeemed:

(a)   at par by the issue of 5,000 Ordinary Shares of £1 each at par.
        Show the balance sheet after redemption.

(b)   at par, out of profits.
        Show the balance sheet after redemption.

(c)   at par, partly by the issue of 3,000 Ordinary Shares of £1 each, at par.
        Show the balance sheet after redemption.

NOTE: Treat (a), (b) and (c) as three separate exercises.

EXERCISE 4.2

The following is a summarised Balance Sheet of Ajax Ltd at 31 December, 19-7 :

	£		£
Issued Capital		Fixed Assets less depn..	21,000
50,000 Ordinary Shares of 50p each	25,000	Stock	7,000
7,000 8% Redeemable Preference Shares of 50p each	3,500	Debtors	5,000
		Bank	6,000
Profit and Loss account	8,500		
Current Liabilities	2,000		
	39,000		39,000

The following transactions take place on 1 January, 19-8 :

(i)   All the preference shares are redeemed at a premium of 10%

(ii)   £5,000 9% Debentures are issued at a discount of 5%, these being paid for immediately.

(iii)   4,000 Ordinary Shares of 50p each are issued at par, these being paid for immediately.

You are required to show the revised Balance Sheet as at 1 January, 19-8 after the above transactions have been completed.

EXERCISE 4.3 EX

The following is a summarised balance sheet of a *private limited company* at 31 December 19-3 :

	£		£
Issued Share Capital			
80,000 Ordinary Shares of £1 each	80,000	Net Assets	85,000
Revaluation Reserve	2,000		
Revenue Reserves	3,000		
	85,000		85,000

The company decides to purchase 10,000 of its own ordinary shares at par and to issue simultaneously 2,000 Preference shares at par.

Show the balance sheet as it would appear after these transactions have taken place.

EXERCISE 4.4 EX

A section of the balance sheet of Pearl Ltd as at 31 December 19-8 is as follows :

Balance Sheet extract

	£
Ordinary shares of £1 each	1,300
Share premium account	520
Retained profits	780
	2,600

The Companies Act 1985 allows companies to issue redeemable shares and the above balance sheet includes redeemable ordinary shares possessing a nominal value of £260.
These are to be redeemed on 1 January 19-9.

Required :

Revised balance sheets as at 1 January 19-9, following redemption, taking separate account of each of the following assumptions :

(a)   The shares were initially issued at par and are redeemed at par.

(b)   The shares were initially issued at par and are redeemed at £1.20 per share. To help to finance the redemption a new issue of 100 shares is made at £1.05 per share.

NOTE   Assume that no other transactions occur on 1 January 19-9

SOLUTIONS

Solution 4.1

(a)

Balance Sheet

	£		£
Issued Share Capital			
20,000 Ordinary Shares £1	20,000	Fixed Assets	20,000
General Reserve	3,000	Current Assets	
Profit and Loss account	6,000	Stock	2,000
	29,000	Debtors	2,000
Creditors	1,000	Bank	6,000
	30,000		30,000

(b)

Balance Sheet

	£		£
Issued Share Capital			
15,000 Ordinary Shares of £1	15,000	Fixed Assets	20,000
Capital Redemption Reserve	5,000		
General Reserve	3,000	Current Assets	
Profit and Loss account	1,000	Stock	2,000
	24,000	Debtors	2,000
Creditors, etc.	1,000	Bank	1,000
	25,000		25,000

(c)

Balance Sheet

	£		£
Issued Share Capital			
18,000 Ordinary Shares of £1	18,000	Fixed Assets	20,000
Capital Redemption Reserve	2,000		
General Reserve	3,000	Current Assets	
Profit & Loss account	4,000	Stock	2,000
	27,000	Debtors	2,000
Creditors	1,000	Bank	4,000
	28,000		28,000

NOTE :   Either General Reserve OR Profit and Loss account may be used to create a Capital Redemption Reserve, so your figures may differ on these accounts.

In each case the creditors' security remains at a total of £20,000 - i.e. there are always £20,000 of assets, which cannot be repaid whilst the company is a going concern.

Solution 4.2

Transaction (i)   Bank reduced by £3,850 - Preference Share Capital reduced by £3,500 and Profit and Loss account by £350 (premium).

Transaction (ii)   Bank increased by £4,750 - Debentures increased by £5,000 (nominal value) - the £250 loss (discount) reduces Profit and Loss account.

Transaction (iii)   Bank increased by £2,000 - Ordinary Share Capital also increased by £2,000.

NOTE: Capital has been reduced by £3,500 with the redemption of the preference shares and this 'gap' has been partly filled by the issue of more shares, to the extent of £2,000. The remaining 'gap' of £1,500 must now be filled by transferring £1,500 from Profit and Loss account to a Capital Redemption Reserve as per Companies Act requirements.

Revised Balance Sheet

Issued Capital	£		£
54,000 Ordinary Shares of 50p	27,000	Fixed Assets less depn.	21,000
Capital Redemption Reserve	1,500	Stock	7,000
Profit and Loss account		Debtors	5,000
(see notes above)	6,400	Bank (see notes above)	8,900
9% Debentures	5,000		
Current Liabilities	2,000		
	41,900		41,900

LESSON 5

BUSINESS AND SHARE VALUATIONS

The value of any business which, in the case of a limited company means the value of its shares, can be determined in a variety of ways for a variety of reasons.

Let us look first at the reasons for valuing a business. The most obvious is for the general interest of the owners, be it the sole trader, the partners or the shareholders. In the case of the sole trader and partnership it may be necessary to place a value on the business for the purpose of calculating Inheritance Tax due on the death of an owner. Where a business is being sold or amalgamated, it is obviously necessary to place a value on it. Similarly where shares are being transferred to a new owner and there is no market value quotation available, it will be necessary to work out the value of those shares. Also, where unquoted shares are being offered to a bank as security for lending, the bank will need to have some means of determining the value of those shares.

There are many methods of valuation of businesses and shares. Some methods are more suitable than others depending on the purpose or reason for valuation. Remember this when answering examination questions on this topic.

What are the various methods then? Perhaps the most obvious method is to look at the most recent balance sheet and add the assets, deducting the liabilities from the total. This will give Capital or Shareholders' stake in the case of a limited company - i.e. the Balance Sheet Value. This is referred to as the 'Assets Basis' or 'Book Value Basis' or 'Going Concern Basis'. Obviously, any fictitious assets would not be included - however, intangible assets such as Goodwill, Patents, Trade Marks *would* be included in the valuation unless the business was to cease to exist due to death of the owner(s), when these items would have no real value any more. If the business was being 'taken over' (i.e. was continuing in another form) then these intangibles *would* represent part of the value of the business.

Our first method of valuation is therefore:

Balance Sheet Basis/Assets Basis/Book Value Basis/Going Concern Basis

Total Assets (including intangibles depending on purpose of valuation)
less   Total Liabilities
=   **value of business**   (Divide by number of shares issued to get value per share).

There are serious limitations on this method of valuation in that the assets may not be reflected on the balance sheet at their true current values. For example, land and buildings may not be shown at current values - depreciation of assets over the years may have been unrealistic - stocks may be valued on an unsuitable basis - debtors may include bad debts.

Another method of valuation is by the :

Liquidation Basis/Break-up Basis/Gone Concern Basis.

This is a means of looking at the business in the most pessimistic way - i.e. what would it be worth in the event of liquidation? Bank managers often value a business in this way before lending!

The formula for this method is obvious - the forced sale value of the assets are added together and liabilities deducted to give the value of the business. Obviously, goodwill would not be included in the assets!

The limitation of this method is that break-up values must be a matter of pure opinion and there is a very wide margin for error.

Other methods of valuation are as follows:

Earnings yield

To illustrate let us look at this simple balance sheet:

Balance Sheet

	£		£
10,000 ordinary shares	10,000	Assets	18,000
Reserves	5,000		
Current liabilities	3,000		
	$\underline{18,000}$		$\underline{18,000}$

Let us assume that the above company makes a profit (after tax) of £4,000. This is the amount which is available to the ordinary shareholders (whether they draw any of it as dividends is not our concern here). £4,000 available on 10,000 £1 shares represents an *Earning Yield* of

$$\frac{4,000}{10,000} \quad x \quad \frac{100}{1} \quad = \quad 40\%$$

In other words, £10,000 of shares are earning a 40% return. If the shares of another similar type of company are earning only 10% we could say that the shares in the first company are worth 4 times the value of the shares in the second company. With shares of a nominal value of £1 in each case therefore, we could say that the shares in the first company are worth £4 against a value of £1 in the second company. Another way to show this would be:

$$\frac{\text{Net Profit}}{\text{Nominal Shares}} \quad x \quad \frac{100}{\text{Yield in other Company}} \quad = \quad \text{Value per share}$$

$$= \quad \frac{£4,000}{£10,000} \quad x \quad \frac{100}{10} \quad = \quad £4 \text{ per share}$$

In the example above we have based the yield on the nominal value of the shares, £10,000. If however, the shares were quoted on the Stock Exchange at a value of £1.60 each then altogether the shares would be worth 10,000 x £1.60 = £16,000. To get an accurate picture of what this £16,000 of value is earning we should therefore use the following calculation :

$$\frac{£4,000 \text{ profit after tax and preference dividends}}{£16,000 \text{ market values of shares}} \quad x \quad \frac{100}{1} = 25\%$$

Comparison with a similar company earning 10% gives :

$$\frac{4,000}{16,000} \quad x \quad \frac{100}{10} \quad = \quad £2.50 \text{ per share}$$

In examination questions the market value of the shares is not usually given so it has been necessary to use the nominal value as in the first example. Note that the profit figure used is after tax *and preference dividends*, and should be *before* allowing for exceptional items.

The drawback to this basis of valuation is that we are looking at what has happened in the past whereas a potential buyer would be more concerned with what might happen in the future.

Let us suppose that the buyer expects a return of 15% on his investment and that the company he is considering buying expects future profits to average £60,000 per annum. What is the value of the company in these terms?

$$\text{Value} = \frac{\text{Expected earnings (£60,000)}}{15} \times \frac{100}{1} = \underline{£400,000}$$

We must also bear in mind that the other companies being used for comparison may *not* be similar companies in many respects. For example, they may have high gearing (i.e. relying on long term loans heavily which means that interest on these will reduce earnings) or a completely different policy on directors' remuneration (again affecting profits).

Dividend Yield

A proportion of the profit earned is usually distributed as a dividend. Let us assume that the company we are looking at declares a dividend of £3,000. As a proportion of issued share capital this works out at a return of :

$$\frac{£3,000}{£10,000} \begin{matrix} \text{(Dividend)} \\ \text{(nominal Value of Shares)} \end{matrix} \times \frac{100}{1} = 30\%$$

The shareholders are getting a 30% return on their £10,000 of capital.

If a similar company has a dividend yield of 20% then we could say that our shares are worth 50% more than the other company's shares (30% against 20%), so using a £1 share as the basis for comparing we could say that our shares are worth £1.50 against a value of £1 in the other company.

The calculation would look like this :

$$\frac{\text{Dividend}}{\text{Nominal Value of Shares}} \times \frac{100}{\text{Dividend Yield in other Company}} = \text{Value per share}$$

$$\frac{£3,000}{£10,000} \times \frac{100}{20} = £1.50 \text{ per share}$$

Once again we have used the nominal value of the shares in our calculation, but to get a truer picture we should use market value. For example, if you bought a £1 share at par (i.e. for £1) and the company declared a dividend of say, 10% then you would receive a cheque for 10p (remember that percentage dividends declared by a company are always based on the nominal value of the share). A 10p return on an outlay of £1 = a true yield of 10%. If, however, you had bought your share at a premium, say for £2, then you would still receive your cheque for 10p but this return would be on an outlay of £2 which is a true yield of only 5%.

Therefore in our above comparison of dividend yields we should use market value of share in place of nominal value. If however, the examination question does not give market value you must obviously use nominal values, but you could make some reference to this in any comments which may be called for.

The limitation of this basis of valuation is that the companies being used for comparison purposes may have different profit retention policies and may be more or less consistent in paying dividends. What are future expectations? Relying on past results can be misleading.

Replacement Cost Basis

The first valuation we looked at in this lesson was the Book Value basis of valuation. The 'accurate' valuation of shares on this basis is obviously very uncertain because the calculations must rely on the amounts shown in the balance sheet as being realistic which in many cases is most unlikely! The assets may well be under or over valued in the balance sheet.

However, it is not unreasonable to expect a prospective buyer to look at the assets in terms of 'what would it cost me to *replace* those assets?' It is not then unreasonable to expect the buyer to value the company on the basis of what he would have to 'fork out' today to acquire those very same assets.

This is valuation of shares on 'Replacement Cost Basis' rather than balance sheet basis. All you need do is to ascertain the current *replacement* values of the various assets, deduct the liabilities and then divide the total by the number of shares on issue to get the value of one share. (NOTE - in the examination, are you being asked the value per share or the overall value of the company?)

Maintainable Earnings Basis

In determining the value of a company, and therefore the value of each share, a prospective buyer could look at the average profits (earnings) over the past x number of years and, if confident that these could be maintained in future, multiply this average profit by x number of years to give a value to the company. In calculating past average profits adjustments may well be made to items making up past profits (e.g. depreciation). In the examination you would be informed of any such adjustments to be made.

Price Earnings Ratio

The PE ratio simply shows the relationships of the price of the share to the earnings of that share. For example if a particular share is priced on the Stock Exchange at £2.50 and in the current year the earnings per share in the company (i.e. Net Profit after tax and preference dividends, divided by total issued shares) worked out at 25p, the PE ratio would be 10. The ratio can be expressed thus :

$$\frac{P}{E} \quad = \quad \frac{£2.50}{£0.25} = \quad 10$$

This means that someone buying the share for £2.50 is purchasing 10 years earning capacity of that share, or it would take 10 years for the share to earn the equivalent of its cost. This assumes of course that the earnings will remain constant over the years. If the price of the share increases then the ratio will increase.

This ratio is used mainly to compare the merits of one company's shares with those of another company's shares and is used a great deal for international comparisons. A ratio of 2 means the shares are earning profits to cover their cost (price) in only 2 years but then the question arises 'Why haven't the high earnings in relation to price caused an increase in demand for those shares so pushing up their price and therefore increasing the gap between earnings and price? What other factors are involved?' The ratio, like all ratios, cannot tell a story on its own - it is only one of many means of determining the merits of particular shares and must be used in conjunction with all the other means.

There is a direct relationship between the PE ratio and the Earnings Ratio we looked at earlier. This must be obvious to you - get out your pen and work out some simple examples. You will find that :

PE 10	=	Earnings Yield of	10%
PE 2	=	"	50%
PE 20	=	"	5%
PE 12	=	"	$8^1/_3$%
PE 1	=	"	100%

and so on. In each case the PE ratio, multiplied by the earnings yield, equals 100.

In comparing these ratios with other companies one must be satisfied that these other companies are truly similar!

Summary of Valuation Bases

(a)   Balance Sheet/Book Value Basis :

$$\frac{\text{Assets less Liabilities at book values}}{\text{Number of shares}}$$

(b)   Liquidation/Breakup/Gone Concern Basis :

$$\frac{\text{Assets at estimated forced sale values, less liabilities}}{\text{Number of Shares}}$$

(c)   Earnings Yield :

$$\frac{\text{Net profit after tax and Preference Dividends}}{\text{Market or Nominal price of Issued Shares}}$$

(d)   Dividend Yield :

$$\frac{\text{Dividend declared}}{\text{Market or Nominal price of Issued Shares}}$$

(e)   Replacement Cost Basis :

$$\frac{\text{Current Replacement Asset Values Less Liabilities}}{\text{Number of Shares}}$$

(f)   Maintainable Earnings Basis :

Average Profits over X years (adjusted) x   X years

(g)   Price Earnings Ratio :

$$\frac{\text{Price of Share}}{\text{Earnings of Share}}$$

Finally - do be careful in the examination to assess the situation outlined in the question. Do not be tempted to show off your knowledge of methods of valuation which are completely irrelevant to the situation in front of you. And remember, that whatever methods are used, the final valuations in real life boil down to final negotiation and haggling! But a guide must precede this.

EXERCISE 5.1

Biscuits Ltd is a private company controlled by X who has deposited his shares in the company with his bank to secure an overdraft. In order to estimate the value of the company's shares the bank obtained the information given below :

Balance Sheet of Biscuits Ltd
as at 31 December, 19-8

	£		£
Issued Share Capital			
£1 Ordinary Shares	10,000	Fixed Assets	11,000
Reserves	4,000		
Profit and Loss account	5,000	Current Assets	13,500
Current Liabilities	5,500		
	24,500		24,500

The company's profit for the year ended 31 December, 19-8 was appropriated as follows :

	£
Net Profit for year	3,000
Ordinary Dividends for year	500
Retained Profit	2,500

At 31 December, 19-8 a professional valuer considered that in the event of a forced sale the company's assets would realise :

Fixed Assets	£17,500
Current Assets	£10,000

Similar private companies have recently been sold at values giving an earnings yield of 10%. On the Stock Exchange ordinary shares of public companies in the same industry as Biscuits Ltd, currently have a dividend yield of 4%.

Required :   A table to be completed in the following form :

Valuation of £1 Ordinary Share
in Biscuits Ltd

1.   Balance Sheet Basis   £_____

2.   Break Up Basis   £_____

3.   Dividend Yield basis   £_____

4.   Earnings Yield Basis   £_____

Confine your calculations to the information provided above.
Comment briefly on the limitations of the valuations you have calculated. Ignore taxation.

EXERCISE 5.2

The summarised balance sheets and profit statements of Ash Ltd, for the past three years are shown below :

Balance Sheets at 31 December

	19-6	19-7	19-8
	£	£	£
Issued Share Capital	20,000	20,000	20,000
Revenue Reserves	22,000	28,000	32,000
Creditors	13,500	13,000	15,000
Bank Overdraft	7,500	4,000	5,000
	63,000	65,000	72,000

Balance Sheets at 31 December (continued)

	19-6	19-7	19-8
	£	£	£
Freehold Properties	15,000	12,000	12,000
Equipment less depreciation	20,000	18,000	16,000
Stock	15,000	19,000	23,000
Debtors	13,000	16,000	21,000
	63,000	65,000	72,000

Profit statements for year ended 31 December

	19-6	19-7	19-8
	£	£	£
Sales	100,000	110,000	120,000
Gain on Sale of Property	–	7,000	–
	100,000	117,000	120,000
Cost of goods and expenses	78,000	103,000	107,000
Depreciation of equipment	2,000	2,000	2,000
Loss on sale of equipment	6,000	–	–
Directors' remuneration	5,000	6,000	7,000
Net Profit	9,000	6,000	4,000
	100,000	117,000	120,000

The issued share capital of Ash Ltd, is wholly owned by the company's directors who are considering an offer from Beech Ltd, to purchase all their shares.

Beech Ltd would pay a total of eight times the 'maintainable earnings' of the company - defined as the average of net profit over the past three years. For this purpose net profit would be calculated after the exclusion of extraordinary items, after charging depreciation at replacement cost instead of at historic cost and after charging annual management salaries of £4,500 instead of directors' remuneration.

You are given the following information regarding the assets of Ash Ltd at 31 December, 19-8

       Freehold Properties - have an estimated net realisable value of £30,000.
       The acquisition of comparable properties would cost £32,000 including legal fees, etc.

       Equipment - was purchased 1 January, 19-6 for £20,000. At 31 December, 19-8 the equipment has an estimated 8 year life, with no scrap value. Comparable new equipment with a 10 year life would cost £25,000 at 31 December, 19-8. The existing equipment, if sold separately from the other assets of the business, would realise only £12,000.

       Stock in Trade - has a net realisable value of £28,000 if sold in the normal course of business, but would realise only £22,000 if sold on closure of the business. The stocks would cost £24,000 to replace.

       Trade Debtors - are all considered good.
       Additional liquidation costs of £1,000 would be incurred if the assets were sold separately.

Similar companies have recently been sold on the basis of an earnings yield of 9% based on current net profit (after directors' remuneration).

Required :
(a)

A table completed in the following form (overleaf), showing valuations for the total equity of Ash Ltd. :

(a)   <u>Valuation</u>

1.   'Maintainable earnings' basis   £_____

2.   Earnings Yield basis (current year) £_____

3.   Book Value basis   £_____

4.   Liquidation basis   £_____

5.   Replacement Cost basis   £_____

(b)   Comment briefly on the offer from Beech Ltd, in relation to the valuations you have obtained.

NB.   Assume that you are making valuations at 31 December, 19-8. Calculate to the nearest £100, and ignore taxation.

EXERCISE 5.3

Mardyke Ltd, has made an offer to acquire the ordinary shares of Floyd Ltd. John, who owns 1,000 £1 ordinary shares in Floyd Ltd, would receive for his entire holding £2,000 in cash plus £1,000 9 per cent debenture stock in Mardyke Ltd.

The debenture stock in Mardyke Ltd, will be quoted on the Stock Exchange when it is issued : debenture stocks in companies which involve similar risks to Mardyke Ltd, are currently valued on a basis which gives a yield of 10 per cent per annum. (For simplicity, redemption dates can be ignored; i.e. assume perpetual debenture stock).

John is considering the offer and hopes the following information will help :

Summarised balance sheet of Floyd Ltd, at 31 December, 19-4.

	£		£
£1 Ordinary Shares	500,000	Fixed Assets at cost less deprn.	680,000
Reserves	340,000		
Current liabilities	460,000	Current assets	620,000
	1,300,000		1,300,000

Excerpt from the profit statement of Floyd Ltd for the year ended 31 December, 19-4 :

	£
Trading profit	138,000
Less interest paid on short-term loans	6,000
Net Profit	132,000
Less dividends for 19-4	60,000
Retained Profit	72,000

According to a recent stockbroker's report 'the property assets of Floyd Ltd are reliably estimated to have a saleable value of £1 million'. It can be assumed that saleable values of the other fixed assets would be negligible and that current assets would realise their balance sheet figures.

The shares of Floyd Ltd are quoted on the Stock Exchange, and shares in quoted companies in the same industry currently have an average price-earnings ratio of 10 and an average dividend yield of 5 per cent per annum.

Required :

(a)   Calculations showing the value of Mardyk's offer for John's shares in Floyd Ltd, and valuations for those shares on four further valuation bases. Adopt widely known valuation bases and state which you have used, in a table as follows :

Valuation basis	Valuation of 1,000 ordinary shares in Floyd Ltd
1. Offer from Mardyke Ltd	£ _____
2.	£ _____
3.	£ _____
4.	£ _____
5.	£ _____

(b)   Comment very briefly on your results and the limitations of the valuation bases you have used.

EXERCISE 5.4

Redlands owns 5,000 ordinary shares in Whitchurch Ltd, a private company. The shares were inherited by Redlands from his father, who died some years ago. Redlands has received an offer of £1.80 for each of his ordinary shares.

The following up-to-date information has been obtained concerning the affairs of Whitchurch Ltd.

Balance Sheet at 31 March, 19-9

	£		£
Issued Share Capital (£1 shares)	100,000	Freehold property at cost	60,000
Reserves	50,000	Plant at cost less deprn.	40,000
Current liabilities	35,000	Stock at cost	42,000
		Debtors	39,000
		Cash	4,000
	185,000		185,000

The profits earned by the business have been consistently in the region of £20,000 per annum and a regular annual dividend of 12% on the nominal share capital is paid. A valuation of the freehold was recently undertaken by a local firm of surveyors and this produced a figure of £120,000. The plant is thought to possess a second-hand value of no more than £15,000, whilst the net realisable value of stock is considered to be in the region of £49,000. Liquidation costs of £5,000 would be incurred if the company's assets were sold separately.

It is discovered that private companies in the locality are normally sold at prices which give an earnings yield of 12%. Quoted companies, engaged in a line of business similar to that of Whitchurch Ltd, currently pay dividends which represent a return of 6% on the market value of their shares.

Required :
(a)   Valuations of Redlands' shares in Whitchurch Ltd, presented in the following manner :

		Valuation of one £1 Ordinary Share
(i)	Book value (net asset) basis	£_____
(ii)	Liquidation (break up) basis	£_____
(iii)	Earnings yield basis	£_____
(iv)	Dividend yield basis	£_____

(b)   Comment on the relevance to Redlands of each valuation.

NOTE   It is essential that candidates show how they arrive at the figures in the answer to this question. Ignore taxation.

The directors of Connecticut plc, who own 50% of the company's ordinary shares, have approached the bank requesting a renewal of the overdraft facility of £50,000 for a further twelve months. Connecticut's share quotation was suspended last month because of irregularities concerning the purchase and sale of the company's shares by one of its directors. The director has since resigned and it is expected that the Stock Exchange will resume dealing in the company's shares in the near future.

The following historical cost information has been extracted from previously published accounts :

Balance Sheet at 31 December 19-2

	£ 000	£ 000
Fixed Assets		
Equipment at cost less depreciation		800
Current Assets		
Stocks	810	
Debtors	580	
	1,390	
Current Liabilities		
Trade Creditors	316	
Proposed dividends	100	
Bank overdraft	24	
	440	
Net Current Assets		950
		1,750
Capital and Reserves		
Ordinary shares (£1 each)		1,000
Reserves		550
		1,550
10% Preference shares		200
		1,750

Profit and Loss Accounts

		19-0	19-1	19-2
Net Profit for the year		126	210	240
Less : dividends	- ordinary shares	80	80	80
	- preference shares	20	20	20
Retained profit for the year		26	110	140

The following additional information is provided :

1. Depreciation of £60,000 per year has been charged on the equipment during each of the last three years. The equipment is old and in need of replacement; annual depreciation based on current replacement cost would be in the region of £76,000.

2. On investigation, the stock in the balance sheet shown above was found to be overvalued by £14,000.

3. The profit for 19-0 was arrived at after deducting an exceptional loss of £56,000 arising from the liquidation of a major customer.

4. It is estimated that the equipment and stocks possess respective liquidation values of £240,000 and £600,000. The debtors would be collected in full and liquidation costs would amount to £52,000.

5.	A recent article in the financial press estimated a dividend yield of 12% and an earnings yield of 20% for other companies in Connecticut's industry.

Required :
(a)	A table, completed in the following form, showing valuations for the entire ordinary share capital of Connecticut plc.

	Valuation
1. Earnings yield basis (based on average earnings for the last three years, after making appropriate adjustments).	
2. Liquidation (break-up basis)	
3. Dividend yield basis	

(b)	Comments on the significance of the above-mentioned valuations, paying particular attention to the request for a renewal of the overdraft facility.

NOTE	(i)	Assume that you are making the valuations at 31 December 19-2
	(ii)	Ignore taxation.

Exercise 5.6 EX

Gurney Ltd is an unlisted company; all the ordinary shares, but none of the preference shares, are held by the directors and their families. The directors have decided to retire and move to the South of France. They wish to discover the likely value of their shares before entering into discussion with potential purchasers. They have been told by friends that, for the purpose of sale as a going concern, the business should be valued on the 'earnings yield' basis. If they fail to agree a price with a buyer, the company will be liquidated.

The following facts and information are provided :

(i)

Balance Sheet of Gurney Ltd at 31 December 1986

	£000	£000
Plant and equipment at cost less depreciation		2,605
Current assets		
Stocks	1,372	
Debtors	896	
Bank	57	
	2.325	
Less: Current liabilities		
Creditors	509	
Proposed dividends (including £40,000 for preference shares)	240	
	749	
Net current assets		1,576
		4,181
Financed by:		
Ordinary share capital		2,000
8% preference share capital, issued 1980		500
Reserves		1,681
		4,181

(ii)	Net reported profits:	£000
	1984	715
	1985	483
	1986	572

(iii)   The company changed from the marginal cost to the total cost basis for valuing stock when preparing the accounts for 1984, but failed to re-state opening stock on the new basis. The relevant values for the opening stock at 1 January 1984 are :

	£000
Marginal cost basis	826
Total cost basis	966

(iv)   The plant and equipment would fetch £1,800,000 in the second-hand market and the stocks would realise £1,406,000 in a forced sale.

(v)   A re-examination of the debtor balances at 31 December 1986 shows £30,000 to be doubtful or bad.

(vi)   In December 1984 the company sold a section of its activities which had contributed £85,000 towards the reported profit for that year.

(vii)   The depreciation charges averaged £200,000 for the years 1984 - 86. The replacement cost of fixed assets in similar condition is significantly lower than book value and would require an annual depreciation charge of £165,000.

(viii)   The cost of liquidating the company is estimated as £31,000.

(ix)   The typical earnings yield of listed companies, engaged in a similar line of business to Gurney Ltd, is 12%.

Required:

(a)   Valuations of the ordinary shareholders' interest in Gurney Ltd on :

(i)   The earnings yield basis. This should be based on 'maintainable' profits, defined as average reported profits for the last three years after making appropriate adjustments.

(ii)   The liquidation basis.

(b)   A full discussion of the merits and demerits of the two methods used above to value Gurney.

Notes: (i)   Assume you are making the valuations at 31 December 1986.

(ii)   Ignore taxation.   (Spring 1987)

Exercise 5.7 EX

Richards Plc suffered a series of trading losses in the first half of the 1980s, which resulted in management changes and a substantial re-organisation of the company's activities between November 1985 and February 1986. This produced an encouraging improvement in the results reported for 1986: profits for the year amounted to £2,000,000 and a dividend of 10 pence per share was paid on 31 December 1986. The balance sheet at 31 December 1986 contained the following information :

Balance Sheet at 31 December 1986

	£000s
Freehold property at cost less depreciation	5,000
Plant and machinery at cost less depreciation	3,350
	8,350
Current assets	6,750
Less: Current liabilities	2,900
Net current assets	3,850
	12,200

Balance Sheet at 31 December 1986 (cont)

Financed by:

Share capital (£1 ordinary shares)	8,000
Reserves	4,200
	__12,200__

During August 1987, Hadlee Plc made an unwelcome takeover bid for the company at a price of £2.90 per share. The directors have advised the shareholders not to sell and informed them that, during the first half of 1987, sales were 15% higher than in the first half of 1986. They have forecast profits of £2,720,000 for 1987 and a leading firm of accountants has approved these figures.

A recent article in the financial press drew attention to the fact that the replacement value of Richards' freehold property is £10,000,000 and the replacement value of the plant and machinery is £6,000,000.

The shares of Richards have, in recent months, been purchased and sold at a price of £2.60 per share. Shares in quoted companies in the same industry as Richards have an average price/earnings ratio of 10 and a dividend yield of 5%.

Required :

(a) Valuations of one £1 ordinary share in Richards Plc. Set out these valuations in your answer book in the following manner:

		Valuation of one £1 ordinary share
(i)	Book value basis	—
(ii)	Replacement cost basis	—
(iii)	Dividend yield basis	—
(iv)	Price/earnings basis - 1986 profits	—
(v)	Price/earnings basis - 1987 forecast profits	—

(b) Discuss the relevance of your valuations to the shareholders in the light of the takeover bid by Hadlee Plc. Advise the shareholders whether or not to sell.

Note : Ignore taxation

(Autumn 1987)

Exercise 5.8 EX

One of your customers, Peter Lubbock, has recently sold his business to a multi-national company and he is keen to invest the proceeds in Graig Security Systems Ltd, a recently established company which installs and monitors sophisticated surveillance systems for domestic and business use. The formation of this company involved a heavy capital investment, but the fixed assets acquired are sufficient to support a significant increase in the level of operations.

The following information is provided relating to Graig Security Systems Ltd:

(1)

Balance Sheet at 30 June 1989

	£000
Fixed Assets	580
Working capital	20
	__600__
Share capital (£1 ordinary shares)	400
16% loan	200
	__600__

(2)   The profits of the company for the year to 30 June 1989, after deducting loan interest, amounted to £130,000. It is the directors' policy to pay out the entire profits each year in the form of dividends, and this policy is expected to continue for the foreseeable future.

(3)   The fixed assets are highly specialised. It is estimated that it would cost £760,000 to replace them, but their break-up value is put at no more than £230,000. Goodwill is estimated to be worth £200,000.

(4)   Peter Lubbock has been invited to acquire 120,000 ordinary shares in the company at a price of £2 per share. The proceeds would be used to repay immediately the loan and to provide much needed working capital requirements.

(5)   An earnings yield of 18% is considered appropriate for companies in this line of business.

Required :

(a) Calculations of the value to be placed on one £1 ordinary share in Graig Security Systems Ltd based on the foregoing information. You should summarise the results of your calculations in the following manner:

	Valuation of £1 ordinary share
(i) Break up basis	
(ii) Replacement cost basis	
(iii) Earnings yield basis	

(b)   Discuss the relevance of each of these three valuations to Peter Lubbock in deciding whether to make the share purchase. Make (and show) any other calculations you consider appropriate.

Notes: (i) Ignore taxation
        (ii) Assume you are making the calculations on 30 June 1989.

(Autumn 1989)

64

SOLUTIONS

SOLUTION 5.1

<u>Valuation of a £1 share</u>

Balance Sheet Basis	£1.90
Break Up Basis	£2.20
Dividend Yield Basis*	£1.25
Earnings Yield Basis**	£3.00

*   Dividend Yield of Biscuits $= \dfrac{500}{10,000}$ (Nominal value as market price is not given)

$= 5\%$ - other companies have a dividend yield of 4% therefore Biscuits' shares could be said to be 25% better in this respect than other companies' £1 shares, and we could regard a £1 share in Biscuits as being worth £1 plus 25% = £1.25, compared with a £1 share in the other companies.

i. $\dfrac{\pounds 500 \text{ dividend}}{\pounds 10,000 \text{ (shares at nominal value)}}$ x $\dfrac{100}{4\% \text{ (yield in others)}}$ = £1.25

**   Biscuits earnings yield = 30%. Other companies have a yield of 10% - therefore a £1 share in Biscuits is worth £3 compared with a £1 share in other companies.

i.e. $\dfrac{\pounds 3,000 \text{ (profit)}}{\pounds 10,000 \text{ (nominal value)}}$ x $\dfrac{100}{10\% \text{ (yield in others)}}$ = £3.00

<u>Limitations of these valuations</u> :

The information is probably out of date when it is used - valuation on balance sheet basis may not be very accurate as assets may be shown at historical cost rather than current values, also depreciation charges may not be realistic - valuation on break-up values depends on opinions of true values - in calculating dividend and earnings yields we are assuming that Biscuits has comparable dividend policies, expectations, etc., as have other companies, and this is probably not so.

SOLUTION 5.2

		<u>Valuation</u>	
1.	Maintainable Earnings basis	£56,000	
2.	Earning Yield Basis	£44,400	
3.	Book Value Basis	£52,000	
4.	Liquidation basis	£64,000	
5.	Replacement Cost Basis	£77,000	(£82,000)

Comments

Beech's offer of £56,000 (1. above) is less than Ash would expect to receive from liquidation! Obviously the liquidation value of £64,000 would be the absolute minimum offer which would be considered by Ash.

Workings :

No. 1.

	19-6	19-7	19-8	
	£	£	£	£
Net Profit	9,000	6,000	4,000	= 19,000

Add Loss on Sale of Property	6,000
	25,000
Less Gain on sale of property	7,000
	18,000
Less Additional depreciation	1,500
	16,500
Add directors' remuneration	18,000
	34,500
Less management salaries	13,500
Adjusted Net Profit over 3 year period	21,000
Average = maintainable earnings of	7,000

$$8 \quad x \quad £7,000 \quad = \quad £56,000$$

No. 2

$$\frac{£4,000}{£20,000} \quad x \quad \frac{100}{9} \quad = £2.22 \text{ per share x } 20,000 = £44,400$$

No. 5
The figure of £77,000 takes account of the fact that new equipment would have a 10 year life whereas Ash's equipment has only an 8 year life. The other answer, £82,000 is acceptable.

SOLUTION 5.3
(a)

<table>
<tr><td></td><td align="center">Valuation Basis</td><td align="right">Valuation of 1,000 ordinary
shares in Floyd Ltd</td></tr>
<tr><td>1.</td><td>Offer from Mardyke Ltd</td><td align="right">£2,900</td></tr>
<tr><td>2.</td><td>Balance sheet (assets) basis</td><td align="right">£1,680</td></tr>
<tr><td>3.</td><td>Liquidation (break up) basis</td><td align="right">£2,320</td></tr>
<tr><td>4.</td><td>Price earnings (earnings yield) basis</td><td align="right">£2,640</td></tr>
<tr><td>5.</td><td>Dividend yield basis</td><td align="right">£2,400</td></tr>
</table>

NOTE:

Re:1 £1,000 9% debentures in Mardyke would produce an income of £90 per year. Stocks in similar companies have a yield of 10% per annum, so to produce £90 per year interest would only involve holding £900 of such stock - therefore Mardyke's £1,000 of stock is in real terms only worth £900 to John. This, plus the £2,000 cash gives the valuation.

Re:2 The balance sheet value of Floyd's shares = $\frac{£840,000}{500,000}$ = £1.68 per share

Re: 3 Assets have saleable value of £1 million plus current assets of £620,000 = £1,620,000 less current liabilities of £460,000 =

$$\frac{£1,160,000}{500,000 \text{ shares}} \quad x \quad \frac{1,000 \text{ shares}}{1} = £2,320$$

Re: 4

$$\text{Net Profit} = \frac{\text{£132,000}}{\text{500,000}} \quad \text{x} \quad \frac{100}{1} \quad = \quad 26.4\% \text{ earnings yield}$$

As shares in similar companies have an earnings yield of 10% (P/E 10 = Earnings yield 10%) we can regard shares in Floyd as being worth more than twice the value (26.4% compared with 10%).

To be exact - $\frac{26.4}{10}$ = £2.64 per share x 1,000 shares = £2,640.

Re: 5

$$\frac{\text{Dividend £60,000}}{\text{Shares £500,000}} \quad \text{(market value not given)} \qquad \text{x} \quad \frac{100}{1} \quad = \quad 12\%$$

Other companies have a yield of 5% - so Floyd's shares are worth

$\frac{12}{5}$ = £2.40 x 1,000 shares = £2,400.

(b)

Basis 2 -	What are the current values of the assets? Using these, we could have a completely different picture.
Basis 3 -	These estimates are based on *opinions* only.
Basis 4 -	This particular year's profits may have been untypical of a normal year - what will be the position next year? How similar are other companies?
Basis 5 -	Distribution of dividend policies are peculiar to a company, therefore it is difficult to compare - e.g. one company may be on an expansion policy at present. Using *market value* of the shares would have given a truer picture.

SOLUTION 5.4

(a)

			Valuation of one £1 ordinary share
(i)		Book value basis	£1.50
(ii)		Liquidation basis	£1.87
(iii)		Earnings yield basis	£1.67
(iv)		Dividend yield basis	£2.00

(b) Valuation (i) depends on how 'true' the balance sheet figures are. We know, for example, that property is undervalued and the figure for plant is determined by the depreciation method used. Again, the methods of valuing stock can produce widely differing figures and we have no knowledge of how many of the debtors will prove to be bad.

Valuation (ii) is a matter of opinions to a large extent and no doubt two separate parties would give two widely differing estimates.

Valuation (iii) - do the companies with whom we are comparing have the same 'ideas' in allowing for depreciation, setting up provisions for bad debts, etc? - because these items affect profit figures. In other words, just how 'similar' are these other companies?

Valuation (iv) - all companies have different distribution of dividend policies and it is difficult to find two companies with comparable policies.

From our limited valuations shown and subject to the comments given it would seem that the offer of £1.80 for each share is a fair one. Redland's final decision must now rest on his views on the future prospects of Whitchurch Ltd.

LESSON 6

COST ACCOUNTING

ABSORPTION AND MARGINAL COSTING

How does a manufacturer work out how much his products have cost him to make? The answer, surely, is obvious - he adds up all his costs of production such as raw materials, labour, power, light and heat, etc, and divides this total by the number of units he has produced. This gives him the cost of one single unit.

This type of cost is known as ABSORPTION COST (or TOTAL COST), i.e. the cost includes *all* the costs incurred in making the product spread evenly and fairly over each item produced.

EXAMPLE

Manufacturing Costs of Producing 1,000 Bicycles

	£
Direct Materials	5,000
Direct Labour	3,000
Prime Cost	8,000
Indirect labour	1,000
Indirect Factory Overheads (e.g. - light, heat, power, factory rates, deprn. of machinery etc.)	5,000
Total Cost of Production	14,000

The cost of producing one bicycle therefore is £14 - using ABSORPTION COST (TOTAL COST) as a basis for calculating cost.

Note that all of the various costs in the above example are distinctly costs of manufacture (factory costs). There are justifications for some producers to include also a proportion of office costs (i.e. Profit and loss account items) such as administration and advertising costs, but normally the cost of production is based on factory costs only and we will therefore work on this basis.

Now consider the costs listed above. If one *extra* bicycle was produced, which of the above costs would increase? The cost of raw materials will certainly increase by 1/1000 in order to produce the *extra* bicycle - i.e. a proportionate increase, but it is unlikely that more labour will be involved in this *extra* production, or light, heat, power, rates or depreciation costs. In other words, *another* bicycle could be produced with only an increase in costs of raw materials.

Therefore, to produce 1,001 bicycles will give an account as follows :

Manufacturing costs of Producing 1,001 Bicycles

	£	
Direct Materials	5,005	(increase of 1/1000)
Direct Labour	3,003	(")
Prime Cost	8,008	
Indirect Labour	1,000	(same)
Indirect Factory Overheads	5,000	(same)
Total Cost of Production	14,008	

68

The cost of producing one *more* bicycle therefore is only £8. However, using ABSORPTION COST methods the cost of *each* bicycle produced is :

£14,005 ÷ 1001 = £13.99!

If your friend asked you, as the manufacturer, to make an extra bike for him, what would you charge him? You don't expect profit because he is a friend - £8 or £13.99? The *extra* bike has really only cost you £8 to produce!

This is MARGINAL COSTING - i.e. concerning yourself only with what *extra* cost has been incurred in making one more item.

Absorption costing is concerned with *total* costs divided by the number of items produced. Marginal Costing is concerned with the *extra* cost of producing another item on the basis that despite increased production, certain costs won't increase at all.

FIXED AND VARIABLE COSTS

Manufacturers have many different types of costs to bear as you can see by looking at the debit items in any manufacturing account. If the manufacturer increases production he expects his manufacturing costs to increase; but by how much? If production was doubled would his total manufacturing costs also double? The answer is 'No' - his costs would increase but they would not double.

This is because certain costs are FIXED - that is to say, they are not affected by changes in the volume of production. An example would be rent. This has to be paid whether production is low or high, and the amount of activity going on in the factory or in the office does not affect in the slightest the amount of rent which has to be paid. There are many other examples - think of as many as you can.

If *all* costs of a manufacturer were fixed then he could double production without any increase at all in his total costs; but some of his costs are not fixed - they are VARIABLE, i.e. they vary as production varies. The best example is the cost of raw materials - obviously, if production and sales increase by 20%, then the cost of materials must increase by 20%. Similarly, salesmen's commission might also increase by 20%. These are perfectly variable costs, but most variable costs move by different degrees, in sympathy with production. If production increases by 20% it may be necessary to increase the work force (labour) costs by only 2%. (This is where efficient management comes in!) How many other examples can you think of?

We know then that all costs must be either fixed or variable. *Fixed Costs* remain constant despite movements in production. *Variable Costs* move up or down (in varying degrees) with production and sales.

However, in the long run, all costs tend to become variable to some extent; the rapidly expanding firm must eventually reach the point where more premises are needed and then the rent, etc. cost increases.

You should now understand why the extra cost of producing one bicycle is only £8 in the last example. Fixed costs remained the same despite the increased production and the only increase in total costs (£8) was due to the variable cost element.

USES OF MARGINAL COSTING

We know that in a given period the *extra* cost of making one more item will be its marginal (variable) cost. Let us now assume that we make radios and our present costs for the production of 5,000 radio sets, which we can sell, are as follows :

69

		£	
Variable Costs	(5,000 sets)	45,000	(i.e. £9 per set)
Fixed Costs		30,000	
Total costs	(5,000 sets)	75,000	(i.e. £15 per set)

The *Absorption Cost* per set is £15. We sell the sets for £25 each. Assume now that a well-known chain of electrical stores comes along and says to you, 'We want to place an order for 1,000 of your radio sets but we are only prepared to pay £12 per set'.

Can we take on this order? Looking at absorption cost to us of £15 per set, it is not on! We would surely lose £3 per set in costs. However, we do realise that the cost of the extra 1,000 sets will only be their *marginal* cost!

We investigate and determine the following :

Without Extra Order			**With Extra Order**		
		£			£
Income = 5,000 x £25		125,000	Income =	5,000 x £25	125,000
Less variable costs				1,000 x £12	12,000
(5,000 x £9)		45,000			137,000
		80,000	Less variable costs		
Less fixed costs		30,000		6,000 x £9	54,000
					83,000
			Less fixed costs		30,000
PROFIT		50,000	PROFIT		53,000

We have made £3,000 more profit by taking on the extra order at a ridiculously low selling price of £12 per set! Because our fixed costs of £30,000 are already covered by the income from normal sales (i.e. 5,000 sets) we do not incur any further fixed costs in making the additional 1,000 sets. All we do incur is the marginal (variable) cost of £9 per set and as the income from this extra order is *£12* per set we actually make a profit of £3 per set on the new bulk order.

£1,000 x £3 = £3,000 - our additional profit!

This illustrates the first basic use of marginal costing - to evaluate orders at special prices.

Remember that the profits shown above will be reduced by administration, distribution, and other office costs (i.e. Profit and Loss account items) which have not, in our example, been taken into account. Obviously these costs will have a bearing on the final decisions to be taken.

Also, remember that in practice the production of 1,000 more radio sets *may* cause certain 'fixed' costs to increase. Rates on the factory, for example, will remain fixed at £x p.a. whether 20 or 20,000 radios are produced but the point will eventually come, with continued expansion, when additional premises are needed - therefore additional rate costs - to cope with the increased production.

BREAK EVEN POINT

A business is said to 'break even' when it reaches the point where total revenue from sales exactly equals total costs - i.e. it is making neither profit nor loss. Up to this point the firm is, of course, making losses and it is therefore very important for a new firm to know how soon it will reach break even point, for once revenue from sales exceeds costs (i.e. past break even point) then profits start to come in.

EXAMPLE

A company has fixed costs of £10,000 per annum. Its variable costs (assume these to be perfectly variable) average out at £2 per unit produced. Each unit is sold for £6.

How many units must be sold per year before the company breaks even?

ANSWER

Ignoring fixed costs for the moment, each unit sold produces an excess revenue of £4 (selling price less variable costs). This excess has to go towards defraying the fixed costs, and anything left over is profit. In other words the £4 excess revenue is a 'contribution' towards fixed costs and profit.

Therefore, how many contributions of £4 are necessary in the year to cover the fixed costs of £10,000? £10,000 divided by £4 = 2,500 - this is the number of units which must be produced in order to break even.

Check this - Revenue from 2,500 units = £15,000 (2,500 x £6). Total cost of producing 2,500 units = 2,500 x £2 (variable cost per unit) = £5,000 plus fixed costs of £10,000 = £15,000.

If 2,501 units are produced and sold then the contribution of this extra unit (i.e. £4) will not be needed to help cover fixed costs (they have been covered by the previous 2,500 units) and it will therefore be regarded as £4 of profit.

It is very important to understand the central role that Contribution plays in marginal costing theory. Revenue less variable costs always equals CONTRIBUTION, and extra contribution (i.e. after fixed costs have been covered) = extra profit!

In a given time the bigger the amount of contribution the bigger the profit (after fixed costs have been covered) because the fixed costs do not go up as contribution goes up.

Diagrammatically :

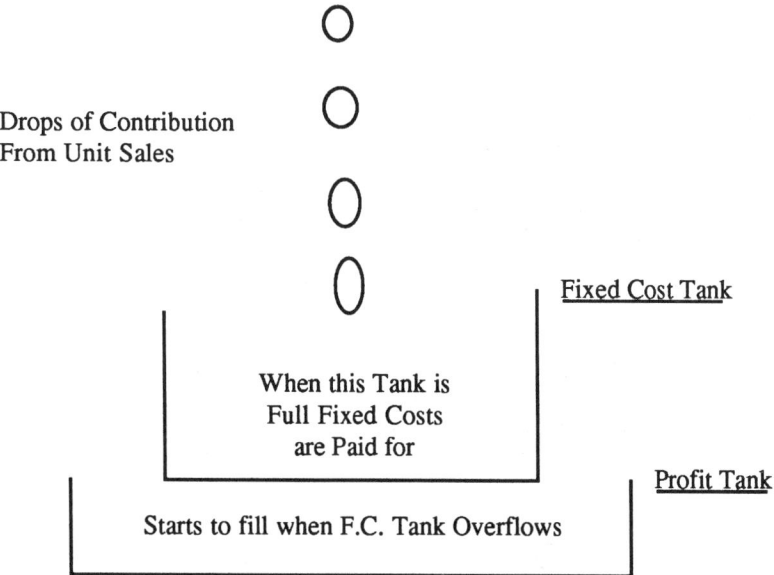

This diagram illustrates why extra contribution is extra profit. If the fixed cost tank is full the extra drops of contribution run straight into the profit tank.

7 1

If there is only enough contribution to fill the fixed cost tank then the business has made neither profit not loss - it has BROKEN EVEN.

Margins of safety

Low profits are not as good as high profits, but losses are a disaster. Every firm has a sales target is wants to reach, at which it will make profits. Break even points are calculated so managers know when the crucial no-loss stage is reached.

However, it is equally useful to know, in advance, *how far above break even the sales target is*. This distance (measured in money or units) is called the *Margin of Safety:*

$$\begin{array}{ll} & \text{Budgeted Revenue/or units} \\ less & \underline{\text{Break even Revenue/or units}} \\ \\ = & \underline{\text{Margin of Safety Revenue/or units}} \end{array}$$

Take the two following similarly profitable products, only one of which the firm will invest in making and selling, which are budgeted as follows:

		Product A £	Ratio %	Product B £	Ratio %
	Revenue	75,000	100	75,000	100
less	Variable Costs	25,000	33	45,000	60
	Contribution	50,000	67	30,000	40
less	Fixed Costs	40,000		20,000	
	Profit	£10,000		£10,000	

Break even for Product A in Revenue $= \dfrac{40,000}{0.67} = £59,701$

Break even for Product B in Revenue $= \dfrac{20,000}{0.40} = £50,000$

Margin of Safety

	Product A £	Product B £
Budgeted Revenue	75,000	75,000
less B/E Revenue	59,701	50,000
Margin of Safety	£15,299	£25,000

Therefore, Product B has a greater margin of safety, i.e. Product B's sales forecast can be more wrong before it really hits trouble (i.e. makes losses).

The Margin of Safety should be expressed in terms of revenue or units but also as a percentage, e.g.

Product A $\dfrac{\text{Margin of Safety (£ or units) £15,299}}{\text{Budgeted Revenue (or units) £75,000}} \times \dfrac{100}{1} = 20.4\%$

Product B $\dfrac{25,000}{75,000} \times \dfrac{100}{1} = 33.3\%$

This shows more clearly the extent to which sales can fall 'with safety'.

It should be clear to you that (for similar budgeted profits) the product, or business, with the lower fixed costs will always have the higher margin of safety. In other words, margin of safety and cost structure are of course linked.

It is usually impossible to accurately predict sales, especially of a new product. So the margin of safety is a very important aspect to consider when launching a new product. If there is a low margin of safety then falling short on sales by a small amount will mean the product makes losses. Under which circumstances, the managers should come up with a better idea!

If Products A and B above were sold for £10 each, then their B/E in units, Budgeted Sales in units and margin of safety in units are:

		A	B
	Budget Sales	7,500 units	7,500 units
less	B/E units	5,970 units	5,000 units
	Margin of Safety in Units	1,530 units	2,500 units
		20.4%	33.3%

This can be a quite important aspect; because what if A's were sold for £10 each and B's for £500 each? Then the margin of safety in *units* would be:

		A	B
	Budgeted Sales in units	7,500	150
less	B/E in units	5,970	100
	Margin of Safety in Units	1,530	50
		20.4%	33.3%

This is valuable information of course. B has the greater margin of safety in *revenue* but lower *in units*. The question for managers then becomes one of "Is it easier to sell 7,500 A's or 150 B's?" The figures help to concentrate the minds of the decision makers! If it was decided to make and sell B's then everyone would know that a shortfall from target of (say) 10 units would be far more serious than a 10 unit shortfall in A's sales target.

EXERCISE 6.1

The XY Co. Ltd is just about to start trading, and the directors estimate that for every unit the company sells, at £10 each, the company will incur variable costs of £8.

Expense payments for the year, which will remain fixed irrespective of the level of sales, will amount to £30,000.

Required :
> A calculation of the sales which the company would have to make in its first year *in order to break even.*

EXERCISE 6.2

At the beginning of 19-1 Deer Ltd was incorporated and manufactures a single product. At the end of the first year's operations the company's accountant prepared a draft profit and loss account which contained the following financial information.

Profit and Loss Account of Deer Ltd for 19-1

	£	£
Sales (200,000 units)		600,000
Less : Prime cost of units manufactured during 19-1		
(500,000 units)	800,000	
Deduct closing stock	480,000	
Prime cost of goods sold	320,000	
Fixed Costs :		
Factory expenses	200,000	
General expenses	100,000	620,000
NET LOSS :		20,000

Additional finance is required, and the directors are worried that the company's bank manager is unlikely to regard the financial facts shown above as a satisfactory basis for a further advance. The company's accountant made the following observation and suggestion :

'The cause of the poor result for 19-1 was the decision to value closing stock on the prime cost basis. An acceptable alternative practice would involve charging factory expenses to the total number of units produced and carrying forward an appropriate proportion of those expenses as part of the closing stock value.'

Required :

(a)   A revised profit and loss account, for presentation to the company's bank, valuing closing stock on the total (absorption) cost basis suggested by the company's accountant.

(b)   Assuming that, in 19-2, the company again produces 500,000 units but sells 700,000 units, calculate the expected profit using each of the two stock valuation bases. Assume also that, in 19-2, sales price per unit and costs incurred will be the same as for 19-1.

(c)   Comment briefly on the accountant's suggestion and its likely effect on the bank manager's response to the request for additional finance.

EXERCISE 6.3

A recent conference of businessmen listened to a lecture on 'Accounting Policies' and were surprised to discover the extent to which the level of reported profit depends on the accounting procedures chosen for the purpose of valuing assets and liabilities. One of the participants suggested that this was a good reason for adopting a prudent approach when measuring profit, and there was some support for this view, though others argued that it was important to adopt a realistic approach rather than a pessimistic approach when preparing company accounts.

Required :

Indicate which accounting policy is likely to produce the more conservative figure for reported profit in each of the circumstances listed below. You should explain your choice.

(a)   Using first in, first out (FIFO) or last in, first out (LIFO) as the basis for valuing stock, assuming prices are rising and there is no change in the volume of stock held.

(b)   Using marginal or total cost as the basis for valuing stock, assuming prices are stable and the volume of stock held is increasing.

(c)   Using marginal or total cost as the basis for valuing stock at the end of the first year of a company's operations.

(d)   Applying the lower of cost and net realisable value rule to separate items of stock and work-in progress or to groups of similar items.

(e) Using the reducing balance *or* straight line method of depreciation during the early years of a particular asset's life.

(f) Valuing freehold property at historical cost less depreciation *or* current cost less depreciation when prices are rising.

EXERCISE 6.4

The summarised profit and loss account of Orchard Ltd for the year to 30 June, 19-9 and the summarised balance sheet at that date are as follows:

Profit and Loss Account

	£	£
Sales		200,000
Less variable cost of goods sold :		
Materials consumed	100,000	
Wages and expenses	40,000	140,000
Contribution towards fixed costs :		60,000
Less fixed costs :		
Depreciation	6,000	
Other expenses	50,000	56,000
NET PROFIT		4,000

Balance Sheet

	£		£
Share capital	70,000	Fixed assets at cost	160,000
Reserves	46,000	Less depreciation	57,000
	116,000		103,000
Creditors for materials	30,000	Stock valued at variable cost	35,000
Bank overdraft	32,000	Debtors	40,000
	178,000		178,000

The company manufactures a single product and has an available capacity capable of producing up to £300,000 of goods each year, valued at selling price. Any increase in the level of business activity would produce proportionate increases in the level of stocks, debtors and creditors.

The directors of Orchard Ltd are disappointed with the results achieve during the year to 30 June 19-9, which represent a return of less than 4% on the equity investment at the beginning of the year. The company is also under strong pressure from its bank to reduce the bank overdraft to £16,000. The directors discover that a demand exists for the product manufactured, significantly in excess of present output.

Required: The level of sales required during the year to 30 June, 19-0 in order to produce a net profit of £13,000.

Ignore taxation.
No dividends are to be paid during any of the relevant years.

EXERCISE 6.5

Ken Dowden and his two brothers are the three directors of a small company, Aluminex Ltd, which manufactures aluminium widgets. The company has banked with you for a number of years and is financially sound. The summarised final accounts for 19-2 are set out below.

Summarised Profit and Loss Account for 19-2

		£	£
Turnover (100,000 units at £5 each)			500,000
Less :	Variable costs	300,000	
	Depreciation	20,000	
	Other fixed costs	120,000	440,000
NET PROFIT			60,000

Summarised Balance Sheet at 31 December, 19-2

		£
Fixed assets at cost		200,000
Less :	Accumulated depreciation	80,000
		120,000
Working Capital		200,000
Bank deposit account		25,000
		345,000
Financed by :		
Share capital		200,000
Retained profits		145,000
		345,000

It is expected that during 19-3 production costs for the existing level of activity will remain unchanged; the selling price is also expected to remain the same. In 19-2 the company worked a day shift only, and existing plant was used to its full capacity. There is a heavy demand for the company's product and the three directors are planning to increase the level of activity. Ken Dowden's brothers believe that it will be possible to sell another 50,000 widgets, without reducing the sales price, but Ken believes that an increase of 30,000 is a more realistic estimate. Two alternative proposals for increasing the level of output are under consideration.

1. Work an evening shift. This would enable the company to produce additional output of up to 50,000 units. The variable cost per unit would be 50% higher than the rate for the day shift, the depreciation charge would remain unchanged and other fixed costs would increase by £2,000.

2. Purchase additional plant costing £120,000, with a capacity of 50,000 units. The plant would be depreciated on the straight line basis over ten years, assuming a nil residual value. The variable cost per unit and annual depreciation charge on the existing plant would remain unchanged but other fixed costs would increase by £40,000.

Under either alternative, working capital requirements would increase proportionately with the level of activity. The balance on the bank deposit account, in the balance sheet set out above, is surplus to operating requirements and could be used to help to finance the planned expansion of activity. Your bank has been approached to finance any shortfall.

Required :

(a). A summarised profit and loss account for 19-3 and a summarised balance sheet at 31 December 19-3, under alternative 1, assuming sales of widgets increase to 150,000 units.

(b) A summarised profit and loss account for 19-3 and a summarised balance sheet at 31 December 19-3, under alternative 2, assuming sales of widgets increase to 150,000 units.

(c) A full discussion of the two alternatives, including an assessment of the effect of the company failing to achieve additional sales of 50,000 units. You should support your discussion with calculations of the break even point on the additional sales (i.e. the amount of *additional* sales required to ensure that profits earned in 19-3 are equal to those earned in 19-2).

1.   Assume that the calculations are being made on 1 January 19-3
2.   The balance on the bank account or the bank overdraft may be treated as the balancing item in the balance sheets you prepare.
3.   The forecast accounts should be presented in columnar format.
4.   Ignore interest payable, if any.

EXERCISE 6.6

Radios Ltd commenced business on 1 January, 19-3. In the years 19-3 and 19-4 the company's production and sales were :

	19-3	19-4
Number of radios manufactured	11,000	10,000
Number of radios sold	9,000	11,000

In both years all sales were made at a constant price of £10 per radio. The company's manufacturing costs in the years 19-3 and 19-4 were :

| | 19-3 | 19-4 |
	£	£
Raw materials	14,300	13,000
Other variable costs	18,700	17,000
Fixed manufacturing costs	68,200	68,200

There were no stocks of raw materials or work-in-progress at the relevant balance sheet dates.

Required :
(a)   Calculations revealing the net profit of Radios Ltd for the years 19-3 and 19-4. Finished goods are to be valued at full cost, including manufacturing overheads.

(b)   A clear explanation (supported by figures) of the difference in net profit of the company in the two years.

NOTE   Ignore taxation.

EXERCISE 6.7 EX

The summarised profit and loss account of Merrill Ltd, a company which manufactures a single product is as follows :

Profit and Loss Account, year ended 30 June 19-2

		£	£
Sales (25,000 units)			1,000,000
Less :	Manufacturing costs		
	- variable	500,000	
	- fixed	180,000	680,000
Gross profit			320,000
Less :	Running costs		200,000
NET PROFIT			120,000

There is strong demand for the company's product, but there is also keen competition from other suppliers. The directors of Merrill Ltd believe that if the sales price remains unchanged, at £40 per unit, turnover will amount to only 23,000 units in the year to 30 June, 19-3. Further estimates show that turnover of 25,000 units could again be achieved if the price were reduced to £39, while a reduction in sales price to £38 would cause turnover to increase to 35,000 units. Variable manufacturing costs per unit and fixed manufacturing costs per annum are expected to remain unchanged whichever of the three options are chosen by the company's director. At 23,000 units, running costs will fall to £165,000 whereas at 35,000 units they will rise to £320,000.

Required :

(a)   Forecast profit and loss accounts of Merrill Ltd for the year ended 30 June, 19-3 under each of the alternatives indicated above.

(b)   Calculations of the net profit ratio (net profit as a percentage of sales) under each of these alternatives.

(c)   An indication of the alternative which you would favour. You should explain your choice and also refer to any further information which might help the decision making process.

NOTE   Assume for the purpose of this question that your calculations are being made on 1 July, 19-2.

Exercise 6.8 EX

Newhaven Photographics Ltd will have free space in one its main retail outlets when a tenancy ends on 30 June 1988. The company has had enquiries about the possible sale of the surplus premises, and has discovered that they would fetch £120,000 if sold at any time during the next five years.

The company's Projects Manager believes that they should instead use the space to market a Japanese personal computer (PC). The following financial forecasts have been prepared:

(i)   The premises are to be refurbished at a cost of £30,000 to be paid for in June 1988. The cost is to be written off over five years on the straight line basis.

(ii)   A stock of 80 PCs is to be purchased and paid for in June 1988. Purchases, for cash, will subsequently be made at the end of each month, commencing July 1988, to replace items sold.

(iii)   Sales, also on the cash basis, are expected to be at the rate of 60 PCs per month, commencing July 1988.

(iv)   The sales price of each PC will be £600 and the purchase price £500.

(v)   Annual running costs, other than depreciation, are estimated at £34,000.

(vi)   The company aims to achieve, annually, a target return of 20% on the initial investment in any project undertaken.

Required:

(a)   Calculations of :

   (i)   The amount of the initial investment at 30 June 1988
   (ii)   The break-even level of sales per annum, in units and value.
   (iii)   The forecast profit per annum.
   (iv)   The margin of safety.
   (v)   The level of sales required to achieve the target return of 20% on the initial investment.

(b)   A discussion of the Project Manager's proposal based on your calculations under (a) and the information provided.

Note : Ignore the time value of money.   (Spring 1988)

Exercise 6.9 EX

The Directors of Presbury Ltd have under consideration two alternative schemes for manufacturing a new product for which they believe there exists a strong demand. The details relating to the two schemes are as follows:
SCHEME A

The company will acquire plant costing £280,000. Fixed expenses (other than depreciation) would amount to £130,000 per annum and variable expenses per unit would be £150.

78

SCHEME B

The company will acquire plant costing £400,000. Fixed expenses (other than depreciation) would amount to £300,000 per annum and variable expenses per unit would be £120.

In both cases the plant is expected to last four years and then be worthless. The straight line method of depreciation is considered appropriate. The finished product will be marketed for £200 per unit irrespective of the level of sales. The forecast level of demand is 7,000 units per annum. The working capital requirements amount to £60,000 under each scheme.

Required :

(a)   For each scheme, A and B, calculate:

      (i)   the number of units which must be produced and sold each year to break even (i.e. where total revenues exactly cover total costs);
      (ii)   the forecast profit per annum;
      (iii)   the margin of safety.

(b)   Calculate the annual level of sales at which the same profit arises under each scheme.

(c)   A discussion of these two alternative schemes of production indicating the main factors to be take into account when choosing between scheme A and scheme B.

Note: Ignore the time value of money.

(Autumn 1988)

Exercise 6.10 EX

The directors of Westburn Granules Ltd require a minimum rate of return on investment of 12% per annum on all new projects. The following estimates are provided in relation to a proposal to sell widgets:

(1)   Initial investment in fixed assets and working capital   £200,000
(2)   Sale price of each widget   £10
(3)   Variable cost per unit sold   £6
(4)   Fixed costs per annum   £25,000
(5)   Turnover per annum   15,000 units

The directors recognise, from past experience, that estimates are liable to error, and they are keen to discover the possible adverse variation in each of the above five estimates before the project must be rejected as non-viable.

Required :

(a)   A calculation of the minimum annual profit required by the directors from the new project.

(b)   A calculation of the annual profit, assuming all the forecasts are achieved.

(c)   Calculations of the extent to which each of the estimates (1) to (5) above, taken individually, can vary before the project becomes unacceptable to the directors. (When making each individual calculation, assume that all the other estimates remain as stated.)

Note: Ignore the time value of money.

(Autumn 1989)

SOLUTIONS

SOLUTION 6.1

Contribution on each unit sold = £2.

To cover fixed costs of £30,000, therefore, 15,000 units must be sold (£30,000 divided by £2). Therefore, total sales = 15,000 units at £10 per unit = £150,000 to break even.

SOLUTION 6.2

(a) *Workings:*

Prime cost of 500,000 units	= £800,000	(£1.60 per unit)
Therefore closing stock = 300,000 x £1.60	= £480,000	(as in question)

Total cost of 500,000 units	= £800,000	(prime cost)
plus	£200,000	(factory expenses)
	£1,000,000	(£2.00 per unit)

Therefore closing stock = 300,000 units x £2.00 = £600,000

Revised Profit and Loss Account for 1981

		£	£
Sales			600,000
Less :	Prime Costs	800,000	
	Factory Expenses	200,000	
		1,000,000	
Less :	Closing Stock	600,000	
Cost of Goods Sold		400,000	
General Expenses		100,000	500,000
NET PROFIT			100,000

Budgeted Profit and Loss Accounts for 1982

(b)		PRIME COST		TOTAL COST	
		£	£	£	£
Sales			2,100,000		2,100,000
Less:	Opening Stock	480,000		600,000	
	Prime Costs	800,000		800,000	
	Factory Expenses	200,000		200,000	
		1,480,000		1,600,000	
Less :	Closing Stock	160,000		200,000	
		1,320,000		1,400,000	
General Expenses		100,000		100,000	
			1,420,000		1,500,000
NET PROFIT			680,000		600,000

(c) The two different methods of valuation simply spread profit differently between accounting years. Using the total cost base, a proportion of fixed costs are carried forward to the next accounting period - which means that *this* period's valuation of closing stock is higher (because it includes some fixed costs) and next period's opening stock will also be higher. A higher *closing* stock means higher profits for that year, but as this valuation then becomes the *opening* stock for the next year, the higher opening stock means *lower* profits in the second year! In other words, the profit 'benefit' in year one, by virtue of a high closing stock figure, is lost in year two by virtue of an equivalent high opening stock figure.

Any bank manager should be fully aware of the effects on profits of different bases of stock valuation and should not be 'swayed' by a change in method of valuation, as in this example.

SOLUTION 6.3

(a) In times of rising prices the LIFO valuation will give a lower stock valuation than if the FIFO valuation base was used. This is because the 'oldest' stock will be being valued at the then (cheaper) cost. A lower closing stock means a lower profit figure shown.

(b) Using marginal cost valuation will give a lower figure for closing stock (therefore a lower profit figure). This is because the marginal cost valuation takes account of the variable costs *only* included in the stock item, whereas 'total cost' includes further elements to boost the stock figure - i.e. a proportion of fixed costs. If the volume of stock is increasing then even more elements of fixed overheads are being included in the stock valuation, so giving a higher closing stock figure, and therefore higher profits. Note however, that marginal cost basis of valuation is not recommended by SSAP 9.

(c) The same answer applies as in (b) above except that with a possible 'slow' first year of operations the same fixed costs will be spread over a smaller number of units of production and the total cost valuation will therefore be that much higher - i.e. going further away from conservatism!

(d) Applying the rule to *separate* items of stock always produces a lower valuation (therefore lower profits). SSAP 9 requires this kind of valuation rather than valuation of *groups* of similar items.

(e) The straight line method will produce a lower depreciation charge in the *early* years - as a result, a higher profit will be shown. Therefore, in the *early* years the reducing balance method will give a higher charge against profits so producing the more conservative profit figure. In later years however, the situation is reversed!

(f) If prices are rising and depreciation is charged on current cost then obviously the depreciation charge is going to be higher - the profits lower - the more conservative approach.

SOLUTION 6.4

The contribution towards fixed costs = 30% - in other words, for every £1,000 of sales made there is a 'contribution' of £300.

The profit at present is £4,000 on sales of £200,000. Therefore, to produce an extra £9,000 profit :

How many 'blocks' of £1,000 of sales are needed?
9,000 ÷ 300 x £1,000 = £30,000 additional sales =

Total sales of £230,000

(Check this : 30% of £23,000 = £69,000 contribution, less fixed costs of £56,000 = £13,000 profit).

SOLUTION 6.5

(a)

Forecast Profit and Loss Account for 19-3 (Alternative 1)

	£	£
Turnover (150,000 @ £5)		750,000
less Variable costs:		
100,000 @ £3	300,000	
50,000 @ £4.50	225,000	
Depreciation	20,000	
Other fixed costs	122,000	
		667,000
Net Profit		83,000

(b)   **Forecast Profit and Loss Account for 19-3 (Alternative 2)**

		£	£
Turnover			750,000
less	Variable costs :		
	150,000 @ £3	450,000	
	Depreciation	32,000	
	Other fixed costs	160,000	
			642,000
Net Profit			108,000

(a)   **Forecast Balance Sheet as at 31 December 19-3 (Alternative 1)**

	£		£
Share Capital	200,000	Fixed Assets @ cost	200,000
Retained Profits	228,000	Less depreciation	100,000
			100,000
		Working capital	300,000
		Bank deposit	
		(balancing figure)	28,000
	428,000		428,000

(b)   **Forecast Balance Sheet as at 31 December 19-3 (Alternative 2)**

	£		£
Share Capital	200,000	Fixed Assets @ cost	320,000
Retained Profits	253,000	Less depreciation	112,000
			208,000
Bank overdraft			
(balancing figure)	55,000	Working Capital	300,000
	508,000		508,000

(c) With alternative (1), the *extra* production gives a contribution of £0.50 per unit to go towards covering the *extra* £2,000 fixed costs. The break even point on the *extra* sales is therefore 4,000 units.

With alternative (2), the extra production gives a contribution of £2 per unit to go towards covering extra costs of £52,000. The break even point on extra sales is therefore 26,000 units.

Alternative (2) is obviously more profitable but is subject to the risk of not achieving a higher break even point.

Working on Ken's brother's estimate of 30,000 extra units, Alternative (1) would produce £73,000 profits (Alternative 2, £68,000) and would leave £58,000 in deposit account (Alternative 2 would have bank overdraft £55,000).

Alternative (1) and an increase in production of only 30,000 units would appear to be the best proposition.

SOLUTION 6.6

		£	£
(a)	Sales in 19-3, 9,000 x £10 =		90,000
	Costs :		
	Opening stock	–	
	Materials	14,300	
	Variable Costs	18,700	
	Fixed Costs	68,200	
		101,200	
	Less Closing Stock (2,000 x £9.20)	18,400 *	
			82,800
			7,200
	Sales in 19-4, 11,000 x £10	110,000	

```
Costs :
Opening stock                         18,400
Materials                             13,000
Variable costs                        17,000
Fixed costs                           68,200
                                     116,600
Less Closing stock (1,000 x £9.82)     9,820  *
                                                        106,780
Profit                                                    3,220
```

*   Valuation of stock per unit

	19-3		19-4	
Total Costs	101,200	= £9.20	98,200	= £9.82
No. of units produced	11,000		10,000	

(b) In 19-4, Radios Ltd sold 2,000 more units yet made a lower profit than in 19-3. This is because the lower production in 19-4 meant that the *fixed* costs were spread over fewer units than they were in 19-3 which naturally increases the cost of production per unit. In addition to this the lower closing stock in 19-4 reduces the portion of fixed costs which are carried forward to the next period.

The profit, per unit, in 19-3 was £0.80 (selling price £10 less cost £9.20). As 2,000 more units were sold in 19-4, this should give an increased profit of 2,000 x 80p = £1,600, but the difference in overheads for 19-4, (9,000 x 62p) £5,580 turns this into a *reduced* profit of £3,980.

LESSON 7

VALUATION OF ASSETS

As you continue your studies of the varying sections of this book you must never forget the basic aim of the producers of financial documents, whether they be the profit and loss acccount, the balance sheet or any other statement, is that they must, as far as is possible, show a 'True and Fair View' of the state of affairs or the organisation to which the report refers. To assist in this aim, over the years various 'rules' have been developed and these were referred to earlier in the book. They cover : a) Going Concern, b) Accruals, c) Prudence d) Consistency, and are called Concepts, but modern financial reporting demands a more precise definition of these rules and, therefore, the Accounting bodies through the Accounting Standards Committee have, and continue to produce, Statements of Standard Accounting Practice that give guidance on specific areas, so that we can achieve the precise aim that we seek. The SSAPs apply to the valuation of assets in the balance sheet etc.

In the balance sheet the assets are split into the following categories :

Fixed Assets

Sub-divided into Tangible Fixed Assets, Intangible Fixed Assets and Investments.

Current Assets

Sub-divided into Stocks, Debtors, Investments, Cash and Bank.

TANGIBLE FIXED ASSETS (SSAP 12)

These are assets which are constantly being used by a business without which the business would not be able to function, e.g. land and buildings, plant and machinery, motor vehicles, etc. They are in permanent use although they will, of course, eventually wear out or become obsolete and have to be replaced. They do not in themselves make the profits for the business (i.e. they are not there to be sold at a profit), but they do allow the business to function in such a way as to make profits.

When these fixed assets are shown in the Company's Balance Sheet they are usually shown at cost (or valuation where the asset has been re-valued in the accounts, usually applying to buildings), less any depreciation that has been charged against the profits over the years of the life of the asset so far.

The resultant figure represents that part of the asset which has not been 'written off' rather than an estimate of its present-day value. For example a machine costing £10,000 which is considered to have a useful life of 10 years would probably be written off in equal amounts of £1,000 per year over that period, but this does not necessarily mean that after 5 years the machine would have a saleable value of £5,000 even though this figure would appear in the Balance Sheet as 'written down value'.

This is an example of the rule of 'going concern' in that because we know that the business will continue into the future, by continuing this policy, the asset, when its useful life has expired, with be worth nothing and this will be the value that will be shown against it in the Balance Sheet. The opposite of going concern is that the business is to be liquidated and then of course we would show in the financial statement, the actual value that we receive for selling that item.

DEPRECIATION is an attempt to spread the cost of an asset over its useful life by charging a certain amount of its cost against continuing years profits. You can devise whatever depreciation method you think appropriate to the particular asset but there are four methods that are commonly used.

1.   The straight line method
2.   The reducing balance method
3.   The usage basis method
4.   The revaluation method

To demonstrate the use of each of these methods we will consider an example of a Company which buys a machine costing £11,000. It is estimated that the machine will last for 5 years, and that at the end of the fifth year it will have a value of £1,000.

Using the straight line method we write off the same fixed percentage each year thus the annual depreciation cost will be £2,000 a year as per the following example :

		£
	Cost	11,000
Less	Scrap Value	1,000
	True Cost to Company	10,000

This, divided by 5 years = £2,000 p.a. depreciation. After 5 years the written down value will be £1,000.

Using the reducing balance method we use a fixed percentage rate but instead of applying it to the original cost we apply it to the written down value at the end of the previous year thus :

Using a rate of 38% and calculating to the nearest £1 :

	£
Cost	11,000
1st year Depreciation 38%	4180
	6,820
2nd year Depn. (38% of 6,820)	2,592
	4,228
3rd year Depn. (38% of 4,228)	1,607
	2,621
4th year Depn. (38% of 2,621)	996
	1,625
5th year Depn. (38% of 1,625)	617
Written down value at end of year 5	1,008

Using the usage basis instead of estimating the asset's life in years we estimate in terms of productive hours and then find an hourly rate, thus :

Estimate of usage in hours :

Year 1 to 3	10,000 per year	=	30,000 hours
Year 4 to 5	8,000 per year	=	16,000 hours
Estimate of life in productive hours		=	46,000 hours

Depreciation Rate per hour :

$$\frac{11,000 - 1,000}{46,000} = 21.7p$$

Depreciation for years 1, 2 and 3 :   10,000 hours at 21.7p per hour = £2,170

You will immediately recognise the effect of these valuation methods all of which are perfectly acceptable, but which as you will see, start with the same cost value and end approximately with the same value but in between times show differing annual charges for depreciation. You must accept that the methods are acceptable, but you must also be aware of the effect of each of the methods on reported accounts, because not only is the profit affected but so are the asset values. For example, at the end of the first year using the straight line basis the asset was shown in books as being worth £9,000 but by using the reducing balance method it is shown as being worth £6,820. In the first instance the profit would have been charged with £2,000 and in the second the first year's profit would have been charged with £4,180.

This is one of the examples that demonstrate the need for SSAPs 2 and 12 which requires companies, in the notes to the annual accounts, to declare the accounting policies that have been used in the preparation of the accounts so that users of the accounts can immediately make a mental adjustment to the figures knowing the repercussions on values, of differing methods of, in this case, depreciation.

The final method of depreciation is the revaluation basis whereby at the end of each year an expert valuation is obtained for the current value of the particular assets and therefore the depreciation charge is the difference between the value placed on the assets at the end of last year and the value placed on it this year. The revaluation method is used primarily for the asset of land and buildings whether the asset is freehold land and buildings or long leasehold. Over recent years property values have substantially increased and, therefore, to show an asset at its original cost would totally distort the current total asset value of the company and therefore SSAP 12 requires companies to periodically undertake the exercise to revalue all its properties and once the new value has been established to effect that valuation in the books. This is achieved by a simple double entry in the books by debiting the Buildings account with the difference between the current value and the value shown in the books at the time and the corresponding credit is shown in a reserve account called a Fixed Asset Revaluation Reserve account. You must understand that this apparent profit is only a 'paper profit' and therefore the reserve is a *capital* reserve not a *revenue* reserve. In other words it cannot be used to pay a dividend.

The current practice is then to depreciate the value of the buildings, not the value of the land - just the buildings.

All requirements of depreciation on fixed assets or tangible fixed assets as they are referred to in the balance sheet are contained in SSAP 12, the main points of which are listed below.

However, before leaving this topic of depreciation, I must ask you again to remember what actually happens when depreciation is provided for (i.e. by debiting the profit and loss account). Profits which would otherwise be available for distribution as dividend, are diverted to some other use (in this case to provide for the eventual replacement of the asset).

e.g.   Results of a year's trading are :

	£
Purchases	1,200
Sales	2,000
Expenses paid (e.g. rent, wages, etc.)	300

NOTE :   A gross profit of £800 has been made but £300 expenses have had to be paid out to make that gross profit - therefore net profit = £500. In other words cash or debtors have increased by £500. (Remember that profits always increase debtors/cash - in this example they have increased by £800 *the gross profit* then have been reduced by the payments of £300 for expenses).

£500 is, then, firmly planted in the business, but this will be drawn on by the owners as their reward for the capital they have invested. If however, we put another entry in the Profit and Loss account - depreciation £100 - this will have the effect of reducing the net profit *FIGURE* by £100, so reducing what the owners can draw on by £100. This ensures that, of the profit lying in the business (i.e. £500 in cash or debtors) £100 will *remain* in the business, so providing a fund for the eventual replacement of the asset. In other words, £100 of profits which would otherwise be available for distribution to the owners are diverted to some other use by a simple book-keeping entry.

Rather than think of these 'saved' funds as being there for the eventual replacement of the asset, we could think of them as a means of recovering, over a number of years, the amount originally spent in purchasing the asset.

I do not apologise for repeating myself on this concept as it is very *important*.

S.S.A.P. 12

ACCOUNTING FOR DEPRECIATION

Depreciation must be charged on all fixed assets except freehold land, but in the case of such land depleting in value (i.e. by extraction of minerals) then depreciation must be provided for.

A fair proportion of the value of the asset should be allocated each year during the expected useful life of the asset.

If the estimated useful life of the asset has to be changed then that part of the asset not yet written off should be 'spread' over the revised remaining useful life.

If a situation arises whereby the expected useful life of the asset is considerably reduced, (perhaps as a result of new technology and obsolescence), and it is therefore obvious that the present written down value of the asset will never be recovered by the normal annual charges for depreciation, then the asset would immediately be written down to its estimated recoverable amount, to be written off over the asset's remaining life. This procedure is in line with the 'prudence' concept - i.e.to write off a large 'chunk' of the asset immediately it becomes evident that the asset has reduced in value.

Where a fixed asset is revalued the depreciation charge should immediately be based on the revalued amount. In the year of revaluation a note should show which part of the yearly depreciation charge is based on the 'old' value and which part on the 'new' value.

If the *market* value of the asset is greater than the book value depreciation must still be charged in the normal way.

The accounts should disclose the method of depreciation used, the useful life (or the depreciation rate), and the aggregate depreciation provided to date.

Intangible Fixed Assets

These are assets not having a 'physical' existence as compared with Tangible assets that do have a physical existence.

Examples of Intangible Assets are :

1. Development costs
2. Patents, Licences, Trade Marks and Brand names.
3. Goodwill

1.   *DEVELOPMENT COSTS*

Forward looking companies constantly spend money on developing new products - figures of £100m a year are not uncommon. To charge such expenditure to the current year's profit would depress the profit considerably and because we are developing for the future we are tempted to treat this expenditure as capital expenditure. However, there is no guarantee that the business will benefit from this and prudence must govern our actions.

SSAP.13 governs this and categorises the expenditure into four categories (say, A,B,C and D - see below) and advises as to how we should deal with each.

S.S.A.P. 13

ACCOUNTING FOR RESEARCH AND DEVELOPMENT

(A)   Where fixed assets are purchased to provide facilities for research and development, these assets should be treated in the accounts like any other fixed asset (i.e. capitalised, then depreciated over their useful life).

(B/C) Other expenditure on research (pure and applied) should be written off in the same year the expenses were incurred.

(D)   Expenditure on development should also be written off in the year the costs are incurred but may be deferred to a future period (i.e. capitalised temporarily) in certain circumstances, i.e. where the development is for a clearly defined project with reasonable certainty of success and profits. In such a case the development expenditure incurred could be 'held over', being shown on the balance sheet in the meantime as an 'intangible fixed asset'. When the benefits from the development start to accrue so the item 'development expenditure' will start to be written down to Profit and Loss account on an annual basis until it has disappeared from the balance sheet.

Movements on deferred development expenditure account should be disclosed in the accounts and the reasons for the treatment of development costs must be clearly stated by way of notes.

NOTE :   Pure research is *finding out.*

Applied research is *using what you have found out,* with a purpose in mind.

This purpose is then *developed* in order to produce something new or improved, and this could be a product, a process or a service.

2.   *PATENTS, LICENCES, TRADE MARKS AND BRAND NAMES*

These are only included in the balance sheet as an asset if they have cost the company money - i.e. purchased.

However, recently, some well known companies have been creating an asset in the form of 'brand names'. These are well known household names of a particular brand of product and the companies concerned obviously consider the 'name' to be worthy of having a value placed on it. At the moment there is much controversy taking place regarding this practice.

As with tangible fixed assets they should be written off over their estimated useful life (SSAP 12)

3.   *GOODWILL (SSAP 22)*

There are many definitions of this asset but it is simply the *difference* between

      (i)   the true asset value of the company being bought
and   (ii)   the price paid for these assets.

It is, if fact, how much extra the buying company must pay to get control of the other company, and could be regarded as the buying of future potential profits.

There have been many definitions of Goodwill, such as 'the benefit arising out of reputation', 'the attraction which brings in custom' and so on. Obviously a good established business will have attracted over the years a certain degree of custom and reputation which helps to maintain or increase its profits. This reputation is valuable to the business and it is reasonable to regard it as a business asset and to call it 'Goodwill'.

Should the business be subsequently sold the purchaser would naturally be expected to pay for the goodwill as well as the machinery, buildings, etc., which he acquires. In this case the purchaser would quite rightly open an account for the asset Goodwill which he has paid for and this would then appear on the assets side of his balance sheet. If, at a later date, he too sells the business then he will sell the Goodwill along with the other assets.

The guidance for the depreciation (amortisation) of the recorded asset 'Goodwill' is contained in SSAP.22, which is currently under review. A summary of the requirements is given below, but basically there are two options :

      (i)   write off the purchased goodwill straight away against the reserves
or
      (ii)   capitalise the goodwill and write it off by the straight line method over an estimate of its useful life.

S.S.A.P. 22

ACCOUNTING FOR GOODWILL

This Standard defines goodwill as being the difference between the value of the business as a whole and the total of the 'fair' values of its various net assets. In most cases you could therefore say that goodwill is the difference between the accepted value of the business and the value of the net assets shown on the latest balance sheet.

Goodwill could therefore be positive (if the accepted value of the business as a whole exceeds the value of the net assets held) or negative (if the accepted value of the business as a whole is less than the value of the net assets held).

The latter case would be possible if the business in question was not, for some reason, particularly attractive to buyers and would in the event of a sale command a price lower than the value of its net assets (i.e. it has a negative goodwill).

Goodwill obviously only exists whilst the business is a going concern and is therefore quite unlike any other asset. The Standard draws attention to the fact that :

1.   It has no relationship whatsoever to any costs incurred in the business.
2.   Factors may contribute to goodwill which cannot possibly be valued (e.g. first-class public-relations management or servicing arrangements).
3.   The value of goodwill may fluctuate according to circumstances at any time.
4.   It cannot effectively be compared with the goodwill of any other business.

Goodwill can be classified into 'purchased goodwill' (where another business, and therefore its goodwill, is purchased), and 'non-purchased goodwill' (where the goodwill has been built up through normal trading but does not appear in the accounts).

SSAP 22 says quite clearly that only *purchased goodwill* should be acknowledged in the accounts - i.e. recognised in financial statements (even if the board of directors are convinced that non-purchased goodwill is there in the business - they must ignore it for the purpose of presenting the accounts!) *See previous notes on 'Brand Names'!*

The Standard goes on to say that 'purchased goodwill', whilst correctly being acknowledged in the accounts immediately on purchase, should then be eliminated from the accounts by immediate 'write-off' (i.e. to reserves). It does, however, permit companies to amortise (write-off) goodwill through the profit and loss account over a period of time (i.e. write it off gradually), consistent with the considered useful economic life of the goodwill purchased. Difficult to determine!

The preference is clearly that of immediate write-off and this should be made against existing reserves. Which reserves? Realised reserves (e.g. P & L a/c balance or general reserve etc.) or unrealised reserves (e.g. revaluation reserve).

If an unrealised reserve is used then transfers must be made over a period to a realised reserve so that, ultimately, the whole 'cost' of immediate write-off of goodwill is written off against realised reserves.

Obviously, if the amortisation method is used - i.e. taking a 'bit' out of profits every year to gradually write off the purchased goodwill - Dr. P & L a/c - Cr. goodwill then the gradual write-off *will* be to realised profits.

Final points to note :

A company using the amortisation method will obviously show a greater 'shareholders funds' than the company which writes off purchased goodwill immediately against reserves. This must be taken into account when interpreting any company accounts.

Finally it must be appreciated that where a company is in the habit of buying-up other companies (and therefore their respective goodwill) the buying company may decide to write-off immediately the goodwill purchased from Company A and amortise over a period the goodwill purchased from Company B. They don't have to be consistent in their treatment!

Investments in Other Companies

For a variety of reasons companies often invest in other companies. It could be that they wish to build up a group of companies which they control or it could be to cement a relationship with a major supplier, or it could simply be that they want to put short term surplus capital to the best possible use.

Investments are shown in the Balance Sheet in two areas :

a) In the area of fixed assets; this refers to those investments that are deemed to be of a reasonable permanent nature.

b) Investments that are intended to be very short term are shown in the Current Asset section of the Balance Sheet.

The valuation placed on each investment is its cost or its current market value if this is lower than the cost (remember prudency - 'never anticipate a profit but provide fully for all known or anticipated losses').

If a reduction in value is required the accounting entries are debit the profit and loss account and credit the investment account.

In the notes that support the accounts the directors are required to give an estimate of the current market value of the investment to be shown alongside the original cost so that users can see the current value of that asset.

Investments in what are called quoted companies, (companies that have a quotation on the Stock Exchange) the valuation is easily obtained by taking the share price in the Financial Times at the date of the year end. Investments in unquoted companies cause a little difficulty and it is left to the Directors to give 'their best estimate' of the current value.

In most cases this cost and current value is adequate but sometimes, between the date of the companies year end and the date of the preparation of the accounts, certain events happen that change the valuations given. The best example of this was in 1987 when a company with a year end of 30th September 1987 produced and published its accounts in December, during which time the stock market 'crashed'. SSAP 17 regulates post balance sheet events and in this case, alongside the cost and the market value at the date of the Balance Sheet, we would have to show the latest valuation with a suitable note.

Current Assets

A current asset is an asset which would become completely liquid (i.e. turn itself into cash) within a fairly short space of time. For example - stock when sold will produce debtors - debtors will pay off their balances and therefore turn into cash, and so on. A rough guide is to regard a current asset as one which will normally be replaced by cash within a period of about 12 months, but a better description is that of an asset which is constantly changing its value as trade takes place, and is therefore always on the move. For example, stock is acquired then sold, so increasing debtors, then the debtors pay up and are therefore reduced in value whilst cash is increased, then cash is used to buy more stock and the 'circle' starts again. A more apt description of these kind of assets is *circulating assets*.

Debtors

Valuation of this item is straightforward - all the debit balances in the ledger representing money due to the business are added up to give a figure representing the total amount due to the business from customers. However, some of these debts may be irrecoverable (e.g. if the customer has gone bankrupt and all dividends have been received from the trustee in bankruptcy) and some may be doubtful.

You should remember the procedures for dealing with these situations from your Stage 1 studies; where it is known that a sum owing from a particular debtor is irrecoverable, it is written off as a bad debt by crediting the debtor concerned (to close his account) and debiting the profit and loss account (as with any expense or loss) so reducing the figure for net profit. This is where the debt is *BAD* - but it may be that a debt is only *DOUBTFUL* in which case it would be wrong to write the account off as irrecoverable The debtors account must be left alone, but the doubtful nature of the debt must be acknowledged in some way, and the accepted practice is :

(a)   to debit profit and loss account (as with a *BAD* debt)

(b)   to credit a Provision for Bad or Doubtful Debts (instead of crediting the debtor's account)

What does this achieve?

(a)   The profit *figure* in the profit and loss account is reduced, so reducing the amount the owners will draw from the business; thereby the business is conserving profits or diverting them to some other use.

(b)   We now have a record (i.e. the Provision for Doubtful Debts account) of the amount of profits being conserved to cover doubtful debts.

Should any of these *doubtful* debts become definitely bad in future years, then the provision we have made will cover this loss. You will see from the above that the procedures and effects are *exactly the same as for depreciation.*

With depreciation we are building up a 'fund' to replace an asset when it has worn out, and with doubtful debts we are building up a 'fund' to replace the debtor if he turns bad. In both cases the 'fund' is being built up by diverting profits, which would otherwise be available for distribution to the owners of the business.

VALUATION OF STOCKS

At the end of a financial period a business must value its stocks so that this valuation can be put into the accounts, for the purpose of obtaining a figure representing the profit for the period. The stock represents, of course, that portion of purchases (or manufacturing) which has *not* been sold at the end of the period and if it is ignored the gross profit will be understated.

The term 'stock' can of course refer to goods which are :

(a)   bought for re-selling;

(b)   raw materials which the manufacturer intends to use in his manufacturing;

(c)   goods which have actually been *made* by the manufacturer himself;

(d)   goods which have been partly made by the manufacturer.

These different kinds of stock are referred to respectively as :

(a)   Stocks of finished goods which appear in the Trading account;

(b)   Stocks of raw materials which appear in the Manufacturing account;

(c)   As in (a) - but are calculated in the Manufacturing account;

(d)   Stocks of Work-in-Progress (W.I.P.) which appear in the Manufacturing account.

Any of these stocks will, of course, also appear in the balance sheet as current assets.

For the present I should like you to regard my references to the term 'stock' as applying to (a) and (b) only, and we will look at manufactured goods and work-in-progress separately later on.

The normal basis used for the valuation of stock is 'at the lower of cost and net realisable value' (SSAP9).

In other words, two different values are looked at - Cost, and Net Realisable Value (NRV) and the lowest figure is used. The full meanings of those terms will be explained as we look at each one.

Cost

This is the purchase price of the goods, plus any expenditure incurred in acquiring the stock, e.g. carriage on purchases. Some businesses may regard a certain proportion of wages as being expenditure incurred in acquiring the stock, whilst others may even include a proportion of other overheads in addition to carriage and wages. Opinions differ on what exactly should be included and the recommendation is that 'cost' should include such part, if any, of the overhead expenses as is appropriate in the circumstances of that particular business.

For the moment we will think of 'cost' as being the purchase price of the goods (or raw materials) only, and just bear in mind that some businesses may add to this a certain amount of overheads. Remember that it is the value of the stock-on-hand (i.e. the unsold/unused stock) which we want to determine.

In determining cost the accountant may use a variety of methods, e.g.

1)   He may add together the actual cost of each individual item of stock in the store room. This is known as the UNIT COST method (not very practicable in many businesses!)

2)   He may take the 'average cost' of the goods held at the *beginning* of the period and as new stocks are acquired calculate a new 'average cost' figure. Any issues of stocks will be at the most recently calculated 'average cost'. This is, of course, referred to as the AVERAGE COST (AVCO) method.

3)   He may *assume* that the first stocks acquired are the first to be disposed of. In other words, the stock on hand at any one time is the most recently acquired stock. Known as the F.I.F.O. method (i.e. First in - First Out).

4)   He may estimate the SELLING price of the stock on hand and then deduct from this an amount equal to the normal gross profit. For example, if selling price is calculated as being £5,000 and the *normal* gross profit margin is 40% of sales, then gross profit = £2,000. Therefore Sales (£5,000) less gross profit (£2,000) = £3,000, this being taken as the cost of the stock in hand. This is know as the ADJUSTED SELLING PRICE method and is mainly used by retailers.

5)   He may *assume* that the last stocks acquired are the first to be disposed of - i.e. that the stock on hand is made up of the *earliest* purchases. This is the L.I.F.O. (Last in - First out) method.

Do note that these are *methods* of valuation only, for the accountant's use, and do not necessarily correspond with the method of physical distribution adopted in the actual stores. It is difficult to imagine the L.I.F.O. method as being in operation by the storekeeper, yet is is a sound method for the accountant to *assume*.

Whatever method is used for determining cost, it should be used consistently by the business and if any major changes are made in the methods of valuation, this fact must be stated by way of a note in the accounts.

Here I should point out that the methods used to value assets apply to all types of companies, sole traders and partnerships *BUT* the SSAPs apply only to Limited Companies. As far as Limited Companies are concerned, the LIFO method is not acceptable because, in times of inflation the method under-states stocks and, therefore, profits - it also under-states assets in the balance sheet.

EXAMPLES

Record of Receipts and Sales or Issues of Stock

Date	Received	Issued or Sold	No. of Units in Stock
January	20 @ £4.50		20
February	10 @ £3.00		30
March		8	22
April	10 @ £7.20		32
May		16	16

The cost value of the stock in hand on 31 May is :

(a)   Using the AVERAGE COST (**AVCO**) method :

Average cost per unit in January	=	£4.50
February	=	£4.00
March	=	£4.00
April	=	£5.00
May	=	£5.00

Therefore at 31 May average cost = 16 x £5.00 = £80

(b)   Using the **F.I.F.O.** method :

The 16 units left are the ones most recently purchased, i.e.

10 @ £7.20 (bought in April)	=	£72
6 @ £3.00 (bought in February)	=	£18
16 Units		£90

(c)   Using the **L.I.F.O.** method :

The 16 units left are the oldest stock - the earliest purchases -
i.e. 16 @ £4.50 (bought in January) = £72

Note the different results obtained by using different methods of valuing cost - each one has its own advantages and disadvantages but providing that the use of any particular method has the effect of showing a 'true and fair view' of the position and results of that business, then the use of that method is justified.

So far we have only determined the *cost* of the stock in hand but we know now of the various methods used to work out 'cost'. As stock valuation is to be at 'the lowest of cost and net realisable value' we must now work out the -

Net Realisable Value

This is simply the price at which the stock could be sold (at the balance sheet date) LESS all expenses that would be incurred in selling it. It is possible for this valuation to work out at less than 'cost' if, for example, some of the stock has deteriorated or gone out of fashion since it was purchased. It may well be that a fashion shop has bought a number of military-style coats at a cost of £7 each, and due to a change in fashion tastes, these could only now be sold at a 'sale' price of £4.

In this case, N.R.V. would be £4 (per coat) less any expenses incurred in selling the coat.

These then are the two different values that must be calculated for our stock-on-hand at the balance sheet date :

(1)   Cost (calculated by one of the methods mentioned above)

(2)   Net Realisable Value

Whichever gives the *lowest* figure is the one which appears in the accounts (i.e. stock account and trading or manufacturing account) and in the balance sheet.

The rule of 'lower of cost and N.R.V.' can in certain circumstances be extended to read 'lower of cost, N.R.V., and Replacement Price (R.P.)'. Generally however replacement price is *not* acceptable except in circumstances when replacement price is the best measure of net realisable value. In the following examples we will assume that circumstances justify the inclusion of Replacement Price.

This means that we can apply the rule of 'lower of cost and N.R.V.' **or** *the extended rule of 'lower of cost, N.R.V. and R.P.'*

Where the stock is made up of different types - e.g. tins of paint of varying qualities - comparison of cost and N.R.V. (and R.P.) needs to be made in respect of each item of stock separately (do *not* compare the *totals*).

EXAMPLE

Stock at 31 December	Cost	N.R.V.	R.P.
	£	£	£
Type A	500	490	495
Type B	1,000	1,300	900
	1,500	1,790	1,395

Valuing each type *separately* and taking the lowest of cost, N.R.V., and R.P. we get the following valuations :

Type A	£490
Type B	£900
TOTAL VALUE	£1,390

Taking the lowest of cost and N.R.V. we have :

Type A	£490
Type B	£1,000
TOTAL VALUE	£1,490

From the above example it can be seen that there are two different ACCEPTABLE valuations according to which method of valuation is used, the lowest *acceptable* being £1,390 and the highest *acceptable* being £1,490. Stock may be valued in any of these ways providing that the method adopted is used consistently from year to year.

The above rules for valuing stock are detailed in Statement of Standard Account Practice 9, which aims to reduce the differences and variations adopted in practice.

Stocks of Manufactured Goods

The procedure for valuing the stock of finished goods in a manufacturing company (i.e. where the goods have been *made* not purchased) is exactly the same as above; COST in this case however, would be the cost of manufacturing the goods which would consist of the following :

	£
Raw Materials Used	xxx
Direct Factory labour	xxx
Main Cost known as PRIME COST	XXX

Plus other factory cost, e.g.
      Factory Power, Factory Rent and
      Rates, Depreciation of Plant,
      Factory Overheads, etc.   xxx

TOTAL FACTORY COSTS   XXXX

From your previous knowledge of manufacturing accounts you will realise that only actual *manufacturing* costs are included in the above total. Office, financial, distribution, advertising and administrative expenses do *not* form part of the cost of manufacture (these are charged to profit and loss account quite separately). Also that the above total is the cost of manufacture of finished goods and partly finished goods (W.I.P.) - a final adjustment of adding opening stock of W.I.P. and deducting closing stock of W.I.P. would produce a figure representing the cost of finished goods only. SSAP 9 recommends that Prime Cost is *not* an acceptable basis as it under-states stock values. Despite this the policy is often adopted by sole-traders and partnerships.

Stocks of Work in Progress

Whatever proportion of costs have gone into the partly finished article determines the cost value.

EXAMPLE

> J.B. Ltd started producing gas detectors on 1 June and by 30 June when accounts were prepared for the month they had produced 200 complete units and 10 units which were exactly half finished as regards materials and in all other respects. No sales had yet been made.
>
> The costs during June were :

	£
Cost of materials used	4,410
Workshop labour	5,840
Workshop sundry expenses	660
Workshop rent	365
Administrative expenses	725
	12,000

At 30 June it was estimated that the net realisable value of each unit was £52.
At the same date J.B. Ltd held stocks of raw materials as follows :

	COST	N.R.V.	R.P
Material A	700	740	750
Material B	200	180	150
Material C	130	140	100
	1,030	1,060	1,000

Required :

A list of all the *acceptable* valuations for finished goods, work-in-progress and raw materials.

Calculations :

(i)   Finished Goods

There are 200 complete units in stock and the total cost of producing 205 units (including 10 x $^1/_2$ completed units) was £11,275 (does not include administrative expenses) - therefore one unit cost :

$$\frac{11,275}{205} = £55$$

200 units therefore have a Factory Cost of £11,000

N.R.V. of each unit is £52 so 200 units   = £10,400

Our table now looks like this :

Factory Cost	N.R.V
£11,000	£10,400

Applying the rule of lower of cost and N.R.V. gives us an acceptable valuation of £10,400.

(ii)   Work-in-Progress

10 x $^1/_2$ units = 5 complete units and by using the figures already calculated above we have :

Factory Cost	N.R.V.
£275	£260

giving an acceptable figure of £260 by applying the rule as before.

(iii)   Raw Materials

The table is already laid out for us in the question so let us apply the rule firstly as *'lower of Cost and N.R.V.'*

Separate Materials	£	
Material A	700	
Material B	180	
Material C	130	
	1,010	Acceptable Valuation

Now we will apply the extended rule of lower of Cost, N.R.V. and R.P.

Separate Materials	£	
Material A	700	
Material B	150	
Material C	100	
	950	Acceptable Valuation

Study the above examples remembering that in practice one certain basis is adopted and used consistently (another reminder of the concepts!).

SSAP 9

STOCKS AND WORK IN PROGRESS

Stocks should be valued at the **lower of cost and net realisable value (NRV)**. The comparison of cost and NRV should be made in respect of each type of stock *separately* - totals should not be compared. (Refer to example page 97).

Valuation at Replacement cost (i.e. where this is lower than NRV) is not acceptable when the effect is to show a loss greater than that which is expected. Remember that the lower the figure for closing stock, the lower the profit, or greater the loss. Where replacement cost is considered to be the best, or only measure of NRV however, then it is acceptable to value stocks at the **lower of cost and replacement cost.**

Net Realisable Value - this is the amount at which the items of stock and work in progress could be sold for, less all further costs of completion and less all marketing, selling and distribution costs of the items concerned.

Replacement Cost - the cost at which identical stock could be purchased or manufactured.

Cost - this comprises net purchase price, including import duties, transport and handling costs.

A manufacturer in valuing his work in progress and finished goods will add to the purchase price of raw materials a proportionate share of direct labour, direct expenses, sub-contracted work, and other factory overheads such as light and heat, power, depreciation of machinery, etc. - i.e. his cost of converting the raw materials. Such cost will *not* normally include distribution or administrative expenses, although with certain types of production such expenses may justifiably be included in cost. The test is 'Can these expenses be reasonably allocated to the manufacturing process?'

The Standard (SSAP 9) recommends the use of 'total cost' basis as opposed to marginal cost for the purpose of valuing stocks of a manufacturer.

Coming back to purchase price - i.e. of the finished goods or, in the case of a manufacturer, raw materials - the purchasing cost per unit can be determined in various ways. LIFO is not recommended by this Standard but the Companies Act 1985 appears to justify its use.

Disclosure in Accounts

The different types of stock (i.e raw materials, W.I.P., finished goods) should be shown separately in the accounts with notes to say how each particular stock was valued - i.e. the method used and the accounting policy followed in valuing. In the case of long-term contracts the accounts should also show the amount of progress payments received to date.

VALUATION OF LONG-TERM CONTRACTS

The work-in-progress of a contractor engaged on a long term contract (such as the building of a large office or college complex) would consist of the partly completed buildings. At the end of his financial year the contractor will need to estimate the value of the partly completed contract (W.I.P.) in order to prepare his final accounts and balance sheet. One way of doing this would simply be to determine how much has been spent on the buildings to date and to do this, costs of materials used, wages paid, and overheads paid would be added together to give the value of the Uncompleted Contract (i.e. the value of the partly completed buildings). The resultant stocks figure would appear in the contractor's final accounts and in his balance sheet.

Now you know of one way to value a contractor's uncompleted contract - simply add up 'TOTAL COSTS TO DATE.'

The profit on such a contract will not be realised until the work is completed and such profit will be the difference between total costs incurred and the contract price. However, in the meantime, the contractor may want to take credit for part of the estimated total profit on the contract, the proportion being determined by the degree of completeness of the contract at that date. For example, if the work is $3/4$ completed then it would be reasonable to take credit in the account for $3/4$ of the expected total profit :
If the total costs for the *whole* of the contract are going to be £800,000 and the total costs incurred to date amount to £500,000, then we could say that the contract is 5/8ths complete and therefore 5/8ths of the total profit expected could be brought into the accounts. When the contract is 7/8ths completed we have taken credit for 7/8ths of the total profit and by the time the contract is 100% completed we will, over the period, have taken credit for the whole of the profit.

We can therefore regard the value of the uncompleted contract to be made up of **total costs incurred to date** plus a **proportion of the expected profit,** but this profit must only be included where it is foreseeable and can be assessed with reasonable certainty.

If, at the time of valuing, there is an expected *loss* on the contract as a whole, then the value of the uncompleted contract would have to be **total costs incurred to date** *less* the **whole** of the expected loss. This is in line with the attitude of 'conservatism in accounting' whereby we can, if we wish, anticipate *part* of an expected profit but must acknowledge the *whole* of any expected loss.

It would seem then that an uncompleted contract can be valued at 'cost to date' or 'cost to date plus a proportion of the expected total profit on the contract'. However, the statement of Standard Accounting Practice No. 9 says that credit for a proportion of the foreseeable profit *must* be taken *unless* the contract is of less than one year's duration. Therefore, a contractor can value his uncompleted contract at cost without the addition of profit if the contract is not expected to last for more than one year. SSAP 9 (Revised) states that there may be conditions whereby the requirements of the Standard apply to contracts of less than one year. This would depend on the company's overall activities. Any progress payments received to date would of course be deducted from these valuations on the basis that that *part* of the uncompleted contract to which the payments relate has in effect been 'sold'.

In assessing the percentage of total profit expected on a contract to be accounted for *now* we must be prudent. For example, on a contract nearing completion we can be reasonably certain of the final outcome, but on a contract in its early stages this can not be so.

EXAMPLE

At year end 31 October 19-8

CONTRACT	£000s	COST INCURRED	ESTIMATED TOTAL COST	CONTRACT PRICE
A		80	100	150
B		50	500	700

Workings of acceptable valuations

	£000s A	£000s B
CONTRACT PRICE	150	700
COST	100	500
PROFIT	50	200
COSTS TO DATE	80	50

99

	PERCENTAGE COMPLETE	£000s A	£000s B
	(80 OUT OF 100)		
	(50 OUT OF 500)	<u>80%</u>	<u>10%</u>
	THEREFORE : VALUATION COSTS TO DATE	80	50
PLUS	ATTRIBUTABLE PROFIT (80% OF £50) (10% OF £200)	<u>40</u>	<u>20</u>
	VALUATION	<u>120</u>	<u>70</u>
BUT	PRUDENCY DICTATES REDUCTION :		
	(40 TO SAY 35 NEARING COMPLETION)	<u>5</u>	(20 TO SAY 5 EARLY STAGES!) <u>15</u>
	ACCEPTABLE VALUATION	<u>115</u>	<u>55</u>

How would we show Contract A in the Books at 31 October 19-8 ?

'A' CONTRACT COST

	£000s		£000s
Bank	80	W.I.P. Valuation	115
Balance to P&L	<u>35</u>		
	<u>115</u>		<u>115</u>

(i) So that in the P&L a/c :

	£000s	
Sales	—	
Opening Stock	—	
Cost	80	
Closing Stock	<u>115</u>	
Cost of Sales		(35)
GROSS PROFIT		35

(ii) In the Balance Sheet

STOCK = <u>£115</u>

This is technically totally incorrect. We value Stock at Cost or NRV. Cost of sales is Cost, *not* Cost plus Profit.

So, in 1988 the SSAP 9 on this aspect was revised.

The accounting entries under the revised SSAP 9 would be :

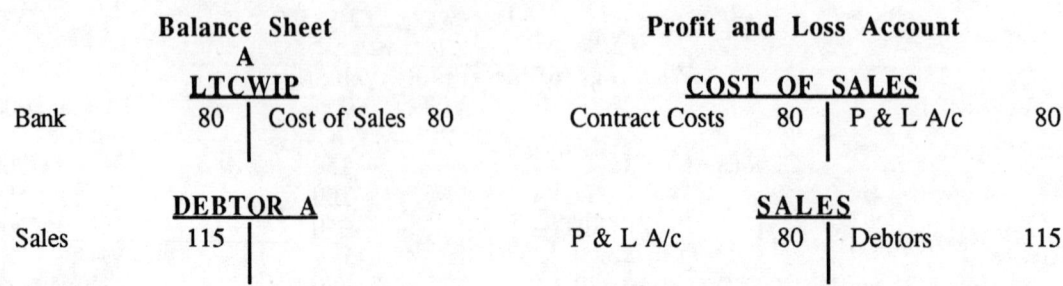

	Balance Sheet **A**			**Profit and Loss Account**		
	<u>**LTCWIP**</u>			<u>**COST OF SALES**</u>		
Bank	80	Cost of Sales	80	Contract Costs 80	P & L A/c	80
	<u>**DEBTOR A**</u>			<u>**SALES**</u>		
Sales	115			P & L A/c 80	Debtors	115

The P&L Account would show the same Gross profit but in a technically correct way, viz :

	£000s
Sales	115
Cost of Sales	80
GROSS PROFIT	35

and in the Balance Sheet :

1.   No stock because it had been 'matched' to the sales
2.   A contract debtor

Double Entry (SSAP 9 Revised)

All contract costs should be debited to a 'Long Term Contract Work in Progress' (LTCWIP) account, as these costs occur (Cr. Bank).

At the end of the financial year the *value of the work done* in that period should be credited to Sales and debited to Contract Debtors. Obviously payments will be received from these Contract Debtors during the year and will of course be credited to them. The final balance of Contract Debtors should be shown in the balance sheet as 'Amounts due on Contracts'.

The *cost of the work done* in the period is, at the year end, credited to LTCWIP account and debited in the P & L account as 'cost of contract sales'. Any losses on contracts will be debited to P & L account (cost of contract sales) and credited to a provision account.

We have therefore :

LTCWIP Account

	£000s		£000s
Bank (Contract costs)	5,000	P&L (cost of contract sales)	3,000
		Provisions for anticipated losses	100
		Contract Debtors (excess paymts. received for work not done)	50
		Balance c/d	1,850
	5,000		5,000
Balance b/d	1,850		

This final balance on LTCWIP account is shown on the balance sheet as a stock figure - i.e. 'Long-Term Contract Stock'.

By showing *cost* of work done and of sales this ensures that stock does not include any profit.

EXERCISE 7.1

A company is incorporated in 1 January, Year 1 and at the end of its first half year of trading, the stock record cards show the following :

Year 1	Type X		Type Y	
	Receipts (units)	Issues (units)	Receipts (units)	Issues (units)
January	100 @ £4.00		200 @ £10.00	
February		80	100 @ £8..50	
March	140 @ £6.00			240
April	100 @ £3.80		100 @ £11.50	
May		140	140 @ £10.00	
June	80 @ £5.00			100

The following additional information is available to you :

N.R.V. and R.P. values of stocks

At 30 June, Year 1	N.R.V.	R.P.
Type X	£950	£1,000
Type Y	2,000	1,800
	2,950	2,800

The value of stock-in-hand includes both types of stock (i.e. only one figure is shown in the accounts for 'stock')

You are **required** to :

(a) Using the FIFO method to determine 'cost', calculate the LOWEST and HIGHEST values at which stock could be valued in the company's balance sheet at 30 June, Year 1 and yet conform with accepted accountancy conventions.

(b) As in (a) but this time using the 'Average Cost' method to determine cost.

Show your answer in the following form :

	Lowest Acceptable Value £	Highest Acceptable Value £
(a) Stock on hand		
(b) Stock on hand		

EXERCISE 7.2

Contractors Limited erect buildings under contract. At 31 March, 19-8 the company had almost completed a college for a local education authority at a contract price of £902,000 which will be received in full on completion.

Cost incurred for work on the contract totalled £700,000 at 31 March, 19-8

Additional work required to complete the building will cost not more than £70,000.

What value(s) would be acceptable for the uncompleted contract?

EXERCISE 7.3

The directors of Trimmer Limited propose to adopt the treatments shown below in the company's published accounts for the year ended 31 December, 19-3.

* Underlining indicates wording in the accounts

1. Accumulated depreciation on motor vehicles _____ £4,375

    This amount relates to vehicles purchased at the beginning of 19-2 for £10,000. Depreciation provided in 19-2 amounted to £2,500, but only £1,875 has been provided in 19-3.

2. Long term contracts in progress, at cost £26,000 plus attributable profit £6,000 _____ £32,000

    This valuation related to two contracts;
    Contract 1, for which £40,000 will be received on completion, is expected to incur total costs of £30,000. Costs incurred to 31 December, 19-3 were £18,000. The profit of £6,000 included in the valuation relates to this contract.

    Contract 2, for which £25,000 will be received on completion is expected to incur total costs of £20,000. Costs incurred to 31 December, 19-3 were £8,000.

3. Depreciation of equipment on replacement cost   £20,000

This amount has been charged in the calculation of profit; depreciation on original cost would have been £11,000 but that amount is not mentioned.

4. Gain on revaluation of freehold property   £134,000

This gain has been included among revenue items in calculating net profit for the year.

5. Acquisition of freehold property, at cost   £92,000

This item, which has been added to freehold property in the balance sheet, includes legal fees of £2,000 paid on acquisition.

6. Current taxation   £17,500

This amount, which relates to corporation tax payable in January 19-4 on profits of 19-2 appears as a current liability in the balance sheet but no amount appears for estimated tax of £14,600 which is payable 1 January, 19-5 on profits of 19-3.

Required :
(a) A list of those transactions which are *acceptable* within the usual accountancy conventions. Simply state the appropriate number of each treatment. (i.e. acceptable numbers .....). Marks may be deducted for treatments incorrectly listed.

(b) A list of those transactions which are *not acceptable* within the usual accountancy conventions, and a brief explanation of why each treatment is not acceptable. Give the appropriate number against each explanation. To gain marks you must give the correct explanation.

NOTE   You are not asked to consider Companies Act requirements.

EXERCISE 7.4 EX

The summarised balance sheet of J. Bolt, a sole trader, contained the following information at 30 June 19-6.

Balance Sheet at 30 June 19-6

	£	£
Fixed Assets at book value		25,000
Current assets		
Stocks	12,000	
Debtors	9,600	
Cash at bank	1,400	
	23,000	
Current Liabilities	7,000	16,000
		41,000
Capital		41,000

Briston Ltd has offered J.Bolt £60,000 in cash for the assets of his business other than the cash at bank. It is thought that the fair values of fixed assets and stocks are £21,600 and £14,700 respectively. The debtors figure includes £500 due from a customer recently declared bankrupt.

Required :
(a) A calculation of the value of goodwill in J. Bolt's business based on the above information.

(b) Explain the difference between 'purchased' and 'non-purchased' goodwill and outline the ways in which these items should be accounted for to comply with SSAP22 entitled 'Accounting and Goodwill'.

(c) Discuss the advantages and disadvantages of the procedures prescribed by SSAP22 to account for purchased goodwill.

EXERCISE 7.5 EX

Canvas Ltd was incorporated in December 19-3 to trade in a single product called 'Como'. The company began trading on 1 January 19-4. Purchases and sales for the five years to 31 December 19-8 when the company discontinued 'Como' in favour of a more profitable line, were as follows :

	Purchases		Sales	
	Units	Price per unit £	Units	Price per unit £
19-4	100	400	80	500
19-5	100	450	80	550
19-6	100	500	80	600
19-7	100	550	80	650
19-8	-	-	80	700

Required :

(a) Using (i) the first in first out (FIFO) basis and (ii) the last in first out (LIFO) basis of stock valuation, calculate the gross profit of Canvas Ltd for each of the five years to 31 December 19-8. You should present you answer in columnar format.

(b) Compare the results of your calculations and consider the relative merits of FIFO and LIFO as bases for valuing stock during a period of inflation.

EXERCISE 7.6 EX

Larchmont Ltd was established on 1 January, 19-3 to manufacture a single product using a machine which cost £400,000. The machine is expected to last for four years and then have a scrap value of £52,000. The machine will produce a similar number of goods each year and annual profits before depreciation are expected to be in the region of £200,000. The financial controller has suggested that the machine should be depreciated using either the straight line method or the reducing balance method. If the latter method is used, it has been estimated that an annual depreciation rate of 40% would be appropriate.

Required :

(a) Calculations of the annual depreciation charges and the net book values of the fixed asset at the end of 19-3, 19-4, 19-5 and 19-6 using :

        (i)   the straight line method;

        (ii)   the reducing balance method.

(b) A discussion of the differing implications of these two methods for the financial information published by Larchmont Ltd for the years 19-3 to 19-6 inclusive. You should also advise management which method you consider more appropriate bearing in mind expected profit levels.

NOTE : Ignore taxation

EXERCISE 7.7 EX

Barber Ltd undertakes long term contract work and makes up its accounts to 31 December each year. The following information is provided relating to a contract to build a sports centre for a local authority :

1.   Contract price, £6,000,000

2.   Date contract commenced, 1 November 1987

3.   Financial details at 31 December

	1987	1988
	£000	£000
Total costs to date	350	4,100
Estimated costs to completion	5,000	1,240
Progress payments received		3,800
Invoiced sales value of work completed during year	—	4,000
Cost of work completed during year	—	3,600

4. The contract was completed on 30 May 1989, by which time total contract costs amounted to £5,400,000. The contract price was received in full by 31 December 1989.

The company complies with the requirements of SSAP 9, entitled 'Stock and Long-Term Contracts' when preparing its accounts.

Required :
(a) Calculate the amount of contract profit, if any, recognised in the accounts for each of the years to 31 December 1987, 1988 and 1989.

(b) Prepare the balance sheet entries in respect of the above contract at 31 December 1987 and 1988.

(c) Compare the standard accounting procedures used to recognise profit on the sale of stocks with those used for recognising profit on long term contracts. Explain why the treatment is different.

(Spring 1990)

EXERCISE 7.8 EX

Gower Ltd was incorporated in December 1985 to manufacture and sell 'widgets'. The company commenced business operations on 1 January 1986 and the trial balance at the end of its first year of trading contained the following information :

Trial Balance at 31 December 1986

	£000s	£000s
Share capital (ordinary shares of £1 each)		1,000
Trade creditors		106
Sales		1,650
Manufacturing costs, other than depreciation	1,100	
Trade debtors	350	
Cash at bank	36	
Administration, selling and distribution expenses	216	
Research and development expenditure	54	
Plant and machinery at cost	1,000	
	2,756	2,756

The company's directors have to decide how to value stock, plant and machinery, and research and development expenditure, for the purpose of the published accounts.

The company's accountant has produced the following information :

(i) Valuations for closing stock :
First in first out basis, £220,000
Average cost basis,   £200,000

(ii) The plant and machinery has an expected working life of four years and can be reduced to its estimated disposal value of £240,000, using either the straight line method or applying a rate of 30% on the reducing balance basis.

(iii) The research expenditure (£14,000) and development expenditure (£40,000) have been incurred in respect of a new process for manufacturing widgets. The new process, which has produced significant savings, became operational on 1 January 1987.

Required :

(a)   On the basis of the above information and the regulations contained in relevant SSAPs, explain how Gower should account for stocks, plant and machinery, and research and development, if the directors wish to report the lowest possible profit figure for 1986.

(b)   Prepare a profit and loss account for 1986, and a balance sheet at 31 December 1986 using conventionally acceptable accounting policies which produce the *lowest* measure of reported profit for the year.

(c)   Prepare a profit and loss account for 1986 and a balance sheet at 31 December 1986, using conventionally acceptable accounting policies which produce the *highest* measure of reported profit for the year.

(d)   Discuss fully the effect of the alternative accounting policies, used in (b) and (c) above, on the levels of profit reported for 1986 and for futures years.

NOTE : Ignore taxation.   (Autumn 1987)

EXERCISE 7.9 EX

Herapath Ltd and Blackwall Ltd are companies in the same line of business but in different geographical areas; each was incorporated on 1 January 1984. The summarised balance sheets and abstracts from the statements of accounting policies for 1984 and 1985 are given below :

SUMMARISED BALANCE SHEETS AT 31 DECEMBER

	Herapath		Blackwall	
	1984	1985	1984	1985
	£000s	£000s	£000s	£000s
Plant at cost	200	200	300	300
Accumulated depreciation	20	40	90	153
	180	160	210	147
Stocks	100	140	130	175
Net liquid assets	30	70	45	105
	310	370	385	427
Share capital	250	250	375	375
Profit 1984	60	60	10	10
1985	—	60	—	42
	310	370	385	427

Abstracts from statements of accounting policies :

	HERAPATH	BLACKWALL
Depreciation	10% on cost	30% reducing balance
Stock valuation	First in first out (FIFO)	Last in first out (LIFO)

FIFO gives the following valuations for Blackwall's stock at 31 December :

1984 £150,000
1985 £210,000

Required :

(a)   Summarised balance sheets for Blackwall Ltd as at 31 December 1984 and 31 December 1985, in the same form as the above presentation, adjusted to comply with the accounting policies used by Herapath. You must show clearly any changes which you make to the reported profit figures.

(b) Calculations of the rate of return on shareholders' equity for each company for each year on the basis of the information provided in the question and, in the case of Blackwall Ltd, on the basis of the statements prepared in answer to part (a)

(c) Explain why it is important for companies to adopt similar accounting policies. You should use the information prepared in answer to parts (a) and (b) to support your explanation.

NOTE : Ignore taxation.

No dividends were paid or proposed for 1984 or 1985

For the purpose of calculations under (b) use year-end balances for shareholders' equity.

(Spring 1986)

SOLUTIONS

SOLUTION 7.1

		Lowest Value	Highest Value
		£	£ £
(a)	Stock on hand	2,700	2,900
(b)	Stock on hand	2,750	2,950

Explanation:

(a)   'Cost' using FIFO method =

Type X   £900 [80 @ £5; 100 @ £3.80; 20 @ £6]

Type Y   £2,090 [140 @ £10; 60 @ £11.50]

giving :

	Cost	N.R.V.	R.P.
	£	£	£
Type X	900	950	1,000
Type Y	2,090	2,000	1,800
	2,990	2,950	2,800

Accepted Forms of Valuation

LOWER OF COST, N.R.V. and R.P.

		£
Separate	- Type X	900
	- Type Y	1,800
		2,700

LOWER OF COST and N.R.V.

		£
Separate	- Type X	900
	- Type Y	2,000
		2,900

The above are the different ways that stock could be valued and the lowest acceptable figure is £2,700 - whilst the highest acceptable figure is £2,900.

(b)   'Cost' using the Average Cost Method = Type X £1,000

	Receipts	Issues	No. of Units in Stock	Total Cost	Average Cost per Unit
				£	£
Jan	100 @ £4		100	400	4
Feb		80 @ £4	20	80	4
Mar	140 @ £6		160	920	5.75
April	100 @ £3.80		260	1,300	5
May		140 @ £5	120	600	5
June	80 @ £5		200	1,000	5

Use exactly the same method to arrive at an average cost figure for Type Y - this should work out at a total average cost of £2,080. Now apply the rules again with these new cost figures.

SOLUTION 7.2

Values of uncompleted contract :

(a)   £700,000 (costs incurred only)*
(b)   £820,000 (costs £700,000 plus proportion of profit)

*   Only acceptable if contract is of less than 1 year's duration (* see paragraph 5 page 99), or where the final outcome of the contract cannot be reasonably assessed.

SOLUTION 7.3

(a)   Acceptable :   No. 1 and 5
(b)   Not acceptable   No. 2,3,4, and 6

Comments

No. 2   As these are *long* term contracts, the attributable profit on Contract 2 should have been included (SSAP9), assuming that the contract is at a stage where the outcome can be assessed with reasonable certainty.

No. 3   Depreciation on historic cost is acceptable, not on replacement cost.

No. 4   This 'book' gain should have been taken to a Revaluation Reserve, not to revenue reserves. It is *not* distributable.

No. 6.   Tax on current profits should have been allowed for, and shown.

LESSON 8

LIQUIDATION OF COMPANIES

It is incorrect to refer to a limited company as going bankrupt - it goes into liquidation. When this happens all the assets of the company are sold and the proceeds of sale used to pay off the liabilities of the company. At the point of liquidation what kind of liabilities is the company likely to have?

It may owe to *trade creditors* for goods supplied, to the *tax* authorities for unpaid taxes, to the local authority for *rates*, to its workers for *wages*, to various lenders for *loans* received in the past particularly *banks* and on *debentures,* and of course to the *shareholders* themselves who have invested their money in the company over the years. Such retained profits are of course Reserves and these are due to the ordinary shareholders, *not* the Preference shareholders who are entitled each year to a fixed rate of dividend out of available profits and having received such dividend have no further claim on profits. If however the preference shares are 'cumulative' (and all preference shares *are* cumulative unless designated as 'non-cumulative') and there are arrears of dividends due to them at the time of liquidation then these arrears would be taken out of existing reserves. This is the only time that a preference shareholder would have any claim on the reserves of the company.

With all these varied liabilities to satisfy, who is going to be paid first and who will be paid last? This is important because the assets will probably not realise sufficient money to pay everybody.

Well, to start with, some of the lenders, e.g. the bank and debenture holders, may have security for their loans. The bank for example may have taken a legal mortgage over the company's premises in which case the sale proceeds of the premises will go direct to the bank to satisfy the loan or overdraft. This applies to any type of creditor who has received security from the company against certain assets. These are 'secured creditors' and provided the assets on which they have security realise sufficient money the secured creditors will be repaid in full. If the assets providing the security do not realise enough to pay off the whole debt then the creditor becomes an unsecured creditor *for the shortfall* and he joins the ranks of the other unsecured creditors for this shortfall.

The first people to be repaid then are the secured creditors. Certain of the unsecured creditors are classed by the Companies Act 1985 and the Insolvency Act 1986 as 'Preferential Creditors', and these will be paid off in priority to the other unsecured creditors who are not classes as 'preferential' by the Acts. These preferential creditors are those to whom the company owes money for :

a)   The last one year's PAYE.
b)   The last one year's payments to subcontractors in the construction industry.
c)   The last six months VAT.
d)   The last one year's betting duty.
e)   The last one year's class 1/2 social security contributions.
f)   The last one year's class 4 contributions.
g)   State pension scheme contributions.
h)   Four months arrears of wages and salaries (limit amount yet to be decided)
i)   Accrued holiday pay.
j)   Advances by any person to enable claims under (g) and (h) above to be paid.

All the above have equal priorities for repayment and if there is not enough to pay them all in full, they will receive dividends in proportion to their claims. Liquidation expenses will, of course, have to be met in full.

With regard to (h) above, wages, the Acts give the right of subrogation to someone who has lent money for the purpose of paying wages. This means that if the bank has lent money for payment of wages then it can 'stand in the shoes' of the workers who have been paid and exercise their right as preferential creditor subject to the 4 months proviso. Obviously the bank would only need to do this when its debt was not covered by security.

So far then we have paid off the secured creditors and the preferential unsecured creditors - if there is still some money left, the unsecured creditors will be repaid providing they have submitted their valid claims. Their priorities are equal and they will receive pro-rata dividends unless there is enough money to pay them off in full in which case there may still be some money left to give to the *shareholders* who are *always, without exception*, left until *last*. The preference shareholders are repaid before the ordinary shareholders.

Let us now summarise the order of repayment.

1st   Secured Creditors (to the extent of their security)*

2nd   Pre-Preferential Creditors - i.e. Liquidator's Costs

3rd   Preferential Creditors

4th   Unsecured Non-Preferential Creditors

5th   Preference Shareholders

6th   Ordinary Shareholders

*   If the security is in the form of a Floating Charge then the proceeds from the assets comprised in the Floating Charge are used first to pay the preferential creditors; whatever is then left goes back to the mortgagee. This applies only to Floating Charges, not to fixed charges.

EXERCISE 8.1

Mulligan Ltd is in financial difficulties. A meeting of creditors is to be held tomorrow to consider the company's affairs.

The Company has sent its bank the following estimated balance sheet at 15 September, 19-2. The Company's auditors certify that the balance sheet is based on the company's accounting records, and that there has been insufficient time to investigate the validity of the amounts in the balance sheet.

	£		£
Issued share capital, £1 shares	40,000	Equipment at cost less deprn.	36,000
Profit and Loss account	41,000	Stocks and contracts-in-progress	184,000
Taxation due	15,000	Debtors	135,000
Loan from Vernon Ltd	30,000		
Sundry creditors	169,000		
Bank overdraft	60,000		
	355,000		355,000

The bank is aware that Mulligan Ltd has been operating profitably, but the financial difficulties have been precipitated by the insolvency of a major customer. From discussions with the company's directors, the bank expects that the contracts-in-progress included in the balance sheet at £50,000 will prove worthless, and that £41,000 of the debts will prove to be bad. Unfortunately the bank's overdraft was secured on the contracts, so that the bank is now in the position of an unsecured lender.

The only preferential creditors are for taxation and £9,000 of the sundry creditors. The remaining liabilities are unsecured.

111

The bank learns that the following proposals are to be considered at the creditors' meeting :

(1)   Immediate liquidation of the company. In these circumstances stocks would realise only £80,000, and the sale value of the equipment would be negligible. The debts would be realised in full, apart from the bad debts previously mentioned.

(2)   A reconstruction in which business associates of the directors would subscribe £40,000 in cash for new shares in the company; from this cash the preferential creditors would be satisfied. The conditions are that non-preferential creditors (including Vernon Ltd and the bank) agree to a reduction in their claims to 90% of the amount presently due, that payment is postponed for one year and that interest during the year is waived.

(3)   A reconstruction in which Vernon Ltd would convert its loan into 30,000 shares of £1, and would subscribe a further £40,000 cash for £1 shares in the company; from this cash the preferential creditors would be satisfied. The conditions are that the remaining non-preferential creditors agree to a reduction in their claims to 80% of the amount presently due, that payment is postponed for three months and that interest during the three months is waived. Vernon Ltd offers a guarantee to lend Mulligan Ltd a further £50,000 to meet payments at the end of the three months if this proves necessary. The bank is confident that Vernon Ltd has the funds available.

The existing shareholders of Mulligan Ltd are prepared to co-operate in the issue of shares under either of proposals (2) or (3). Under those proposals bad debts and valueless contracts would be written off and preferential creditors would be paid immediately. The bank overdraft would be frozen (at the appropriately adjusted level) and a new bank account opened for subsequent transactions.

Assume that the bank charges 10% per annum on overdrafts, and that the £60,000 shown in the balance sheet includes interest to date.

Assume for convenience that an adopted proposal would be implemented immediately on 21 September, 19-2.

Ignore liquidation or reconstruction expenses and any changes which may have occurred between 15 September and 21 September, 19-2.

Use the figures given throughout; do *not* add extra safety margins in any of your calculations.

Required :
(a)   A calculation of the amount the bank would receive under the first proposal if the information given proves accurate.

(b)   Balance sheet for Mulligan Ltd at 21 September, 19-2 under proposal (2), after making appropriate provisions on the assumption that the company will continue to trade.

(c)   Balance sheet for Mulligan Ltd at 21 September, 19-2 under proposal (3), after making appropriate provisions on the assumption that the company will continue to trade.

(d)   Consider the relative merits of the three proposals from the bank's viewpoint.

EXERCISE 8.2

Fastfoods Ltd is in financial difficulties.

The company's estimated balance sheet at 28 April, 19-6 is shown below :

	£		£
Issued share capital		Freehold property at cost	17,000
(£1 ordinary shares)	25,000	Equipment at cost less deprn.	122,000
Profit & Loss account	7,000	Stocks at cost	25,000
10% Debenture stock	12,000		
Sundry creditors	103,000		
Bank overdraft with Eastern Bank	17,000		
	164,000		164,000

Fastfoods Ltd operates a number of retail outlets for 'take-away' cooked food; most of these outlets are rented. Its largest supplier is Catercorp Ltd which holds all the debenture stock and is also a trade creditor for £60,000: the latter amount is included with sundry creditors in the balance sheet.

The sundry creditors in the balance sheet also include preferential creditors for £11,000.

The bank overdraft is secured by a charge over the freehold property of Fastfoods Ltd, and the debenture stock is secured by a floating charge over the company's assets.

A meeting of the creditors of Fastfoods Ltd has been called for tomorrow, to consider the following alternatives:

(1)   Immediate liquidation of the company, which would result in the following estimated amounts for realised assets :

	£
Freehold Property	14,000
Equipment	51,000
Stocks	10,000

(2)   An offer of support from Catercorp Ltd which would permit the reconstruction of Fastfoods Ltd.

Under the reconstruction, the debentures held by Catercorp Ltd would be converted into £1 ordinary shares at par, and for every £100 of the £60,000 trade debt owed to Catercorp Ltd there would be issued 55 £1 ordinary shares in the reconstructed company. The balance of the trade debt owed to Catercorp Ltd would be written off against the assets of Fastfoods Ltd.

The existing shareholders of Fastfoods Ltd would receive one £1 ordinary share in the reconstructed company for every five presently held.

A further 30,000 £1 ordinary shares in Fastfoods Ltd would be issued to Catercorp Ltd in exchange for the introduction of £30,000 cash; these new funds would be sufficient to enable the reconstructed company to meet the remainder of its liabilities as they fall due.

It has been estimated by the Management of Catercorp Ltd that after reconstruction, Fastfoods Ltd should earn regular net profits of £12,000 per year.

Assume that Catercorp Ltd can currently earn 15% per annum on new investments involving similar risks to those which would be incurred by investing in Fastfoods Ltd.

Assume that the adopted proposal would be implemented immediately.

Use the figures provided, without deducting expenses for liquidation or reconstruction, and without adding safety margins to your calculations.

Required :

(a)   Calculations showing the total amount Catercorp Ltd would receive if Fastfoods Ltd were liquidated.

(b)   Numerical comparisons showing which of the two proposals is more advantageous to Catercorp Ltd.

(c)   Calculation of the annual net profit the reconstructed Fastfoods Ltd would need to earn in order to provide Catercorp Ltd with the same financial results as it would obtain from liquidation.

(d)   Comment briefly on which of the two proposals you consider the Eastern Bank might be inclined to support.

NOTE   Ignore taxation.

EXERCISE 8.3 EX

Western Bank today received the following balance sheet relating to its customer, Home Builders Ltd.

Balance Sheet at 10 April, 19-5

	£		£
Issued share capital	40,000	Equipment at cost less deprn.	16,000
Profit and Loss account	16,200		
Taxation due	8,000	Work-in-progress at cost :	
Loan from Propinvest Ltd		Site A 93,000	
(secured on site A)	71,000	Site B 49,000	142,000
Loan from Western Bank			
(secured on site B)	40,000	Stocks and other work-in-progress	41,000
Trade creditors	35,000	Debtors	17,200
Overdraft (Western Bank)	6,000		
	216,200		216,200

The balance sheet was accompanied by a statement from the company's auditors stating that the balance sheet has been based on the company's accounting records, but there has been insufficient time to assess the validity of certain items in the balance sheet, particularly with regard to the net realisable value of current assets.

Home Builders Ltd has had cash flow problems for some time, and the balance sheet has been prepared for presentation to a meeting of creditors to be held tomorrow for the consideration of the company's financial situation.

From discussions with Home Builders Ltd and its accountants, Western Bank has ascertained that the only preferential creditors are for taxation and £2,000 of the bank's overdraft, which was advanced for wages. The secured creditors are as stated in the balance sheet; sites A and B are small developments containing houses at different stages of construction.

Three proposals are to be discussed at the creditors' meeting as follows :

(1)   Immediate liquidation of the company. The estimated net proceeds of realisation would be :

	£
Equipment	5,000
Work-in-progress	
Site A	60,000
Site B	30,000
Stocks and other work-in-progress	20,000
Debtors	15,000

(2)   An offer from the local government authority to take over site A for £64,000, and site B for £36,000. These amounts would be paid to the secured lenders on completion of all work on the sites, which can be assumed to be exactly one year from the date of the creditors' meeting. The remaining assets would be sold immediately for the amounts shown for liquidation above, and lenders on sites A and B would be treated as unsecured creditors for the balance of their loans.

(3)   An offer from Octopus Ltd to acquire the Share Capital of Home Builders. Preferential creditors would be paid immediately in full. In one year's time all other creditors (secured or unsecured) would be paid 90 pence in the £ on their current claims against Home Builders Ltd. The financial reliability of Octopus Ltd is undoubted.

The existing shareholders of Home Builders Ltd would be prepared to co-operate with proposal (3).

Assume that Western Bank earns 15% per annum on all its lending, and that the amounts shown in the balance sheet include accrued interest to date.

Assume for convenience that any adopted proposal would be implemented immediately on 24 April, 19-5 with payments being received immediately, unless otherwise stated.

Ignore expenses of realisation and liquidation, and any interest charges or changes in the situation between 10 April and 24 April, 19-5.

Use the figures given throughout; do not add extra safety margins in your calculations.

Required :
(a)   Calculations showing clearly the amounts Western Bank would receive under each of the three proposals.

(b)   An examination of the relative financial merits of the proposals from the viewpoint of Western Bank.

EXERCISE 8.4 EX

The following is the summarised balance sheet of Founder Ltd at 31 August, 1977

	£		£
Issued share capital - £1 shares	25,000	Freehold building	52,000
Revenue Reserves	19,000	Equipment less deprn.	34,000
	44,000	Stocks	40,000
10% debentures 1984/6	40,000	Sundry debtors	45,000
Sundry creditors	43,000		
Bank overdraft	44,000		
	171,000		171,000

The bank overdraft is secured by a charge over the freehold building.

The debentures, which are all held by Reave Ltd, are secured by a floating charge over the assets of Founder Ltd and are repayable between 1984 and 1986.

Founder Ltd has had difficulty in meeting its financial obligations, and a meeting of creditors has been called to consider its affairs. The following proposals are to be considered at the meeting :

(a)   *Immediate liquidation of the company*

In these circumstances it is estimated the company's assets would realise the following amounts :

	£
Freehold building	28,000
Equipment	11,000
Stocks	13,000
Debtors	40,000

Liquidation costs can be ignored.

Preferential creditors for £9,000 are included among sundry creditors in the balance sheet.

(b)   *Amalgamation of Founder Ltd with Reave Ltd*

Preferential creditors would be paid in full. Secured creditors would be paid the estimated realisable value [as shown in (a) above] for their security, and all unsecured amounts would be paid at the rate of 40p in the £ in final settlement of the creditors' claims. Shares would be purchased by Reave Ltd at 1p each.

(c)   *Injection of £30,000 new funds into Founder Ltd*

Certain shareholders, with a majority of shares in Founder Ltd, are of the opinion that the company is merely suffering from a temporary shortage of finance. They consider that the provision of new share capital of £30,000 would stabilise the company's financial situation and enable it to earn average profits of £9,000 per year (after meeting all interest charges). Potential subscribers to the new share capital are available.

The company would first pay its preferential creditors. It would then make immediate payments on account to reduce the amounts owing to both non-preferential sundry creditors and the bank by 20p in the £. However, it would need a year's moratorium on the remaining 80% of these liabilities, during which time repayment would not be required and interest would be waived. A separate bank account, to be maintained in credit, would be open for trading transactions.

At the end of the moratorium period the outstanding current liabilities would revert to their normal commercial status; the non-preferential sundry creditors would become payable and the bank overdraft would be reduced at a rate of at least £5,000 per year.

Assume that :

(i)   the current rate of interest on all forms of borrowing is 10%;

(ii)   the £44,000 overdraft in the balance sheet includes interest to date;

(iii)   an adopted proposal would be implemented immediately;

(iv)   no changes have occurred since the balance sheet date.

Required :
(a)   Calculations showing the amounts which would be received by the bank and non-preferential sundry creditors under each of the proposals.

(b)   A careful explanation of the relative merits of the proposals from the different viewpoints of the bank, the non-preferential sundry creditors and the shareholders.

Exercise 8.5 EX

The following is the summarised balance sheet of Lion Ltd at 30 April 1988:

	£000	£000
Freehold property at book value		70
Plant and machinery at book value		200
		270
Current assets:		
Stocks	82	
Debtors	57	
	139	
Creditors : amounts due within one year		
Creditors	95	
Bank overdraft	105	
Taxation and national insurance	20	
	220	
Net current assets		(81)
		189
Creditors: amounts due after one year		
12% debentures repayable 1990		50
		139
Financed by capital and reserves		
Ordinary share capital (£1 shares)		200
Profit and loss account		(61)
		139

The 12% debenture holders have a first charge on the freehold property and the bank has a second charge.

The demand for Lion's products has collapsed over the last five years owing to the availability of cheap imports. Trading losses are mounting steadily and a meeting of creditors has been called to examine Lion Ltd's affairs. The following alternative proposals are put forward by the directors of Lion:

A. Liquidation of the company

It is estimated that business assets, if sold individually, would realise the following amounts:

	£000
Freehold property	120
Plant and machinery	18
Stocks	57
Debtors	50

Liquidation costs are estimated at £5,000. The amount due for tax and National Insurance and £10,000 of the creditors are 'preferential'.

B. Sale of Company to Gulf Plc

Gulf, which is Lion's main supplier and also the debenture holder, is willing to purchase the shares for a token sum and take over the business as a going concern. Under the scheme, the preferential creditors would be paid in full, the debentures would be converted into ordinary shares and the remaining creditors and the bank would receive the full amount owing in twelve months time. These debts would not attract further interest over the twelve month period.

Assume that:

(i)   The bank lends money at 12%.
(ii) The calculations are being made on 1 May 1988.
(iii) Piecemeal liquidation could occur, in which case cash would be received immediately; alternatively, the company could be sold to Gulf at once.

Required:
(a)   Prepare a statement showing the distribution of the proceeds assuming the liquidation option is chosen. Show clearly the amount received by each provider of finance.

(b)   Examine the two proposals from the bank's point of view.

(Spring 1988)

SOLUTIONS

SOLUTION 8.1

(a)

	£
Stocks	80,000
Debtors	94,000
	174,000
Less tax	15,000
	159,000
Less creditors	9,000
	150,000

to satisfy :	£
Loan	30,000
Unsecured creditors	160,000
Bank	60,000
	250,000

This means a dividend of 60% (£0.60 for every £1)
Therefore the bank would receive £36,000.

N.B. You must remember that in liquidation, the preferential debts such as taxation, and the secured debts are the first to be paid. The unsecured creditors then share what is left, and if this is not sufficient to pay them in full there will be nothing left at all for the shareholders.

(b)

Balance Sheet as at 21 September, 19-2

	£		£
Issued Share Capital	80,000	Equipment at cost less depreciation	36,000
Less Profit & Loss account	*25,000	Stocks/Contracts	134,000
	55,000	Debtors	94,000
Loan - Vernon Ltd	27,000	Cash	16,000
Creditors	144,000		
Bank	54,000		
	280,000		280,000

	£
* Balance was	+ 41,000
Less : bad debts & contracts	91,000
	− 50,000
Add : gains from non-preferential creditors reducing their claims	25,000
	− 25,000

(c)

Balance Sheet as at 21 September 19-2

	£		£
Issued Share Capital	110,000	Equipment at cost less deprn.	36,000
Less Profit & Loss account	6,000		
	104,000	Stocks/Contracts	134,000
Creditors	128,000	Debtors	94,000
Bank	48,000	Cash	16,000
	280,000		280,000

(d)

Under the proposals the bank can expect :

Proposal 1	Proposal 2	Proposal 3
£36,000 *NOW*	£54,000 in 1 year	£48,000 in 3 months

To effectively compare the relative merits of the above we must convert them to a common time basis - e.g. *ONE YEAR FROM NOW* -

The bank can expect to get *in 1 year's time* under Proposal :

1.	2.	3.
£36,000 plus 1 year's interest of £3,600 =		£48,000 plus $3/4$ year's interest of £3,600 =
£39,600	£54,000	£51,600

1. assumes that the assets would realise the amounts stated.

2. and **3.** assume that payment would be made at the times stated.

Whilst **2.** appears to be the most attractive, it is by no means certain that the company would be in a position to keep its promise to pay back the bank at the end of one year - there are lots more creditors who are relying on the same promise!

Number **3.** is more attractive in that Vernon is taking an active interest in the company and therefore providing some kind of security, although, in view of all the other creditors involved, it is still doubtful that the bank would be paid as promised.

SOLUTION 8.2

(a)

	£	
Realisation of :		
Property	14,000	
Equipment	51,000	
Stocks	10,000	
Total amount received	75,000	
Less bank's secured claim	14,000	Leaving £3,000 owing to bank
	61,000	
Less preferential claims	11,000	leaving £92,000 non-preferential creditors
	50,000	
Less debentures	12,000	all satisfied
Available for unsecured creditors	38,000	to satisfy £95,000 as above
Allows a dividend of	38,000	= 40p in the £
	95,000	

Therefore - Catercorp Ltd receives :

as debenture holders	12,000
as creditors 60,000 x 40p	24,000
Total	36,000*

(b) Under Proposal 2 Catercorp Ltd would receive £1 ordinary shares as follows :

For the debentures	12,000	
For debt 600 x 55	33,000	
For cash	30,000	
	75,000	shares.

Other shareholders would own 5,000 shares, therefore Catercorp Ltd would own $\frac{75}{80}$ of the new company's share capital and would thus have claim to $\frac{75}{80}$ of £12,000 profit per annum

=   £11,250 income p.a.

Under Proposal **1** Catercorp Ltd would receive £36,000 and would *not* have to part with £30,000 cash for shares so it could invest a total of £66,000 at 15% per annum (see question) giving an income of £9,000 per annum.

Therefore proposal **2** is more advantageous to Catercorp Ltd.

(c)   £9,000 per annum would come as a result of liquidation. To receive this same amount from profits of the reconstructed company, the company would only need to make regular profits of :

$$9,900 = \frac{75}{80} \text{ of total profit.}$$

Therefore, total profit must = $\frac{9,900}{75} \times \frac{80}{1}$ = £10,560 per annum

£10,560 annual profits would provide £9,900 $\frac{(75)}{(80)}$ for Catercorp Ltd. Therefore, the expected £12,000 per annum profits could afford to be an optimistic view and still be advantageous to Catercorp Ltd.

(d)   In liquidation the bank would receive £14,000 from security plus [3,000 x 40p see (a) above] £1,200 = £15,200.

With a reconstruction the bank would stand a chance of getting its full debt of £17,000 repaid together with charges and interest and would therefore probably support this option.

120

LESSON 9

CASH AND WORKING CAPITAL

CASH

A Balance Sheet shows the financial state of a business as at a particular date. It has been described as a 'photograph' of a business and these 'photographs' are usually taken once a year. In this respect always remember that someone can change overnight!

Whilst we can get a certain amount of information as to how a business is progressing by comparing one year's balance with another it is often desirable to know what has gone on in the period between the balance sheet dates.

Quite often a trader is puzzled as to why, after a year of good profits, he has a bigger bank overdraft at the year end than he had at the beginning. In explaining to him we would point out that whilst profits have the effect of increasing cash, via debtors, it is rare that the cash (or bank) balance at the year end has increased by the same amount as profits for the period for the following reasons :

(i)   Some of the cash from profits may still be in the form of debtors, or EXTRA cash may have been received from debtors.

(ii)   some of the cash may have been applied to the purchase of more stock.

(iii)   some of the cash may have been utilised in paying creditors (who supply us with stock) or creditors may have been allowed to build up, so saving our cash.

(iv)   Payments may have been made in purchasing fixed assets (such transactions do not of course affect profits) or there may be cash receipts from the sale of fixed assets.

(v)   Extra cash may have come in from new issues of shares or debentures or cash may have gone out in repayment of redeemable shares or debentures.

(vi)   Dividends may have been paid out of profits, and so on ......

All of the above reasons could be summarised in the form of a Cash Flow Statement whereby we show *Sources* of cash and *Uses* of cash in the period. The cash book would of course give us all the information we need but there would be far too many items to analyse. We need something concise so that what has happened to cash can be seen almost at a glance. Most of the items in the cash book would refer to receipts from debtors,payment to creditors, payment of rent, wages, etc. If we take one figure, the net profit figure for the period, then we have in fact taken the *net* effect of all those numerous items just mentioned which make up the trading and profit and loss account. This figure will start off our Cash Flow Statement as a Source of cash. All the other figures which go into our statement will simply account for the reasons why the profit figure is not wholly represented by cash at this point in time. The difference between the final totals 'Sources' and 'Uses' will account for the difference in the cash (bank) balances at the beginning and end of the period in question.

Let us look as some examples :

Balance Sheet as at start

	£		£
Capital	5,000	Cash	5,000

During Month 1 - Any trader buys £2,000 of stock for cash - therefore :

Balance Sheet as at end of Month 1

	£		£
Capital	5,000	Stock	2,000
		Cash	3,000
	5,000		5,000

Cash Flow Statement for Month 1

		£
Sources		
Profits		-
		-
Uses		
Increase in stock		2,000
		2,000

Applications exceed Sources by £2,000 - i.e. cash has decreased by £2,000

During Month 2 - Any trader sells £1,000 of stock for £1,500 cash - therefore :

Balance Sheet at end of Month 2

	£		£
Capital	5,000	Stock	1,000
Profit and Loss account	500	Cash	4,500
	5,500		5,500

Why has cash increased by £1,500 in month 2 when only £500 profit has been made? Because £1,000 of stock has been converted into cash and an additional £500 of cash has come in from profits.

Cash flow Statement for Month 2

	£
Sources	
Profits	500
Decrease in Stock	1,000
	1,500
Uses	
NIL	NIL

During Month 3 - £500 of stock is sold on credit for £750

Balance Sheet as at end of Month 3

	£		£
Capital	5,000	Stock	500
Profit and Loss account		Debtors	750
(£500 + £250)	750	Cash	4,500
	5,750		5,750

Despite a profit of £250, cash remains the same. This is because the reduction in stock of £500 which should have been converted into cash has been applied to debtors and similarly with the £250 profit.

Cash Flow Statement for Month 3

	£
Sources	
Profits	250
Decreases in stock	500
	750
Uses	
Increases in Debtors	750
	750

So once again we have accounted for the 'movements' in cash.

During Month 4 - Stock is bought for £800 cash. £400 of stock is sold for £550, on credit.

Balance Sheet at end of Month 4

	£		£
Capital	5,000	Stock	900
Profit and loss account	900	Debtors	1,300
		Cash	3,700
	5,900		5,900

Profits of £150 have been made yet cash has reduced by £800. This is because the whole of the cash which should have been received (£550) has been applied to debtors, and another *£400* of cash has been utilised in increasing stock (if you are wondering what has happened to the *other* £400 spent on stock - well, this found its way into 'debtors' as part of the £550 mentioned above!).

Cash Flow Statement for Month 4

	£
Sources	
Profits	150
	150
Uses	
Increase in Debtors	550
Increase in Stock	400
	950

i.e. a decrease in cash of £800.

During Month 5 - Stock is purchased on credit for £1,000 and is immediately sold for £1,600 on credit. Also fixed assets are bought for £1,000 cash.

Balance Sheet as at end of Month 5

	£		£
Capital	5,000	Fixed Assets	1,000
Profit and Loss account	1,500	Stock	900
Creditors	1,000	Debtors	2,900
		Cash	2,700
	7,500		7,500

The cash balance has reduced by £1,000 in month 5. this is because the whole of the cash which *should* have been received from the sale of £1,600 has been applied to debtors - also, £1,000 of cash has been *saved* by purchasing stock on credit (i.e. stock is acquired without having to pay for it there and then, and this is equivalent to a receipt of cash). Also, of course, £1,000 cash is spent on fixed assets.

Cash Flow Statement for Month 5

	£
Sources	
Profits	600
Increase in Creditors	1,000
	1,600
Uses	
Increase in Debtors	1,600
Purchase of fixed assets	1,000
	2,600

i.e. a decrease in cash of £1,000

What it all amounts to is this :
Sources of cash are :

1.   Profits
2.   Increase in creditors (cash is saved)
3.   Decreases in debtors (cash benefits)
4.   Decreases in stock ('saving' of cash as stock is not replaced)

Uses of cash are :

1.   Losses
2.   Decreases in creditors (extra payments being made)
3.   Increases in debtors (less cash coming in)
4.   Increases in stock (more cash going out for this)

Other Sources are :

(i)   Cash from a share/debenture issue/loans
(ii)   Sale of fixed assets

Other Uses are :

(i)   Redemption of Shares/Debentures/Loans
(ii)   Purchase of fixed assets
(iii)   Drawings of proprietor or payment of dividends to shareholders

SUMMARY
Any increase in an asset (other than cash) must be at the expense of cash - i.e. a use of cash.

Any decrease in an asset (other than cash) must be a gain to cash - i.e. a source of cash.

Conversely, any increase in a liability must be a gain to cash.

Any decrease in a liability must be at the expense of cash.

EXAMPLE

From the following balance sheets we will prepare a Cash Flow Statement for the period 19-9.

Balance Sheets

	19-8 £	19-9 £		19-8 £	19-9 £
Issued Share Capital	30,000	40,000	Fixed Assets (cost)	47,200	64,000
Share Premium	1,500	2,500	Less depreciation	6,200	8,900
General Reserve	4,000	6,000		41,000	55,100
Profit and Loss account	7,000	10,000			
	42,500	58,500	Stock	7,000	11,000
Debentures	5,000	3,000	Debtors	5,000	3,700
			Bank	1,000	500
Creditors	3,500	4,800			
Dividends Proposed	3,000	4,000			
	54,000	70,300		54,000	70,300

As good a start as any is to calculate the cash flow from profits. The Profit and Loss account has increased by £3,000 *after* transferring to General Reserve £2,000 and after appropriating a dividend of £4,000. Therefore the company must have made a net profit of £3,000 + £2,000 + £4,000 = *£9,000*. This is the figure taken down from the Profit and Loss account proper to the appropriation account and is therefore *after* charging depreciation in the Profit and Loss account. You know from the revision topics that the entry in the Profit and Loss account does not affect the cash in any way (unlike other items in Profit and Loss account such as rent, wages, etc.) - it is a book keeping entry only (Dr. Profit and Loss. Cr. Provision for Depreciation account) - a non-cash debit. As we want to know how much cash has come in from profits we must *add* the current year's charge for depreciation, £2,700, on to our calculated net profit figure of £9,000, so making *£11,700*. Then we can look at all the *other* items in our balance sheets.

Cash Flow Statement for 19-9

Sources	£	Uses	£
Profits	11,700	Repayment of Debentures	2,000
Issue of Shares	10,000	Dividend Paid	3,000
Share Premium	1,000	Purchase of Fixed Assets	16,800
Increases in Creditors	1,300	Increase in Stock	4,000
Decrease in Debtors	1,300		
	25,300		25,800

i.e. The bank balance is £500 worse off than before - check this with the balance sheets.

Note that the dividend *proposed last year* (£3,000) would have been *paid this year*.

A cash flow statement in this simple form is, in my opinion, a most useful analysis and an understanding of its construction will be of great benefit to you when answering questions concerned with cash flow. It will also help you to understand the construction of 'Sources of Applications of Funds Statements' which will be dealt with in the next lesson.

WORKING CAPITAL

When a business commences to operate, the first transaction is of course the injection of capital into the concern. A sole trader provides a sum of money with which to start off his business; the partners in a firm each provide their various sums of money to get the firm started in business; and the limited company sells its shares in order to get the necessary capital together with which to start trading.

Let us suppose that a particular business concern starts off with a contribution of £10,000 capital, and that £5,000 of this capital is used to purchase premises from which the business will operate and a further £2,000 is used to buy furniture, fittings and equipment. In other words a total of £7,000 is put into Fixed Assets - which are here to stay! The business has not yet started to operate (i.e. by trading or manufacturing) but has simply set itself up. The work has not yet started. Out of the original £10,000 capital provided, £7,000 has been spent on this 'setting up' of the business - which leaves £3,000 for the business to *work with*. this is the amount which the business has to utilise to make its profits.

To start with, some of this £3,000 will be used to buy stock - this will subsequently be sold and the business will then have debtors - the debtors will eventually 'pay up' so producing cash - this cash will then be used to pay off the creditors who have provided the business with stock on credit - more stock will then be purchased, then sold and the debtors will pay up, so creating cash - and so on. All of this activity with the £3,000 left over from the initial capital of £10,000! This £3,000 of capital is *working* in order to make profits and is the firm's Working Capital.

If the firm makes some profits then these will increase the capital which the firm has to work with - i.e. its working capital. The larger the profits are the larger the firm's working capital will become.

Let us look at an example to see how this works out.

EXAMPLE

The balance sheet of A. Trader at 31 December, Year 1, is as follows :

	£		£
Capital	6,000	Fixed Assets	2,500
Creditors	500	Stock	2,000
		Debtors	1,500
		Bank	500
	6,500		6,500

The balance sheet tells us that out of the initial £6,000 capital provided, £2,500 has been tied up in fixed assets, so leaving £3,500 of capital for the firm to work with - i.e. its working capital.

During January, Year 2 the following transactions occur :

	£
Receipts from debtors	1,200
Payments to creditors	400
Purchase of stock on credit	700

The balance sheet at 31 January, Year 2 will now look like this :

	£		£
Capital	6,000	Fixed Assets	2,500
Creditors	800	Stock	2,700
		Debtors	300
		Cash	1,300
	6,800		6,800

Working capital is still the same - £3,500. Why? Because no extra working capital came in from profits (there were none in January) or elsewhere, and no further working capital has been tied up in fixed assets.

During February, Year 2 the following transactions occur :

> £800 stock sold on credit for £1,000
> £200 paid to creditors
> £750 spent on fixed assets

The balance sheet at 28 February now looks like this :

	£		£
Capital	6,000	Fixed Assets	3,250
Profit and Loss account	300	Stock	1,900
Creditors	600	Debtors	1,400
		Cash	350
	6,900		6,900

Working capital is now £3,050 - i.e. £6,000 of capital plus £300 extra capital in the form of retained profits, of which £3,250 has been tied up in fixed assets, thereby leaving £3,050. At the end of January working capital was only £3,500 but it has been increased by the amount of the profits (£300) and then decreased by the purchase of fixed assets (£750).

What do we know about *working capital* then? We know that it is that part of the capital put into a business which is not tied up in fixed assets and is therefore available to work with in order to make profits. And when we talk of capital 'put into a business' we don't mean just the initial investment (e.g. the proceeds from shares) but also any new capital which may come into the business (e.g. new issue of shares/loans) *and* any new capital which finds its way into the business (e.g. from profits) and is LEFT IN (e.g. retained profits in the form of Reserves). To sum up this section let us have a look at another balance sheet.

Balance Sheet as at 19-0

	£		£
Issued Share Capital	10,000		
Share premium	3,000	Premises	12,000
General Reserve	2,000	Machinery, etc.	4,000
Profit and Loss account	4,200	Stock	7,000
	19,200	Debtors	2,000
Debentures 1990/95	3,500	Bank	1,000
	22,700		
Creditors	3,300		
	26,000		26,000

From this we can say that the capital obtained from issuing shares is £10,000 plus the premium on the issue, £3,000, and that of the new capital generated over the years in profits, a total of £6,200 has been retained in the company. All this makes a total investment of £19,200 by the shareholders. In addition, £3,500 loan capital has been obtained by issuing debentures which gives us a grand total of £22,700 long term capital.

How much of this is 'tied up'? - £16,000 in fixed assets.

This leaves £6,700 (£22,700 less £16,000) to work with - i.e. the *Working Capital*.

How important is *Working Capital?*

It can be described as the circulating blood of a business - once it stops circulating the business is dead - and it there is not sufficient of it, then the business has to struggle for its life. Let me illustrate that.

MOVEMENTS IN WORKING CAPITAL

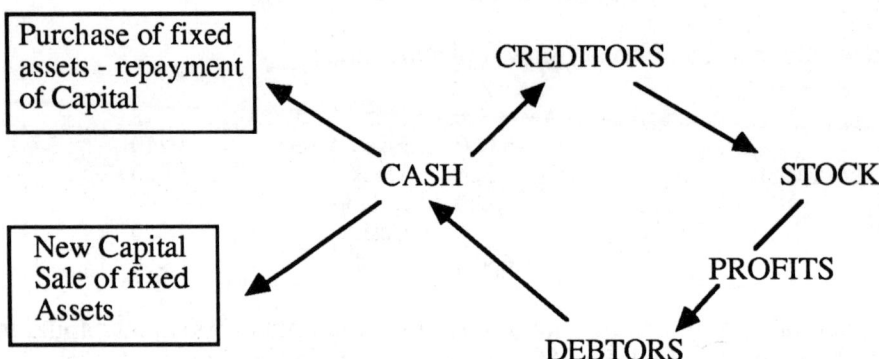

The above shows how working capital revolves, and as it revolves, profits are made (as stock is sold to debtors) - the faster it revolves the faster the profits are made. You will note from the diagram how new capital can be injected into the flow of working capital, and how working capital can leave the flow as capital is repaid (i.e. redeemable shares or long term loans being paid off) or fixed assets purchased. All short term loans (e.g. bank overdraft) would be classed as 'creditors' as they would soon be due to be repaid.

A business gets into difficulties when working capital is depleted too much. The cause of this could be due to heavy losses being made or it could be due to diverting too much working capital into fixed assets. This latter cause is the most common and is referred to as 'overtrading'. For example, a business which is getting in a lot of new orders from customers is obviously going to be very pleased with itself, but to satisfy this increased demand for its products, the business may have to erect new factories or machinery or to buy other new fixed assets. This, we know involves depleting the store of working capital and unless the business has adequate resources of working capital, it may well find that after buying all the additional fixed assets, it has no capital left to work with! This is where the business resorts to heavy borrowing and great reliance on extended trade credit in order to purchase stocks of raw materials and goods. And if the creditors start pushing for payment, the business may find that the only way to repay its debts is to sell some of its fixed assets! The next step is then usually bankruptcy or liquidation as no business can continue to function without its full complement of fixed assets.

If, of course, the depletion of working capital referred to (through buying more fixed assets) is quickly replaced by the extra profits coming in from increased trade, then all is well, and such is usually the case when a business is expanding gradually and steadily. The danger is when the business expands too rapidly (unless its store of working capital is very large, which is unlikely).

A prudent businessman will therefore expand his business at a rate which is consistent with the working capital available, and will know at what point he should draw the line by refusing new orders and contracts. Let us look at an example of overtrading.

128

Balance Sheet of a Company as at 31 December, Year 1

	£		£
Share Capital	50,000	Fixed Assets	35,000
Profit and Loss account	10,000	Stock	10,000
	60,000	Bank	30,000
Creditors	15,000		
	75,000		75,000

Normal Profits = £7,500 p.a.
Working Capital = £25,000 (i.e. capital of £50,000 plus retained profits of £10,000 of which £35,000 has been 'tied up').

The company is offered a contract which would double its normal profits but which would involve purchasing another factory and equipment at a cost of £80,000. To purchase these fixed assets the company obtains a bank overdraft of £50,000 which, together with its existing bank balance pays for the assets.

Balance Sheet of a Company NOW

	£		£
Share Capital	50,000	Fixed Assets	115,000
Profit and Loss account	10,000	Stock	10,000
	60,000		
Creditors	15,000		
Bank Loan	50,000		
	125,000		125,000

Working Capital = MINUS £55,000.

The problems are :

(i)   Stock must be bought and the company must rely very heavily on credit for this.

(ii)   The working capital which has gone will only be replaced slowly as profits are made.

(iii)   If stock is not turned over quickly there will be no money to pay the creditors' bills as they become due, there being no working capital to fall back on.

In effect the company is now being run mainly with other peoples' *short term* money, these people having a bigger stake in the business than the shareholders themselves have. If these short term creditors do not get paid as the debts become due, they could push the company into liquidation.

The above illustrates how very important it is for a business to maintain an adequate supply of working capital at all times.

You should now have a very good idea of what working capital is and I want you now to look at it from another angle, which is this :

'Working capital is the excess of total current assets over total current liabilities'
- i.e Current Assets minus Current Liabilities = Working Capital.

Go back NOW (not later!) to every balance sheet illustrated in this topic and check the above formula against each balance sheet to find the working capital. It should of course be the same in each case, as when we calculated it by the other method. Turn back the pages ..
......

If total current assets are £7,000 and current liabilities are £4,000, then the working capital is £3,000.

In other words, if all the current liabilities were paid off in full, there would still be £3,000 of current assets left to work with - the business is not wholly dependent on its short term creditors.

Read these words again and consider their significance in the examples we have looked at during the course of this topic.

Changes in Amount of Working Capital

We have already seen some of the things which can increase or decrease the amount of working capital available such as purchase of fixed assets (decrease); issue of more shares (increase); making of profits (increase), etc.

In deciding whether a certain kind of transaction will affect the amount of working capital available, it might be easier to think of working capital in the terms of 'current assets less current liabilities'. From this is should be obvious that the amount of working capital will not be affected in the slightest by a transaction that increases or decreases current assets *and* current liabilities by the same amount; nor by a transaction which increases current assets *and* decreases current assets by the same amount. Such transactions respectively could be :

(i)   Purchase of stock on credit (stock increases - Creditors increase)

(ii)   Payment made to a creditor (cash decreases - Creditors decrease)

(iii)   Receipt of cash from a debtor (cash increases - Debtors decrease)

In other words if a transaction does not affect any item *outside* of the working capital 'circle' in the following balance sheet, then it does *not* affect the amount of working capital available. All changes caused by transactions (i) to (iii) above occur **within** the 'circle' :

Balance Sheet

	£		£
Share Capital	10,000		
Profit and Loss account	3,000	Fixed Assets	14,000
	13,000		
Debentures	4,000		
Current Liabilities		**Current Assets**	
Creditors	2,500	Stock	2,000
		Debtors	2,000
		Cash	1,500
	19,500		19,500

Some examples of transactions which *will* affect an item outside of the 'circle' and will therefore affect the working capital are :

(i)   New debentures, £1,500 issued - current assets (cash) increases whilst debentures increase - current liabilities remain the same - result is an increase in working capital.

(ii)   Purchase of fixed assets - current assets (cash) decreases whilst fixed assets increase - current liabilities remain the same - result is a decrease in working capital.

(iii)   £1,000 stock sold for £1,400 on credit - current assets (stock) decrease by £1,000 - current assets (debtors) increase by £1,400 - this gives a net increase in total current assets of £400 whilst Profit and Loss account increases by this amount. Current liabilities remain the same - result is an increase in working capital of £400.

(iv)   The £400 profit in (iii) is paid out as dividend - current assets (cash) decrease whilst Profit and Loss account decreases - current liabilities remain the same - result is a decrease in working capital.

And so on .... Now think up some transactions yourself and decide how these would affect working capital, if at all. Play around with little balance sheets as above - use plenty of paper and transmit your thoughts, imaginary decisions, etc. to this paper. This is one of the best ways of becoming permanently familiar with any topic in accountancy.

Current ratio (Working Capital Ratio)

In deciding whether a business has *enough* working capital it is not sufficient to calculate the amount. For example £30,000 of working capital may be more than enough for a small manufacturing firm but to a large public company it would be hopelessly inadequate.

A useful indication is to calculate the current ratio, that is, what proportion do the current assets bear to the current liabilities? If the current assets total £12,000 and the current liabilities total £6,000, then the current ratio is two to one indicating that the current assets cover the current liabilities twice over. The ratio is expressed .....

$$\frac{\text{Current assets}}{\text{Current liabilities}}$$

If the current liabilities are covered twice by the current assets then the business is in a fairly strong position as regards its ability to meet its immediate commitments.

There is no 'rule of thumb' here because different types of business require different levels of cover. For example, a retail business dealing in cash sales would require a lower current ratio than a business dealing with long term contracts where the turnover is slow and in the meantime there is the need to carry large stocks and possibly debtors. If the working capital of the business cannot support much of these stocks and debtors until sales take place and payment is received, then there is a need to rely heavily on 'outside support' in the form of short term credit, and too much reliance on short term support can be dangerous. The business must be in a position to satisfy the claims of these short term creditors easily and hence the need for adequate cover.

Generally speaking, a 1.5 - 2.0 to 1 current ratio would be reasonable to adequate whilst a 3 to 1 ratio may indicate that the business is carrying too much stock or too many debtors - in other words the ratio is too high; but always consider the type of business.
A business with a very inadequate amount of working capital can only rectify this by gaining access to more *long term* or permanent capital, (e.g. long term loans, share issues, etc.)

EXERCISE 9.1

Indicate with a tick in the appropriate column what effect each of the following transactions will have on the amount of working capital.

		Effect on Working Capital		
		increase	decrease	none
1.	Purchase of stock on credit			
2.	Repayments of debentures			
3.	New issue of shares			
4.	Receipt of cash from debtors			
5.	Profit on sale of stock			
6.	Proposed dividend			
7.	Sale of fixed asset			
8.	Increase in provision for depreciation			
9.	Payment made to a creditor			

EXERCISE 9.2

The directors of Gifts Ltd are reviewing the company's financial estimates.

A summary of the company's estimated balance sheet at 31 December, 19-1 is shown below.

	£		£	£
Issued share capital £1 Ordinary shares	60,000	Goodwill		8,300
General Reserve	22,000	Freehold property		27,800
Profit and Loss account	14,500	Plant at cost	39,900	
Trade creditors	7,500	Less: accumulated		
		depreciation	16,600	23,300
		Quoted investments -		
		(market value £10,400)		11,000
		Stocks		17,200
		Trade debtors		10,000
		Cash in hand and bank		6,400
	104,000			104,000

The following information relates to expectations for the year ending 31 December, 19-1

	£
Credit Sales	120,000
Purchases	60,000
Depreciation for the year	4,500
Net profit	7,000

It can be assumed that all transactions will take place at an even rate throughout the year.

The directors are considering making the following amendments to the estimated figures :

1. A bonus (scrip) issue of 20,000 ordinary shares, to be capitalised from the general reserve.

2. A transfer of £5,000 from Profit and Loss account to the general reserve.

3. The average period of credit taken from suppliers to be amended to 2 months.

4. £2,300 to be written off goodwill.

5. Freehold property to be shown in the accounts at £40,000 on the basis of a professional valuation.

6. Depreciation for the year to be increased to £6,000.

132

7.   Quoted investments to be reduced to the estimated market value in the accounts.

8.   Trade debtors to be reduced by a provision of £1,000 for doubtful debts.

9.   The average period of credit allowed to customers to be amended to two months.

Required :
A statement showing how *each* of the proposed amendments would affect the cash balance shown in the estimated balance sheet of Gifts Ltd at 31 December, 19-1, compared with the previously estimated position.

Consider each item independently and state your answer in the form :

1.   <u>Increase £</u> ....   <u>or decrease £</u>..............................   <u>or no change</u> ....
2.   Etc.

You are not required to present an amended balance sheet or to comment on your answers.
NOTE   Ignore taxation.

EXERCISE 9.3

The directors of Dumble Ltd are considering the company's estimated financial situation in 19-6. The following estimates relate to the company's expected activities in 19-6.

	£
Sales	240,000
Purchases	150,000
Depreciation	7,000
Net profit	13,000

It is estimated that 60 per cent of the company's sales will be on credit and 40 per cent for cash.

Consistent with the above information, the estimated balance sheet for the year ending 31 December 19-6 is shown below :

	£		£	£
Issued Share Capital	75,000	Freehold Property at cost		54,000
Profit and Loss account	55,000	Plant at cost	62,000	
		Less: deprn.	18,000	44,000
Trade creditors	16,000	Stocks		28,000
		Trade Debtors		18,000
		Bank		2,000
	146,000			146,000

It can be assumed that all transactions will take place at an even rate throughout the year.

The directors are interested in the effects which would occur if the following changes were made to the estimates :

1.   80 per cent of sales to be made on credit and 20 per cent for cash.

2.   Depreciation for 19-6 to be amended to £11,000

3.   The average period of credit to be taken from suppliers to be amended to two months.

4.   A provision of £2,000 to be made for doubtful debts at 31 December, 19-6

5.   Freehold property to be revalued at £60,000.

A statement showing the net profit, bank balance or overdraft, and the current ratio (working capital ratio) for 19-6 which would result from making each individual amendment. For any items which are unaffected by an amendment, show the appropriate figures derived from the original estimates.

Consider each amendment independently and present your answer in a table as shown below :

Amendment	Net profit 19-6	Bank Balance (or overdraft)	Current Ratio
1			
2			
3			
4			
5			

NOTES :
1)   Ignore taxation
2)   Assume that the amendment will not alter the amount of bank interest payable.

EXERCISE 9.4

Simon is puzzled by the accounts of Retail Ltd. He says :

'I have calculated the company's funds generated from operations by adding back depreciation to net profit. The amounts came to £29,000 in 19-5 and £35,000 in 19-6 but, despite modest dividends and fixed asset acquisitions, the company started 19-5 with a bank balance of £5,000 and finished 19-6 with an overdraft of £13,000. Why?

You are provided with the following figures for Retail Ltd :

Balance Sheets at 31 December -

	19-4 £ 000	19-5 £ 000	19-6 £ 000
Issued share capital	100	100	100
Reserves	33	42	58
Proposed dividends	8	10	8
Trade Creditors	28	36	39
Bank Overdraft	-	5	13
	169	193	218
Fixed assets at cost, at beginning of year	126	137	149
Additions during year	11	12	13
	137	149	162
Less : Depreciation	38	48	59
	99	101	103
Stock	25	32	35
Trade debtors	40	60	80
Bank	5	-	-
	169	193	218

Profit Statement for year ended 31 December -

	£ 000	19-5 £ 000	£ 000	19-6 £ 000
Sales: for cash		200		150
on credit		300		400
		500		550
Deductions				
Opening stock	25		32	
Purchases	357		388	
	382		420	
Less: Closing Stock	32		35	
Cost of goods sold	350		385	
Sundry expenses	121		130	
Depreciation	10		11	
		481		526
Net profit		19		24
Proposed dividend		10		8
		9		16

It can be assumed that all sundry expenses were paid in the year in which they were incurred and that trade creditors relate only to purchased goods.

Required :

Numerical statement showing that the cash receipts and payments which explain the changes in the bank account of Retail Ltd in 19-5 and 19-6 so far as the information available permits.

NOTE   Ignore taxation.

EXERCISE 9.5

Henry plans to start a wholesale business on 1 January, 19-5. On that date he will introduce £10,000 capital, which will be paid into a business bank account, and he will immediately make cash purchases of £6,000 equipment and £3,100 stock-in-trade. In 19-5 he will keep his stock of goods replenished at £3,100.

Henry expects that he will receive a credit period of five weeks from his suppliers (apart from the initial cash purchase of goods) and that all his customers will take a credit period of eight weeks. He expects to earn a gross profit margin of 40% on selling price of all sales. The gross profit margin is stated before charging the following costs, which will remain fixed irrespective of the level of sales.

	Estimates for the year ending 31 December, 19-5
	£
Wages	5,000
Rent	4,000
Sundry expenses	4,000
Depreciation	600

Wages, rent, and sundry expenses will be paid as they are incurred. It can be assumed that all transactions involving credit will take place at an even rate throughout a year of 50 weeks (for ease of calculation).

Henry asks his bank to provide a temporary overdraft to finance his working capital requirements.

He explains :

'I estimate that I will make a net profit of £2,400 during the year. I shall withdraw only £1,400 for my own needs during the year, so the retained profit of £1,000 will be ample to ensure that there is no overdraft outstanding at the end of the year'.

Required :

(a)   A calculation of the sales Henry would have to make in 19-5 in order to achieve the net profit of £2,400 which he expects.

(b)   Henry's balance sheet at 31 December, 19-5 assuming that he makes a net profit of £2,400 during 19-5, of which he withdraws £1,400.

(c)   A numerical statement summarising the funds flows which caused the change in Henry's bank account from the opening balance of £10,000 to the position at 31 December, 19-5 shown in your answer to part (b).

(d)   A calculation of the sales Henry would have to make in 19-5 in order to have a nil bank balance at 31 December, 19-5. Assume that Henry withdraws £1,400 from net profit, as before.

NOTE   Ignore taxation and bank interest.

EXERCISE 9.6 EX

The following is a summary of the accounts of Pudsey Ltd, a trading company, for 19-3

Summarised Profit and Loss account for 19-3

	£ 000s	£ 000s
Sales		1,600
Less: Cost of goods sold		960
GROSS PROFIT		640
Less: Running costs - variable	160	
- fixed	300	460
NET PROFIT		180

Summarised Balance Sheet at 31 December 19-3

	£ 000s	£ 000s
Fixed assets at cost		1,000
Less: Accumulated depreciation		200
		800
Current Assets		
Stock	160	
Trade debtors	200	
Bank balance	10	
	370	
Current Liabilities		
Trade creditors	80	
Working capital		290
		1,090
Financed by :		
Share capital		700
Retained profit		390
		1,090

The directors plan to expand the level of business activity in 19-4. There is a strong demand for the company's product, and there exists sufficient capacity to increase sales substantially. Any increase in sales will result in a proportionate increase in cost of goods sold, stock, trade debtors and trade creditors. The fixed running costs include depreciation of fixed assets, £50,000, computed on the straight line basis.

Required :

(a)   A calculation of the level of sales required to increase net profit to £300,000

(b)   The forecast balance sheet at 31 December 19-4 assuming that the level of sales calculated under (a) is achieved. The bank balance may be inserted as the balancing item in the balance sheet you prepare.

(c) An explanation for the difference between the net profit of £300,000 and the *net* change in the bank balance during 19-4. You should support your explanation with an appropriate numerical statement.

NOTE Ignore dividends and taxation.

EXERCISE 9.7 EX

The accountant of Wiley Ltd has prepared the following estimated balance sheet as at 31 December, 19-2 for the company's directors.

Estimated Balance Sheet as at 31 December, 19-2

	£	£		£
Ordinary share capital				
£1 shares		500,000	Freehold property at cost	600,000
			Less: Depreciation	100,000
Reserves at 1 January,				500,000
19-2	250,000			
Add : Net profit for			Stock valued at marginal cost	590,000
19-2	50,000	300,000	Trade debtors	160,000
		800,000		
Loan repayable in 3 years time		250,000		
Trade creditors		140,000		
Bank overdraft		60,000		
		1,250,000		1,250,000

The directors are disappointed with the estimated net profit for 19-2 and the estimated financial position as at 31 December, 19-2 displayed in the balance sheet shown above. The following suggestions are made for consideration by the company's accountant.

(i) A bonus (capitalisation) issue of shares to existing shareholders on the basis of one additional £1 share for every two shares held at present.

(ii) Increase the depreciation charged on the freehold buildings from £20,000 to £30,000.

(iii) Arrange for a loan of £100,000 also repayable in 3 years' time, to be made to the company on 31 December, 19-2.

(iv) Value stock at total cost, £680,000, for the purpose of the accounts. The 19-1 accounts included stock at marginal cost of £400,000 and the corresponding figure for total cost at that date was £470,000.

(v) Offer cash discounts for prompt payment in respect of future sales. If this course is followed it is estimated that sales will be unaffected, but discounts of £3,000 will be allowed during the period October-December, 19-2 and trade debtors at the year end will amount to £120,000.

Required :

Taking each course of action *separately*, a statement showing the following :

(a) net profit for 19-2

(b) bank overdraft (or balance) at 31 December, 19-2

(c) working capital at 31 December, 19-2 - and

(d) liquidity ratio, defined as the ratio of trade debtors + bank balance (if any) to current liabilities at 31 December, 19-2.

Consider each course of action *separately* and present your answer in a table, as shown overleaf :

137

Course of Action	Net profit £	Bank over-draft (or balance) £	Working Capital £	Liquidity Ratio £
i)				
ii)				
iii)				
iv)				
v)				

NOTE   Ignore taxation
Assume that no course of action will alter the amount of bank interest payable.

EXERCISE 9.8 EX

William, who has been in business for many years, has decided to set up a new company called Griffin Ltd in Exmorth. William plans that his company should take over some fixed assets from an existing business for £40,000 and stock for £15,000; none of the other assets or liabilities of the former concern is to be acquired.

The company will begin trading on 1 January, 19-0 and William who has expert knowledge in these matters, expects sales at an even rate amounting to £150,000 during the first year of business. The gross profit margin will be 20% on sales, and William expects his stock to turn over six times during 19-0, based on the average of opening and closing stocks. It is intended to allow debtors seventy two days' credit, and suppliers are expected to allow forty five days for the payment of amounts due to them. Expenses, other than depreciation, debited to the profit and loss account will amount to £15,000. Depreciation is to be charged at 10% on the cost of fixed assets.

The bank have agreed to provide certain limited overdraft facilities for the new venture. The borrowing limit will be set so that William's current assets will be double his current liabilities at 31 December, 19-9. It will be necessary for William to arrange sufficient share capital to ensure compliance with this condition.

Required :
(a)   The estimated balance sheet of Griffin Ltd at 31 December, 19-0 showing clearly the share capital, which would have to be raised at the outset, and a bank overdraft consistent with the information given above.

(b)   A calculation of the revised figure for stock at 31 December, 19-0 assuming that the bank introduces an alternative requirement that the liquid ratio (ratio of debtors to current liabilities) at 31 December, 19-0 should be at least 1.2:1, and that the company decides to achieve this by increasing the rate of stock turnover.

NOTE   Ignore taxation and interest on the bank overdraft. All sales and purchases are to be on credit. Assume a 360-day year throughout.

EXERCISE 9.9 EX

The directors of Weardale plc have acquired a franchise to manufacture and sell a new product, designated 'Trent', in Great Britain for a period of six years. The franchise requires a payment of £2 on each item sold. The company has plenty of spare accommodation and has under consideration two alternative methods for manufacturing 'Trent'.

Method A   This involves the acquisition of plant costing £240,000. The estimated costs per unit manufactured are materials £7 and labour £4. Fixed overhead costs per annum, excluding deprecation and interest, are estimated at £20,000.

Method B   This involves the acquisition of more sophisticated plant costing £900,000. The estimated costs per unit manufactured are materials £5 and labour £3. Fixed overhead costs per annum, excluding depreciation and interest, are estimated at £75,000.

The following additional information is provided for both methods :

(i)   The plant is expected to last six years and then have a zero residual value. The company uses the straight line method of depreciation.

(ii)   An initial stock of raw materials, sufficient to manufacture 5,000 units of 'Trent' is required. Subsequent purchases will be made, on a monthly basis, to replace items used up, and one month's credit will be received on these items - i.e. stock, other than the initial purchase, is financed by suppliers.

(iii)   'Trent' will be sold for £15 per unit, and one month's credit will be allowed to customers.

(iv)   The directors are fairly confident that sales of 100,000 units per annum can be achieved.

(v)   The finance required for the project will be raised by issuing debentures carrying a 10% rate of interest.

Required :

(a)   For each method calculate :

(i)   The amount of the initial investment assuming that the expected level of sales is achieved.

(ii)   The break-even quantity of sales per annum.

(iii)   The expected profit per annum

(iv)   The quantity of sales at which the same profit is earned under each method.

(b)   A detailed comparison of the two methods based on the calculations made in answer to (a) above.

NOTES
    Ignore inflation and taxation
    Sales and production occur at a steady rate throughout the year.

EXERCISE 9.10 EX

The following estimated profit and loss account and balance sheet for 1987 has been prepared for Compton Ltd, a trading company:

Forecast Profit and Loss Account for 1987

		£000s	£000s
Sales			900
Less:	Purchases	720	
	Stock decrease during 1987	30	
Cost of goods sold			750
Gross profit			150
Less:	Depreciation	40	
	Other running expenses	50	90
Net Profit			60

Forecast Balance Sheet at 31 December 1987

	£000s	£000s
Fixed assets		
Freehold property at cost less depreciation		200
Plant and machinery at cost less depreciation		125
		325
Current assets		
Stocks	110	
Trade debtors	150	
	260	
Current liabilities		
Trade creditors	60	
Bank overdraft	40	
	100	
Net current assets		160
		485
Financed by:		
Share capital (£1 ordinary shares)		300
Reserves		185
		485

It is to be assumed that 1987 consists of twelve months, each of thirty days, and transactions take place at an even rate throughout the year.

The directors intend to undertake an expansion of business activity at the beginning of 1988, and plan to approach the bank for finance at that time. The directors are worried that the bank manager is unlikely to be impressed by the figures above and are considering ways of improving the financial appearance of the company. The following ideas are put forward at a board meeting:

(i) Restate the freehold property at its recent professional valuation of £300,000.

(ii) Extend the period of credit taken from suppliers to 45 days for purchases made on and after 1 October 1987. This change will not affect the company's creditworthiness.

(iii) Offer customers a cash discount of $2^1/_2$% for payment within 30 days. This offer to take effect for sales made on and after 1 October 1987. All the company's customers are expected to take advantage of this offer with the level of sales being unaffected.

(iv) Arrange for a loan of £50,000 to be made to the company on 31 December 1987. The loan will carry interest at 15% per annum and be repayable on 30 June 1988.

(v) Make a bonus (capitalisation) issue of two additional £1 shares, at par value, for every three shares held at present. The issue to be made during December 1987.

(vi) The average period for which stocks are held to be amended to 72 days. Additional purchases to be made during October to put this policy into effect.

Required : Taking each course of action separately, set out a statement showing the following:

Course of action	Net Profit for 1987 £	Bank balance (or overdraft) at 31 Dec. 1987 £	Working capital at 31 Dec. 1987 £	Working capital (current) ratio at 31 Dec. 1987 £
(i)				
(ii)				
(iii)				
(iv)				
(v)				
(vi)				

For any items unaffected by a course of action, show the original figure derived from the accounts above.
NOTES: (i) Ignore taxation (ii) Assume no course of action will alter the amount of bank interest payable.

(Autumn 1987)

SOLUTIONS

SOLUTION 9.1

	Effect on working Capital		
	Increase	Decrease	None
Purchase of stock on credit			√
Repayment of debentures		√	
New issue of shares	√		
Receipt of cash from debtors			√
Profit on sale of stock	√		
Proposed dividend		√	
Sales of a fixed asset	√		
Increase in provision for depreciation			√
Payment made to creditor			√

SOLUTION 9.2

Item   1, no change; 2, no change; 3, increase £2,500; 4, 5, 6, 7 and 8, no change; 9, decrease £10,000.

NOTE -

With the exception of items 3 and 9 the amendments involve book entries only which do not affect cash.

Item 3   One-sixth (2 months) of purchases on credit = £10,000 of creditors, an increase of £2,500 which benefits cash.

Item 9   One-sixth of credit sales = £20,000 debtors, an increase of £10,000, to the detriment of cash.

SOLUTION 9.3

Amendment	Net Profit	Bank balance (or overdraft)	Current Ratio
	£	£	
1	13,000	(4,000)	2.6 to 1
2	9,000	2,000	3.0 to 1
3	13,000	11,000	2.28 to 1
4	11,000	2,000	2.88 to 1
5	13,000	2,000	3.0 to 1

Workings :

Amendment 1

Total sales remain unchanged so net profit remains unaltered. As more sales are on credit the debtors will increase which will be to the detriment of bank balance. 80% of sales = £192,000 compared with 60% credit sales on original estimates - i.e. £144,000 - an increase of £48,000 or an increase of one-third. Therefore, outstanding debtors will increase by one-third - i.e. from £18,000 to £24,000, an increase of £6,000. Bank will therefore reduce by £6,000. The original current ratio was 3:1 but now the current assets are stock £28,000, debtors £24,000 *to* creditors £16,000 and bank overdraft £4,000 = £52,000 to £20,000 = 2.6.

141

Amendment 2

An increase in depreciation of £4,000 will reduce profits by £4,000 but will not affect cash or any other current asset of current liability.

Amendment 3

Purchases in total remain the same. One-sixth of a year credit gives outstanding creditors of £25,000 - an increase of £9,000. This will benefit cash.

Amendment 4

Debtors change and the net profit figure, but not bank.

Amendment 5

The only items affected are Freehold Property and Revaluation Reserve - nothing else - i.e. Debit Property, Credit Revaluation Reserve.

SOLUTION 9.4

Cash Receipts and Payments 19-5

	£	£
Receipts		
From debtors		280,000
From cash sales		200,000
		480,000
Less Payments		
To creditors	349,000	
Expenses	121,000	
Dividend paid (for 19-4)	8,000	
Purchase fixed assets	12,000	
		490,000
Reduction in cash		10,000

Cash Receipts and Payments 19-6

	£	£
Receipts		
From debtors		380,000
From cash sales		150,000
		530,000
Less Payments		
To creditors	385,000	
Expenses	130,000	
Dividend Paid (for 19-5)	10,000	
Purchase fixed assets	13,000	538,000
Reduction in cash		8,000

Note to student : The reductions in cash shown above can be checked against the bank balances in the balance sheets.

In 19-5 credit sales were £300,000 but as debtors increased by £20,000 between 19-4 and 19-5, only £280,000 of cash was actually received in 19-5. Similarly although purchases were £357,000, creditors were £8,000 more in 19-5 and so, only £349,000 had actually been paid to creditors in 19-5.

If this question had asked for a statement accounting for the change in cash you could have produced a Cash Flow Statement along the lines covered in this lesson but the question asked specifically for a statement showing the cash *receipts* and *payments*. Any variation on the above *presentation* would be allowed provided the required information was all there.

SOLUTION 9.5

(a)   Sales had to be enough to cover fixed costs of £13,600 and provide a profit of £2,400. Therefore, £16,000 is needed. As all the costs stated in the question are fixed, we need a *gross profit* of £16,000 and as the gross profit margin is 40% of sales, the sales figure needs to be **£40,000** to give a gross profit of £16,000.

Balance Sheet

(b)	£		£
Capital	11,000	Equipment	6,000
		Less depreciation	600
			5,400
Creditors	2,400		
Bank overdraft (balancing figure)	1,500	Stock	3,100
		Debtors	6,400
	14,900		14,900

NOTE   Creditors = 5 weeks' purchases. If sales are £40,000 and Gross Profit is £16,000, the cost of goods = £24,000, and 1/10 = £2,400.

Bank Summary

(c)		£	£
	Opening balance		10,000
	Receipts from debtors (sales less outstanding debtors)		33,600
			43,600
	Less :		
	Initial purchase of stock	3,100	
	Payments to creditors	21,600	
	Payment of expenses	13,000	
	Purchase of equipment	6,000	
	Drawings	1,400	45,100
	Closing overdraft		(1,500)

(d)   The emergence of debtors £6,400 and creditors £2,400, means a net decrease in cash available from sales (£40,000) of **£4,000** (i.e. £4,000 is tied up in Working Capital). So, for every £1,000 of sales made, £100 cash will be 'tied up'.

As £1,000 of sales produces £400 (40%) of gross profit, Henry will be left with £300 towards repaying the overdraft - therefore £1,500 is needed. How many £300s will be required to cover this?

Answer : FIVE. Therefore 5 x £1,000 additional sales are required making *total* sales of £45,000 to produce a nil bank balance.

143

LESSON 10

STATEMENTS OF SOURCE AND APPLICATION OF FUNDS

In the last lesson we looked at Cash Flow Statements as a concise means of showing an overall picture of cash flows in and out of a business during a particular period. We also saw that cash was only a part of working capital as a whole and we could therefore prepare in addition to our Cash Flow Statement a Working Capital Flow Statement which would show all those things which have increased (sources) and decreased (uses) not just cash, but working capital as a whole. We would be accounting for the change in working capital (current assets less current liabilities) over a period of time.

Both types of flow 'statements' would, in effect, select certain information from the profit and loss account and balance sheet prepared at the end of a period and summarise this information - obviously a very useful aid in assessing the financial position of a business.

Such is the importance of these statements that a statement of standard accounting practice (S.S.A.P. 10) has been issued stating that companies with a turnover of £25,000 or more per annum should prepare a statement of Source and Application of Funds and that this statement should form part of the audited accounts.

The statement is required to show the profit or loss for the period with adjustments for items not affecting funds. (e.g. book entries such as depreciation), the purchase and sale of fixed assets, the issue and repayment of shares and long-term loans, dividends paid, tax paid, and the increase and decrease of working capital sub-divided into its individual components.

From studying these requirements it would appear that we do not want a statement accounting for movements in cash alone - a cash flow statement - or a statement accounting for movements in working capital overall - a working capital flow statement - but instead, a combination of the two. Thus, our new 'Statement of Source and Application of Funds' will show movements in cash *and* working capital during a period of time.

EXAMPLE

X Ltd Balance Sheets

	Year 1 £	Year 2 £		Year 1 £	Year 2 £
Share Capital	40,000	50,000	Fixed Assets (cost)	77,400	102,000
General Reserve	11,000	14,000	Less depreciation	27,400	33,500
Retained Profits	4,500	7,800		50,000	68,500
Debentures	7,000	5,000			
Current Liabilities			Current Assets		
Taxation	5,700	6,500	Stock	19,000	21,000
Creditors	6,300	7,200	Debtors	8,000	6,300
Proposed Dividends	4,500	6,000	Bank	2,000	700
	79,000	96,500		79,000	96,500

N.B. No fixed assets were sold during Year 2.

From the above information prepare a Statement of Source and Application of Funds for Year 2 :

(i) The first step is to determine the funds generated from trading - i.e. the profit before tax. The profit and loss account has increased by £3,300 and this is *after* transferring £3,000 to General Reserve *after* providing for a proposed dividend of

£6,000 and taxation of £6,500. Therefore, the profit *before* any of these appropriations were made must have been - £3,300 + £6,000 + £6,500 = *£18,800*

(ii) The depreciation charge in year 2 was £6,100 (the difference between Year 1 and Year 2), and our profit of £18,800 was *after* charging for this so the £6,100 must be added back to show the true inflow of funds from profits.

(iii) Share capital has increased by £10,000 and as this was not a bonus issue, funds have been increased by £10,000 (source).

(iv) Funds have been applied in paying off £2,000 of debentures.

(v) Year *1's* proposed dividend of £4,500 and taxation liability of £5,700 will have been *paid* during Year 2 - i.e. application of funds.

(vi) Fixed assets were purchased for £24,600 (an application of funds).

NOTE - in comparing the balance sheets we have not concerned ourselves with changes in current assets and current liabilities, *except* for proposed dividends and tax paid, both items being different from other current liabilities in that they are appropriations from Profit and Loss account. At the moment we are not concerned with the other items.

Let us now put the above information into a Statement in the form used as illustration in SSAP 10 :

X Ltd

Statement of Source and Application of Funds
for the period 1 January to 31 December, Year 2.

	£	£
Source of Funds		
Profits before tax		18,800
Adjustments for items not involving a movement		
of funds : Depreciation		6,100
		24,900
Issue of shares for cash		10,000
		34,900
Application of Funds		
Repayment of Debentures	2,000	
Dividends paid	4,500	
Tax paid	5,700	
Purchase of fixed assets	24,600	36,800
		(1,900)

What does the above tell us? that funds show a net decrease of £1,900 in the year - but how can we reconcile this? To do this we must be aware that SSAP 10 excludes appropriations of profit for dividends and taxation from its concept of working capital - in other words it does not regard such appropriations as a movement of funds. In this sense then, only actual *payments* of tax and dividends affect funds. With this in mind, the 'net funds' (SSAP 10's definition of working capital) for Year 1 and Year 2 are calculated as follows :

	Year 1 £	Year 2 £
Current Assets	29,000	28,000
Less: Current Liabilities (excluding appropriations		
of profit - i.e. tax and dividends)	6,300	7,200
Net Funds	22,700	20,800

This shows a decrease of £1,900 which agrees with our Statement.

To finish off the Statement of Source and Application of Funds we must now add a final section, thus :

(continuation of Statement of Source and Application of Funds above) -

	£	£
Increase (Decrease) in Working Capital		
Increase in Stocks	2,000	
Decrease in debtors	(1,700)	
Increase in creditors	(900)	
Decrease in Bank	(1,300)	(1,900)

This section *reconciles* the movements of fund observed earlier with the movements in working capital. In preparing this final section of the Statement, think of each individual item (current assets and liabilities) *in isolation*. For example, if stock increased by £2,000 (see above) *in isolation,* what would happen to working capital overall? It would increase. If creditors increased by £900 what would happen? Working capital would decrease ...... and so on.

Our Statement therefore consists of three main headings :

	£
Source of Funds	
Application of Funds	⎯⎯⎯
	═══════
	£
Increase (Decrease) in Working Capital	⎯⎯⎯
	═══════

Whenever you are asked to prepare a Statement of Source and Application of Funds I would recommend that you use the above form although variations on this would be acceptable to the examiner.

S.S.A.P. 10

Statement of Source and Application of Funds

The requirements of this Statement are fully covered in Lesson No.10.

EXERCISE 10.1

From the following balance sheets prepares a Statement of Source and Application of funds for the period Year 2.

Balance Sheets

	Year 1 £	Year 2 £		Year 1 £	Year 2 £
Share Capital - £1 shares	70,000	100,000	Fixed Assets		
Revaluation Reserve	10,000	-	Plant and Equipment		
General Reserve	12,000	17,000	at cost	51,400	70,300
Retained Earnings	9,500	13,500	Less depreciation	8,400	14,300
	101,500	130,500		43,000	56,000
8% Debentures	20,000	25,000	Premises (valuation)	60,000	60,000
Current Liabilities			Current Assets		
Corporation tax	13,500	16,000	Stock	44,000	61,000
Creditors	23,000	27,500	Debtors	28,000	32,000
Dividends Proposed	10,500	15,000	Bank	-	5,000
Bank overdraft	6,500	-			
	175,000	214,000		175,000	214,000

NOTE During Year 2 there was a bonus issue of 10,000 shares of £1 each.

EXERCISE 10.2

From the following balance sheets prepare a Sources and Application of Funds Statement for the period Year 2.

Balance Sheets for Year 1 and Year 2

	Year 1 £	Year 2 £		Year 1 £	Year 2 £
Ordinary Shares	80,000	95,000	Machinery (cost)	82,060	96,060
Redeemable Pref. Shares	12,000	7,000	Less: Depreciation	9,420	12,350
Share Premium	4,000	4,500		72,640	83,710
Retained Earnings	11,200	9,900	Goodwill	12,000	9,000
Capital Redemption Reserve	-	5,000			
Debentures	6,000	8,000	Stock	16,500	24,900
Creditors	3,700	3,150	Debtors	9,600	14,690
Proposed Dividends:			Bank	14,520	10,110
Ordinary	8,000	9,500	Rates prepaid	600	200
Preference	960	560			
	125,860	142,610		125,860	142,610

During Year 2 there was a bonus issue of 5,000 Ordinary Shares of £1 each.

EXERCISE 10.3

The directors of Green Ltd are reviewing the company's financial requirements for the year to 31 August, 19-6.

The summarised balance sheet of Green Ltd at 31 August, 19-5 showed :

	£		£	£
Ordinary Share Capital	40,000	Goodwill		6,000
Profit and Loss account	36,200	Freehold warehouse		26,000
Trade creditors	19,800	Fittings & Equip. at cost	20,000	
Bank overdraft	3,000	Less: depreciation	8,500	11,500
		Stock in trade		23,000
		Trade debtors		32,500
	99,000			99,000

The company's plans are based upon the following expectations for the year to 31 August, 19-6 :

Issue for cash of 10,000 £1 ordinary shares at a premium of 50p per share in October, 19-5.

New equipment will be purchased for £7,000 cash on 1 September, 19-5. Goodwill will be written down by £3,000.

Stock in trade at the end of the year will be £29,000.

The following trading transactions, etc. will occur at an even rate throughout the year.

	£
Sales	240,000
Purchases	186,000
General Expenses	35,000
Directors' salaries	8,000

The period of credit allowed to customers will be two calendar months and the period of credit taken from suppliers will be $1^1/_2$ calendar months. All amounts (including debtors and creditors outstanding at 31 August, 19-5) will be paid in full at the end of the credit periods. No amounts for general expenses or directors' salaries will be outstanding at the end of the year.

Depreciation on all equipment held at the end of the year will be provided at the rate of 10% per annum (on cost).

Required :

(a)   A statement of the estimated sources and applications of funds of Green Ltd. for the year ending 31 August, 19-6
Ignore taxation.

(b)   A statement showing how the following alternative assumptions would affect the cash available to the company at 31 August, 19-6 compared with the previously estimated position.

(Specify your answer in each case as either **Increase £ ......** or **Decrease £ ......** or **No change.** Comments on your answers are not required).

(i)   Freehold shop revalued in accounts at £34,000
(ii)   Period of credit allowed to customers $1^1/_2$ months.
(iii)   Period of credit taken from suppliers 1 month.
(iv)   Depreciation provided for year increased to 15% on cost.
(v)   Remainder of goodwill written off.

EXERCISE 10.4

Balance Sheets of ABC Ltd

	Year 1	Year 2		Year 1	Year 2
	£	£		£	£
Share Capital	100,000	120,000	Fixed Assets (cost)	140,000	170,000
Share Premium	15,000	18,000	Less: Provision for		
General Reserve	30,000	34,000	depreciation	81,000	87,000
Profit and Loss				59,000	83,000
Appropriation A/c*	6,200	8,700			
Debentures	25,000	20,000	Stock	58,000	65,200
Reserve for Corpn. Tax	14,000	16,000	Debtors	43,200	55,000
Current Liabilities	30,000	38,500	Bank	60,000	52,000
	220,200	255,200		220,200	255,200

	£
*Net profit in Year 2	37,500
Less: depreciation for year	6,000
	31,500
Less: estimated tax for year (to reserve)	16,000
	15,500
Less: Transfer to General Reserve	4,000
	11,500
Less: Dividend paid	9,000
	2,500
Add: Profit and Loss Appropriation A/c	
Balance from Year 1	6,200
Profit and Loss Appropriation A/c	
Balance c/fwd at end of Year 2	8,700

Prepare a statement showing the sources and applications of funds for Year 2.

EXERCISE 10.5

The balance sheets of Boswell Ltd at 31 March, 19-2 and March, 19-3, appear below :

	31 March 19-2 £	31 March 19-3 £		31 March 19-2 £	31 March 19-3 £
Issue Share Capital	30,000	40,000	Freehold property at cost	25,000	25,000
Profit and Loss account	27,000	23,000	Equipment (see note)	18,000	22,200
Corporation Tax due:			Stock in trade	16,400	17,800
1 January, 19-3	6,000	-	Debtors	13,600	14,000
1 January, 19-4	-	4,000	Bank	2,000	1,000
Creditors	12,000	13,000			
	75,000	80,000		75,000	80,000

NOTE Equipment movements during the year ended 31 March, 19-3 were :

	Cost £	Depreciation £	Net £
Balance at 31 March, 19-2	30,000	12,000	18,000
Additions during year	9,000		
Depreciation provided during year		3,800	
	39,000	15,800	
Disposals during year	4,000	3,000	
Balance at 31 March, 19-3	35,000	12,800	22,200

The company's summarised profit calculation for the year ended 31 March, 19-3 revealed :

	£	£
Sales		100,000
Gain on sale of equipment		400
		100,400
Less:		
cost of goods and trading expenses	86,600	
Depreciation	3,800	90,400
Net Profit		10,000
Corporation tax on profits of the year		4,000
Retained profit of the year		6,000

During the year ended 31 March, 19-3, Boswell Ltd made a bonus issue of 10,000 £1 ordinary shares by capitalisation from the Profit and Loss account.

Required : A statement of Source and Application of Funds for the year ended 31 March, 19-3.

EXERCISE 10.6 EX

The following balance sheet has been prepared for Cohen Ltd at 31 December, 1979 :

Balance Sheet at 31 December, 1979

	£	£		£	£
Ordinary share capital			Freehold property at cost		400,000
£1 shares		800,000	Plant and machinery at cost	1,446,600	
10% redeemable preference share			Less: depreciation	617,900	828,700
capital		300,000			
Reserves		625,000	Investments at cost		230,000
		1,725,500			
12% Debentures 1990		500,000	Current Assets		
			Stock	1,063,700	
			Debtors	682,300	
Current Liabilities					1,746,000
Trade creditors	476,200				
Taxation due 30.9.1980	196,000				
Dividend	60,000				
Bank overdraft	247,000	979,200			
		3,204,700			3,204,700

The directors of Cohen Ltd are concerned about the fact that the present overdraft is close to the facility allowed by the company's bank. The financial director has prepared the following estimated statement of funds for 1980 :

Estimated Statement of Funds for 1980

	£	£
Sources		
Profit before taxation		437,100
Add: items not involving the outflow of funds -		
Loss on sale of plant (note 1)		3,500
Depreciation		247,600
Funds generated by trading activities		688,200
Funds from other sources :		
Sale of investments (note 2)		175,000
Sale of plant (note 1)		2,000
Ordinary share capital (note 3)		240,000
		1,105,200
Applications		
Dividend paid - ordinary shares	60,000	
preference shares	15,000	
Redemption of preference shares (note 4)	300,000	
Taxation paid	196,000	
Purchase of plant and machinery	206,500	777,500
		327,700
Changes in working capital items		
(Increase) in trade creditors	(43,400)	
Increase in debtors	59,700	
Increase in stock	103,500	
Increase in net liquid funds	207,900	327,700

NOTES ON THE ABOVE ACCOUNTS (overleaf) :

150

1.   Plant which had cost the company £25,000 some years ago will be sold for £2,000.

2.   This represents the proceeds arising from the sale of 20,000 shares which had cost the company £7.00 each in 1970.

3.   As the result of the share issue the company's authorised and issued ordinary share capital will consist of one million ordinary shares of £1 each.

4.   The preference share capital is to be redeemed at par value, on 1 July, 1980.

5.   The freehold property is to be revalued during 1980. It is expected that a firm of professional valuers will place a figure of approximately £660,000 on the property, and this revised figure will be written into the books.

6.   Tax payable on the estimated profits for 1980, including the capital gain on the sale of investments, will be £203,800 and the directors propose to pay a final dividend of 10p on each ordinary share.

Required :   The estimated balance sheet of Cohen Limited at 31 December, 1980 presented in vertical format and taking account of the above information. You should show clearly how the figure for reserves, appearing in the forecast balance sheet, has been calculated.

NOTE   Ignore Advance Corporation Tax.

EXERCISE 10.7 EX

Maximon Ltd is a well established company engaged in the manufacture and sale of metal products. The following information is obtained from the company's financial records.

Balance Sheet at 30 June

	19-1 £	19-1 £	19-2 £	19-2 £
Fixed Assets at cost		637,100		767,300
Less: Depreciation		297,500		321,400
		339,600		445,900
Trade investments at cost		106,000		106,000
Current Assets				
Stock and work-in-progress	230,200		260,100	
Trade debtors and prepayments	135,800		196,400	
Bank balance	-		9,300	
	366,000		465,800	
Less: Current Liabilities				
Trade creditors and accruals	96,800		101,700	
Taxation due : 31 March 19-2	63,800		-	
31 March 19-3	-		61,000	
Dividend payable	60,000		66,000	
Bank overdraft	71,000		-	
	291,600		228,700	
Net Current Assets		74,400		237,100
		520,000		789,000
Financed by :				
Ordinary share capital (ordinary shares of £1 each)		200,000		220,000
Share premium account		-		30,000
Reserves		320,000		339,000
		520,000		589,000
15% debenture		-		200,000
		520,000		789,000

Profit and Loss Accounts, year ended 30 June

	19-1 £	19-2 £
Operating Profit	160,500	176,000
Less: finance charges -		
bank interest	9,200	-
debenture interest	-	30,000
Net profit before taxation	151,300	146,000
Less: Taxation	63,800	61,000
Profit after taxation	87,500	85,000
Less: dividend proposed	60,000	66,000
Retained profit for the year	27,500	19,000

NOTES

1.   On 31 January, 19-2 a rights issue was made of one ordinary share for every ten ordinary shares currently held. For the purpose of this issue the ordinary shares were valued at £2.50 each.

2.   The debenture is secured on the company's freehold property which is included amongst fixed assets in the balance sheet shown above.

3.   During the year ended 30 June, 19-2 the company disposed of fixed assets which cost £65,200 some years ago for £17,900. A loss of £9,600 arising on disposal has been deducted in arriving at operating profit for the year.

Required :

(a)   The statement of source and application of funds of Maximon Ltd, for the year ended 30 June, 19-2 in accordance with the provisions contained in Statement of Standard Accounting Practice No. 10 entitled 'Statements of Source and Application of Funds'.

(b)   An examination of the respective financial positions of Maximon Ltd at 30 June, 19-1 and 31 June, 19-2 and a discussion of the financial developments which have occurred during the intervening period. The financial statement prepared under (a) and relevant accounting ratios should be used to support your analysis.

NOTE   Ignore advance corporation tax.

EXERCISE 10.8 EX

The following financial information is provided in respect of the affairs of Pontcanna plc.

Balances at :	1 January 19-1 £ 000	31 December 19-1 £ 000
Stock and work in progress	876	921
Trade debtors less provision for doubtful debts	534	617
Trade Creditors	261	309
Plant at cost	1,300	1,500
Debenture interest outstanding	-	18

Transactions during 19-1 included :	£ 000
Receipts from customers	2,160
Purchases	1,245
Administration and other expense paid in cash	702
Purchase of plant, 1 January 19-1	200
Issue of 12% debentures for cash 1 January 19-1	300

Plant is depreciated at the rate of 10% per annum on cost. The provision for doubtful debts at 31 December, 19-1 has been increased by £54,000.

Required :

(a)   The following financial statements for 19-1 :

(i)   Profit and Loss account
(ii)   Source and application of working capital
(iii)   Receipts and payments of cash

The statements should be presented in the following form :

	Profit & Loss Account	Source and Application of Working Capital	Receipts and Payments of Cash
	£ 000	£ 000	£ 000
Inflows :			
Less Outflows:			
Purchases			
Payments			
Administration and other expenses etc.			
Net inflow (outflow)	_____	_____	_____

(b)   The following reconciliations based on the figures calculated in your answers to (a).

       (i)   Net profit or loss with net increase or decrease in working capital.
       (ii)   Net increase or decrease in working capital with net increase or decrease in cash.

(c)   An explanation of the various ways in which financial information contained in the profit and loss account and the statement of source and application of working capital may be used to assess corporate progress.

NOTE   It is essential that candidates show how they arrive at each of the figures in their answer to this question.

EXERCISE 10.9 EX

The draft balance sheet of Langusta Ltd as at 31 December 1987, together with comparative figures for the previous year, is as follows:

	1987	1986
	£000	£000
Tangible fixed assets at cost or valuation	1,360	940
Less: Accumulated depreciation	98	72
	1,262	868
Current assets		
Stock and work in progress	346	338
Debtors	175	150
Cash at bank and in hand	7	—
	528	488
Creditors: Amounts falling due within one year		
Creditors and accruals	106	101
Bank overdraft	—	37
Taxation due 30 September 1987	—	65
Taxation due 30 September 1988	91	—
Proposed dividends	36	55
	233	258
Net current assets	295	230
Total assets less current liabilities	1,557	1,098
Creditors falling due after one year		
Debentures redeemable 1990	200	200
	1,357	898

Financed by Capital and Reserves

Ordinary share capital (£1 each)	500	400
Preference share capital(£1 each)		250
Share premium account	80	–
Property revaluation reserve	310	–
Capital redemption reserve	70	
Debenture redemption reserve	140	120
Plant replacement reserve	75	52
Profit and loss account	182	76
	1,357	898

The following additional information is provided:

(i) The balances of tangible fixed assets are made up as follows :

	Land and Buildings	Plant and Machinery	Total
Cost or valuation	£000	£000	£000
Balance at 31 December 1986	700	240	940
Additions	–	110	110
Revaluation	310	–	310
Balance at 31 December 1987	1,010	350	1,360
Accumulated depreciation			
Balance at 31 December 1986	–	72	72
Charge for the year	–	26	26
Balance at 31 December 1987	---	98	98

(ii) 100,000 ordinary shares were issued on 1 January 1987 at £1.80 per share. All the preference shares were redeemed at par on the following day.

Required :

(a) A reconstruction of the profit and loss account for 1987 so as to disclose the figure for profit before tax.

(b) The statement of source and application of funds for 1987, prepared in accordance with the provisions of SSAP10 as far as the information permits.

(c) An explanation of how the balances on the share premium account and capital redemption reserve have arisen.

(d) State, giving your reasons, whether the balances on each of the following accounts are distributable as dividends:

Property revaluation reserve
Capital redemption reserve
Debenture redemption reserve.

NOTES :

(i) Ignore advance corporation tax
(ii) Land and buildings are not depreciated
(iii) An interim dividend was not paid for 1987.

(Spring 1988)

SOLUTIONS

SOLUTION 10.1

Statement of Source and Application of Funds
for the period Year 2

	£	£
Source of Funds		
Profits before tax		40,000
Adjustments for items not involving a movement		
of funds : Depreciation		5,900
		45,900
Issue of shares for cash		20,000
Issue of debentures		5,000
		70,900
Application of Funds		
Corporation Tax paid	13,500	
Dividends paid	10,500	
Purchase of plant	18,900	42,900
		28,000

Increase (Decrease) in Working Capital	£
Increase in Stock	17,000
Increase in Debtors	4,000
Increase in Creditors	(4,500)
Increase in Bank	11,500
	28,000

Profit and Loss

Workings

Reconstructed Appropriation Account - Year 2

	£		£
Proposed Dividends	15,000	Balance b/d	9,500
Corporation Tax	16,000	NET PROFIT - (Balance	
General Reserve	5,000	figure)	40,000
Balance c/d	13,500		
	49,500		49,500

The Revaluation Reserve has obviously been utilised to make the bonus issue.

NOTE   That the appropriations for tax and dividends in Year 1 would have been *paid* (application of funds) in Year 2.

SOLUTION 10.2

Statement of Source and Application of Funds
for period Year 2

	£	£
Source of Funds		
Profits before tax		21,760
Adjustments for items not involving a movement		
of funds : Depreciation		2,930
		24,690
Issue of shares for cash		10,000
Premium on shares		500
Issue of Debentures		2,000
		37,190

Application of Funds

Purchase of machinery	14,000	
Payment of dividends		
Ordinary	8,000	
Preference	960	
Redemption of Preference Shares	5,000	27,960
		9,230

Increase (Decrease) in Working Capital

Increase in Stock	8,400
Increase in Debtors	5,090
Decrease in prepayments	(400)
Decrease in creditors	550
Decrease in Bank	(4,410)
	9,230

Workings

Reconstructed P & L Appropriation Account -Year 2

	£		£
Proposed Dividends		Balance b/d	11,200
Ordinary	9,500	NET PROFIT - (Balance	
Preference	560	figure)	21,760
Capital Redemption Reserve	5,000		
Goodwill written off	3,000		
Bonus issue of shares	5,000		
Balance	9,900		
	32,960		32,960

SOLUTION 10.3

(a) A good starting point is to prepare an estimated balance sheet from the information given, as at 31 August, 19-6, viz :

	£		£	£
Ordinary Share Capital	50,000	Goodwill		3,000
Share Premium	5,000	Warehouse		26,000
Profit and Loss account*	47,500	Fittings	27,000	
Creditors (1½ months)	23,250	Less: depreciation	11,200	15,800
		Debtors (2 months)		40,000
		Stock		29,000
		Bank (balancing figure)		11,950
	125,750			125,750

Calculation of Profit and Loss account balance

	£		£
Stock	23,000	Sales	240,000
Purchases	186,000		
	209,000		
Less stock	29,000		
	180,000		
General expenses	35,000		
Salaries	8,000		
Depreciation	2,700		
NET PROFIT	14,300		
	240,000		240,000
Written off Goodwill	3,000	Balance b/d	36,200
Balance	* 47,500	Net profit b/d	14,300
	50,500		50,500

Answer

(a)

Statement of Source and Application of Funds

	£
Source of Funds	
Profits before tax	14,300
Adjustments for items not involving a movement	
of funds: Depreciation	2,700
	17,000
Issue of shares at premium	15,000
	32,000
Application of Funds	
Purchase of new equipment	7,000
	25,000
Increase (Decrease) in Working Capital	
Increase in Stock	6,000
Increase in Debtors	7,500
Increase in Creditors	(3,450)
Increase in Bank	14,950
	25,000

(b)

(i) No change	(ii) Increase of £10,000	(iii) Decrease of £7,750
(iv) No change	(v) No change.	

SOLUTION 10.4

Sources and Applications of Funds Statement

	£	£
Sources of Funds		
Profit before tax	31,500	
Add: items not involving movement		
of funds : Depreciation	6,000	
	37,500	
Issue of Shares	20,000	
Premium on shares	3,000	60,500
Application of funds		
Purchase of fixed assets	30,000	
Repayment of debentures	5,000	
Payment of tax	14,000	
Payment of dividend	9,000	58,000
NET INCREASE		2,500
Increase (Decrease) in Working Capital		
Increase in Stock		7,200
Increase in Debtors		11,800
Increase in Current Liabilities		(8,500)
Decrease in Bank		(8,000)
NET INCREASE		2,500

LESSON 11

CASH BUDGETS

In Lesson 9 we saw how easily we could account for changes in a bank balance from one period to another by the use of a Cash Flow Statement. Whilst in the examples studied we were looking back in time to see what *had* happened to cash we could of course prepare such a statement based on estimated future profit and loss accounts and balance sheets in order to see what *will* happen to cash in the next period.

However, in looking ahead, we may wish to be more precise than this and we may want a comprehensive statement which shows details of all receipts and payments of cash which are likely to occur every month for the next 3, 6, 9 or 12 months, and which will show the estimated bank balance at the end of each month throughout the period in question.

Such a statement is called a Cash Budget or Cash Forecast and can be an invaluable guide to a business in ensuring that sufficient cash will be available to meet various future commitments, or in determining future cash requirements by way of loan or overdraft.

When banks are approached by customers requiring overdrafts they are often told that 'the overdraft will never exceed £x as that is ample for our requirements' - the trouble is that the customer then finds that cash is not coming in as fast as he thought it would, and in certain months the overdraft limit is well exceeded. There are always good reasons of course! It is because of this that banks employ cash forecasts (or budgets) on a large scale in assessing advance propositions. Not only does it indicate the more realistic requirements of their customer, it is also a good guide to prospects of repayment of the advance, If a budget reveals that the proposed overdraft is likely to reach a high peak in certain months then both the bank and the customer are prepared for this.

A cash budget is a very useful type of 'crystal ball' *provided that the estimates on which it is based are good ones!*

In the examination you are often asked to prepare such a budget from given information. You will obviously want to know how much cash will be received and how much will be paid out in each month and the examiner will probably do his best to 'hide' the information you need in order to simulate a real situation. It is up to you to unravel the information required from the facts given in the question, and to do this you need to think logically and to apply common sense to your approach.

The receipts and payments need to be analysed of course to show how much will be received from sales, sale of assets, issue of shares, etc., and how much will be paid for purchases, overheads, purchase of assets etc.

In its simplest form your cash budget is going to look like this :

Cash Budget for Quarter to 31 March

	Jan £	Feb £	March £
Receipts for month	800	400	200
Total receipts for month	800	400	200
Payments for month	600	1,100	500
Total payments for month	600	1,100	500
Bank balance at start of month (+ or −)	+100	+300	−400
Add receipts (as above)	800	400	200
	900	700	−200
Less payments (as above)	600	1,100	500
Bank balance at end of month (+ or _)	+300	−400	−700

The budget is made up of vertical columns for each month in question and various 'labels' to the left of these columns showing what the various receipts and payments are in respect of, and I strongly recommend that this structure be built up first of all *before* attempting to put any figures into your budget. To try to build up your budget piecemeal can cause you unnecessary confusion and waste valuable time, but by constructing your plan first you can see exactly where you are going, and it is then that much easier to get there. In other words, use method - let me illustrate this by giving you an examination question and then going through it with you in a methodical manner :

QUESTION

Wheeler's bank account was overdrawn £1,900 on 31 March 19-9 against an overdraft limit of £2,000. On that day he asked the bank to increase the limit to £5,000 on the following grounds :

'I have made a special export contract to sell £2,000 of goods each month for the next 3 months. The contract gives me a profit margin which is higher than usual, and I shall have to make additional purchases for £1,500 each month to meet the contract. The snag is that I have to pay for all my purchases in the month I buy them, but I shall have to wait two months to receive cash for each month's deliveries under the contract, so I shall not see any money until June. I need the £3,000 increase in the overdraft to cover the purchases while I wait for payment.

My estimated overall position for the next three months is :

	April £	May £	June £	TOTAL £	£
Normal sales	5,000	6,250	6,250		17,500
Contract sales	2,000	2,000	2,000		6,000
					23,500
Running expenses	900	1,000	1,000	2,900	
Purchases :					
for normal sales	4,000	5,000	5,000	14,000	
for contract	1,500	1,500	1,500	4,500	21,400
				PROFIT	2,100

In addition, I am owed £5,000 for sales made in March which I shall receive in April; I always receive cash in the following month for my normal sales. Naturally I have to pay running expenses in the month they occur. I hold no stocks worth mentioning so all my purchases each month are necessary to make the sales. There is never any variation in profit margin on my normal sales'

The bank agreed to an overdraft limit of £5,000 subject to a reduction to £4,000 at the end of June (and other reductions in later months). It was agreed that, if necessary, Wheeler would reduce his purchases for normal sales to keep within the overdraft limits.

It can be assumed that all receipts and payments occur on the last day of each month.

Required:
(a)   An analysis showing for the three months to 30 June, 19-9 Wheeler's bank overdraft at the end of each month if his original estimates are followed precisely.

(b)   If there are any months in which Wheeler's purchases would have to be reduced in order to keep the agreed overdraft limits, state the months and the amounts by which purchases would have to be reduced.

        Ignore interest on overdraft.

Approach to Answer

On looking through the question your first thought is probably 'where do I start?' and you may spend ten minutes reading through the question, which is wasted time - you should be writing within seconds of seeing the question. Let your eyes jump to that part of the question which says 'Required'. A cash budget for the three months to 30 June? Start writing your heading and to the right of your paper enter headings for April, May and June, viz :

Wheeler's Cash Budget to 30 June, 19-9

	April £	May £	June £

Then write in your first 'label' on the first line of the budget - make this **'Receipts'**: - *Now* go through the question quickly to find out what kind of receipts you are going to be dealing with - do *not* worry about amounts for the present. It is easy to determine that the only receipts will be from 'normal sales' and 'contract sales' so write these labels under your heading of 'Receipts' and draw total lines so completing the first section of your budget (no amounts yet), viz :

Cash budget ....

	April £	May £	June £
Receipts :			
Normal Sales			
Contract Sales			

The next heading is **'Payments'** - again go quickly through the question to find out what *kind* of payments are involved in this period. You will find these to be 'purchases for normal sales', 'purchases for contract sales' and 'running expenses'. Write in your labels and draw total lines.

160

Continue now, without the need to look at the question, to write in the standard labels for the final part of your budget - i.e. 'bank balance at start of month', add 'total receipts', less 'total payments' to give 'bank balance at end of month'.

Your budget should now look like this :

Cash Budget ....

	April £	May £	June £
Receipts:			
Normal Sales			
Contract Sales	___	___	___
	═══	═══	═══
Payments:			
Purchases for normal sales			
Purchases for contract sales			
Running expenses	___	___	___
	═══	═══	═══
Bank balance at start of month			
Add: Receipts (as above)	___	___	___
Less: Payments (as above)	___	___	___
Bank balance at end of month	═══	═══	═══

This whole process should take only a few minutes and you have hardly referred to the question so far. You can now see exactly where you are heading and already you are at an advantage over those candidates still chewing their pens in that you pen is working already!

Now we can look for the figures to put in our budget. Deal with one thing at a time so that your attention is concentrated on one particular section of the question at a time and work *across* the budget.

Starting with receipts from normal sales we are told that these are received in cash in the following month. Therefore normal sales of £5,000 in March will be received in April (enter under **April**); normal sales of £5,000 in April will be received in May (enter); and normal sales of £6,250 in May will be received in June (enter).

Wheeler has to wait two months for the cash from contract sales so April's contract sales of £2,000 will be received in June (enter under **June**).

Now, on to payments - *all* purchases are paid for in the same month they are bought so these can be taken straight from the question and entered in the budget. Running expenses are obvious and are taken straight from the question again.

Finally, add up the receipts and payments and enter totals in the bottom section of the budget. Then enter the opening bank balance in the budget, an overdraft of £1,900 (straight from the question), and finish off the additions and subtractions.

Your final answer appears thus :

Cash Budget ....

	April £	May £	June £
Receipts:			
Normal Sales	5,000	5,000	6,250
Contract Sales	-	-	2,000
	5,000	5,000	8,250
Payments:			
Purchases for normal sales	4,000	5,000	5,000
Purchases for contract sales	1,500	1,500	1,500
Running expenses	900	1,000	1,000
	6,400	7,500	7,500
Bank balance at start of month	−1,900	−3,300	−5,800
Add: Receipts (as above)	5000	5,000	8,250
	3,100	1,700	2,450
Less: Payments (as above)	6,400	7,500	7,500
Bank balance at end of month	−3,300	−5,800	−5,050

If you tackle all cash budgets in this way you should be able to deal in a relaxed manner with anything the examiner decides to give you.

The second part of the question needs some careful reasoned thought. Let us look at it for the practice :

The agreed overdraft limit is £5,000 for April and May, reducing to £4,000 in June.

We can see from the above that Wheeler has exceeded the limit by £800 in May. To keep to the limit he must therefore reduce the purchases for normal sales by £800 (i.e. from £5,000 to £4,200). This will reduce total purchases in May to £5,700 (£6,500 less £800). The May column of the Cash Budget would then appear thus :

	May £	
	−3,300	Balance
Add	5,000	Normal Sales
	+1,700	
Less	1,000	Running Expenses
	+700	
Less	5,700	Total Purchases
	−5,000	Balance

We have rectified Wheeler's position in May by reducing his purchases for normal sales by £800. How does this affect the June figures? Well, the question tells us that Wheeler does not hold any stocks, which means that all purchases are disposed of in the same month in which they are bought. If, therefore, he is buying £800 less in May for normal selling, then his normal sales in May must also be reduced (he obviously cannot sell more than he has bought!). As the proceeds of May's normal sales are not received until June, the figure in the June column of our cash budget (which represents the receipts from normal sales) will be reduced. But by how much will these sale proceeds be reduced? Not by £800 as this is the *cost* price of the reduced purchases - sales will be reduced by the corresponding *selling* price of £800 worth of purchases. How can we find the selling price of goods which cost £800?

162

Well, the question tells us that there is never any variation in the profit margin on normal sales, so let us see what this profit margin is by looking at the figures in the question :

> Purchases (for normal sales) in April, £4,000 were sold for £5,000 (i.e. a 'mark-up' above cost of 25%).
> Purchases (for normal sales) in May, £5,000 were sold for £6,250 (a mark-up again of 25%).
> The same thing happened in June.

What then is the selling price of £800 of purchases? - £1,000 (£800 + 25%)

Right then - the proceeds from May's normal sales which are receivable in June, will be reduced by £1,000 - i.e. from £6,250 to £5,250 - and the June column of our Cash Budget will now look like this :

	June £	
Balance at start	−5,000	(brought forward from May)
Add: receipts from		
Normal Sales	5,250	
Contract Sales	2,000	
	+2,250	
Deduct :		
Running Expenses	1,000	
	+1,250	(+1,250)
Deduct : Purchases		
(Normal and Contract)	6,500	(5,250)
Balance at month end	−5,250	(−4,000)

The final balance of £5,250 is £1,250 over the limit, so purchases for normal sales in June must be reduced by this amount. the original figure for total purchases therefore, £6,500 must be reduced to £5,250. The figures in brackets above are, then, our final figures.

Summary of answers to this part of the question :

> 'Wheeler's purchases for normal sales would have to be reduced by £800 in May, and by £1,250 in June, in order to keep within the overdraft limits'.

This question is a good example of the type of searching you are expected to do in order to extract from the question the information you want. Do not move on until you can follow every single aspect of it!

EXERCISE 11.1

The balance sheet of Plunket's Speciality food Shop at 31 August, 19-1 was :

	£		£	£
Plunket's capital	13,750	Leasehold premises at cost	10,000	
Trade Creditors	3,000	Less: accumulated depn.	2,000	
Bank overdraft	1,050			8,000
		Fittings at cost	5,000	
		Less: accumulated depn.	1,000	4,000
		Stock in trade		5,000
		Trade debtors		800
	17,800			17,800

On the basis of past performance, Plunket expects that his sales during the coming six months will be :

September	October	November	December	January	February
£8,000	£8,000	£10,000	£20,000	£6,000	£6,000

Plunket allows credit to some of his regular customers, and the proportions of cash and credit sales are usually :

	Cash Sales	Credit sales
November	80%	20%
December	60%	40%
All other months	90%	10%

Customers who buy on credit normally pay in the following month. Plunket's gross profit margin is consistently 25% of his selling price. He normally maintains his stocks at a constant level by purchasing goods in the month in which they are sold; the only exception to this is that in November he purchases in advance 50% of the goods he expects to sell in December.

Half of the purchases each month are made from suppliers who give a 2% cash discount for immediate payment and Plunket takes advantage of the discount. He pays for the remainder (without discount) in the month after purchase.

Expenditure on wages and other running expenses of the shop are consistently £2,000 per month paid in the month in which they are incurred.

Leasehold premises and fittings are depreciated at 10% per annum on cost price in Plunket's accounts.

Required :
(a) The preparation of :
(i) a cash budget showing Plunket's bank balance or overdraft for each month in the half year ending 28 February, 19-2.
(ii) Plunket's balance sheet at 28 February, 19-2.

(b) If Plunket's bank manager considered it necessary to fix the overdraft limit at £3,500, explain what Plunket should do in order to observe the limit.

EXERCISE 11.2

The directors of Smith Ltd are considering the company's trading estimates for the six months to 31 October, 19-0.

It is expected that the balance sheet on 30 April, 19-0 will be as follows :

	£		£
Issued share capital	30,000	Fixed assets, at cost	56,000
Profit and loss account	18,500	Less: depreciation	20,000
			36,000
Trade creditors	11,000		
Expense creditors	5,500	Stock in trade	28,000
Bank overdraft	17,000	Trade debtors	18,000
	82,000		82,000

In the absence of certain adjustments considered later, the transactions for the half year ended 31 October, 19-0 have been estimated as follows :

	£
Purchases	72,000
Expenses	36,000
Sales	120,000

The above transactions will take place at a constant rate throughout the period, as did the transactions of the preceding six months. All payments are made to creditors and received from debtors in the month after a transaction occurs.

In addition to the above items, Smith Ltd must buy an essential fixed asset for £9,000 at some time during the six months to 31 October, 19-0.

The company's overdraft limit is currently £17,000, but the bank is pressing for a reduction. There is to be a limit of £12,000 from the end of May until 31 October, 19-0 after which the overdraft limit will be reduced to £6,000.

The company's directors are considering the following *alternative* methods of securing funds :

(i)   A reduction of stock by £8,000 (from the figure of £28,000 which is normally maintained). Sales per month would be reduced by £7,000, on which the gross profit margin lost would be 30%. Monthly expenses would be reduced by £1,500.

(ii)   A discount of $2^1/_2$% would be offered to debtors who paid promptly. It can be assumed for the purposes of calculation that (net) payment would be received at the time of sale. It is expected that 50% of debtors would take the discount; the remaining 50% of debtors would continue to take one month's credit.

Either alternative would be put into effect from 1 May, 19-0. That is to say, stocks would be run down £8,000 in May by curtailing purchases, *or* sales in that month would be eligible for the $2^1/_2$% discount.

Assume that bank interest would not be significantly different under either alternative, and that it can be ignored.

The company does not contemplate any transactions which are not mentioned above.

Required :

(a)   Calculations showing the reduction in net profit per month resulting from each alternative method of providing funds. Comment briefly on your results.

(b)   A monthly cash budget for the half year ending 31 October, 19-0 adopting the superior of the alternatives calculated above. Assume that the fixed asset will be bought and paid for at the earliest possible date, provided the payment will not cause the overdraft limit to be exceeded.

(c)   Your answer to the following questions :

         If someone offered the company a loan of £8,000, what is the absolute maximum rate of interest per month which it would be worthwhile for Smith Ltd to pay, if the company could repay the loan and interest at its convenience after 31 October 19-0?

         Adopt calendar months throughout, and ignore differences in length.
         Ignore taxation.

EXERCISE 11.3

Morgan has established a manufacturing company, Morgan Ltd which has not yet started manufacturing or selling. The company's balance sheet at 20 September, 19-2 is as follows :

	£		£
Issued share capital	21,000	Equipment at cost	18,000
		Stock in trade	3,000
	21,000		21,000

Morgan has asked your advice regarding working capital needs. He gives the following estimates for the company's first year's trading :

	Estimates for year ending 30 September 19-3 £	Estimated credit period (weeks)
Sales	60,000	6
Materials	24,000	4
Wages	18,000	1
Rent	5,000	2
Sundry expenses	6,000	3
Depreciation	1,800	-
Directors' remuneration	3,000	-
Retained profit	2,200	-
	60,000	

The estimated credit period are based on the average time Morgan expects to delay before paying for goods or services received, and on the average time he expects his customers to delay payment for the goods sold by Morgan Ltd. It can be assumed that all transactions involving credit will take place at an even rate throughout a year of *50 weeks* (for ease of calculation).

Director's remuneration will be drawn in full at the end of the year, just prior to the balance sheet date. Stock-in-trade will be maintained at the opening level of £3,000.

Morgan would like to obtain an overdraft to finance the company's working capital needs. For the purpose of calculations assume that all overdraft requirements will be granted, and any surplus cash will be retained in the bank account.

Ignore taxation and bank interest.

Required :

(a)   A cash budget which will be sufficient to reveal the maximum overdraft requirements, on the basis of the information available. For this purpose it can be assumed that all cash transactions (except directors remuneration) occur at exactly weekly intervals (e.g. the first week's wages are paid on Monday of Week 2, etc.). Do not continue the cash budget for more weeks than necessary.

(b)   The estimated balance sheet of Morgan Ltd at 30 September, 19-3 on the basis of the information available.

(c)   Assume that Morgan wishes to pay for all materials at an average interval of one week (instead of four weeks) in order to obtain discounts. Calculate the increase or decrease in -

(i)   The maximum overdraft

and   (ii)   the bank overdraft/balance in the balance sheet at 30 September, 19-3.

Ignore the discount saving for calculation purposes.

(d)   Assume that the credit period taken by customers proves to be eight weeks.
Calculate the increase of decrease in

(i)   the maximum overdraft

and   (ii)   the bank overdraft/balance in the balance sheet at 30 September,19-3.

EXERCISE 11.4

Mason has a business as a jobbing builder and decorator. Towards the end of September 19-4, he asks his bank to increase his overdraft limit to meet certain expenditures on a contract he is undertaking,.

The contract will take three months to complete and Mason will receive £12,000 for this work in January 19-5. His costs on the contract work will include wages of £2,000 per month in the months of October and November, and £1,000 in December. In addition he will purchase materials for the contract amounting to

£2,500 in October and £800 in November. Wages are all paid in the month in which they are incurred, but Mason will obtain one month's credit on his purchases for the contract.

Mason also undertakes other work which has been running at a consistent level of £9,000 per month in recent months; this level is expected to be maintained in the last three months of 19-4. These customers take an average credit period of two months. For this work Mason normally incurs wages of 30% of the sales value, and purchases materials equal to 30% of the sales value every month. The wage and material costs are entirely variable with changes in sales value, and both are paid in the month in which they are incurred.

Mason incurs £2,500 in general expenses each month. These can be considered as fixed irrespective of the level of sales activity, and are paid in the month in which they are incurred.

Assume that Mason's overdraft on 30 September, 19-4 is £4,000 and that the bank agrees an overdraft limit of £8,000 for the last three months of 19-4, after which the limit will be reviewed. Mason agrees, if necessary, to reduce his normal sales activity in order to keep within the overdraft limit.

Assume that all receipts and payments occur on the last day of each month.

Required:
(a)   An analysis showing, for the three months to 31 December, 19-4 Mason's bank overdraft at the end of each month if his original estimates are followed precisely.

(b)   If there are any months in which Mason's normal sales would have to be reduced in order to keep to the agreed overdraft limits, state the months involved and the corresponding amounts by which sales would be reduced.

NOTE   Ignore bank interest and confine your calculations to the transactions specified above.

EXERCISE 11.5 EX

Norman Berman is a trader whose draft balance sheet as at 30 June, 19-2 is as follows :

Balance Sheet at 30 June 19-2

	£ 000s		£ 000s	£ 000s
Capital				
Balance at 1 July 19-1	120	Fixed assets at cost		89
Add: Net Profit	24	Less: Depreciation		31
Less: Drawings	(18)			58
Balance at 30 June 19-2	126			
Current Liabilities		Current Assets		
Trade creditors	32	Stock in trade	64	
		Trade debtors	35	
		Bank	1	100
	158			158

There is a buoyant demand for Berman's products, and sales have increased steadily over the years. The following forecasts and estimates are made for the year ending 30 June, 19-3.

1.   Forecast monthly sales are as follows :

19-2. July-December £40,000 per month
19-3. January-June £45,000 per month
19-3. July-December £50,000 per month

2.   The gross profit margin will be 20% on sales.

3.   It is Berman's policy to maintain stocks, at the end of each month, sufficient to cover the expected sales for the following two months.

4.	The period of credit allowed to customers and obtained from suppliers is expected to remain the same as for the year ended 30 June, 19-2 - i.e. one month.

5.	Berman has sufficient accommodation for the planned increase in sales, but vehicles and equipment costing £20,000 will need to be purchased and paid for in December 19-2.

6.	Wages and general expenses (including an allowance for bank interest) are paid for in the month that they are incurred and will amount to £5,000 per month.

7.	The depreciation charge for the year is to be £12,000.

8.	Berman will withdraw £2,000 each month for personal use.

9.	Berman's bank has agreed to provide any overdraft facilities required during the year ended 30 June, 19-3 and will charge interest at a rate of 18% per annum.

Required :
(a)	A forecast cash statement, showing the bank balance or overdraft at the end of each month, for the year ending 30 June,19-3.

(b)	Berman's forecast profit and loss account for the year ending 30 June 19-3.

(c)	Berman's forecast balance sheet at 30 June 19-3.

(d)	A discussion of the respective merits of bank overdraft finance as compared with loan finance, in the light of Berman's requirements, assuming that he could alternatively finance the purchase of vehicles and equipment by raising a five year loan at a fixed interest rate of 15% per annum.

NOTE	Ignore taxation.

	Assume for the purpose of the question that your calculations are being made on 1 July, 19-2 and that the year to 30 June, 19-3 consists of twelve months of equal length.

EXERCISE 11.6 EX

The summarised final accounts of Michael, a trader, for the year ended 30 June, 19-1 are as follows :

Profit and Loss Account year ended 30 June,19-1

		£	£
Sales			480,000
Less: Cost of goods sold			360,000
Gross profit			120,000
Less:	Depreciation	10,000	
	General expenses	96,000	106,000
Net Profit			14,000

Balance Sheet as at 30 June, 19-1

	£		£	£
Capital	97,000	Fixed assets at cost		100,000
		Less: Depreciation		30,000
Trade creditors	60,000			70,000
		Current Assets		
		Stock in trade	45,000	
		Trade Debtors	40,000	
		Bank	2,000	
				87,000
	157,000			157,000

168

Michael has approached your bank for a loan to finance the acquisition of additional freehold premises. The premises are situated next door to his existing premises and occupation could be obtained on 1 October, 19-1. The premises would cost £50,000 and payment would be made during the month of October. There is a heavy demand for the goods which Michael sells and he is confident that from 1 October monthly sales can be increased by 20% if the additional premises are obtained. The gross profit percentage would remain unchanged and general expenses, inclusive of an allowance for bank interest at 15%, would increase by £1,200 per month from 1 September. Michael intends to employ two sources of finance for the planned expansion.

1.   He will offer customers a discount of 2 % for immediate payment on all sales made from 1 October, 19-1 onwards. He expects half the customers to take advantage of this offer. The remaining customers will take the same period of credit as in the previous year.

2.   He has asked for a bank overdraft facility of £20,000 for the next twelve months.

Michael expects creditors to increase in proportion to sales; the stock-in-trade balance will remain at £45,000. The depreciation charge on existing fixed assets will remain unchanged. The additional buildings will be depreciated on the straight line basis assuming a life of twenty years; for this purpose the buildings are considered to comprise £40,000 of the planned expenditure on premises referred to above. General expanses are paid monthly for cash; Michael draws £ 1,000 from the business bank account each month to cover personal expenditure.

Required :

(a)   Michael's estimated profit and loss account for the year ended 30 June, 19-2 and estimated balance sheet at 30 June, 19-2.

(b)   Calculations of the estimated maximum overdraft Michael will require during the year to 30 June, 19-2 and of his bank balance or overdraft at 30 June, 19-2.

(c)   An assessment of Michael's plans for expansion.

NOTE
1.   There are no seasonal fluctuations in the level of activity in Michael's trade
2.   Purchases and sales take place evenly during the year
3.   Your calculations under (a) and (b) should be based on the assumption that the bank agrees to finance the planned expansion.

EXERCISE 11.7 EX

Canton Ltd was recently incorporated and plans to commence trading on 1 June,19-9. During May the company will issue 200,000 ordinary shares of £1 each at par and the cash will be subscribed at once. During the same month £ 130,000 will be spend on plant and £50,000 will be invested in stock, resulting in a cash balance on 1 June of £20,000.

Plans for the twelve months commencing 1 June 19-9 are as follows :

1.   Stock costing £40,000 will be sold each month at a mark-up of 25%. Customers are expected to pay in the second month following the sale.

2.   Month-end stock levels will be maintained at £50,000 and purchases will be paid for in the month following delivery.

3.   Wages and other expenses will amount to £6,000 per month, payable in the month during which the costs are incurred.

4.   Bad debts are expected to be incurred at the rate of 2% of sales.

5.   Plant will have a ten year life and no scrap value. Depreciation is to be charged on the straight line basis.

169

Required :

(a)   A cash budget for Canton Ltd which will be sufficient to reveal the maximum overdraft requirement on the basis of the information available. Do not continue the cash budget for more months than necessary.

(b)   The company's estimated trading and profit and loss account for the year ending 31 May, 19-0 and estimated balance sheet at 31 May, 19-0.

(c)   A calculation of the *additional* sales which would be needed in order to produce *additional* profits sufficient to cover a dividend of 6% on the issued share capital. For this purpose you may regard depreciation and 75% of wages and other expenses as fixed costs and the remainder as directly variable with output.

NOTE

The company's bank has agreed to provide the necessary overdraft facilities.

EXERCISE 11.8 EX

Castellane Ltd is a company trading in a single product. Its summarised profit and loss account for the year ended 31 December, 19-9 and balance sheet at 31 December, 19-9 were as follows :

Profit and Loss Account

		£	£
Sales (200,000 units)			432,000
Less:	Cost of goods sold	240,000	
	Depreciation : 10% on cost	20,000	
	Wages and salaries	42,000	
	Other expenses	90,000	392,000
Net profit			40,000
Taxation			16,000
Retained profit			24,000

Balance Sheet

	£		£
Share capital	100,000	Fixed assets at cost	200,000
Reserves	50,000	Less: depreciation	63,000
	150,000		137,000
Trade creditors	20,000	Stock	40,000
Tax due 30 September 19--0	16,000	Trade debtors	36,000
Bank overdraft	27,000		
	213,000		213,000

The cost of goods sold varies directly with the number of units sold, whilst depreciation, wages and salaries and other expenses are fixed for sales up to 350,000 units per annum.

The demand for Castellane Limited's product is responsive to price changes, and investigations have revealed that a reduction in the price charged to customers to £2 per unit would enable sales to be increased to 300,000 units per annum. Accordingly, the directors advertised the lower price to come into effect for sales made on and after 1 January, 19-0. The company's policy is to maintain stocks at the equivalent of two months' sales at cost. Arrangements have been made for stock to be delivered on 1 January, 19-0 sufficient to accommodate the planned increase in sales activity. The company will receive from suppliers in 19-0 the same period of credit as was received in 19-9, i.e. one month. Wages and salaries and other expenses accrue evenly throughout the year and are paid on the last day of the month to which they relate.

The directors of Castellane are under no pressure from their company's bank to reduce the overdraft. Nevertheless they say that they 'would prefer to be in the black because we don't like borrowing'. Accordingly, they have approached a form of debt factors who have agreed to take over the debt collecting function beginning with sales made during the month of January 19-0. In view of Castellane's excellent history of debt collection, the debt factors will pay the company on the last day of each month 98% of the book value of debts taken over for that month. The company at present pays bank interest at the rate of 14% per annum on the outstanding balance.

Required :
(a)   A calculation of the value of the purchases to be made during January 19-0.

(b)   A cash budget for 19-0 showing the bank balance or overdraft at the end of each month.

(c)   A forecast profit and loss account for the year to 31 December, 19-0 and forecast balance sheet at that date. Taxation should be provided at 40% on the forecast profit for the year,

(d)   Brief comments on the financial effects of the directors' decision to employ the services of a firm of debt factors.

NOTE   There is no seasonal variation in the level of business activity.
Assume a 360 day year consisting of twelve months of 30 days each.

EXERCISE 11.9 EX

Alan Cheep is the managing director of Shedford Sports Ltd which runs a chain of shops selling sportswear and equipment. The company owns some of the shops and rents the others. Cheep has the opportunity to purchase two of the shops (currently rented from Newbolt City Council) at a total cost of £120,000 payable in two equal instalments on 31 January 1989 and 31 January 1990. Cheep has decided to approach the company's bank to finance the acquisition. His accountant has prepared the following forecasts and estimates:

(i)

FORECAST BALANCE SHEET AT 31 DECEMBER 1988

	£	£
Fixed assets at cost less depreciation		425,000
Current assets		
Stocks of sportswear and equipment	172,000	
Due from credit card companies	22,500	
Balance of cash at bank	1,500	
	196,000	
Less: current liabilities		
Trade creditors	42,000	
Net current assets		154,000
		579,000
Financed by:		
Share capital		200,000
Reserves		379,000
		579,000

(ii)

FORECAST REVENUES AND EXPENSES FOR 1989

Quarter	1st	2nd	3rd	4th
	£	£	£	£
Sales	200,000	220,000	250,000	240,000
Purchases of stock	135,000	165,000	165,000	150,000
Wages	26,000	27,000	27,000	28,000
Other expenses	43,000	41,000	43,000	40,000

(iii)   The balance outstanding from credit card companies at the end of each quarter is consistently in the region of 10% of quarterly sales. All other sales are for cash.

(iv)   Suppliers allow one months credit and you may assume that purchases accrue evenly within each quarter.

(v)   Wages include monthly director's remuneration of £2,500 for Alan Cheep.

(vi)   Other expenses include a charge for depreciation of £7,000 in the first quarter and £8,000 for each of the remaining three quarters.

(vii)   Wages and other expenses (excluding depreciation) are paid in the quarter in which they are incurred.

(viii) Interest is charged by the bank at 12% per annum and debited to the customer's bank statement on 30 June and 31 December. The interest charge for each half-year is to be based on the estimated cash deficiency (if any) mid-way through each half-year, i.e. on 31 March and 30 September respectively.

(ix)   Closing stock at 31 December 1989 is estimated at £180,000.

Required:

(a)   A cash budget prepared on the quarterly basis for 1989. Show the cash surplus or deficit at the end of each quarter.

(b)   A forecast of the profit for 1989.

(c)   A forecast balance sheet at 31 December 1989.

(d)   An estimate of the time it will take to repay the bank overdraft, assuming the forecast quarterly trading results for 1989 are repeated in future years.

NOTES:
(i)   Assume a corporation tax rate of 30% on reported profit.
(ii)   No dividends are to be paid in the foreseeable future.
(iii)   Assume each quarter consists of 90 days.
(iv)   Ignore credit card charges.

(Autumn 1988)

EXERCISE 11.10 EX

Mr Dimbula, a sole trader, has been in business for a number of years. The summarised trading and profit and loss account for the year to 30 September 1989 was as follows:

Summarised Trading and profit and loss account
Year to 30 September 1989

	£000	£000
Sales (all on credit)		600
Less: Variable costs: purchases	420	
Fixed costs: general expenses, etc	140 *	560
Net Profit		40

* General expenses include depreciation of £8,000 on fixed assets.

Dimbula believes that sales and profits can be increased by changing the credit terms for his product for which there exists a strong demand. The following plans and estimates are made on 1 October 1989:

(1)   In October 1989 Dimbula will issue a circular informing customers that the period of credit allowed will be increased from one to two months on all sales from 1 January 1990.

(2)   The more favourable credit terms will produce an increase in monthly sales, over present levels, of 20% from January 1990.

(3)   The period of credit received from suppliers will remain unchanged at one month.

(4)   It is Dimbula's policy to maintain stocks at a level equivalent to expected sales over the following two months. Stocks at 30 September 1989 were £70,000, to cover expected sales in October and November.

(5)   General expenses accrue evenly during the year and, depreciation apart, are paid on a monthly basis.

At 30 September 1989 Dimbula's bank balance stood at £10,000. The bank has agreed to provide overdraft facilities to cover any cash requirements over the forthcoming twelve month period.

Required :

(a)   A cash budget showing the forecast bank balance or overdraft at the end of each month during the year to 30 September 1990.

(b)   Calculate the **extra** profit resulting from the new credit policy in the year to 30 September 1990.

NOTES:

(i)   Trading transactions occurred at an even rate during the year to 30 September 1989.
(ii)   Assume that each year consists of twelve months of equal length.
(iii)   Assume you are making the calculations on 1 October 1989.

(Autumn 1989)

SOLUTIONS

SOLUTION 11.1

(a)   (i)

Cash Budget

	Sep. £	Oct. £	Nov. £	Dec. £	Jan. £	Feb. £
Receipts:						
Cash sales	7,200	7,200	8,000	12,000	5,400	5,400
Credit sales	800	800	800	2,000	8,000	600
	8,000	8,000	8,800	14,000	13,400	6,000
Payments:						
Cash purchases	2,940	2,940	7,350	3,675	2,205	2,205
Credit purchases	3,000	3,000	3,000	7,500	3,750	2,250
Wages and expenses	2,000	2,000	2,000	2,000	2,000	2,000
	7,940	7,940	12,350	13,175	7,955	6,455
Bank balance at start of month	− 1,050	− 990	− 930	− 4,480	− 3,655	+ 1,790
Add Receipts (as above)	8,000	8,000	8,800	14,000	13,400	6,000
	6,950	7,010	7,870	9,520	9,745	7,790
Less Payments (as above)	7,940	7,940	12,350	13,175	7,995	6,455
Bank balance at end of month	− 990	− 930	− 4,480	− 3,655	+ 1,790	+ 1,335

(a)   (ii)

Estimated Balance Sheet as at 28 February, 19-2

	£		£	£
Capital (31 August 19-1)	13,750	Leasehold premises at cost	10,000	
Add net profit	2,185	Less: depreciation	2,500	
	15,935			7,500
		Fittings at cost	5,000	
Trade creditors	2,250	Less depreciation	1,250	
				3,750
		Stock-in-trade		5,000
		Trade debtors		600
		Bank		1,335
	18,185			18,185

NOTE:

Net profit is arrived at, viz:	£
Sales	58,000
Gross Profit = 25% of £58,000	14,500
Less wages and expenses	12,000
	2,500
Less depreciation	750
	1,750
Add discounts received	435
Net Profit	2,185

<u>Creditors</u>

February sales = £6,000

Cost of these sales = £4,500 (which gives a gross profit of £1,500 which is 25% of sales)

Half of £4,500 is paid immediately so leaving £2,250 still owing at end of February.

<u>Depreciation</u> is for half a year only!

The balance sheet in the question shows creditors (£3,000 and debtors (£800) at 31 August, 19-1, so we can assume that these represent purchases on credit in August, and sales on credit in August respectively.

(b) If Plunket did not have to purchase the extra goods in November in readiness for the following month, he would only go overdrawn £ 805 in November, and would be in credit for the following months. However, Plunket probably *has* to purchase in advance to ensure having sufficient stock in December to meet the heavy demand.

Another alternative would be for him to utilise some of the £5,000 stock-in-trade which is normally maintained at this level, so saving on purchases in certain months.

Probably the best course would be for Plunket to reduce the proportion of *credit* sales he allows in November and December, thereby receiving more cash from sales in these months.

(Note to student: Calculate by how much the percentages of credit sales would need to be reduced in order to stay within the overdraft limit).

SOLUTION 11.2

(a) (i) If sales are reduced by £7,000 per month then 30% of this will be lost in profits - i.e. £2,100 less profits. A reduction in expenses of £1,500 per month will have the effect of increasing profits by £1,500. A decrease of £2 ,100 and an increase of £1,500 = *a net decrease of £600*.

(ii) If $2^1/_2$ % discount is allowed to half of the debtors per month this is equivalent to an extra expense of £250 per month ($2^1/_2$% of £10,000) - This will *decrease profits by £250*.

Alternative (ii) is the superior of the two.

Cash Budget based on Alternative (ii)

(b)

	May £	June £	July £	August £	Sept. £	Oct. £
Receipts						
Credit Sales	18,000	10,000	10,000	10,000	10,000	10,000
Cash Sales	9,750	9,750	9,750	9,750	9,750	9,750
	27,750	19,750	19,750	19,750	19,750	19,750
Payments						
Purchases	11,000	12,000	12,000	12,000	12,000	12,000
Expenses	5,500	6,000	6,000	6,000	6,000	6,000
Fixed Asset			9,000			
	16,500	18,000	27,000	18,000	18,000	18,000
Bank balance at start	−17,000	−5,750	−4,000	−11,250	−9,500	−7,750
Receipts	27,750	19,750	19,750	19,750	19,750	19,750
	10,750	14,000	15,750	8,500	10,250	12,000
Less: Payments	16,500	18,000	27,000	18,000	18,000	18,000
Bank balance at end	−5,750	−4,000	−11,250	−9,500	−7,750	−6,000

175

(c)   With such a loan, there would be no need to offer cash discounts - so providing the interest on the loan cost less than £250 per month it would be worthwhile. Therefore the maximum rate of interest would have to be :

$$\frac{25}{8,000} \quad \text{x} \ 100 = 3.125\%$$

SOLUTION 11.3

(a)

Cash Budget

(£) Week:	1	2	3	4	5	6	7
Balance at start of week	-	-	(360)	(820)	(1,400)	(2,460)	(3,520)
Sales Receipts							1,200
							2,320
Payments :							
Purchases					480	480	480
Wages	-	360	360	360	360	360	360
Rent	-	-	100	100	100	100	100
Sundry expenses	-	-	-	120	120	120	120
	-	(360)	(820)	(1,400)	(2,460)	(3,520)	(3,380)

MaximumOverdraft

Balance Sheet

(b)

	£		£
Issued Share Capital	21,000	Equipment at cost	18,000
Profit and loss account	2,200	Less: Depreciation	1,800
			16,200
Creditors	1,920		
Expenses due	360	Stock	3,000
Wages due	360	Debtors	7,200
Rent due	200		
Bank	360		
	26,400		26,400

(c)   Payment for purchases of materials at one week intervals would reduce creditors to £480, being a reduction of £1,440, which is equal to a reduction in cash - i.e. the overdraft would increase to *£1,800*. It would involve additional payments in weeks 2, 3 and 4 of £480 which would increase the maximum overdraft by £1,440.

(d)   An increase in the period of credit given to customers to 8 weeks would mean that debtors at 30 September, 19-3 would be £9,600 - an increase of £2,400 which is equal to an application of cash of £2,400, so giving an overdraft of £ 2,760. Increasing the credit means that Morgan would be paying out £1,060 (see budget) in weeks 7 and 8 without any cash coming in from sales to offset this. His maximum overdraft would therefore be increased by 2 x £1,060 = *£2,120.*

NOTE to Students :

There are other ways of arriving at the answers - the main thing is to arrive at the correct answer fairly quickly!

SOLUTION 11.4

(a)

Cash Budget

	October £	November £	December £
Receipts			
Normal Sales	9,000	9,000	9,000
Payments			
Contract Wages	2,000	2,000	1,000
Purchase of materials for contract	-	2,500	800
Normal Wages	2,700	2,700	2,700
Normal purchases	2,700	2,700	2,700
General expenses	2,500	2,500	2,500
	9,900	12,400	9,700
Bank balance (overdraft) at start	(4,000)	(4,900)	(8,300)
Receipts	9,000	9,000	9,000
	5,000	4,100	700
Less: Payments	9,900	12,400	9,700
	(4,900)	(8,300)	(9,000)

(b) November's overdraft must be reduced by £300, so normal sales must be reduced thereby reducing wages and purchases of materials for that month. For every £100 reduction in sales there would be a saving on these expenses of £60 (60% of sales). Therefore to 'save' £300, sales would need to be reduced by £500 (300 + 60 x 100).

December's overdraft would now stand at £8,700, and to reduce this by £700 would involve reducing sales by £1,166 (700 + 60 x 100).

Receipts from debtors in the period in question would not be affected because of the 2 months' credit period.

LESSON 12

ACCOUNTING RATIOS AND GEARING

Ratios

When a banker is considering lending money to a business many factors will be taken into account in arriving at a decision of whether to lend or not. The past record of the business customer will obviously be relevant and first hand knowledge of the character, integrity and abilities of the trader, the partners or the directors will certainly influence the decision. In addition the good banker will apply sound reasoning to the proposition put to him, taking into account those aspects of the law and current banking practice which are relevant to that situation. All of this will form a major part of your 'Practice of Banking' studies in the future.

Before arriving at a final decision the banker will want to see the profit and loss accounts and balance sheets of the business for past years in order to observe its state of 'financial health' and progress, good or otherwise. Often these accounts will provide information on the capabilities of management within the business. Here, the manager is looking at what has already happened (i.e. past accounts) - he will also want to see what is likely to happen in the future and will therefore need to study projected accounts and statements - i.e. records of what the position is likely to be in the future on the basis of estimates. Again, the detailed study of this area will form part of your future 'Practice of Banking' studies.

As the banker interprets the accounts in front of him he will obviously be making comparisons - for example he will note that sales have increased between one year and another or that profits are 'down on last year' etc., etc. It is not sufficient however to note these things in isolation. A weakness in one area may be compensated for by increased strength in another area. He must, therefore, look at the whole picture and note relationships between items, particularly changing relationships.

To do this he will employ a technique known as *ratio analysis* whereby he will analyse the relationship between one item in the accounts and another.

There are scores of ratios which *can* be calculated and commented on. Many of them however reveal very little useful information and become merely an academic exercise. We are now going to look at a few standard ratios which are regularly employed and which do provide useful 'pointers'. For the purpose of illustrating these ratios we will use a simple set of accounts and balance sheet as a reference basis :

Trading and Profit & Loss Account

	£		£
Stock	4,000	Sales	60,000
Purchases	38,000		
	42,000		
Less: Stock	6,000		
Cost of Goods sold	36,000		
Gross Profit	24,000		
	60,000		60,000
Various Expenses	11,500	Gross Profit	24,000
Interest on Loan	500		
Depreciation	3,000		
Net Profit	9,000		
	24,000		24,000

178

Dividend paid	9,000	Balance b/fwd	10,000
Balance c/d	10,000	Net Profit	9,000
	19,000		19,000

Balance Sheet

	£		£
Issued Share Capital	30,000	Fixed Assets	39,000
Reserves	10,000		
		Current Assets	
Long Term Loans	5,000	Stock	7,000
		Debtors	4,000
Current Liabilities	6,000	Bank	1,000
	51,000		51,000

RATIOS APPLIED :

Gross Profit Margin

Formula

$$\frac{\text{Gross Profit}}{\text{Sales}} \quad x \quad \frac{100}{1} \quad = \quad \%$$

$$= \quad \frac{24,000}{60,000} \quad x \quad \frac{100}{1} \quad = \quad 40\%$$

This is a key ration for most types of business, and is simply the gross profit expressed as a percentage of sales. It measures the efficiency of the main area of activity (i.e. buying and selling). Remember that the gross profit has to cover all expenses (in the profit and loss account) and leave something over for final profit (net profit). In types of businesses which naturally have many overheads (e.g. hotel and catering industry) the gross profit needs to form a large percentage of sales in order to cover those overheads - i.e. a large gross profit margin. Other businesses with few expenses can manage with a low profit margin.

The main thing is that the margin should remain at a fairly constant level year by year and should therefore be compared with previous years. This is because as sales increase (or decrease), cost of goods sold should increase or decrease in proportion, so that although the gross profit *amount* changes, its relationship with the changed sales figure is the same.

If there is a significant change in this percentage figure it should be investigated. If it has fallen it could be due to increased costs of supplies not being passed on to selling price, or it could be due to reduced selling prices whilst cost of supplies remains the same. The latter reason is sometimes accompanied by a large increase in volume of sales (as a result of cut selling price).

Try altering the sales and cost of goods sold figures in the above model and observe the results with these comments in mind.

Net Profit Margin

Formula

$$\frac{\text{Net profit (before tax and dividends)}}{\text{Sales}} \quad x \quad \frac{100}{1} \quad = \quad \%$$

$$= \quad \frac{9,000}{60,000} \quad x \quad \frac{100}{1} \quad = \quad 15\%$$

This is an extension of the gross profit margin, i.e. allowing for expenses.

By comparing this return with previous years attention can be drawn to any disproportionate increases in expenses generally. For example, using the model accounts above, if we increase sales by 100% *and* increase expenses by 100% then the return remains at 15%. Now - if sales have increased then there should have been *some* increase in our net profit return because some of the expenses will be *fixed* (i.e an increase in sales does not cause a proportionate increase in the expense - e.g. rates) and a doubling of sales should *not* cause a doubling of *all* expenses (only the perfectly variable ones).

Again alter the figures in the model and observe the results first-hand.

Return on Ordinary Shareholders Capital (on Equity)

Formula $\dfrac{\text{Net Profit before tax and dividends}}{\text{Ordinary Share Capital plus reserves}}$ x $\dfrac{100}{1}$ =   %

= $\dfrac{9,000}{40,000}$ x $\dfrac{100}{1}$ =   22.5%

This is sometimes referred to as *'return on equity'* and shows what has been earned from the ordinary shareholders' provision of funds (i.e. their share capital plus what they have left in the business as reserves). It shows how effectively the ordinary shareholders' funds are being used by the management - in this example to create a return of $22^{1}/_{2}$% before tax which is good. If the return had been, say, 5% then the ordinary shareholders might be thinking that their money would be earning more in the bank or building society without the same risk, and this ratio tends therefore to be of more interest to the ordinary shareholders than to others, e.g. the bank. Note that *preference* share capital is not counted in this ratio.

Return on Long Term Capital Employed

Formula $\dfrac{\text{Net Profit before interest, tax and dividends}}{\text{Total Issued Share Capital plus reserves}}$ x $\dfrac{100}{1}$ =   %
                                    plus long term loans

= $\dfrac{9,500}{45,00}$ x $\dfrac{100}{1}$ =   21% (approx)

Whereas the previous ratio showed how effectively the ordinary shareholders' funds were being used in the business, this ratio shows how effectively *all* of the long term capital at the company's disposal is being used. Our model company has £45,000 of long term funds to 'play around with' and has generated a return of profit of over 21% which is an indication of pretty efficient management.

To a lender such as the bank this is a very useful indicator of how efficiently funds available are being used.

Return on Gross Assets

The last two ratios measured the efficiency with which companies were using the long term capital available to them. An extension of this would be to see how effectively the company was using the long term *and* the short term capital (i.e. creditors, proposed tax, bank overdraft etc.). This, on the basis that creditors etc. are providing funds to the company for its use, even if on a short term. We are now, therefore, looking at *all* the providers of finance - long and short-term - i.e all of the liabilities, which is the same, of course, as saying all of the assets, hence 'return on gross assets'.

The ratio would be expressed :

$$\frac{\text{Net Profit before Interest}}{\text{Total Assets}} \qquad x \quad 100 \quad = \quad \%$$

This shows how effectively total finance available to the company is being utilised.

A useful indicator, but one not readily accepted by all accountants, as short term credit can fluctuate so much, particularly where a business has seasonal trade. The two previous ratios - long term capital - are more meaningful in that they are generally more consistent.

NOTE

The last three ratios we have looked at are sometimes described loosely as 'Return on Capital Employed', without distinguishing between shareholders' capital, long term capital and total assets.

Ratio of Sales to Long Term Capital Employed

Formula
$$\frac{\text{Sales}}{\text{Long Term Capital}}$$

$$= \qquad \frac{60,000}{45,000} \qquad = \underline{\underline{1.33}}$$

This ratio measures the extent to which the capital employed 'brings in' the sales - not as important as seeing *how much profit* (as shown by the previous ratios).

Shareholders' Stake Ratio (i.e. Proprietorship Ratio).

To what extent are the owners (the shareholders) financing their own business, or conversely, what proportion of the total assets are financed by outsiders?

This ratio is found by taking the shareholders' total stake (share capital plus reserves) and expressing this as a percentage of the total assets.

Formula
$$\frac{\text{Share Capital + Reserves}}{\text{Total Assets}} \qquad x \quad 100$$

$$= \qquad \frac{40,000}{51,000} \qquad x \quad \frac{100}{1} \quad = \quad 78^1/_2 \text{ (approx)}$$

The shareholders' stake represents the amount of assets which are likely to *stay* in the company and is regarded by creditors (including banks) as a 'cushion of security' for them. A high percentage, as in this example, indicates a strong financial position with little reliance on outside funds.

It would be reasonable to expect that at lease 50% of assets are being financed by the owners themselves. Less than this and it isn't really *their* business! However, lenders such as banks will often accept a lower percentage but would be very uneasy if the percentage went below $33^1/_3\%$.

Having said this, one should not dismiss a low percentage off-hand without looking at the 'make-up' of these outside providers of finance. For example, the owners may only be financing 30% of total assets but perhaps long term loans (e.g. debentures) are financing another 40% - i.e. the company is 'high geared' (see pages 187/189) as a result of deliberate policy. There are occasions when a company benefits from being high geared (see later in lesson). Therefore it is very important to consider the make-up of that part of assets not being financed directly by the owners themselves. If there is heav y dependence on *short term* credit then this would certainly cause concern.

Current Ratio

Formula	$\dfrac{\text{Current Assets}}{\text{Current Liabilities}}$	=	? to 1
=	$\dfrac{12,000}{6,000}$	=	2 to 1 (i.e. 2:1)

We have already looked at this particular ratio in Lesson No. 8 and it should therefore be familiar to you. However, to recap, it is the ratio which gives an indication of the ability of the business to pay its short term debts (creditors, bank overdraft, etc.) without having to resort to selling off fixed assets. In other words it shows the ability to pay debts as they become due, and therefore the degree of solvency.

The *type* of business must be considered in deciding whether the ratio shown is adequate or not. A business which has, by its nature, to rely on large credit facilities (e.g. builders) is going to have to have a substantial current ratio (say, at least 2 to 1) in order to feel 'comfortable' at any one time, whereas a business which deals mainly in cash and has no real outlay on materials and labour before receipt of sales income would be quite 'comfortable' with a ratio of 1.5 to 1.

The *average* type of business in the UK has a current ratio of just over 1.5 to 1 so you must decide whether the business in question is average (regarding dependence on credit) or not.

In looking at this current ratio we are assuming that all current assets are fairly liquid - i.e. stock *is* selling and producing debtors who will pay cash within a fairly short space of time.

Suppose however, that stock is *not* selling and that if forms a substantial proportion of total current assets - in this case the current ratio is going to show a misleading picture. This is why an assessor of any accounts will, after looking at the current ratio of the business, now look at the :

Liquid Ratio

Formula	$\dfrac{\text{Current Assets LESS stocks}}{\text{Current Liabilities}}$		
=	$\dfrac{5,000}{6,000}$	= 0.83 to 1	(0.83:1)

We are now saying 'suppose stock is not selling quickly, then we cannot rely on these to provide *quick liquidity*' and we must therefore rely on the other current assets (usually debtors and bank) to provide immediate liquidity to meet any demands from short term creditors.

A very rough 'rule of thumb' here is to regard a 1 to 1 ratio as good - in other words, if a business can cover its current liabilities once over by using its debtors and cash only then it is unlikely to find itself in a position whereby it cannot meet demands for payment of debts. In all probability stock *is* selling and this adds to this ability.

You would normally expect to see a ratio of from 0.75 to 1 to 1.5 to 1, again depending on the *type* of business in question. Too high a ratio could mean that *too much* is being held in debtors (bad debts?) and bank - i.e. funds not being utilised effectively.

This ratio - 'Liquid Ratio' is sometimes referred to as the 'Quick' or 'Acid' ratio.

Stock Turnover

Formula

$$\frac{\text{Cost of Goods Sold}}{\text{Average Stock}} = \text{No. of times per year}$$

$$= \frac{36,000}{5,000 \text{ (average)}} = \underline{\underline{7.2}}$$

This ratio shows the speed with which the business turns over its stock (i.e. clears the stock room and replaces stock). A turnover of 4 indicates that as stock turns over 4 times in a year, then stock remains in the storeroom for an average of $^1/_4$ of a year - 3 months - before being sold.

The turnover of 7.2 indicates that stock is held for about 7 weeks on average before being sold. Note that where opening and closing stocks are given the average of these can be taken in your calculations.

Whether the turnover figure is satisfactory or not depends on the type of business. For a business dealing in very expensive and specialised equipment a turnover of 4 may be considered reasonable, but if the business in question was a fishmonger then something would be very wrong!

Obviously, with any business, the faster the turnover the better, because this is where profits are being made.

A comparison from year to year of this ratio may reveal interesting possibilities. For example, a quickening of turnover may be due to holding smaller stocks on average (and hence a danger of running out of stock!) or, ideally, due to increased sales. A slowing down of turnover could be due to a drop in demand, or holding too much stock (some of this 'excess' stock may in fact be 'bad stock').

If we look at the above formula the other way around this will immediately give us the number of days (or weeks) that stock takes to sell, viz :

$$\frac{(5,000) \text{ Average Stock}}{(36,000) \text{ Cost of Goods Sold}} \quad x \quad 365 \text{ days (52 weeks)} = 50 \text{ days (7 weeks)}$$

For the manufacturer the following formula could also be looked at :

a)

$$\frac{\text{Average Stock of Raw Materials}}{\text{Cost of Raw Material Used}} \quad x \quad 365 \text{ days} \qquad = \text{x days}$$

b)

$$\frac{\text{Average Stock of Work-in-Progress}}{\text{Cost of Goods Manufactured}} \quad x \quad 365 \text{ days} \qquad = \text{x days}$$

a)   Gives an indication of how long raw materials are 'lying around' before being processed.

b)   Shows the production time taken.

These are obviously good pointers to efficiency within the factory and comparisons with previous periods can provide very useful information.

Period of Credit Taken from Debtors

Formula $\quad$ $\dfrac{\text{Debtors (per Balance Sheet)}}{\text{Credit Sales for year}}$ $\quad$ x $\dfrac{365}{1}$ $\quad$ = $\quad$ No. of days

The above is an indication of how quickly, *on average*, the business collects its debts. The debtors in the formula must represent average debtors and this is why in examination questions you are often told to assume that sales occur evenly throughout the year. By taking these debtors as a proportion of total credit sales you can arrive at the proportion of the year taken as credit.

In normal trade 4/5 weeks credit is usually acceptable and if the period indicated exceeds this then an investigation is called for, unless there are circumstances to give good reason for excessive periods being granted.

Period of Credit Taken from Creditors

Formula $\quad$ $\dfrac{\text{Trade Creditors (per Balance Sheet)}}{\text{Purchases on credit for year}}$ $\quad$ x $\dfrac{365}{1}$ $\quad$ = $\quad$ No. of days

This gives similar information as in the previous ratio, but refers to creditors rather than debtors - i.e. how quickly the business pays its debts. Remember that when a business is experiencing a shortage of cash it will delay payment to creditors as long as possible and thus risk possible bankruptcy proceedings.

Cash Operating Cycle

You are now familiar with calculating stock turnover (how many days stock is held before being sold - on average) and in calculating how many days credit is obtainable from suppliers - again on average.

Obviously the difference between these two periods is of great importance to the business. If, for example the stock turnover was 28 days and the period of credit taken from suppliers was 30 days then this means that purchased stock is being sold two days before it has to be paid for. This could be expressed thus :

	Days
Stock Turnover	28
Credit from Suppliers	(30)
	(2)

This is a benefit to cash flow provided that the stock was actually *sold for cash* - i.e. cash is received before it need be used to pay the creditors. However, most businesses sell on credit and the cash from the sale may not be received for some time, even though the goods have actually been sold. Going back to the above example let us assume that debtors take, on average, 40 days to pay.

We now have the following situation :

	Days
Stock turnover	28
Credit to customers	40
Credit from suppliers	(30)
	38

184

i.e. a cash operating cycle of 38 days - the stock takes 28 days to sell and there is a further waiting period of 40 days before cash is received from the sale. A total waiting period of 68 days against which can be offset the 30 days allowed by creditors, so leaving 38 days during which the business has to 'carry', or finance, the cost of the stock. Obviously, the shorter this period is, the better.

Let us now consider a manufacturer who is additionally concerned as to how long raw materials remain in stock before being used, and how long work in progress takes to become finished goods. In other words, the period of waiting for cash (i.e. the cash operating cycle) starts with the purchase of the raw materials and ends when debtors pay for sales. During this period manufacturing costs are being added at each stage of production. We must therefore calculate separate periods of holding 'stock' for :

a) Raw materials - viz:

$$\frac{\text{Stocks of Raw Materials}}{\text{Cost of Raw Materials Used}} \quad x \quad 365 \text{ days} \quad = x \text{ days}$$

b) Work in Progress - viz:

$$\frac{\text{Stocks of W.I.P.}}{\text{Cost of Goods Manufactured}} \quad x \quad 365 \text{ days} \quad = x \text{ days}$$

c) Finished Goods - viz:

$$\frac{\text{Stocks of Finished Goods}}{\text{Cost of Goods Sold}} \quad x \quad 365 \text{ days} \quad = x \text{ days}$$

Then, adjustments must be made for periods of credit taken and given, to give a final cash operating cycle of so many days. Calculations would look like this :

	Days
Raw Materials Turnover	25
W.I.P. Turnover	20
Finished Goods Turnover	40
Credit to Customers	35
Credit from Customers	(28)
	92

Comparisons of the individual figures and the overall figure (92 days) with previous periods and with other similar business can effectively highlight changes in policy and in efficiency at various stages of production and selling.

Interest Cover

This ratio indicates to what extent the profits (*before* interest - known as Operating Profit) cover the liability for interest, and is calculated thus :

$$\frac{\text{Net Profit } \textit{before} \text{ Interest}}{\text{Interest Charges}}$$

Obviously the greater the cover the better for the business - e.g.

<u>Company A.</u>

$$\frac{\text{Net Profit before Interest £10,000}}{\text{Interest Charges £5,000}} \quad = \quad \text{Interest Cover of 2}$$

Whereas -

<u>Company B</u>

$$\frac{\text{Net Profit before Interest £10,000}}{\text{Interest Charges £1,000}} = \text{Interest Cover of 10}$$

Company B is finding it far easier to cover its interest charges than is Company A whose burden of interest charges is too great in relation to the profits being earned. Therefore the lower the interest cover ratio the more vulnerable is the business to demands from the providers of the loans in question.

A business which generates sufficient profits (before interest) to cover the interest commitments many times is obviously in a much stronger position. There is no 'rule of thumb' guide but a cover of 4/5 times would seem to be just about adequate.

The following remaining ratios could, and have, been examined so you must know them. I am not convinced as to their value in assessing a business because there are so many factors which could make nonsense of the indications given by the ratios - you must judge for yourself - think about it and discuss with colleagues and lecturers - get involved!

Fixed Asset Turnover and Total Asset Turnover

These are expressed respectively as :

a) $$\frac{\text{Sales}}{\text{Average Fixed Assets}} \quad : \quad 1$$

b) $$\frac{\text{Sales}}{\text{Average Total Assets}} \quad : \quad 1$$

The idea is that the greater the ratio is, will indicate how effectively the business is using its fixed, or total, assets. Imagine, for example, a business with £10,000 of assets generating sales of £100,000 - this gives a ratio of 10 : 1.

In its early years however the same business may only, using the same assets, generate sales of £50,000 giving a ratio of only 5 : 1.

Obviously, as the business develops and increases sales, the ratio will increase until the point is reached where more assets have to be purchased to cope with the increased sales - this will reduce the ratio immediately!

Think of the few surviving cotton mills in Lancashire using assets purchased 50 years ago - their ratio is very high but the companies concerned are living from day-to-day hoping they will survive.

Too many factors are involved for these ratios to be very meaningful - but you *must* be aware of them and of their limitations. This attitude, of course, applies in varying degrees to all ratios. Remember this!

Finally -

All of the above ratios can provide useful pointers as to how a business is operating but a ratio in isolation is meaningless - the overall picture must be looked at, and comparisons made wherever possible - i.e. comparisons with previous years in order to see the trend, and comparisons with similar businesses in the same trade. Only by doing this can ratios perform any useful function.

Remember that in analysing a particular year's accounts that there may be exceptional circumstances in that particular year - e.g. strikes, fires, legislation, new management etc.

The mere effect of a change of stock valuation policies (i.e. LIFO instead of FIFO for stock valuation) will create havoc in the accounts for that year for the purpose of interpreting. A 'one-off' purchase of an expensive fixed asset will obviously affect the current ratio even though this purchase may make the company much stronger in the future (but does the interpreter know this?). Seasonal trade in business can give wrong indications particularly where the 'season' coincides with the year end accounts (either way).

Overtrading - i.e. too much reliance on short-term credit, is considered dangerous and is usually frowned upon by bankers, but most of the successful companies today have gone through a period of overtrading to get where they are now!

Having looked at the various ratios etc., a good banker will, having taken heed of the limitations just referred to, clinch his final decision, one way or the other, by reference to *knowledge of his customer*.

In the examination you may be asked to calculate ratios and comment on the information produced. Do remember, that your comments on the possible significance of your ratios can command a lot of marks - therefore don't be content with simply working out ratios. Make your comments brief, but good.

Gearing

How do companies finance their activities? Apart from using credit given by suppliers and bank overdrafts for their day to day working capital requirements the bulk of their capital, used mainly for the purchase of fixed assets, is got by issuing shares and taking out long term loans. Some companies rely solely on the issue of shares as their source of capital, whilst others will issue debentures or loan stock either as a means to supplement share capital or to provide the bulk of their capital requirements.

It is important to note that shareholders receive part of the profits as dividends, the size of which depends on the amount of profit made - large profits mean large amounts *available* for shareholders (whether the profits are distributed, or not); no profits means that nothing is available for the shareholders. The providers of long term loans however (e.g. debenture holders) are entitled to a *fixed* rate of interest irrespective of the level of profits (or losses). Another important difference between dividends paid on shares and interest paid on debentures is that corporation tax is based on profits *before* payment of dividend but *after* payment of interest on debentures (i.e. debenture interest is charged in the profit and loss account).

The implications of these differences, between a company relying mainly on shares to provide capital and a company relying mainly on debentures can be great, and therefore it is important to note how a company's capital structure is *geared*.

Gearing expresses the relationship between the proportion of fixed interest capital, e.g. debentures *and* Preference Shares, to ordinary share capital. Where a company has a large proportion of its capital in the form of debentures *and* Preference Shares in relation to ordinary shares it is said to be *high geared :* conversely, when ordinary shares form the greater proportion of capital, with debentures and Preference Shares being the small proportion, the company is *low geared*.

Let us study some examples in order to see the impact of these different gearing structures :

EXAMPLE 1.

A Ltd and B Ltd each have total capital of £100,000 as follows :

	A Ltd £	B Ltd £
£1 Ordinary Shares	20,000	80,000
12% Debentures	80,000	20,000
	100,000	100,000

A Ltd is high geared at 4 to 1 (Debentures to shares) - 400%
B Ltd is low geared at 1 to 4 (Debentures to shares) - 25%

If both companies now make a profit (before tax) of £10,000 the position will be :

	A Ltd £	B Ltd £
Net Profit	10,000	10,000
Less Debenture interest	9,600	2,400
Available to ordinary shareholders	400	7,600
Earnings per share (i.e. maximum possible dividend)	2%	$9^1/_2$%

Which of these companies would you prefer to be a shareholder of? Obviously the low geared one. The reason for this situation is that with relatively low profits of £10,000 a disproportionately large slice of the profit was needed to finance the fixed amount of debenture interest, leaving little left for the shareholders.

Let us no look at the position in a period of high profits, say £20,000 per year before tax :

	A Ltd £	B Ltd £
Net Profit	20,000	20,000
Less Debenture interest (12%)	9,600	2,400
Available to ordinary shareholders	10,400	17,600
Earnings per share	52%	22%

This time the high geared company has produced the best return for shareholders. The reason for the reversal of fortune is that once the debenture interest has been paid for by profits, each extra £1 of profit is available to be spread over a relatively small number of shares, whereas in the low geared company there is more profit 'to spare' after payment of debenture interest, but this profit has to be spread over a much greater number of shares. Another way to observe the above situation is to say that despite large profits the main providers of finance (the debenture holders) still only receive their fixed 12% interest which amounts to cheap capital in the high profit situation.

Taxation

Whether profits are low or high, a company's bill for corporation tax will be that much smaller if the greater part of its capital is obtained by issuing debentures, because the interest on these is charged in the profit and loss account, so reducing the taxable profits of the company. This tax advantage is known as a 'tax shield' and makes debentures a popular means of finance.

Preference Shares

All the shares referred to so far we have assumed to be ordinary shares. If however, a company issues preference shares these will have a fixed rate of *dividend* (as debentures have a fixed rate of *interest*) and can, for purposes of gearing, be treated in the exact same way as we treated debentures in our calculations. The only thing to bear in mind when doing this is the fact that whereas debenture interest is payable whether profits are made or not, preference dividends are only paid if sufficient profits are made to meet the fixed dividends. However, with cumulative preference shares any unpaid dividends are carried forward as arrears to be set off against any future profits.

Debt/Equity Ratio

Gearing is measured by the debt/equity ratio which is expressed thus :

$$\frac{\text{Long Term Loans } plus \text{ Preference Shares}}{\text{Ordinary Share Capital + Reserves}} \times 100$$

EXERCISE 12.1

The following are summaries of revenue accounts for 19-9 and balance sheets at 31 December, 19-9 :

	Whiz Ltd £ 000s	Bang Ltd £ 000s
Revenue Accounts		
Cost of goods sold *(materials used)**	840	110
Wages, depreciation, expenses, etc.	120	100
Net Profit	40	40
Sales	1,000	250

italic refers to Bang Ltd

Balance Sheets

	Whiz Ltd £ 000s	Bang Ltd £ 000s
Issued ordinary shares	60	60
Issued 5% preference shares	–	40
Retained profit	40	30
5% debentures	–	40
Bank overdraft	–	20
Creditors	100	40
	200	230
Fixed assets	100	80
Stocks *(and work-in-progress)**	70	80
Debtors	9	70
Bank	21	–
	200	230

italic refers to Bang Ltd

Whiz Ltd is a supermarket firm; Bang Ltd is engaged in heavy constructional engineering.

Required :

(a) A table completed in the following form :

	Whiz Ltd	Bang Ltd
Current ratio		
Liquid ('quick' or 'acid') ratio		
Rate of stock turnover per annum		
Net earnings for ordinary shareholders as percentage of equity		
Earnings on long term capital employed (i.e. ordinary and preference shares and debentures)		
Net profit as a percentage of sales		

(b) Comment on the implication of the differences between the two companies revealed in part (a)

EXERCISE 12.2

The following information is provided relating to the affairs of two companies engaged in similar trading activities:

	A Ltd	B Ltd
	£	£
Ordinary Share Capital	800,000	500,000
15% Debentures	200,000	500,000

Each company earned a trading profit before finance charges of £110,000 in Year 1 and £190,000 in Year 2.

Corporation tax is charged at 50% on the trading profits after finance charges have been deducted.

The company pays out as dividends its entire after-tax profits.

Required :

(a) Summary profit and loss accounts, dealing with the results of each of the two companies' activities during Year 1 and Year 2, so far as the information given above permits.

(b) Calculations of after-tax profits, expressed as percentages of ordinary share capital for each company in respect of both Year 1 and Year 2.

(c) A discussion of the returns earned for shareholders over the two-year period.

EXERCISE 12.3

The following forecasts are provided in respect of Grassington Ltd a company trading in a single produce, for 19-4 :

	£ 000s
Sales	2,700
Purchases	1,800
Cost of goods sold	1,830
Average trade debtors outstanding	300
Average trade creditors outstanding	160
Average stock held	305

All purchases and sales are made on credit, and trading transactions are expected to occur at an even rate throughout the year.

Required :

(a)   Calculations of the rate of payment of creditors, the rate of collection of debtors and the rate of stock turnover.

(b)   A calculation of the expected cash operating cycle (i.e. the time lag between making payment to suppliers and collecting cash from customers in respect of goods purchased and sold) for 19-4.

(c)   Using the information provided, explain any one method by which the directors *might* achieve a reduction of £20,000 in the company's bank overdraft requirement at 31 December, 19-4 and demonstrate the effect on the cash operating cycle.

NOTE   Assume a 360 day year for the purpose of your calculations.

EXERCISE 12.4

The following information is provided in respect of three companies, of which one is a steel manufacturer, another is a grocery store chain and the third is a finance company. Extracts from the accounts of each of these companies are reproduced below.

Profit and Loss Account extracts

	Company A £ 000s	Company B £ 000s	Company C £ 000s
Turnover/Revenue	3,029	1,556	206
Net Profit	45	67	43

Summarised Balance Sheets

	Company A £ 000s	Company B £ 000s	Company C £ 000s
Fixed assets at book value	257	1,094	6
Stock	236	241	–
Debtors	9	201	1,347
Other assets	66	286	413
	568	1,822	1,766
Shareholders' equity	320	1,200	410
Long-term liabilities	64	321	578
Current liabilities	184	301	778
	568	1,822	1,766

Required :

(a)   Calculate the following accounting ratios for each of the three companies :

(i)   net profit percentage
(ii)   total asset turnover
(iii)   rate of return on gross assets
(iv)   liquidity ratio (assume that the 'other assets' are non-current for the purpose of this calculation).

(b)   Indicate which company you believe is the steel manufacturer, which is the grocery store chain and which is the finance company.
Briefly explain your choice using clues obtained from calculating the accounting ratios and from examining the accounting information provided.

EXERCISE 12.5 EX

Manufacturer Ltd and Bank Ltd are two independent companies which have no financial connection with each other.

The following are summaries of balance sheets at 31 December, 19-4 and excerpts from the companies' profit and loss accounts for the year ended 31 December, 19-4. :

	Manufacturer Ltd	Bank Ltd
	£ 000s	£ 000s
Issued Share Capital	13,000	2,000
Revenue Reserves	7,000	5,200
10% debentures	29,000	800
Current taxation	1,000	1,000
Trade creditors	43,000	–
Overdraft	7,000	–
Current and deposit accounts	–	91,000
	100,000	100,000
Fixed assets, less depreciation	39,000	4,000
Goodwill	6,000	–
Unquoted investments	1,000	9,000
Advances	–	59,000
Stock-in-trade	17,000	–
Trade debtors	37,000	–
Cash and liquid assets	–	28,000
	100,000	100,000
Net Profit before taxation	*1,800*	*1,600*
after charging depreciation of	1,200	100

The companies' businesses are entirely concerned with the activities which their names suggest.

Required:

(a) A list comparing, in numerical terms, *six* aspects from the accounts which you consider reveal the most important differences or similarities between the two companies. Use ratios where appropriate.

(b) A brief discussion of your figures in part (a), with particular regard to the apparent financial stability of the two companies, and the usefulness or limitations of the comparisons you have made.

EXERCISE 12.6 EX

The following are the summarised revenue accounts and balance sheets of Aix Limited.

Revenue Account for years ended 31 December

	1978		1979	
		£ 000s		
Sales		800		1,000
Less: Opening stock	110		130	
Costs of production	500		700	
Closing stock	(130)		(170)	
Cost of goods sold	480		660	
Running expenses (including interest charges)	260		362	
		740		1,022
Net profit		60		78
Proposed dividend		-		40
Retained Profit		60		38

Balance Sheets as at 31 December

	1978	1979
	£ 000s	
Ordinary Share Capital	200	200
Retained profit	100	138
12% Debentures, issued 1 January 1979	–	200
Bank Overdraft	10	–
Dividends	–	40
Creditors	110	120
	420	698
Fixed assets	170	338
Stock	130	170
Debtors	120	160
Bank	–	30
	420	698

No dividends were paid during either 1978 or 1979.

Required :

(a)   A calculation of the following accounting ratios and percentages for 1978 and 1979 presented in the following tabular format :

	1978	1979
Liquid ratio		
Average rate of stock turnover		
Net profit as a percentage of sales		
Earnings as a percentage of long-term capital employed		
Net earnings for ordinary shareholders as a percentage of equity		
Ratio of sales to long-term capital employed		

For the purpose of your calculations equity and long-term capital employed are to be included at their estimated figures at 30 June in each year, assuming no seasonal variations in the level of business activity.

(b)   Comments on the implications of the differences between the above ratios and percentages between the two years.

NOTE   Ignore taxation.

EXERCISE 12.7 EX

The following are the summarised accounts of two trading companies, each of which has recently approached your bank requesting a loan of £150,000 to acquire the shares of a director who is about to retire.

Revenue Accounts for 19-5

	Easthope Ltd £000s	£ 000s	Quilter Ltd £ 000s	£ 000s
Turnover		2,050		2,620
Less: Cost of sales		1,435		1,890
Gross profit		615		730
Less: Depreciation	50		120	
Other indirect expenses	445	495	480	600
Net Profit		120		130

Balance Sheet at 31 December 19-5

	£ 000s	£ 000s
Ordinary share capital	500	600
Retained profit	100	300
	600	900
Current Liabilities	260	300
	860	1,200
Premises	50	430
Other fixed assets	355	245
Current assets	445	525
	860	1,200

You discover that neither company needs to replace fixed assets in the near future. The 19-5 results are expected to be repeated for the next few years, and the directors plan to pay out the entire profits in the form of dividends.

Required:

(a)   The following calculations, ratios and percentages presented in a tabular format for each company:

	Easthope	Quilter
Funds generated from operations		
Proprietorship ratio		
Working capital ratio		
Net profit as a percentage of sales		
Return on year-end balance of shareholders' equity		

(b)   Based on your findings under (a), state the areas in which Easthope appears to be stronger and the areas in which Quilter appears to be stronger

(c)   To which company would you be more willing to grant loan facilities? Give your reasons

NOTE   Ignore taxation.

EXERCISE 12.8 EX

The cash balance of Wing Ltd has declined significantly over the last twelve months. The following financial information is provided.

Year to 31 December		19-2	19-3
		£	£
Sales		573,000	643,000
Purchases of raw materials		215,000	264,000
Raw materials consumed		210,000	256,400
Cost of goods manufactured		435,000	515,000
Cost of goods sold		420,000	460,000

Balance at 31 December		19-2	19-3
		£	£
Debtors		97,100	121,500
Creditors		23,900	32,500
Stocks :	Raw materials	22,400	30,000
	Work-in-progress	29,000	34,300
	Finished goods	70,000	125,000

All purchases and sales were made on credit.

Required:
(a)   An analysis of the above information, which should include calculations of the cash operating cycle (i.e. the time lag between making payment to suppliers and collecting cash from customers) for 19-2 and 19-3

(b)   A brief report on the implications of the changes which have occurred between 19-2 and 19-3.

NOTE   1. Assume a 360 day year for the purpose of your calculations, and that all transactions take place at an even rate.

2. All calculations are to be made to the nearest day.

EXERCISE 12.9 EX

The summarised profit and loss appropriation account and summarised balance sheet of Dexter Ltd for 1986 are as follows :

Profit and Loss Account 1986

	£000s
Net profit before tax	200
Less: Corporation tax	60
	140
Less: Dividends	100
	40

Balance Sheet at 31 December 1986

	£000s
Fixed assets and net current assets	1,070
Financed by:	
Share capital (£1 shares)	1,000
Retained profits	70
	1,070

The directors plan to expand the level of operations by acquiring the assets of an existing business, engaged in similar activity, for £1,000,000 on January 1 1987. The directors need to decide whether to raise £1,000,000 by making a rights issue to existing shareholders or issuing a 12% debenture. The terms of the rights issue would be to issue shares at £2.50 each on the basis of two additional shares for every five shares currently held.

Forecast profits of the expanded company *before* interest charges, if any, for the next three years are as follows :

	£000s
1987	520
1988	240
1989	600

The directors plan to pay out the entire post-tax profit of each of the years in the form of a cash dividend.

Mainstream corporation tax should be charged at the rate of 30% on profits before tax.

Required :

(a)   Forecast profit and loss accounts for each of the years 1987 to 1989 inclusive and the forecast balance sheet at the end of that period, assuming the expansion is financed by a rights issue.

(b)   Forecast profit and loss accounts for each of the years 1987 to 1989 inclusive and the forecast balance sheet at the end of that period, assuming the expansion is financed by issuing a 12% debenture.

(c)   Calculations of the debt:equity ratio and the rate of return on shareholders' equity. Base your calculations on the figures given for 1986 and your answers under (a) and (b) above.

(d)   A discussion of the advantages and disadvantages of the alternative methods of financing the expansion (as in (a) and (b) above). Your discussion should make reference to the position of (i) the shareholders of Dexter Ltd and (ii) the management of Dexter Ltd.

NOTES :

(i)   Assume that you are making the required calculations in answer to this question on January 1 1987.

(ii)   In the balance sheets you prepare in answer to (a) and (b) above, insert the figure for fixed assets and net current assets as the balancing figure.

(Autumn 1987)

EXERCISE 12.10 EX

The following information has been extracted from the accounts of Hardings Ltd for the year to 31 March 1989.

Trading items

	£000s
Sales	1,620
Purchases	930
Cost of goods sold	900

Summarised Balance Sheet at 31 March 1989

		£		£
	Fixed assets at cost	400,000	Share capital	400,000
Less:	Accumulated depreciation	170,000	Retained profit	142,500
		230,000		542,500
	Investments	50,000		
	Stock *	150,000		
	Trade Debtors *	180,000	Trade Creditors *	77,500
	Bank balance *	10,000		
		620,000		620,000

* Assume that each of these balances remained steady over the 12 months to 31 March 1989

There is a strong demand for the goods traded in by Hardings Ltd, and an expansion plan is currently being put into operation. Plant costing £150,000 is to be purchased and paid for in June 1989 and from 1 July,

196

the scale of trading operations is expected to increase by 25%. Each of the components of the operating cycle, in days, is to remain unchanged. The present bank balance is just sufficient to support the current level of operations, and the company's bank has agreed to provide overdraft finance to meet cash requirements arising over the forthcoming 12 months.

The following information has been extracted from the forecast profit and loss account of Hardings Ltd for the year to 31 March 1990 :

Profit and Loss Account extracts, Year to 31 March 1990

	£000
Trading profit before depreciation :	
April - June	30
July - March	130
	160
Less : Depreciation	60
	100
Add :	
Extraordinary profit on the sale (1 June 1989) of the investments shown in the above balance sheet	15
	115

Required :

(a)   Calculate for the financial year to 31 March 1989, in days :
   (i)   the rate of stock turnover
   (ii)   the rate of collection of debts
   (iii)   the rate of payment of creditors
   (iv)   the cash operating cycle.

(b)   Calculate the *additional* working capital requirement which results from the implementation of the expansion proposals.

(c)   Calculate the overdraft requirement on 1 July 1989 (assume that the whole of the *additional* working capital requirement arises on 1 July 1989 for the purpose of this calculation).

(d)   Prepare Hardings' forecast balance sheet as at 31 March 1990.

(e)   Assess, briefly, the financial implications of the plans for expansion from the viewpoint of the lending bank.

NOTES :
   (i)   Ignore interest payable on any bank overdraft
   (ii)   Ignore taxation.
   (iii)   Assume a 360 day year for the purpose of your calculations. No dividends are to be paid for the year to 31 March 1990.

(Spring 1989)

SOLUTIONS

SOLUTION 12.1

(a)

	Whiz Ltd	Bang Ltd
Current Ratio	1 : 1	2.5 : 1
Liquid Ratio	0.3 : 1	1.17 : 1
Stock Turnover	12	1,375
Net earnings for ordinary shareholders	40%	44%
Earnings on long-term capital	40%	$23^1/_2$%
Net profit as % of sales	4%	16%

(b) As Whiz Ltd has a quick turnover of stock with most of its sales being for cash, a 1 to 1 current ratio is probably quite high enough - there is no need to 'carry' large stocks of debtors at any time; therefore there is no need for a high cover. This is in contrast to Bang Ltd who, because of the type of business, need to 'carry' large stocks and debtors for some time before payment from sales comes in. However, a cover of 2.5 to 1 seems adequate to meet this need. It would seem that, bearing the types of businesses in mind, both companies have an adequate current ratio.

The liquid ratio of Whiz Ltd is on the low side indicating a large dependence on stocks, but this would be expected of a supermarket type of business and would not therefore cause any particular concern. Liquid cover of more than 1 to 1 for Bang Ltd gives adequate cover commensurate with the type of business.

A stock turnover of 12 (indicating one month holding of stock on average) seems right for a supermarket, whilst the need to carry large stocks for long periods of time in order to complete heavy engineering contracts would lead one to expect a low stock turnover as shown for Bang Ltd.

The net earnings for ordinary shareholders are better for Bang Ltd than for Whiz Ltd but the reverse is true for the return on long-term capital. This is because Bang Ltd is highly geared, with large issues of debentures and preference shares. Returns for both companies indicate efficient use of funds.

Bang shows a much more attractive profit as a percentage of sales - i.e. the 'slow nature' of sales for Bang Ltd compare with 'supermarket speed' of sales for Whiz Ltd is compensated for by the higher proportionate return which one could say is relevant to the risks involved.

SOLUTION 12.2

(a)

Summary Profit and Loss Accounts

Year 1

	A Ltd £	B Ltd £		A Ltd £	B Ltd £
Debenture Interest	30,000	75,000	Trading Profit	110,000	110,000
Profit before Tax	80,000	35,000			
	110,000	110,000		110,000	110,000
Corporation Tax	40,000	17,500	Profit before Tax	80,000	35,000
Dividends	40,000	17,500			
	80,000	35,000		80,000	35,000

198

Year 2

	A Ltd £	B Ltd £		A Ltd £	B Ltd £
Debenture Interest	30,000	75,000	Trading Profit	190,000	190,000
Profit before Tax	160,000	115,000			
	190,000	190,000		190,000	190,000
Corporation Tax	80,000	57,500	Profit before tax	160,000	115,000
Dividends	80,000	57,500			
	160,000	115,000		160,000	115,000

(b)

	A Ltd	B Ltd
Year 1	5%	3.5%
Year 2	10%	11,5%

(c)

The gearing ratio of A Ltd is 1 to 4 - i.e. it is low geared, the bulk of its finance being obtained from shares rather than debentures. B Ltd's gearing ratio is 1 to 1 - i.e. it is relatively high geared.

In Year 1 when profits are relatively low the high geared company (B Ltd) needs to find a disproportionately large slice of the profits to finance the fixed debenture interest, leaving little left for the shareholders. On the other hand, A Ltd, the low geared company, with few debentures has a relatively small amount of fixed interest to pay to debenture holders leaving more for the shareholders.

In Year 2 when profits are higher the amount of fixed interest is small in comparison to total profits so that a large amount of profit is available for a relatively small number of shares in the high geared company, B Ltd.

The effects of this is shown in (b) above where it can be seen that whilst A Ltd's return to shareholders doubles with the increased profits, B Ltd's return more than trebles.

Finally, the high geared company's (B Ltd) corporation tax is much smaller than the other company's because the large amount of interest payable by B Ltd reduces the taxable profit.

SOLUTION 12.3

(a)

Payment of creditors $= \dfrac{160}{1,800} \times \dfrac{360}{1}$ days $=$ **32 days**

Payment from debtors $= \dfrac{300}{2,700} \times \dfrac{360}{1}$ days $=$ **40 days**

Stock Turnover $= \dfrac{1,800}{305} = 6$ $=$ **60 days**

(b)

Cash Operating Cycle	Days
Credit from suppliers	(32)
Credit to customers	40
Stock of finished goods	60
Cash Operating Cycle	68

(c)

(i)   If payment to creditors could be extended from 32 days to 36 days (still a reasonable period without taking undue advantage of suppliers) this would increase average creditors by one-eighth, i.e. by £20,000 which should benefit cash by this amount. The time lag for receipt of cash would be reduced by 4 days to 64 days.

(ii)   If credit to customers could be reduced by 3 days to 37 days (without upsetting them!) this would decrease average debtors by $7^1/_2\%$ - i.e. by £22,500. Cash would benefit and the time lag would be reduced by 3 days to 65 days.

(iii)   If average holdings of stock could be reduced by £20,000 this would benefit cash, and increase stock turnover above 6 so reducing the number of days that stock is generally held before being sold. Obviously this would reduce the 'time lag'.

NOTE   The question asks for only *one* method.

SOLUTION 12.4

a)

	Company A	Company B	Company C
(i)	1.5%	4.3%	20.9%
(ii)	5:1	0.85:1	0.1:1
(iii)	7.9%	3.7%	2.4%
(iv)	0.05:1	0.7:1	1.7:1

b)

Company A	Grocery
Company B	Steel Manufacturer
Company C	Finance Company

LESSON 13

TAXATION IN COMPANY ACCOUNTS

The profits of a limited company are subject to a special kind of taxation - Corporation Tax. The tax is payable on net profit earned by the company in the year, but the actual figure shown in the profit and loss account is not used to assess the corporation tax due. Instead the tax authorities adjust the figure of net profit by computing their own figures for certain items, such as depreciation and others shown in the company accounts.

Do not get the impression that the company alters the figures in its Profit and Loss account in order to agree with the Inland Revenue - the profit as shown by the Profit and Loss account remains in the accounts and a separate statement is prepared to show the *ADJUSTED* net profit figure on which corporation tax is based.

EXAMPLE

Profit and Loss account of Company

	£		£
Various expenses	18,000	Gross Profit	36,000
Depreciation	8,000		
Net Profit	10,000		
	36,000		36,000

Statement of Profit for Tax Purposes

		£
Net profit as per Profit and Loss account		10,000
Add back depreciation		8,000
		18,000
Less: 'Depreciation' Allowance given by Inland Revenue		5,000
Net profit subject to Corporation Tax	=	13,000

Thus, a percentage of £13,000 is payable by the company to the Inland Revenue.

When is the tax payable? Up to the present time the due date varied considerably between companies incorporated before April 1965, but for companies incorporated after this date the due date for payment was nine months after the end of the company's financial year. The 1987 Budget proposes that these differences be phased out and this means that a due date of nine months after the year end will very soon apply to all companies.

The application of corporation tax is limited to the earnings (profits) of limited companies. The tax which is applied to the earnings of individuals, partnerships and other organisations is Income Tax.

The present system of taxation is called the *IMPUTATION SYSTEM*. You must know how this works and the main elements of the system are : *

(i)   Limited companies will continue to pay corporation tax on the profits they earn.

(ii)   Income tax will *not* be deducted from dividends paid to shareholders, who will therefore receive the full amount of the dividends. The idea here is that the profits paid out as dividends have already been subjected to a tax (corporation tax) and should therefore not be taxed again.

(iii)   The company having paid out the dividends must now pay over to the Inland Revenue an *ADVANCE PAYMENT OF CORPORATION TAX*, the amount being equal to $3/7$ths of the total dividends paid. The *rest* of the corporation tax (referred to as *MAINSTREAM CORPORATION TAX*) will be paid over when due, which, would be 9 months after the end of the financial year.

Let us see the application of this by way of examples. *For ease of calculations I will assume throughout all examples a corporation tax rate of 50% and an income tax rate of 30%. You will be told on the examination paper which rates to assume.*

EXAMPLE

Z Ltd makes a total profit of £30,000 and declares a dividend of 14% on its issued capital of 100,000 £1 shares. Assume Corporation Tax to be at a rate of 50%.

NOTE :
(i)   Z Ltd has a corporation tax liability of £15,000
(ii)   Z Ltd pays dividends of £14,000 to shareholders
(iii)   Z Ltd pays £6,000 ($3/7$ths of £14,000) to the Inland Revenue as Advance Corporation Tax.
(iv)   On the due date Z Ltd pays over the remaining corporation tax (the Mainstream Tax) of £9,000.

*   In outlining the system I am assuming a corporation tax rate of 50% and an income tax rate of 30%.

This is basically how the new tax system works. The shareholder receives his dividend in full without further deduction of income tax and his evidence that his dividend has been subjected to corporation tax before it left the company, is in the form of a 'tax credit' which is attached to his dividend warrant. This tax credit is equal to $3/7$ths of his dividend.

One more point. The *Mainstream* Corporation Tax payment by the company *must be equal to at least 20% of the taxable profits*. Therefore, in the above example (Z Ltd), the mainstream tax must be at least 20% of £30,000 -i.e. £6,000. It is in fact £9,000, so that is fine. Suppose however, that Z Ltd has paid a dividend of *28%* .... using the same figures as before :

NOTE
(i)   Corporation Tax liability = £15,000
(ii)   Z pays dividends of £28,000
(iii)   Z pays £12,000 ($3/7$ths of £28,000) as Advance Corporation Tax
(iv)   This leaves only £3,000 of mainstream tax due, but the mainstream *must* be at least 20% of profits - i.e. 20% of £30,000 = £6,000, which must be paid on the due date.

In this example therefore, the company has paid a total of £18,000 corporation tax (being the advance payment of £12,000 plus the minimum allowable mainstream payment of £6,000) whereas its total liability should only have been £15,000. The surplus paid, of £3,000 can be used to set off any future corporation tax liability, but *at all times* the mainstream tax must be equal to at least 20% of taxable profits.

Companies Investing in Other Companies

Where a company buys shares in another company it will receive dividends like any other shareholder. This income is referred to as *FRANKED INVESTMENT INCOME*.

On receipt of a dividend of say, £14,000 the company (A) will obviously receive also a 'tax credit' of £6,000 ($^3/_7$ths of the dividend) as evidence that this amount has been paid as Advance Corporation Tax by the other company (B).The £14,000 received will appear on the credit side of company A's profit and loss account as investment income, plus the tax credit of £6,000 - i.e *this amount is shown gross*.

If, in the same year, Company A pays its own shareholders a dividend of £21,000, then it would normally have to pay to the Inland Revenue Advance Corporation Tax of £9,000 ($^3/_7$ths of £21,000); but it can now set off the tax credit of £6,000 (on the dividend received from Company B) and pay only the difference of £3,000 as Advance Corporation Tax. Obviously, the eventual mainstream payment will be £6,000 more - in other words, the £6,000 used as set off has still got to be paid eventually - but that has not to be paid over until much later.

Study this example which covers all the points made so far :

> X Ltd made profits of £120,000 in Year 1 and paid a dividend of £42,000. In the same year, X Ltd received dividends of £14,000 from its holding of shares in Y Ltd.

> In Year 2, X Ltd made a profit of £150,000 and paid a dividend of £140,000. Dividends of £14,000 were received from Y Ltd, in Year 2.

Show how much X Ltd paid as Advance Corporation Tax in Years 1 and 2, and show the amount of Mainstream Corporation Tax paid in each year. Assume Corporation Tax to be 50%.

ANSWER

Year 1	£	£
Corporation Tax Liability		60,000
Advance Corporation Tax	18,000	
Less: set off of tax credit on Franked		
Investment Income ($^3/_7$ths of £14,000)	6,000	
	12,000	
Mainstream Corporation Tax	48,000	
Total Tax paid	60,000	

Year 2

Corporation Tax Liability		<u>75,000</u>
Advance Corporation Tax	60,000	
Less: set off of tax credit on Franked		
Investment Income ($^3/_7$ths of £14,000)	<u>6,000</u>	
	54,000	
Mainstream Corporation Tax		
(minimum of 20% of taxable profits)	<u>30,000</u>	
Total Tax paid	<u>84,000</u>	

The surplus payment of £9,000 can be set off against a future corporation tax liability.

Note carefully these additional points :

1. The rate of $^3/_7$ths for Advance Corporation Tax (ACT) is the rate which applies when the income tax standard rate is 30%. A dividend which *pays* to the shareholder £7,000 carries with it a 'tax credit' of £3,000 making the gross income of the shareholder £10,000, which has borne income tax of 30%. As the rate of income tax changes, so does the rate for ACT. For example, with an income tax rate of 33%, the ACT rate would be $^{33}/_{67}$ of dividends paid, and so on. Note how the ACT rate and the income tax rate always make up to a total of 100 - e.g. $^{30}/_{70}$; $^{32}/_{68}$; $^{35}/_{65}$, etc. Usually in an examination you are told the ACT rate, but if you were not told and you knew the income tax rate you would be able to easily calculate the ACT rate.

2. You have been told that the Mainstream Tax must be equal to at least 20% of the taxable profits. This is when Corporation Tax is 50% and Income Tax 30% - i.e. the 20% minimum is the *difference* between the corporation tax and income tax rates. If corporation tax was 53% and income tax 34%, the minimum mainstream tax would be 19% of the taxable profits.

3. ACT is payable to the Inland Revenue quarterly (31 March, 30 June, 30 September, 31 December) with 14 days' grace beyond these dates. Therefore, a dividend *paid* in February, Year 1 would incur ACT payable by 14 April, Year 1.

4. ACT is set off against the corporation tax liability for the *accounting year in which the dividend is actually paid*. For example, if a company with a year end of 31 December has a corporation tax liability of £10,000 based on the profits of Year 1, and at 31 December, Year 1 it *declares* a dividend, then such dividend will not actually be *paid* until January or February, Year 2, in which case the ACT on that dividend would be set off against the corporation tax liability on the profits of *Year 2*, the year in which the dividend was *paid*. The ACT figure would therefore need to be 'held over' in a Deferred Taxation account * until Year 2's profits had been ascertained and the corporation tax liability calculated. The actual *payment* of this ACT would of course be made on 14 April, Year 2 (see note 3)

* See **Deferred Taxation** section.

Treatment in the accounts

Dividends paid or proposed are shown in the profit and loss appropriation account at the amounts to be *paid* to shareholders. Thus, a dividend of £7,000 which incurs ACT of, say, £3,000 would be debited as £7,000 - i.e. net of the 'tax credit'. If such dividend was only proposed, the £7,000 would appear as a current liability in the balance sheet.

Franked Investment Income is shown on the credit side of profit and loss account at the amount actually received *plus* the amount of the 'tax credit' which would accompany the cheque received. Therefore with an ACT rate of $^3/_7$ths, a dividend cheque received for £6,370 would be grossed up to £9,100 and this latter amount would appear in the profit and loss account.

Annual Charges

So far, we have been talking about *DIVIDENDS* paid and received on *SHARES*. Interest payments on loans (the best example being Debentures) are different in that these are *CHARGES* against profits rather than appropriations of profits. In other words, when an interest payment is made this payment has *not* been subjected to corporation tax. The amount paid is shown in the profit and loss account (not the appropriation section) and thereby reduces the figure of taxable profits (like rent and wages, etc.). So, the interest payment does not attract corporation tax like the dividend payment, and the Inland Revenue are naturally anxious that it should be taxed! Because of this, the recipient of *INTEREST* must pay *INCOME TAX* on the amount of interest received, and the company making the interest payment is obliged to deduct income tax from the interest due and to pay over to the debenture holder the *net* amount only. Thus, a debenture holder who is due to receive £100 interest will in fact receive only £70 if the income tax rate is 30%. The company must then pay this £30 over to the the Inland Revenue. The company is, in effect, acting as a collecting agent for the Inland Revenue.

EXAMPLE

ABC Company Limited

Annual Interest on £100,000 6% Debentures = £6,000

Payment to Debenture Holders = £6,000
Less: Income Tax (30%) = £1,800 = £4,200

Profit and Loss Account (debit side)		*Interest on Debenture Account*			
Debenture Interest (gross)	£6,000	Bank	£4,200	P & L a/c	£6,000
		Inland Rev.	£1,800		
			£6,000		£6,000

Bank Account (credit side)		*Inland Revenue Account (credit side)*	
Interest on Debentures	£4,200	Interest on Debentures	£1,800

The accounts above show that the bank account has been reduced by the net payment of interest - the interest account is now closed off as the interest has been paid - the Inland Revenue account shows a credit balance (a liability) of £1,800 representing the tax collected by ABC Company Ltd and due to be paid over to the Inland Revenue. Note that the interest appears *GROSS* in the profit and loss account.

If ABC Company Ltd held Debentures in XYZ Company Ltd then ABC would receive payment of interest from XYZ *less income tax*. In other words, XYZ Company, when making interest payments will not treat ABC Company any differently from other Debenture holders - all interest will be paid less tax.

The company receiving the net payment of interest (in this case ABC) refers to this income as *UNFRANKED INCOME*. Do not confuse this with franked investment income which refers to dividends from shares. The amount of tax which has been deducted (by XYZ) from this receipt of interest can now be set off by ABC Ltd, against its own liability for *INCOME TAX* in respect of its own payments of *interest* (£1,800 in the above example), and pay over to the Inland Revenue the difference only.

EXAMPLE

Straw Ltd has debenture holdings in Hay Ltd. Straw has also issued its own debentures. Straw will therefore *pay* interest on debentures (net) and *receive* interest (net) on debentures in Hay Ltd. The latter is of course Unfranked Income.

Year 1

(a)   Straw has tax of £200 deducted from its Unfranked Income
(b)   Straw deducts tax of £300 from the interest due to its own debenture holders.

Straw Ltd now sets off the £200 against its income tax liability and pays over to the Inland Revenue the difference of £100.

All receipts and payments of interest must be shown in the accounts at the *gross* figures - i.e. before deduction of income tax.

DEFERRED TAXATION (SSAP 15 - Revised)

Deferred taxation is defined as 'the tax attributable to timing differences'.

Timing differences are the differences between profits or losses calculated *for tax purposes* and profits or losses as reported in the profit and loss account, where the latter includes items of expenses and gains on which tax allowances or claims relate to other financial periods of time.

The profit shown in the profit and loss account (reported profit) is usually quite different from the taxable profit figure on which the corporation tax liability is calculated. This is because certain income and expenditure taken into account in calculating taxable profit, refers to different periods than those same items shown in the profit and loss account. In other words there is a 'timing difference'. To explain this properly let us look at the following profit and loss account of a company which started trading on 1 January 19-5 :

Profit and Loss Account for 19-5

	£ 000s	£ 000s
Gross Profit		60
Add: Interest Receivable		4
		64
Less: Expenses -		
Provision for bad debts	2	
Depreciation on plant and machinery	10	
Miscellaneous expenses	34	46
Net profit before tax (i.e. Reported Profit)		18

NOTE
i)   Interest receivable is still outstanding £1,000
ii)   The plant and machinery was purchased 1 January 19-5 at a cost of £100,000 with an estimated life of 10 years.

The above statement is prepared on the accruals concept - i.e. the account is credited and debited with what is due in respect of 19-5, irrespective of whether the amounts concerned have yet been received or paid.

206

However, that part of interest not yet received (£1,000) will not be taxed until it is actually received, which will be in a future period. The provision for bad debts (£2,000) will not be allowed for tax purposes until (if) they become definite bad debts - again in a future period.

The Inland Revenue in determining taxable profits allow a 25% writing down allowance, on a reducing balance basis for purchases of plant and machinery. It is obvious from the above profit and loss account that the company is depreciating plant and machinery at 10% p.a. This means that £15,000 of allowance for depreciation is being held over for future years.

Calculations of Taxable Profit for 19-5

	£ 000s
Net Profit per account	18
Less: timing difference on Interest Received	1
	17
Less: timing differences on written down allowance on plant and machinery	15
	2
Add: timing difference on provision for bad debts	2
Taxable Profit	4

I will continue to assume a corporation tax rate of 50% for ease of calculation, in which case the corporation tax payable for 19-5 will be £2,000 (50% of taxable profit). If however the tax had been based on *reported* profit of £18,000 the tax payable would have been £9,000. This difference of £7,000 is caused by 'timing differences' as shown above and although it does not have to be paid yet it is nevertheless a *potential* future liability and is therefore referred to as 'deferred tax' and held in a deferred tax account.

Let us analyse this £7,000 potential future liability :

a)   When the outstanding £1,000 of interest is received in the next period it will incur tax of £500 (50% of £1,000).

b)   An additional allowance of £15,000 over and above the depreciation charge in profit and loss account, has been given in 19-5 and this represents a saving in tax of £7,500 (50% of £15,000). Suppose however that, on 1January 19-6 the company sold the £100,000 of plant and machinery for £90,000 (its balance sheet value)! Obviously the company would then have to 'give back' this saving of £7,500 to the tax authorities. Therefore, at the end of 19-5 this £7,500 is a *potential* liability and must be shown as such in deferred tax account.

c)   Should the £2,000 provision for bad debts become a real bad debt in the future it will then qualify for tax relief of £1,000, and is therefore a *potential* tax benefit. This £1,000 will be held in deferred tax account but obviously on the opposite (debit) side of the account to the potential liabilities (credits) in a) and b) above.

NOTE   Items a), b) and c) account for the net potential deferred tax liability of £7,000 which will show as a credit balance on deferred tax account at 31 December 19-5. Obviously, adjustments will be made to this account each year. Going on to 31 December 19-6, and assuming that the same plant and machinery is held by the company, a further 25% writing down allowance will be given, *but on the reduced balance of £75,000* - i.e. £18,750. As the company will again charge only £10,000 depreciation to its profit and loss account this means that £8,750 of allowances is being held over for future years - a saving on tax of £4,375 (50% of £8,750). As with the extra allowance in 19-5 this 'saving' will be added to the *potential* tax liability in deferred tax account.

The balance on deferred tax account is a contingent liability, and that part of the balance referring to writing down allowances of plant and machinery would only become payable if a sale of the plant took place. Even if a sale *did* take place it is more than likely that another batch of plant and machinery would be purchased to take its place (attracting the 25% reducing balance allowance), so no money would actually be paid over to the Inland Revenue.

If a company revalues its premises (debit premises account, credit revaluation reserve) it has created a 'paper profit' which, if the premises were to be sold at the new valuation would be liable to capital gains tax. Therefore on revaluation taking place, there is an immediate *contingent* liability for tax which must be held in a deferred tax account - debit premises account, say £30,000, credit revaluation reserve £21,000, credit deferred tax account £9,000 (assuming 30% capital gains tax).

Of course, this contingent liability would never become a real liability (i.e. payable) unless the property in question was actually sold.

Remember that ACT (refer back) awaiting set-off against future corporation tax will be 'nestling' on the debit side of deferred tax account.

The Liability Method

In computing deferred tax in all the above examples I have assumed that the future *potential* liability (or reversal of liability in the case of provision for bad debts) would be at the corporation tax rate of 50%.

SSAP 15 (revised) however insists that the deferred tax liabilities be calculated at the rate of tax it is estimated will be applicable *when the timing differences might reverse* - i.e. at the expected long term tax rate. Obviously in some periods of time this has got to be guesswork!

It should be clear from the above that in many cases the balance on a deferred tax account can usually be regarded as a liability which will never actually have to be paid, particularly if the company in question is firmly established and therefore unlikely to be selling its properties in the near future, and is constantly buying new fixed assets and therefore constantly qualifying for depreciation allowances.

For practical purposes therefore a banker could regard the contingent liability of deferred taxation (in the case of successful and expanding companies) as being part of the shareholders' stake. If, however, the company in question is 'dodgy' the banker must look at deferred taxation account as a very real liability, as in the event of liquidation all benefits being held over would become payable to a *preferential creditor!* - i.e. the tax authorities. SSAP15 (Revised) states that timing differences referred to above should only be accounted for (i.e. transfers to deferred tax account made) if it is *probable* that such liabilities (or assets) *will* crystalise - i.e. become a reality.

If it is considered probable that a potential liability (or asset) will *not* crystalise (e.g a company buying plant and machinery, or revaluing premises, considers that these assets are not going to be disposed of) then these 'potentials' need not be placed to deferred tax account. Such unprovided deferred tax must however be disclosed as a *note* analysed into its various parts.

It is important for a banker to look closely at the deferred tax position when assessing a company's accounts and balance sheet. If a company has adopted the proposals in SSAP 15 then very little deferred tax may be shown in the accounts - this does not mean to say that there is no potential liability! Some of the reserves may well have to be committed to satisfying a liability to the tax authorities and the notes to the accounts should be read carefully. However, as said earlier there is very little risk with a sound and expanding company that any deferred tax liability will ever have to be paid.

SSAP 8

TREATMENT OF TAXATION UNDER THE IMPUTATION SYSTEM IN COMPANY ACCOUNTS

See Lesson No. 13 - 'Taxation in Company Accounts'. Note in particular, the following points :

1.   The Profit and Loss account should show ;

(a)   Corporation tax based on the year's income;
(b)   Corporation tax as a result of transfers between deferred taxation account and Profit and Loss account;
(c)   Tax on franked investment income;
(d)   Irrecoverable ACT;
(e)   Overseas taxation details.

2.   Dividends proposed or paid must be shown in the Profit and Loss account net of the tax credit - i.e. at the amount which will actually be paid.

3.   Franked investment income must be shown in the Profit and Loss account at the amount of dividend actually received (or receivable) *plus* the amount of the tax credit - i.e. gross.

4.   On the balance sheet dividends proposed should be included in current liabilities net of the tax credit. The ACT on proposed dividends should be included as a current liability.

SSAP 15 (Revised)

ACCOUNTING FOR DEFERRED TAXATION

The requirements of this Standard are fully covered in this Lesson No. 13.

EXERCISE 13.1

Maydee Ltd made a profit of £85,000 in Year 1 and paid a dividend of £21,000 whilst in Year 2 a profit of £100,000 was made and a dividend paid of £84,000.

In both years interest was paid on £40,000 of $6^1/_2\%$ Debentures.

The following amounts were received from investments in other companies :

	Year 1	Year 2
	£	£
Franked Investment Income	1,400	2,100
Unfranked Income (net)	560	700

Assume corporation tax to be at the rate of 50% of profits and income tax to have a rate of 30%.

From this information, complete the following table :

209

	Year 1	Year 2
	£	£
Mainstream Corporation Tax		
Advance Corporation Tax		
Income Tax Liability		

EXERCISE 13.2

The following summarised trial balance was extracted from the books of Imputation Ltd, in preparing the company's final accounts for the year ended 30 September, 19-4 :

	£	£
Debenture interest paid (gross)	8,000	
Deferred taxation		68,000
Franked investment income received (net)		14,000
Reserves at 30 September, 19-3		110,000
Sales		600,000
Share capital		200,000
Sundry assets	592,000	
Sundry costs	512,000	
Sundry creditors		120,000
	1,112,000	1,112,000

Adjustments have yet to be made for the following items :

1. Corporation tax on income (including franked investment income) for 19-4 is calculated at £50,000).

2. A cash payment of £21,000 will be made to shareholders on 1 February, 19-5 in respect of a proposed dividend.

Imputation Ltd commenced trading in 19-7.
Assume a basic rate of income tax of 30%, and an Advance Corporation Tax rate of $3/7$. Ignore 'additional' Advance Corporation Tax.

Required :

The profit and loss account of Importation Ltd for the year ended 30 September, 19-4 and the balance sheet for that date, set out in good style, and showing the dates on which tax liabilities will be payable.

EXERCISE 13.3

The following is a summarised Profit and Loss account of Pearl plc for the year 19-4.

Profit and Loss Account for year ending 31 December 19-4

	£ 000s	£ 000s
Gross Profit		140
Add: Interest Receivable		20
Royalties Receivable		12
		172
Less:		
Depreciation on machinery	34	
Provision for bad debts (increase)	6	
Other expenses	85	125
Net Profit before tax		47

NOTE
i) Balance on deferred taxation account at 1 January 19-4 was £117,000 (credit)
ii) Machinery was purchased on 1 January 19-3 for £340,000 and has an expected life of 10 years.

210

iii)   Interest receivable is still outstanding £5,000 and royalties receivable still outstanding amount to
        £6,000.
iv)   During the year premises were revalued from £160,000 to £200,000.
v)   Assume a corporation tax rate of 40% and a capital gains tax of 30%.

Required :

A calculation of the balance on Deferred Taxation account at 1 January 19-5. State whether the balance is debit or credit.

EXERCISE 13.4 EX

Transit Ltd commenced trading in 1976. Following trial balance was extracted from the company's books for the preparation of its *first* annual accounts for the year ended 30 June, 1977 :

	£	£
Assets (all current)	192,500	
Franked investment income received (net of tax credit)		6,500
Operating profit (after bank interest of £4,000 but before invest. income)		29,000
Share capital		20,000
Sundry creditors		150,000
Interim dividend paid 25 June, 1977	13,000	
	205,500	205,500

It has been calculated that the company's corporation tax on its operating profit of £29,000 will be £12,000.

Assume an advance corporation tax rate of $^{35}/_{65}$ths.

Required :

The Profit and Loss account of Transit Ltd for the year ended 30 June, 1977 together with the balance sheet at that date, so far as the information permits. Show the dates on which tax liabilities will be payable, but in all other respects comply with standard accounting practice.

.

EXERCISE 13.5 EX

The following trial balance was extracted from the books of Gladstone Limited at 31 December, 19-9.

Trial Balance

	£	£
Share capital (ordinary shares of £1 each)		1,000,000
Reserves at 1 January 19-9		554,000
Deferred taxation account		160,000
Trade creditors		356,000
Taxation due 1 January 19-0		160,500
Fixed assets at book value	1,557,900	
Current assets	1,057,600	
Interim dividend	70,000	
Advance corporation tax	30,000	
Capital gain on disposal of land		59,000
Trading profit for 19-9		426,000
	2,715,500	2,715,500

The following additional information is provided :

(i)   The corporation tax due on the 19-8 profits, payable 1 January 19-0 has been agreed at £174,500.

(ii)   The taxable trading profits for 19-9 are estimated at £250,000, on which corporation tax is payable at 52%.

(iii)   Corporation tax is payable at an effective rate of 30% on the capital gain which arose on the sale of land during 19-9.

(iv)   The directors have decided to make a transfer to the deferred taxation account of £104,000 for 19-9

(v)   The directors propose to pay a final dividend of 10.5p per share for 19-9.

Required :
            The profit and loss account and balance sheet of Gladstone Limited for 19-9 in a form suitable for publication, so far as the information permits .

NOTE   Advance corporation tax (ACT) should be taken at $3/7$ths for the purpose of your calculations.

EXERCISE 13.6 EX

Lancaster Ltd was incorporated and commenced business in January 19-2. The following trial balance was extracted form the books at 31 December 19-2.

	£	£
Share capital (ordinary shares of £1 each)		1,000,000
Trade creditors		264,500
Operating profit ✓		315,000
Royalties		90,000
Dividends received		7,000
Fixed assets at cost (purchased January 19-2)	200,000	
Provision for depreciation at 31 December 19-2)		40,000
Stock, debtors and cash	1,469,500	
Interim dividend paid	35,000	
Advance corporation tax	12,000	
	1,716,500	1,716,500

The following additional information is provided :

1.   Royalties consist of £65,000 received in cash and £25,000 outstanding at the year end. ✓

2.   The royalties outstanding give rise to a timing difference as defined by SSAP 15 entitled 'Accounting for Deferred Taxation'. ✓

3.   The directors intend to claim a first year allowance of 25% on the fixed assets purchased in January 19-2. No provision for deferred taxation will be made in respect of the resulting timing difference as the directors are in possession of reliable evidence which supports their opinion that it will not reverse in the foreseeable future.

4.   Corporation tax is payable at 52% on *taxable* profits of £220,000. ✓

5.   The directors propose to pay a final dividend of 14p per share for 19-2. ✓

Required :
            The profit and loss account of Lancaster Ltd for 19-2 and balance sheet at 31 December 19-2, not necessarily in a form for publication, but complying with the provisions in SSAP 15.

NOTE
            Advance corporation tax should be taken as $3/7$ths for the purpose of your calculations.

EXERCISE 13.7 EX

The summarised trial balance of Barbican Ltd at 31 March 1988 contained the following information :

Trial Balance at 31 March 1988

	£000	£000
Retained profit at 1 April 1987		260
Operating profit for the year before tax		450
Trade creditors and accruals		372
Share capital : shares of £1 each		1,000
Deferred tax account		54
Fixed assets at cost	1,250	
Accumulated depreciation at 31 March 1988		820
Interim dividend paid	73	
Advance corporation tax (ACT)	85	
Overprovision for corporation tax in previous year		10
Stock, debtors and cash	1,558	
	2,966	2,966

The following information is provided in respect of the year to 31 March 1988:

(i) Taxable profits amount to £400,000 and net originating timing differences, expected to reverse at a future date, amount to £50,000

(ii) The directors propose to pay a final dividend of 15p in the £.

(iii) A corporation tax rate of 27% should be used and Advance Corporation Tax may be taken as $\frac{25}{75}$ for the purpose of your calculations.

Required :

The profit and loss account of Barbican Ltd for the year to 31 March 1988 and the balance sheet at that date, not necessarily in a form suitable for publication, but complying with the provisions of SSAP 8 and SSAP 15.

(Autumn 1988)

SOLUTIONS

SOLUTION 13.1

	Year 1	Year 2
	£	£
Mainstream Corporation Tax	34,100	20,000
Advance Corporation Tax	8,400	35,100
Income Tax Liability	540	480

Workings
Year 1 -

Tax liability on profits (50% of £85,000)		42,500
ACT ($^3/_7$ of dividend of £21,000)	9,000	
Less: tax credit on Franked Invest. Income	600	8,400
Leaving Mainstream of		34,100

In Year 2 the mainstream tax comes out at less than 20% of taxable profits - therefore the minimum payable is 20% of £100,000 = £20,000. The excess paid (£5,100) will be set off against future mainstream liabilities.

SOLUTION 13.2

Profit and loss account of Imputation Ltd

	£		£
Sundry costs	512,000	Sales	600,000
Debenture Interest	8,000	Franked Investment	
Net Profit	100,000	Income (gross)	20,000
	620,000		620,000
Dividends proposed	21,000	Net Profit	100,000
Corporation Tax	50,000	Balance b/d	110,000
Balance c/d	139,000		
	210,000		210,000

Balance Sheet as at 30 September, 19-4

		£		£
Share Capital		200,000		
Reserves		139,000	Sundry Assets	592,000
(1)	Deferred Tax	59,000		

Current Liabilities

		£
(2)	Mainstream Corporation Tax	44,000
(3)	Advance Corporation Tax	9,000
Proposed Dividend		21,000
Creditors		120,000
		592,000

	£
	592,000

NOTE

(1)   As the dividend is not to be paid until the 19-5 financial year, the relevant ACT (£9,000) will have to be set off against *that* year's corporation tax which is not yet known. In the meantime, therefore, it is held in Deferred Taxation Account whilst awaiting set off.

(2)   Against this amount could be set off any ACT in respect of any dividends *paid* during 19-4 (i.e. declared at 30 September, 19-3) and any such ACT would at present be nestling in deferred tax account awaiting set off. As we do not have this information we must ignore it and pay over the full amount of corporation tax. However, there is a tax credit on the Investment income of £6,000 which we know can be used to reduce the ACT liability for 19-4 and we are assuming that such liability is nestling in deferred tax account, amount unknown. Therefore we can only deduct the £6,000 tax credit from the corporation tax liability of £50,000.

This £44,000 liability is payable 9 months after the end of the financial year - i.e. 30 June, 19-5.

(3)   As the dividend will be paid in February 19-5 the ACT on this dividend will be payable to the Inland Revenue at the end of that particular quarter - i.e. 31 March plus 14 days grace - 14 April, 19-5.

(4)   Presumably the income tax deducted from debenture interest has either been paid over or is included in sundry creditors.

SOLUTION 13.3

Deferred Taxation Account

		£	19-4		£
			Jan 1	Balance	117,000
Re :	Bad Debts Provision	2,400		Re: Machinery	20,400
19-4					
Dec. 31	Balance c/d	151,400		Re: Interest	2,000
				Re: Royalties	2,400
				Re: Premises	12,000
		153,800			153,800

			19-4		
			Dec. 31	Balance b/d	151,400

LESSON 14

CAPITAL INVESTMENT APPRAISAL

The subject of economics should have made you aware of the fact that all resources are limited in supply and because of this there is a need to utilise resources in such a way as to obtain the maximum benefits from them. To do this it is necessary to choose between various alternatives available, and one economist sums this up by saying that 'he who chooses best, fares best'. This applies to individuals in their everyday life, to the management of large and small firms and to the governments of countries.

As we are concerned in the subject of accountancy, with the activities of businessmen, we will confine our examples of 'choosing' to this field.

The management of any business (say a company) is constantly having to make decisions on *what* to produce, *where* to produce, *how* to produce, and *how much* to produce, and some method has to be applied to ensure that whatever decisions are taken they are the right ones and the best ones. This means it is necessary to look at all of the various alternatives available and to choose that one which is going to give the most benefit to the company.

For example, a company may have to decide whether to replace its existing machinery with new and up-to-date machinery and having decided to buy new machinery it then has to choose between different makes and types of machinery, each having a different cost and each one capable of affecting output in a different way. At the same time a choice has to be made whether to actually buy for cash or on hire purchase or whether to hire the machinery.

Examples of choice could go on indefinitely but all we need be aware of is the fact that in choosing between various alternatives, each with its own attractions, it is necessary to determine *which* of the alternatives will benefit the company most.

In deciding which alternative offers the most benefits which factors will the company consider? Obviously, the *COST* of each alternative and the effect on *PROFITS* which each alternative will have. If it is a matter of choosing between two alternative projects, each of which will produce exactly the same profits then obviously cost will be the sole deciding factor and the project which costs the least will be chosen.

Most decisions however, are not as straightforward as this.

The appraisal of capital projects can utilise various methods - e.g. Discounted Cash Flow, Payback or Rate of Return. We will look at each method in turn.

DISCOUNTED CASH FLOW

EXAMPLE 1.

FACTS - A company is considering whether to replace existing machinery (with a future life span of 5 years) with more up-to-date machinery (also with a future life span of 5 years) at a cost of £15,000. The utilisation of the new machinery will increase profits by £5,000 per annum. Is is worth it?

DECISION - We cannot compare *cost* of £15,000 with *income* of £25,000 (£5,000 p.a. for 5 years) and say outright that it is worth it to purchase the new machinery. Why not? Because the £15,000 has to be paid out *now* whilst the proceeds will be received a little at a time over *future* years. We must bear in mind that money in our hands *now* can be earning interest for us.

216

We cannot compare present values with future values - we must compare like with like. You must understand this before we proceed. The cost of the machine has a *PRESENT* value to us of £15,000. What is the *present* value of £5,000 p.a receivable over the next 5 years? In other words how much would we need to invest *now* (at current interest rates) in order to receive an income of £5,000 p.a. over the next 5 years? A set of interest tables may tell us that £17,000 invested now at x% interest would produce an income of exactly £5,000 p.a. over the next 5 years - therefore the proceeds from using the new machinery have a *PRESENT VALUE* of £17,000.

We can now compare two *PRESENT VALUES*, viz:

1) Present value of cost of machine   = £15,000
2) Present value of proceeds from new machine   = £17,000

It is obviously worth it to purchase the new machine because the proceeds have a higher value than the cost!

What we have done in the above example is to compare two values, by bringing both values to a common basis in time - *now!* We have then been able to effectively compare two *PRESENT VALUES*. We have in fact used a Discounted Cash Flow technique - i.e. looked at future cash flows (the £5,000 p.a. for 5 years) and discounted these future values to *present values*. If we did *not* buy the machine but instead we invested our £15,000 at current interest rates of x%, then we would receive *less* than £5,000 per annum over the next 5 years so it is obviously beneficial to buy the machine and thereby receive £5,000 per annum.

If you understand this example, then you understand Discounted Cash Flow (D.C.F.). Whatever the question, you are going to be faced with various alternatives, some of which will show *future* values and some of which will show *present* values. You simply convert the future values to present values (by using interest tables) and then compare all of your present values in order to find the best one.

In the following examples I do not want you to worry about interest tables. For now, let me do this, and accept the figures I quote from the tables.

EXAMPLE 2

FACTS - A company has to choose which of two new machines it should buy. Machine 'A' will cost £20,000 and will increase profits by £5,000 per annum for 6 years, when the machine will be sold for scrap for £500.

Machine 'B' will cost £28,000 and will increase profits by £7,000 per annum for 6 years when it will then be sold for scrap, £100.

DECISION - Present value of cost of Machine A = *£20,000.*
Present value of receipts of £5,000 per annum for 6 years = £22,000. (i.e. interest tables tell us that it would be necessary to invest £22,000 *now* at x% interest, in order to receive an income of £5,000 per annum for 6 years). Present value of £500 receivable after 6 years (scrap value) - from tables - = £250.

TOTAL PRESENT VALUE OF ALL RECEIPTS = £22,250
Present value of cost of machine B = *£28,000.*
Present value of receipts of £7,000 per annum for 6 years (from interest tables) = £30,000, and the present value of £100 (scrap) receivable after 6 years (from tables) = £50.

TOTAL PRESENT VALUE OF ALL RECEIPTS = £30,050

From the above we can see that both machines are good buys in that the proceeds from using either machine have a higher present value than their respective cost - but which gives the greater benefits?

Machine A

Proceeds	=	£22,250	(present value)
Less cost	=	20,000	" "
NET Present Value		£2,250	

Machine B

Proceeds	=	£30,050	(present value)
Less cost	=	28,000	" "
NET Present Value		£2,050	

Machine A has a higher Net Present Value (N.P.V.) than Machine B - i.e. there is a greater gain in having Machine A.

What have we done in this example? We have converted the total proceeds from each machine into *present* values then deducted the present value of the cost of each machine from the proceeds, so giving a *NET* present value (N.P.V.) for each machine; and we have then compared the NPV of Machine A with the NPV of Machine B.

EXAMPLE 3

FACTS - A company has a machine which requires overhauling. To overhaul it would cost £7,000 and it would then have a life of 6 years when it would have a scrap value of £300. Maintenance costs per year would be £200.

An alternative is to sell the machine now for £3,000 and buy a new replacement for £10,000. The new machine would have a scrap value of £700 at the end of 6 years. Maintenance costs for the new machine would be £100 per annum. Whatever alternative is chosen, the profits from the machine will be the same. What should the company do?

DECISION - Alternatives available :

A)   Overhaul existing machine

B)   Sell machine and buy a new one.

Re. Alternative A) :

Cost of this alternative = £7,000 plus the present value of £200 per year, payable for 6 years, less the present value of £300 (scrap) receivable in 6 years' time, therefore :

		£
Present value of initial cost	=	7,000
P.V. of £200 per year for 6 years at x% p.a. interest (taken from interest tables)	=	800 *
Present value of total costs		7,800
Less: P.V. of £300 receivable in 6 years (from interest tables)	=	150
TOTAL COSTS AT PRESENT VALUES		7,650

(* £800 invested now at x% would produce £200 p.a. for 6 years).

Re. Alternative B) :

Cost of this alternative = £10,000 less £3,000 proceeds from sale of old machine, plus the present value of £100 per year payable for 6 years less the present value of £700 (scrap) receivable in 6 years time, therefore :

		£
Present value of initial cost	=	10,000
Less : sale proceeds of old machine	=	3,000
		7,000
P.V. of £100 per year for 6 years*	=	400
Present value of Total Costs	=	7,400
Less : P.V. of £700 receivable in 6 years*	=	320
TOTAL COSTS AT PRESENT VALUES	=	7,080

*From interest tables

The question tells us that profits will be the same whichever alternative is chosen so we are only therefore concerned with choosing the alternative which bears the least cost - i.e. Alternative (B).

SUMMARY

The Discounted Cash Flow technique is used to discount all *future* receipts or payments to *present* values so that comparisons can be made in order to highlight the alternative which is most beneficial to the business, either because it produces more receipts or involves less cost. Study this statement carefully.

There are many ways in which a question can be presented to you, but you have only to sort out the various alternatives and then compare these alternatives, bearing in mind that it is no use comparing future values with present values. Do not continue this topic until you thoroughly understand everything up to this point.

Remember that *all* future values must be discounted to present values.

Using Interest Tables

You will find at the end of the book two pages headed 'Table of Factors for Use with Questions on Discounted Cash Flow'. The first page (Appendix A) gives factors for interest rates of !0%, 14% and 15%, and this is the page we are now going to study using the *10%* table as our model. You may find it more convenient to detach this page for ease of working.

Column 1 - Future Value of £1

This tells us that £1 invested now, at 10% per annum compound interest, will be worth £1.1 at the end of one year; £1.772 at the end of six years; and £2,594 at the end of ten years.

To find out how much *£500* (invested now) will be worth at the end of one, six or ten years, we simply multiply £1.1, £1.772, or £2.594 by 500 - e.g. £500 invested now will be worth £1,297 at the end of 10 years.

Column 2 - Present Value of £1

This tells us that £1 which is receivable in one year's time has a *present* value of £0.909, or, that £1 which we are due to receive in 7 years time has a *present* value of £0.513.

Looking at it another way - it would be necessary to invest £0.909 now (at 10%) in order to receive £1 in one year's time and it would be necessary to invest £0.513 now in order to receive £1 in 7 years' time.

If we want to know the present value of £600 which we are due to receive in 8 years' time, then we find out from the table the present value of *£1* due to be received in 8 years' time, (i.e. £0.467) and multiply it by 600 (i.e £280.2). It would therefore be necessary to invest £280 now in order to receive £600 in 8 years' time. Using this column let us work out the present value of the following amounts which we are due to receive over the next 4 years :

We are to receive £500 per annum at the end of *each* of the next 4 years.

ANSWER :

						£
P.V. of £500 receivable after	1 year	=	.909 x 500	=		454.5
P.V. of £500 " "	2 years	=	.826 x 500	=		413.0
P.V. of £500 " "	3 years	=	.751 x 500	=		375.5
P.V. of £500 " "	4 years	=	.683 x 500	=		341.5
			TOTAL PRESENT VALUE			1,584.5

In other words in order to receive £500 per annum for the next 4 years it would be necessary to invest £1,584 *now* at 10% interest.

Column 3 - Present Value of £1 received per year.

Whereas column 2 told us the present value of £1 receivable after 2 years, 3 years or 4 years etc., this column tells us the present value of £1 receivable *every* year for the next 2,3 or 4 yeas etc.

For example, if we were due to receive £1 *every* year for the next 4 years then these receipts would have a present value of £3,170 (i.e. £3.170 invested now, would give us an income of £1 every year for the next 4 years). If we were due to receive £500 per annum for the next 4 years, these receipts would have a present value of £3.170 x 500 = £1.585.

Compare this answer with the example I used when looking at column 2, where I calculated the present value of £500 receivable after 1 year, then the present value of £500 receivable after 2 years - then 3 years - then 4 years - finally I added them all up to give a total present value of £1,584.5.

In other words, column 3 is nothing more than a running addition of the items in column 2! The small difference in the two answers is due to a 'rounding off' of the factors and is not important.

That long-winded example using column 2 was, then, unnecessary. I could have used column 3 to give me an answer much quicker.

To sum up - if you want to know the present value of £x which will be received after, say, 4 years, then use column 2. If however you want to know the present value of £x which will be received *every* year for the next, say, 4 years then use column 3.

Column 4 - Annual value of £1 received now

This tells us that £1 invested now at 10% would allow us to withdraw £1.100 for 1 year, or £0.576 per annum for 2 years, or £0.163 per annum for 10 years before our investment would disappear completely (i.e. become nil). If therefore we invested today, £2,000 and we wanted to know how much we could withdraw every year for the next 5 years so that at the end of this time our balance would be exactly 'nil', the answer would be *£528*. (0.264 x 2,000). Let us check this answer by asking 'What is the present value of £528 receivable *every* year for the next 5 years'? Using column 3 the answer is 3.791 x £528 = £2,001.648, or near enough to £2,000 (our original investment).

Which column to use ?

You will probably have gathered from the above that you could use any column for any purpose, but the obvious answer is to use the column which gives you your information in the quickest, most convenient way.

To get you used to using these tables, I should like you to answer the following questions using the *14%* table of factors :

QUESTIONS :

(1)   How much will an investment made now of £1,000, be worth in 7 years' time?

(2)   What is the present value of £2,500 which is receivable in 7 years' time?

(3)   What is the present value of £600 which is receivable *EVERY* year for the next 3 years? Use column 2 to calculate this.

(4)   As in Question 3, but this time use column *3* to calculate the present value.

(5)   An investment of £400 now would allow me to draw exactly £ _____ every year for the next 9 years.

(6)   What is the total present value of the following receipts :

        £1,000 to be received every year for 5 years,
then   £1,400 to be received at the end of the 6th year,
then   £1,500 to be received at the end of the 7th year.

(7)   A lease being offered to me will cost me £1,000 per year for the next 8 years and will then be renewed for a further 2 years at a cost of £300 per year. What is the total cost in terms of present values?

Check your answers on page 245 You should have at least 6 correct before being satisfied with yourself.

You now know enough about D.C.F. to tackle any question set before you, and you are only lacking in one respect - you need practice at doing it yourself. In three examples I went through with you on pages 216 to 219. I was using a fictitious table of factors for x% in order to bring out the principles involved. I now want you to turn back to those examples and work them yourself using first the 10% table of factors then again using the 14% table. Make all calculations to the nearest £1. Having done this, compare your answers with those below:

ANSWERS - to Examples 1-3

Example 1			At 10%	At 14%
			£	£
P.V. of receipts of £5,000 p.a. for 5 years		=	18,955	17,165
Less: Cost of machine (P.V.)		=	15,000	15,000
	N.P.V.	=	3,955	2,165

The machine is worth purchasing.

221

Example 2 - Machine 'A'

		At 10% £	At 14% £
P.V. of proceeds of £5,000 p.a. for 6 years	=	21,775	19,445
P.V. of proceeds of £500 receivable in 6 years	=	282	228
		22,057	19,673
Less: Cost of machine (P.V.)	=	20,000	20,000
N.P.V.	=	+ 2,057	− 327

Machine 'B'

		At 10%	At 14%
P.V. of proceeds of £7,000 p.a. for 6 years	=	30,485	27,223
P.V. of proceeds of £100 receivable after 6 years	=	56	45
		30,541	27,268
Less: Cost of machine (P.V.)		28,000	28,000
N.P.V.		+ 2,541	− 732

At 10% Machine B has a higher N.P.V. than Machine A.
At 14% Machine A has a higher N.P.V. than Machine B.

Example 3

		At 10% £	At 14% £
Overhauling Machine :			
P.V. of initial cost	=	7,000	7,000
P.V. of £200 costs per annum for 6 years	=	871	778
Total P.V. of costs		7,871	7,778
Less: P.V. of £300 receivable after 6 years	=	169	137
N.P.V. of costs		7,702	7,641
Sell and replace machine : P.V. of initial cost		10,000	10,000
Less: proceeds of sale (P.V.)		3,000	3,000
		7,000	7,000
P.V. of £100 costs p.a. for 6 years	=	435	389
Total P.V. of costs	=	7,435	7,389
Less: P.V. of £700 receivable after 6 years	=	395	319
N.P.V. of costs		7,040	7,070

To sell and replace the machine is the cheaper of the two alternatives, at both rates of interest.

Have you tackled those questions satisfactorily? If not, then you must apply more study to this topic and try the exercises again. *This is important.*
Let us now look at an examination question :

> Joe Blake has a cafe business. He is considering moving to larger premises close to his existing cafe; he may require a bank loan and he has asked for your financial advice regarding the proposed move. He supplies the following information :
>
> 'The annual revenue and costs for my existing premises are reasonably stable and can be set out as follows '

	£	£
Sales		11,000
Cost of food supplies, etc.	5,500	
Rent	1,000	
Expenses (wages, light, heat etc.)	2,000	
Deprn. of equipment	400	
		8,900
Net Profit		2,100

'The present business would have to come to an end in 5 years time when my premises are scheduled for redevelopment. In that case I would get virtually nothing for the goodwill of the business or the equipment. Whatever happens I intend to retire in 10 years time so I would get a job at about £2,000 per year in the intervening period. Of course I could sell the business now for about £5,000 (goodwill, equipment, stocks) and still take a job at about £2,000 per year for the next 10 years.

If I move I shall take the equipment and stocks with me; they originally cost £4,200 and have a written down value of £2,000 in my books.

For the new premises I estimate :

	£	£
Sales		17,000
Cost of food supplies, etc.	8,500	
Rent	1,500	
Expenses (wages, light, heat etc.)	3,500	
Deprn. of equipment	700	
		14,200
Net Profit		2,800

There will be the cost of moving to the new premises of about £500 and outlay on new equipment and stocks of £3,500. In 10 years time I should then be able to sell the goodwill, equipment, stocks in the new premises for about £7,000.'

It can be assumed that Blake's estimates of general expenses for both premises include an amount for routine renewals of equipment, so that any problems of replacing items of equipment during the 10 year period can be ignored.

Blake's cost of capital can be taken as 14% per annum in all relevant years. Assume that sale of goodwill/equipment or outlay on new equipment/stocks would occur immediately and that all annual amounts will occur at year ends.

Ignore taxation.

Required :

A numerical analysis which will assist Blake in his assessment of the problem.

Suggested Answer

Alternatives available :

(a)　continue the existing business

(b)　sell the business and take a job

(c)　move to new premises

Re Alternative (a)

		£
P.V. of income of £2,500 pa. (profit + depreciation) for 5 years = 3.433 x £2,500	=	8,582

P.V. of income of £2,000 p.a. (job) in 6th, 7th,
8th, 9th and 10th year =   .456
                                             .400
                                             .351
                                             .308
                                            _.270_
                                            1.785   x £2,000   =   _3,570_
                                                     Total P.V. of Income   =   12,152
                                                     <u>Less</u>: cost of doing this =   _nil_
                                                     N.P.V. of income   12,152

Re Alternative (b)

                                                                                        £
P.V. of income from sale of business   =   5,000
P.V. of income of £2,000 p.a. from job for 10 years
= 5.216 x £2,000   =   _10,432_
                                                     Total P.V. of income   =   15,432
                                                     <u>Less</u>: cost of doing this =   _nil_
                                                     N.P.V. of income   =   15,432

Re Alternative (c)

P.V. of income of £3,500 p.a. (profit + depreciation)
for 10 years = 5.216 x £3,500   =   18,256
P.V. of £7,000 (sale of assets) receivable in 10 years
= .270 x £7,000
                                                                             =   _1,890_
                                                     Total P.V. of income   =   20,146
<u>Less</u>: cost of moving (P.V.) =   £ 500
Cost of new equipment (P.V.)   £3,500
                                                                             =   _4,000_
                                                     N.P.V. of income   =   16,146

Alternative (c) will produce the greatest benefits followed by (b), then (a).

Your final figures may differ by a *few* pounds depending on how you have used the tables - do not worry about this.

Note how depreciation is added back to profits; this is because we are concerned with *CASH* flow - the same applies to any other 'non-cash' debits in profit and loss account.

It is important to show the factors you have used in your answer so that in the event of you making an arithmetical error the examiner will be able to see that your method and choice of factor is correct.

Comparison of Annual Values

In the examples we have looked at, the various alternatives have had equal life spans, but in some of the exercises at the end of this lesson it will be necessary to compare net present values over different life spans. This makes no difference whatsoever to your working or to the comparisons you make *provided there is no mention of replacements at the end of the assets' life span.* Up to the time of writing all examination questions have stated that, for example, production will cease, or the lease will expire, etc. at the end of the given time periods.
If however, you were told that one machine had a life span of 6 years whilst the other machine would last for 9 years and that these machines would be *replaced* at the end of their life spans (i.e. production would continue beyond the periods of 6 years and 9 years) then it would be misleading to compare the N.P.V.s calculated over the two different time periods. You should instead compare the *annual* value of each alternative. This is found by

taking the N.P.V. of a particular alternative and dividing it by the discounting factor given in the interest tables for that time period.

An example will illustrate this :

A company has to choose between employing equipment X and equipment Y. Equipment X will cost £13,000 and will bring in revenue of £3,000 per year, before charging depreciation, for the next 10 years. Equipment Y will cost £17,000 and will bring in revenue, before charging depreciation, of £5,000 per year for the next 6 years. At the end of their respective lives the equipment will be valueless but will then be replaced by new equipment. Assuming 10% per annum cost of capital, prepare an analysis of these two options.

Equipment X

		£
P.V. of £3,000 x 10 years = 6.145 x 3,000	=	18,435
Less: cost	=	13,000
N.P.V. =		5,435

Equipment Y

P.V. of £5,000 x 6 years = 4.355 x 5,000	=	21,775
Less: cost	=	17,000
N.P.V.		4,775

As the equipment is to be *replaced* we cannot compare the N.P.V.s, so we must find the *ANNUAL* values :

Equipment X

$$\frac{\text{(N.P.V.)} \quad 5,435}{\text{(10 Year factor)} \quad 6.145} \qquad = \qquad £884$$

Equipment Y

$$\frac{\text{(N.P.V.)} \quad 4,775}{\text{(6 year factor)} \quad 4.355} \qquad = \qquad £1,096$$

Check	£884 annually for 10 years	= 884 x 6.145	= £5,432
	£1,096 annually for 6 years	= 1,096 x 4.355	= £4,773

Note how comparison of the N.P.V.s and comparison of the Annual Values give quite different results. Equipment Y is shown as the best buy, other considerations being equal.

Although, as I said earlier, questions on this particular type of situation have not *yet* appeared in an examination, you will find that Exercise 14.11 EX requires a knowledge of annual values.

Limitations of Information

Questions in examinations usually ask you to comment on your final results. In order to do this you must be very aware that the use of D.C.F. techniques in determining the best courses of action is *only a guide*. The final results shown by our exercises cannot be taken as being 100% accurate for the following reasons :

All future payments and income are based on estimates, which can be upset by many factors such as inflation, depressions, changes in consumers' tastes etc., strikes etc. In the question we have just looked at we have *assumed* that Blake's profits and costs would remain the same year after year - we have assumed that he would be able to get a job at £2,000 p.a. and that he would be fit enough to carry on, etc. - we have ignored the possibility of changes in taxation or interest rates - we have ignored deductions from his salary for tax, national insurance, etc.

Your calculations may show one option to be better than another on the basis of present values but the difference in the present values of the two options may be a very marginal difference, and if one of these options would involve much more effort, time and risk than the other, then obviously this will influence the decision.

This should give you an idea of the limitations of forecasts and obviously in practice, some allowances would be made for inaccurate estimates, etc. Despite these drawbacks however, you must agree that *any* forecast is better than none, and provided reasonable care is taken in estimating, then the final forecast *can* provide a fairly accurate guideline to follow.

D.C.F. techniques are used a great deal by many businesses, as you can imagine, and they are sometimes referred to under a heading of 'Investment Appraisal' or 'Capital Budgeting'. Because they are used a lot in business, the bank manager is increasingly being approached by customers 'armed' with forecasts based on D.C.F. and it is therefore essential that the manager be in a position to understand and to assess the reliability of these forecasts. Naturally the bank wants to confirm that the money it is lending is being used in the most advantageous way.

The D.C.F. Yield method (Internal Rate of Return)

This method utilises present value concepts but does not require the choosing of a rate of interest in evaluating. The object is to *find* a rate of interest that will make the present value of the expected income from an investment equal, as near as possible, the present value of the cash outlay (costs) involved for that particular investment.

For example, we are considering two different projects, 'A' and 'B'. Project A will cost immediately £11,000 and will bring in profits of £2,500 per annum for 6 years, whilst Project B will cost immediately £6,000 and will bring in profits of £1,200 per annum for 6 years. We are not given a rate for cost of capital but we *are* given the following table of factors to work on :

Table of factors for n = 6 years

Interest Rate (per cent)	Present Value of £1 $(1+r)n$	Present Value of £1 received per year $\frac{1-(1+r)n}{r}$	Annual Value of £1 received now $\frac{r}{1-(1+r)n}$
2	0.89	5.60	0.18
4	.79	5.24	.19
6	.70	4.92	.20
8	.63	4.62	.22
10	.56	4.36	.23
12	.51	4.11	.24
14	.46	3.89	.26

Note that the constant factor in this table is 'number of years' rather than 'rate of interest'.

Taking Project A first. Our aim is to find a rate of interest (see first column of the table) which will make the present value of the expected income (£2,500 p.a. for 6 years) *equal to* the cost (£11,000 payable immediately). We can use trial and error to do this - let us take the factor 4.62 (interest rate 8%) from the table and multiply this by £2,500. 2,500 x 4.62 = £11,550 which is £550 more than our present value of cost. Let us try a lower factor then, say 4.11 (12%). 2,500 x 4.11 = £10,275 which is £725 *below* the cost. Therefore the DCF yield must be the rate in between the two we have tried - i.e. 10% (factor 4.36). 2,500 x 4.36 = £10,900 which is as close as we are going to get to equating present value of income with present value of cost. The DCF yield or internal rate of return for Project A is 10%.

If we adopt a similar trial and error procedure for Project B we will arrive at an answer of 6% (factor 4.92 x 1,200 = £5,904).

A Quicker Way

As we have been looking for a factor which, multiplied by the yearly income, would equate as near as possible to cost, we could have called this unknown factor 'X'. Therefore for Project A we have a formula :

$$2,500 \times X \quad = 11,000$$

$$= \frac{11,000}{2,500} \quad = X = 4.40$$

The nearest factor to 4.40 in the table is 4.36 = *10%*.

Conclusion

Project A has a higher rate of return (10%) than Project B (6%) and is therefore the superior of the two projects - but is A acceptable at all? If the current cost of capital is less than 10% then Project A is acceptable. In other words, if the yield rate is higher than the company's cost of capital, it is acceptable.

Cost of Capital

How does one choose the rate of interest applicable to a particular investment project? Cost of capital is determined by the *type* of capital available to the company - i.e. share capital, long term loans and bank overdrafts. Each of these providers of finance costs the company a different percentage in the form of dividend and interest rates. Obviously, any proposed investment project has to generate a return at least sufficient to cover the cost of the company's acquired capital.

What do the various providers of finance to the company cost?

1)   Ordinary Shareholders' dividend (%)
2)   Preference Shareholders' dividend (%)
3)   Long term loans - as the interest on these is an allowable expense for tax we are only concerned with the *net* cost of such interest. For example, if we are dealing with 12% Debentures and the corporation tax rate is 45% the net cost would be calculated thus :

   Assuming £100 of debentures, the net taxable profit is reduced by £12 due to the interest payment. This means that the company saves in tax 45% of £12 = £5.40. Therefore, the net cost to the company is only 6.6% (£12.00 less saving of £5.40).

4)   Bank overdrafts - although the interest rate constantly changes this interest is, like debentures, an allowable expense for tax and to find the *net* cost we adopt the same procedure of calculation as with debentures.

We therefore have four main types of providers of finance, each costing a different rate, and each providing finance in different proportions. It is therefore necessary to find an *average* rate - i.e. the *WEIGHTED AVERAGE COST OF CAPITAL (WACC)*. This is calculated as follows :

(i)   Each source of finance is calculated as a proportion of *total* sources of finance.
(ii)   These proportions are then multiplied by the net cost of each source to give 'weighted costs'.
(iii)   All weighted costs (one for each source of finance) are added together to give the *WEIGHTED AVERAGE COST OF CAPITAL*.

EXAMPLE

A company's sources of finance are as follows :

	Sources of Finance £ 000	Proportion of Total				Net Cost of Finance	WACC
Shareholders' Equity (Capital + Reserves)	2400	$\frac{2400}{4000}$	=	0.60	X	18%	10.80
Preference Shareholders	900	$\frac{900}{4000}$	=	0.225	X	6%	1.35
Debentures	500	$\frac{500}{4000}$	=	0.125	X	7%	0.875
Bank Overdraft	200	$\frac{200}{4000}$	=	0.05	X	8%	0.40
	4000						13.425

Using discount tables this would be rounded down to 13%, or up to 14%.

Effects of Inflation

Inflation obviously cannot be ignored and in making DCF calculations inflation could be built into the rates used. However, it is preferable (and sometimes necessary for an examination) to make all estimates regarding various alternatives in *real terms*. This can be done by using one of two methods, viz :

METHOD 1

Calculate NPV in the normal way - i.e. the way you are used to - but adjust the *cash flows* concerned for inflation.

EXAMPLE

A particular investment a company is considering will involve an immediate initial cash outlay of £30,000 and will then produce an inflow of cash of £7,000 p.a. for the next 6 years. The company's *money* cost of capital (what you are used to being faced with in previous examples) is 14% and the expected average rate of inflation over the period is 5%

		Cash Flows (£)	Cash Flows Adjusted for Inflation (£)		PV Factor*		NPV
Year	0	(30,000)	(30,000)		-		(30,000)
	1	7,000	7,350	x	0.877	=	6,446
	2	7,000	7,718	x	0.769	=	5,935
	3	7,000	8,104	x	0.675	=	5,470
	4	7,000	8,509	x	0.592	=	5,037
	5	7,000	8,934	x	0.519	=	4,637
	6	7,000	9,380	x	0.456	=	4,277
							1,802

*   See 14% rates in Appendix A NPV in *Real Terms*.

All that we have done is to adjust the cash flows for 5% inflation by adding 5% to the £7,000 after 1 year, so making an adjusted income of £7,350, then 5% (of £7,350) added to this after 2 years and so on. In other words the 5% has been compounded. This has given us a new set of cash flows which we have then discounted in the normal way.

The positive NPV of £1,802 shows that the project is worthwhile.

228

What would have shown had we not adjusted the cash flows for 5% inflation?

		£
PV of £7,000 p.a. x 6 years = 7,000 x 3,889 =		27,223
less immediate outlay		30,000
	NPV -	2,777

A negative NPV indicating that the project is not worthwhile!

Where an examination question gives the money cost of capital *and* the general rate of inflation, you are expected to work out NPV in *real terms* - i.e. on the basis of the *real cost of capital,* as in the above example.

METHOD 2

This is just a quicker way of working out NPV in real terms. Instead of increasing cash flows by the compounded rate of inflation you just need to change the *money cost of capital* rate to the *real cost of capital* rate and using this rate proceed in the normal manner you have become accustomed to throughout this lesson.

To convert the money cost of capital rate to a *real cost of capital* rate you should use the following formula :

$$\text{Real cost of Capital Rate} = \frac{\text{Money Cost of Capital } \textit{less} \text{ Rate of Inflation}}{1.00 \; \textit{plus} \; \text{ Rate of Inflation}}$$

EXAMPLE

A company is considering a project which will need a £60,000 immediate cash outlay and which will then produce cash receipts of £25,000 p.a. for the next 4 years. The company's money cost of capital is *18% and the average general rate of inflation is expected to be* $3^1/_2\%$ *p.a.* Calculate the NPV in real terms.

PROCEDURE

Convert 18% to real terms using the above formula -

$$\textit{Real} \text{ Cost of Capital} = \frac{0.18 - 0.035}{1.00 + 0.035} = \frac{0.1450}{1.035} \qquad = \textit{14\%}$$

PV of 25,000 p.a. x 4 years = 25,000 x 2.914	=	£72,850
Less: immediate outlay	=	60,000
NPV in real terms	=	12,850

It does not matter which method you use in the examination provided you come up with the right answers!

Other Methods of Assessing Investment Decisions

There are other methods which can be applied in order to decide whether a project is worthwhile or not, or whether to adopt Project A of Project B, etc. These other methods are not as reliable however as the DCF method and they are subject to far more limitations than the DCF method.

Two of the most commonly used methods, other than DCF are :

1) **The Payback Method** - this is concerned with how long the cash proceeds from a particular investment (project) would take to 'pay back' the capital outlay on the investment.

e.g. - A company has to choose between two investments (i.e. projects, different machines, etc.) 'A' and 'B'. The following table shows estimated costs and proceeds from each investment.

Cash Profits Per Year

Investment	Cost	Year 1	Year 2	Year 3	Year 4
	£	£	£	£	£
A	8,000	4,000	2,000	2,000	2,000
B	8,000	6,000	2,000	1,000	500

Investment A will 'pay back' its initial cost in *3* years.

Investment B will 'pay back' its initial cost in *2* years.

On this basis, Investment B is the more attractive, but the limitations to this method are obvious :

(a) Investment A produces better profits than B *after* the payback period.

(b) For *both* investments, profits receivable after the payback period are completely ignored.

(2) **Return on Capital Employed Method** (or Accounting Rate of Return Method)

This method considers how much money each proposed scheme earns as a percentage of the capital investment to begin with. (We assume the capital costs were incurred at the start of the project in all these techniques). This is rather like finding out the best interest rate on investing money in a bank :

		Freezer	Butcher	Hardware
(A)	Net Profit	£27,000	£25,000	£21,000
(B)	Initial Investment	£15,000	£10,000	£6,000
(C)	As a percentage of B, i.e. the percentage return on the capital employed	180%	250%	350%
(D)	Life of Project in Years	6	6	6
(E)	Yearly Return C÷D	30%	42%	58%

Quite clearly the hardware store shows the best earnings, in percentage terms, from the amount of capital invested. From a return on capital point of view the hardware store is the best option.

A problem with this method is that it deals in percentage terms rather than in absolute numbers. From an absolute point of view things could be different. The project which *earns the most money* in 6 years is the Freezer with a surplus of £27,000. The Hardware option requires less initial capital and that is why its *percentage* return is better. When considering projects using this method, care must be taken not to recommend a project with a wonderful return on capital; but which earns peanuts in absolute terms.

For instance, which is *really* the better option - 1 or 2 below?

	1	2
Initial Capital Investment	£100	£15,000
Net Profit	£60	£6,000
Return on Capital Employed	60%	40%

Obviously the scale of project is so different that a return on capital comparison is meaningless. No one who wants to invest £15,000 is going to be interested in a £100 alternative.

In our example, if we assume the shop owner has got £15,000 ready to invest, he would only use £6,000 of it on the Hardware store. The problem would then be what else to do with the remaining £9,000. If there were only low-interest rate investments available, it might be that the £21,000 hardware surplus *plus* the interest earned on the £9,000 came to less than the £27,000 Freezer surplus. In this case the combined Hardware plus Bank interest surplus might be less than £27,000. In which case an overall poorer return on capital would have been made. It is essential therefore to compare like with like. If £15,000 is to be invested, *all* the investment must be taken into consideration.

SUMMARY.

The return on capital employed method of choosing the best project is a good method assuming :

(i)   projects are of the same scale,   and
(ii)   other suitable investment opportunities exist for any unused otherwise-idle funds.

FINALLY

The topic of DCF has caused much concern amongst students. I think you will agree that it is a very relevant topic and one with which every banker should be very familiar - it is not difficult provided you know the basic principles involved and dealing with the questions can be a very interesting experience.

In answering a question on DCF you must have a good method of approach and I would suggest the following :

1)   Extract from the question the various alternatives available, and write these down -
        e.g.   a) Sell the business
                                    b) Convert the business
                                    c) Buy the new business

2)   Deal with each alternative separately. for example, with regard to alternative a) extract from the question details of *all* costs and *all* receipts relevant to a) - make a note of these and convert all future values to present values by using the tables. Then calculate the *NET* present value of this alternative.

3)   Do as in 2) with alternatives b) and then c).

4)   Compare the NPVs of all the alternatives and choose the one which is most advantageous.

        Present you answer in an orderly manner - this makes it easier for you and the examiner.

EXERCISE 14.1

Turner wants a new machine for his workshop. He comes to you with the following problem :

'I have to decide whether to buy or lease the machine. In either case it will have a useful life of 6 years. The alternatives are :

i)   Buy for £6,600. The machine is very specialised, so its resale value at any time after acquisition can be ignored.

ii)   Contract to lease the machine for a fixed period of 3 years at £2,000 a year. I would then have the option of renewing the lease annually at a cost of £1,000 per year (for a further 3 years).

The machine will give a net saving (after running costs) of £5,000 per year in labour costs and material wastage, so there is no doubt that I should have it.

I can find the money to purchase outright but is it worth it? I estimate that my cost of capital is 14% per annum because I could always earn that much on other projects'.

All receipts and payments (unless immediate) occur end-year.

Required :
(a)   A numerical analysis (confined to aspects specified in the above information) which will assist Turner in his decision.

(b)   Comment briefly on any other aspects which might need to be considered in a practical situation.

EXERCISE 14.2

Mr Jones is a respectable customer and he approaches your bank for a loan of £2,000. He tells you :

'I own the lease of a shop which I bought for £4,000, 7 years ago. The lease still has 7 years to run so I can say that the cost of the remaining lease is £2,000.

At the moment I am letting the shop at £1,000 per annum, and I could continue to do so until the end of the lease, but I think I can do better than this. I could convert the shop to a launderette at a cost of £5,000 and this would give me a net profit (after depreciation of £600) of £1,400 every year for 7 years. This represents £9,800 of profit from an outlay of only £5,000 which is an excellent return.

I can provide £3,000 towards the cost of this venture and I therefore need a loan of £2,000 from you. The lease would be given to you as security and incidentally I have been offered £6,000 for the sale of the lease'.

(Take this as being a genuine offer).

Assuming cost of capital to be 10% per annum, prepare a numerical analysis showing the relative profitability of the choices available to Jones.

EXERCISE 14.3

Grimrod is considering two different projects ('A' and 'B') and is unsure as to which one he should undertake. He asks for your help and provides the following information.

Project A will cost immediately £13,000, and will earn for him cash receipts of £3,500 per annum for 6 years. Project B will cost immediately £5,000, and will provide cash receipts of £1,500 per annum for 6 years. Using the following table of factors you are required to calculate the DCF yield (internal rate of return) to the nearest 2% per annum, for each project.

232

Table of factors for n = 6 years

Interest Rate (per cent)	Present Value of £1 $(1+r)^n$	Present Value of £1 received per year $\frac{1-(1+r)^n}{r}$	Annual Value of £1 received now $\frac{r}{1-(1+r)^n}$
2	0.89	5.60	0.18
4	.79	5.24	.19
6	.70	4.92	.20
8	.63	4.62	.22
10	.56	4.36	.23
12	.51	4.11	.24
14	.46	3.89	.26
16	.41	3.68	.27
18	.37	3.50	.29
20	.34	3.33	.30
22	.30	3.17	.32

EXERCISE 14.4

Goldsmith requires some equipment for his firm. The following methods of acquisition are available.

(i)   Purchase of the equipment for cash
(ii)   Purchase of the equipment under a hire purchase contract, involving an initial deposit and two annual payments.
(iii)   Hire of the equipment.

You are given the following information :

Cash price of equipment	£10,000
Period of use in Goldsmith's firm	5 years
Sale value at end of use	£1,000
Initial deposit under hire purchase contract	£4,000

Two subsequent payments under hire purchase contract, one year and two years after initial deposit - £4,000 per year.

Annual rental under hire contract, payable at the end of each year of (5 years) service - £2,500 per year.

In all cases maintenance and running expenses would be borne by Goldsmith.

Goldsmith's estimated cost of capital over the 5 year period is 10% p.a.

Required :
(a)   Calculate which is the best method of acquisition on the basis of the available information.

(b)   Comment very briefly on any further aspects which may be relevant to the decision.

EXERCISE 14.5

John Smith is a garage proprietor who has sought your assistance regarding a business project.
He explains :

'I have an option to purchase, for £5,000, a 6-year lease of an undeveloped plot of land next to my garage. I plan to install an automatic car washing plant on the plot. The equipment will cost £8,000 and should last until the end of the lease, when it will be valueless.

It is impossible to be precise about the revenue from the automatic car wash, but I estimate that net cash receipts, after meeting wages, supervision and maintenance, will be about £3,500 per year.

That was my original plan, but today I discovered that I could sub-let the plot to a neighbouring caravan dealer at £1,500 per year for the life of the lease. Now I am in difficulty in comparing the alternatives open to me.'

Assume that Smith's cost of capital will be 10% per annum in all relevant years, that outlays on the lease and equipment would occur immediately and that all annual amounts would occur end-year.

Required : (See Table of Factors at the end of this book - Appendix B)

(a) Calculate, for each alternative, the DCF yield (internal rate of return), to the nearest 2% per annum;

(b) Calculate, for each alternative, the net present values;

(c) Calculate the net cash receipts per year from the automatic car wash which would produce the same net present value as sub-letting to the caravan dealer;

(d) Explain to Smith the implications of your calculations.

NOTE Ignore taxation.

EXERCISE 14.6

John owns a manufacturing firm. He is considering the replacement of some old equipment used in the manufacture of widgets. He believes that replacement will be very profitable, but he asks your assistance in reviewing his analysis, which follows :

Old Equipment	£	£
Cost	20,000	
Less : accumulated depreciation	12,000	
Current book value		8,000
Working capital		2,000
Value invested		10,000
Annual revenue from sale of widgets		8,000
Less: labour, materials, running costs		6,800
Net revenue per year		1,200
New Equipment		
Cash purchase price	13,000	
Less: trade-in allowance on old equipment	8,000	
Net purchase price		5,000
Working capital		6,800
Value invested		11,000
Annual Revenue from sale of widgets		16,000
Less: labour, materials, running costs		12,000
Net revenue per year		4,000

Return on investment

(calculated as Net revenue x 100)
            Value invested

Old Equipment £1,200 x 100   12 per cent
         £10,000

New Equipment £4,000 x 100   36 per cent
         £11,000

John informs you that he would get only £7,300 cash for the old equipment if he sold it independently now instead of trading it for new equipment.

Both old and new equipment have an economic life of four years: at the end of that time there will be no market for the sale of widgets and neither old nor new equipment will have any salvage value.

Working capital consists of the total amounts required to finance stocks and debtors associated with widgets under each alternative; under either alternative the full amount shown as working capital would be recovered when production of widgets ceased.

John's cost of capital is 10% per annum in all relevant years. Assume that annual revenues and costs occur end-year.

Ignore taxation.

Required : Your analysis of the choices available to John. State briefly which choice you would recommend on the basis of the information available.

EXERCISE 14.7 EX

Hi-Fi Ltd manufactures sound reproduction equipment. Some of its employees have discovered a method of improving the performance of cassette tapes, and the company has patented the invention.

The company's operations do not at present include the processing of tapes, and it is therefore faced with a decision on how it might best exploit the invention.

Hi-Fi Ltd has received two offers from other companies. Splice Ltd is prepared to buy the patent for £30,000, whereas Mainbrace Ltd seeks exclusive use of the process in exchange for a royalty on the tapes produced. In the latter case, Hi-Fi Ltd has estimated that £9,000 per year would be received for 7 years; by which time the patent would be valueless.

Two other possibilities are being considered by Hi-Fi Ltd :

A) Processing and marketing could be subcontracted to a tape manufacturer. If this approach is taken, it is estimated that net receipts, after meeting all costs, will be £8,000 per year. However, these amounts could be maintained for 8 years, after which the patent would be valueless.

B) Hi-Fi Ltd could acquire equipment to undertake the process itself, and market the tapes with its other products. The company could lease premises and some equipment, and it is estimated that net receipts after meeting annual outlay costs would amount to £17,000 per year for 9 years. However, the company would also have to purchase items of equipment for £45,000 and would have to tie up working capital of £15,000. The equipment would be valueless at the end of the 9 years, but the working capital would be run down in the normal course of business at the end of the project's life.

Assume that :

(i) the cost of capital for Hi-Fi Ltd in all relevant years is 10% per year.

(ii) the payment from Splice Ltd would be received immediately; the outlay on equipment and investment in working capital would be made immediately; and all annual amounts would occur at the end of the appropriate years.

Required :
(a) A numerical analysis of the options available to Hi-Fi Ltd.

(b) A discussion (based on the results of the numerical analysis) of the factors to be taken into account by the company in their deliberation.

NOTE Ignore taxation.

Campbell and McCarthy own an engineering firm. They have asked you financial advice regarding the replacement of their existing equipment for the manufacture of flibbets.

Campbell explains :

'I am not keen on the idea. The new equipment would cost £25,000, but it will be worthwhile using for only 5 years. It should yield a new revenue (after all costs except depreciation) of £25,000 in the first year, declining by £5,000 per year thereafter, We would have to keep higher stocks of raw materials and finance more debtors, so about £6,000 additional working capital would be needed above the present level of £4,000 required with our existing equipment.

If we bought the new equipment we could sell the existing equipment for only £5,000, although it has a written down value of £15,000 in the firm's books. It is still serviceable and would yield a net revenue (after all costs except depreciation) of £5,000 per year if we did not replace. After 5 years the market for flibbets will almost certainly be negligible, and whatever equipment we have then will not be worth anything, even as scrap.

Taking the current realisable value of the existing equipment as the basis for depreciation, the status quo offers us a net profit of £4,000 per year :

	£
Net revenue before depreciation	5,000
Depreciation (straight line)	1,000
Net profit	4,000

As a return on capital that is pretty good; £4,000 per year on the current realisable value of £5,000 is 80%.

Compare the new equipment. That will involve a £10,000 loss on the sale of the old equipment, which we cannot charge in our accounts against reserves because we have no reserves. So £2,000 per year will have to be charged against future profits, which added to straight line depreciation of £5,000 per year on the new equipment, gives an outlay cost equivalent to £7,000 per year.

Thus :

		£ thousands			
End of Year	1	2	3	4	5
Net revenue before depreciation	25	20	15	10	5
Less 'outlay cost'	7	7	7	7	7
	18	13	8	3	(2)
Less: annual profit foregone on existing equipment	4	4	4	4	4
Net profit (Loss)	14	9	4	(1)	(6)

'Averaged over the 5 years those net profit figures come to £4,000 per year. On an investment of £31,000 (new equipment of £25,000 plus working capital £6,000) that yields a return of about 13%. We have access to ample funds, but we estimate our cost of capital at 14% per annum, so the new equipment is unattractive.'

McCarthy objects:

'Although I agree with Campbell's basic figures and forecasts, I cannot accept his juggling. The new equipment will pay for itself in the first year; that is good enough for me, and I want to go ahead'.

Assume that the working capital levels mentioned by Campbell would apply throughout the 5 years, that the cash outlay on the new equipment (less the amount received for the existing equipment) would occur immediately, and that all other receipts and payments would occur end-year.

Required :

(a) Your own numerical analysis of the alternatives.

(b) Comments on your results in relation to the views expressed by Campbell and McCarthy.

NOTE   Ignore taxation.

EXERCISE 14.9 EX

Monstrosities Ltd is considering an investment in equipment for making garden gnomes. The company has to choose between the following alternatives :

(1)   Installation of a production line for a single type of gnome for an outlay of £9,000.

It is estimated that regular annual sales of £90,000 would be obtained, and that the corresponding annual expenditure on wages, materials, etc. would be £87,400.

(2)   Installation of a production line capable of producing a variety of different types of gnome.

In this case outlay would be £16,000 and the regular annual sales are expected to be £150,000. Annual expenditure on wages, materials, etc. would be £145,800.

In either case, the production line is expected to continue in production at the levels mentioned above for eight years. At the end of that time the production line in either case would be scrapped, and no salvage value would be obtained

The company could provide an outlay of £9,000 from its own resources, but it would have to borrow the additional £7,000 if it chose the second alternative. The company's directors are reluctant to incur debt and are therefore inclined to adopt the first alternative.

Assume that Monstrosities Ltd will have a cost of capital of 12% per annum in all relevant years and that outlay on the purchase of equipment would occur immediately, and that all annual amounts will occur end-year.

Required : (See Appendix B for tables)
(a) Calculations, for each alternative, of the DCF yield (internal rate of return) to the nearest 2% per annum.

(b) Calculations, for each alternative, of net present value, to the nearest £100

(c) A calculation of the DCF yield the company would obtain on its additional £7,000 outlay if it decides to borrow in order to undertake the second alternative.

(d) A succinct report, explaining to the directors of Monstrosities Ltd how your figures in (a), (b) and (c) might help their decision.

EXERCISE 14.10 EX

Graham is a customer of the Downshire Bank. He has a variety of investment interests and he has approached the bank regarding the possibility of a loan for the exploitation of a gravel deposit on land which he owns. He explains :

'I shall have to make an outlay of £12,000 on equipment and I estimate that the deposit will bring in net cash flows (after all costs except depreciation) of £15,000 per year for five years. At the end of the fifth year I shall have to spend £5,000 on land reclamation in accordance with the requirements of the local authority.

Alternatively I could take up an offer made by Local Aggregates Ltd who would pay me £10,000 per year for five years for the right to exploit the gravel. They would bear the cost of land reclamation.

237

At the moment I am undecided about the alternatives; one problem is that if I exploit the deposit myself the net cash flows are uncertain. I wonder what net cash flows would be needed to make the value equal to the offer made by Local Aggregates Ltd?'

Assume that Graham's cost of capital will be 10% per annum in all relevant years, that the outlay on equipment will be made immediately and that all annual payments will be made at the end of the year.

Required :
(a)   Calculations showing the net present values of Graham's alternatives.

(b)   A calculation (to the nearest £100) of the annual net cash flows for five years which would be necessary to make Graham's exploitation of the deposit equal in value to the offer from Local Aggregates Ltd.

EXERCISE 14.11 EX

The directors of Solway Ltd are considering the expenditure of £20,000 on the modernisation of one of the Company's workshops. The following information has been prepared on the proposal :

	£	£
Existing Workshop		
Remaining economic life 10 years		
Anticipated annual gross revenue		10,000
Less: Labour, materials etc.	7,000	
Depreciation	1,000	
		8,000
Annual net profit		2,000
Cost (15 years ago)		25,000
Less: Accumulated depreciation		15,000
Book value now		10,000

Modernised Workshop	First 5 years of operation		Last 5 years of operation	
Economic life 10 years				
	£	£	£	£
Anticipated annual gross revenue		20,000		16,000
Less: Labour, materials etc.	11,000		9,000	
Deprn. on existing book value	1,000		1,000	
Deprn. on additional expenditure	2,000		2,000	
		14,000		12,000
Annual net profit		6,000		4,000
Book value of existing workshop				10,000
Additional expenditure				20,000
Book value now				30,000

One of the directors proposes that the company should reject the modernisation of the workshop, on the following grounds :

> 'The extra investment would bring us an additional net profit of £4,000 per year in the first five years and additional profit of £2,000 per year in the remaining five years of operation. On average over the 10 years that is £3,000 per year, which gives a return on investment of 15% per annum. That is less than the 20% return we are getting on the existing workshop, so that it is obvious we should reject the modernisation proposal.'

You are provided with the following additional information :

(1)   The existing workshop has a negligible market value, but the site on which it is built has a market value of about £9,000

(2)   Operations of the existing workshop involve an investment of £3,000 in working capital. Operations of the modernised workshop would require additional working capital of some £5,000. In both cases working capital would be maintained at a constant level until the end of the workshop's operating life.

(3)   The directors assume that the company's cost of capital is 15% per annum in all relevant years. Assume that receipts and costs (apart from initial outlays) occur end-year.

Required :

(a)   A numerical analysis of the options available to Solway Ltd, based solely on the information provided
(b)   Brief comments on two further aspects that you consider may be relevant to the decision.

NOTE   Ignore taxation in both parts of the question.

EXERCISE 14.12 EX

Stamford Ltd specialises in the production of plastic sports equipment. The company has recently developed a new machine for automatically producing plastic cricket bats. The machine cost £150,000 to develop and install, and production is to commence at the beginning of next week. It is planned to depreciate the £150,000 cost evenly over four years after which time production of plastic cricket bats will cease. Production and sales will amount to 30,000 bats each year. Annual revenues and operating costs, at April 19-3 prices, are estimated as follows :

Sales (£9.60 each)	£288,000
Variable manufacturing costs	£200,000

This morning a salesman has called and described to the directors of Stamford Ltd a new machine ideally suited to the production of plastic cricket bats. This item of equipment is distinctly superior to Stamford's own machine, reducing variable costs by 30% and producing an identical product. The cost of the machine, which is also capable of producing 30,000 cricket bats per annum, is £190,000.

Assume the following :

1.   Annual revenues and operating costs arise at the year end.

2.   The general rate of inflation is 10% per annum.

3.   The company's *money* cost of capital is 21%.

4.   The existing machine could be sold immediately for £12,000.

5.   If purchases, the new machine could be installed immediately.

6.   Either machine would possess a zero residual value at the end of four years.

Required :
(a)   Calculations of the net present value of the two options open to management using the *real* cost of capital.

(b)   Advice to the management as to which course should be followed, and an explanation of the significance of your calculations under (a).

NOTE   Ignore taxation

Use the following table of factors for n = 4 years.

Table of factors for n = 4 years

Interest rate (per cent) r	Present value of £1 $(1+r)^{-n}$	Present value of £1 received per year $\dfrac{1-(1+r)^{-n}}{r}$
10	0.68	3.17
11	0.66	3.10
12	0.64	3.04
13	0.61	2.97
14	0.59	2.91
15	0.57	2.85
16	0.55	2.80
17	0.53	2.74
18	0.52	2.69
19	0.50	2.64
20	0.48	2.59
21	0.47	2.54
22	0.45	2.49

EXERCISE 14.13 EX

The directors of Burley Ltd are considering two mutually exclusive investment projects in respect of which the following information is provided :

	Project A £	Project B £
Initial capital outlay	80,000	100,000
Net cash inflows, year :		
1	40,000	20,000
2	60,000	30,000
3	10,000	50,000
4	5,000	50,000
5	5,000	50,000

The initial capital outlay will occur immediately and you may assume that the net cash inflows will arise at the end of each year.

Burley's estimated cost of capital over the five year period is 12%.

Required :
(a) Numerical assessments of the two projects based on the following methods of investment project appraisal.
  (i) Payback
  (ii) Net present value (NPV)

(b) Comment on the relative merits of the two methods of investment project appraisal in the light of your findings under (a)

NOTE   Ignore taxation.

Factors for the Present Value of £1 applying a Discount Rate of 12%

Year	Factor
1	0.893
2	0.797
3	0.712
4	0.636
5	0.567

240

EXERCISE 14.14 EX

The directors of Catalan Plc are considering a plan for the manufacture and sale of widgets. This requires an immediate investment in plant of £200,000 and in working capital of £60,000.

The estimated annual net cash flows, from the purchase and sale of widgets at May 1988 prices, are as follows :

Year	£
1	80,000
2	90,000
3	90,000
4	50,000
5	30,000

In addition the plant will be sold for £12,000 and working capital disinvested at the end of year 5. The following further assumptions should be made :

(i)   Annual cash flows arise at the year end.
(ii)   The general rate of inflation is 8% per annum
(iii)   The company's *money* cost of capital is 19%

Required :

(a)   Calculate the payback period of the project

(b)   Calculate the net present value of the project using the *real* cost of capital for discounting purposes

(c)   List the main advantages of each of the above methods of investment appraisal.

NOTE : Ignore taxation   (Spring 1988)

Table of Factors for the Present Value of £1

Years	1	2	3	4	5
7%	0.935	0.873	0.816	0.763	0.713
8%	0.926	0.857	0.794	0.735	0.680
9%	0.917	0.842	0.773	0.709	0.651
10%	0.909	0.826	0.751	0.683	0.620
11%	0.900	0.812	0.731	0.659	0.594
12%	0.893	0.797	0.712	0.636	0.567
13%	0.885	0.783	0.693	0.613	0.543
14%	0.877	0.769	0.675	0.592	0.519
15%	0.870	0.756	0.658	0.572	0.497
16%	0.862	0.743	0.641	0.552	0.476
17%	0.855	0.731	0.624	0.534	0.456
18%	0.847	0.718	0.609	0.516	0.437
19%	0.840	0.706	0.593	0.499	0.419
20%	0.833	0.694	0.579	0.482	0.402

SOLUTIONS

SOLUTION 14.1

Alternatives :   (a)   Buy machine
               (b)   Lease machine

Re: (a)

	£
Present cost	6,600

Re: (b)

			£	
P.V. of £2,000 p.a. x 3 years	=	2.322 x 2,000 =	4,644	
P.V. of £1,000 payable in year 4	=	.592 x 1,000 =	592	
P.V. of £1,000 payable in year 5	=	.519 x 1,000 =	519	
P.V. of £1,000 payable in year 6	=	.456 x 1,000 =	456	6,211
		Present Cost		**6,211**

Comments

It appears to be cheaper to lease the machine and there is an added advantage in that any after 'sales' problems should be dealt with promptly. Also, the option to renew the lease after 3 years allows a review of the overall situation - e.g. improved models may then be available.

The disadvantage with leasing is that tax advantages in the form of writing down allowances go to the hiring firm, not to Turner. It would therefore be cheaper for him to buy the machine and thereby qualify for such allowance.

Note to student : If you assumed that payments on the lease commenced *immediately* rather than at the year end, your present cost figure would be £7,080 - no doubt that Turner should buy. This answer is acceptable.

SOLUTION 14.2

Alternatives :   (a) continue to let
               (b) convert to launderette
               (c) sell lease

Re: (a)

			£	£
P.V. of £1,000 pa.a. x 7 years	=	4.868 x 1,000 =		4,868

Re: (b)

			£	£
P.V. of £2,000 p.a. x 7 years	=	4.868 x 2,000 =	9,736	
Less: present cost			5,000	4,736

Re: (c)

		£
Present income	=	6,000

Comments

Jones' best alternative is to sell the lease. Not only is this the most remunerative of the three choices, it is the least arduous as he would not have the work involved in collecting rents or managing the business, and he could use this free time to earn money in other ways. This comment is of course subject to the estimates regarding profits and interest rates being reasonable ones.

Note to student: The profit of £2,000 p.a. is arrived at by adding the non-cash debit of depreciation to the actual net profit figure - never overlook this aspect : you are concerned with *cash* flows only. The final comment about estimates being reasonable is a relevant comment in all DCF answers.

SOLUTION 14.3

This can be solved by trial and error :

Project A		= £3,500 x	?	= outlay of £13,000

Try 14%	= £3,500 x	3.89	= £13,615 (too much)
Try 18%	= £3,500 x	3.50	= £12,250 (too little)
Try 16%	= £3,500 x	3.68	= £12,600 (the nearest!)

Answer 16%

A much quicker way is to regard the unknown factor as being 'y'.

Then -   3,500 x y   = £13,000

Therefore $\frac{£13,000}{£3,500}$ = y   = 3.71

The nearest factor to 3.71 is 3.68 = **16%**

Project B

£1,500 x y   = £5,000

Therefore, $\frac{£5,000}{£1,500}$ = y   = 3.33 = <u>20%</u>

SOLUTION 14.4

(a)   Alternatives :   (i) Purchase of equipment for cash
                                   (ii) Purchase of equipment on H.P.
                                   (iii) Hire of equipment

Re: (i)   £
P.V. of cash payment   10,000
Less: P.V. of sale proceeds (.621 x 1,000)   621
                                    P.V. of Cost   9,379

Re: (ii)
P.V. of deposit   4,000
P.V. of £4,000 p.a. for years 1 and 2 (1.736 x 4,000)   6,944
                                                                  10,944
Less: P.V. of sale proceeds (.621 x 1,000)   621
                                    P.V. of Cost   10,323

Re: (iii)
P.V. of £2,500 p.a. for 5 years (3.791 c 2,500)   9,477
                                    P.V. of Cost   9,477

Option (i) is best, *but* it must be noted that when equipment is bought for cash or on H.P. a writing down allowance of 25% is given by the Inland Revenue thus effecting a considerable saving in taxation. Such an allowance is not given when the equipment is on hire.

Another point to bear in mind is the fact that equipment on rental or H.P. may command better servicing/repair facilities than would be obtained by outright purchase. It might also be possible to opt out of the rental agreement should the need arise.

Note to student: You are always asked to comment on your results - do not omit to do this. For example, if the best alternative is only *marginally* the best and this particular alternative involves more risk or effort than the others, then the others may well be the best, Always question the accuracy of the estimated cost of capital rate - if interest rates prove to be substantially different then the order of preference for the various alternatives may well be completely changed.

243

SOLUTION 14.5

Alternatives :   (A)   Purchase lease for car wash
                (B)   Sub-let land

(a)   **Re. A**   Total outlay = £13,000 (lease and equipment)
£3,500 (income) x 'y' (unknown factor) = £13,000 (outlay)

$$\text{Therefore 'y'} = \frac{13,000}{3,500} = 3.71 = \mathbf{16\%} \text{ (nearest)}$$

Re. B   Total outlay = £5,000 (lease)
£1,500 (income) x 'y' = £5,000 (outlay)

$$\text{Therefore 'y'} = \frac{5,000}{1,500} = 3.33 = \mathbf{20\%}$$

Therefore, sub-letting is better

(b)   **Re. (A)** N.P.V. = £1,500 x 4,36* = £15,260
                             Less immediate outlay   13,000
                             N.P.V.   =   2,260

             Re. (B) N.P.V. = £1,500 x 4.36* = £6,540
                             Less outlay   5,000
                             N.P.V.   –   1,540

* NOTE Cost of capital is 10%

Therefore, car wash is better.

(c)   N.P.V. of sub-letting = £1,540 [(as in (b)]
           Car Wash   ? x 4.36 = £14,540 (a figure which, if we deduct the £13,000 outlay, will leave a N.P.V. the same as with sub-letting)

$$\text{£? x } 4.36 = £14,540$$
$$\text{£?} = \frac{14,540}{4.36} = \mathbf{£3,335 \text{ cash receipts per year}}$$

(d)   DCF yield shows sub-letting to be the best alternative, but N.P.V. shows the car wash as the most attractive proposition.

If Smith's cost of acquiring capital is 10% then the additional outlay on the car wash would be worthwhile and provided the car wash produces *more* than £3,335 per year there is a benefit in doing this, the benefit becoming greater as this figure is exceeded.

SOLUTION 14.6

Alternatives :   (A)   Continue with old equipment
                (B)   Purchase new equipment
                (C)   Cease manufacture

Re. (A)		£
P.V. of £1,200 per annum income for 4 years = 1,200 x 3.170	=	3,804
P.V. of working capital returnable in 4 years = £2,000 x 0.683	=	1,366
	N.P.V.	5,170

<u>Re.(B)</u>

P.V. of £4,000 per annum income for 4 years = 4,000 x 3.170		=	12,680
P.V. of £6,000 receivable in 4 years (working capital) = 6,000 x 0.683		=	<u>4,098</u>
			16,778
Less immediate net cost (£13,000 less 'trade-in')			<u>5,000</u>
			11,778
Less extra working capital needed with new equipment			<u>4,000</u>
		N.P.V.	<u>7,778</u>

<u>Re. (C)</u>

Sale of old equipment (immediate)		7,300
Return of working capital (immediate)		<u>2,000</u>
	N.P.V.	<u>9,300</u>

Comment :

It would appear to be far better for John to 'sell up' - not only should he benefit financially but he is free of risk and effort *in addition*. Time spent manufacturing can now be used to earn in some other way, so adding to the benefits.

NOTE TO STUDENT :

Working Capital injections are *cash flows* and when a business ceases, the working capital is returned to the owner.

In this question, as in many others of this type, there was a lot of information which you did not know - e.g. current book values, return on investment. You are only interested in *cash flows*, in and out.

Answers to Questions on page 221 on the Use of Interest Tables

Q1	£2,502
Q2	£1,000
Q3	£1,392.6
Q4	£1,393.2
Q5	£ 80.8
Q6	£4,671
Q7	£4,812

NOTE: Because of 'rounding off' of factors in the tables your answers may differ from the above by a *few* pounds depending how you have used the columns. This is not important

LESSON 15

PUBLISHED ACCOUNTS OF LIMITED COMPANIES

Sole traders and partnerships are not obliged by law to keep proper accounts, or to divulge information to anyone (except the Inland Revenue) as to the financial state of their business.Their argument if they had to give one, might be 'it's nothing to do with you!' Which is true - but a limited company cannot say this, because what goes on in a company has a lot to do with a lot of people - i.e. shareholders or potential shareholders who are investing their money (or intend to) in the company, and they are therefore concerned to see how it is being used.

For this reason every limited company (whether private or public) is obliged by law to keep proper books of account and to regularly publish financial statements which are available for anyone to see if they so wish. In addition, all shareholders and debenture holders must receive copies of these statements before each annual general meeting, and copies must be kept at all times at the company's registered office. The law not only insists on these statements and accounts being produced, but also states what *kind* of information must be disclosed in the statements. All accounts must of course be audited (i.e. professionally checked) and the Auditor's Report attached to the statements. The law which insists on all this is contained in the relevant sections of the 1985 Companies Act.

Remember that *all* companies must present *full* accounts to their members and this lesson is concerned with just what information has to be shown in those accounts and by what format.

As one of the main occupations of a bank is concerned with the lending of money to limited companies, it is very desirable that bankers should be aware of what information has, and has not, to be disclosed in the accounts of their customers. This is in addition to being able to assess the bank's risk from a study of the company's accounts.

Unlike other topics in accountancy, this one demands more than anything else a good memory, although much of what follows does appeal to reason and understanding to a small extent. The requirements of the Companies Acts with regard to the published accounts of limited companies are detailed below and you should study them. Examination questions on this topic (and they appear regularly) demand a very comprehensive knowledge of these requirements. The acts refer to three kinds of statement, viz :

(i)   The Profit and Loss Account (which is intended to include the Trading and Manufacturing Accounts as well as the Profit and Loss Appropriation Account).

(ii)   The Balance Sheet.

(iii)   The Directors' Report.

We will look at the requirements for each in turn, assuming that these are the accounts being presented to the members.

THE PROFIT AND LOSS ACCOUNT

The account presented to members will not be a detailed account showing every single expense, etc. but will be a summary of the main items. However, certain items of information *must* be shown, *either* in the account itself, *or* by separate notes.

Such items are :

1.   *Turnover (i.e. Sales)*
     Must be shown, irrespective of amount, together with a breakdown of the types of sales making up the total and a breakdown of the geographical markets where the sales took place. These breakdowns of information may be omitted if disclosure of such information would seriously affect the company's interest - the fact that such information has not been disclosed must then be stated in notes to the accounts.

2   *Staff costs*
     These must be broken down as follows :

(a)   (i)   Wages and salaries

      (ii)   Social Security costs - i.e. National Insurance and State Pensions

      (iii) Other pension costs - i.e. company pension schemes

(b)   Notes to the accounts should show the average number of persons employed during the year in categories according to the company's activities.

3.   *Depreciation*
     Depreciation of fixed assets must be shown in the profit and loss account as must provision for diminution in value of a fixed asset. Any amounts written back (i.e. because they are no longer necessary) to profits should also be shown.

     Where *additional* depreciation has been provided for (e.g. based on a revaluation) this must be shown separately.

     Any amounts written off *goodwill* (which *must* be depreciated systematically over its useful life) should be shown - as should the amount written off any *development costs* which have been capitalised. In the latter case a note should give the reasons for capitalising the development costs in question.

4.   *Writing Down if Investments*
     Any *temporary* reduction in the value of an investment treated as a fixed asset should be shown separately from a *permanent* reduction in value. If any amount is *written back* because the reduction in value no longer applies this too should be shown.

5.   *Interest Payable*
     This must be disclosed, showing separately :

      (i)   Interest on loans from group companies

      (ii)   Interest on bank loans and overdrafts and other loans due to be repayable entirely within 5 years

      (iii) Any other kind of loans not covered by the above.

6.   *Directors' Emoluments*
     The following detail must be shown :

      (i)   Total fees and total of 'other' emoluments - i.e. expenses, pension contributions paid on behalf of the directors, and value of 'benefits in kind' (e.g. company car, house etc.)

      (ii)   Total of pensions paid to directors (unless as a result of the director's own contributions).

(iii)   Total compensation paid for 'loss of office'.

NOTE

The following detail need only be shown where the *total* directors' emoluments exceed £60,000 :

(i)   The number of directors whose emoluments fall within the brackets £0-£5,000; £5001-£10,000, and so on, in bands of £5,000. Do not include those working mainly outside the UK.

(ii)   The emoluments of the chairman (unless working mainly outside the UK).

(iii)   The emoluments of the highest paid director (not his name) if he is not the chairman (unless working mainly outside the UK).

(iv)   The number of directors who have declined their right to receive emoluments during the year and the amounts so waived.

7.   *Other Employees' Emoluments of over £30,000 p.a.*
The number of employees must be shown who receive £30,001 - £35,000; £35,001 - £40,000 and so on in bands of £5,000. (Do not include those working mainly outside the UK).

8.   *Hire of Plant and Machinery*
Must be shown

9.   *Auditors' Fees*
Must be shown (include expenses)

10   *Rents Received*
These must be shown after deduction of ground rents, rates, etc.

11.   *Income from Investments*
Income should be shown from quoted and unquoted investments separately.

12.   *Profit or Loss on Sale of Fixed Assets*
Must be shown (this is a requirement of Statement of Standard Accounting Practice. SSAP No. 12).

13.   *Taxation*
Profit or loss before and after taxation should be clearly shown

Full computations of tax on profits from ordinary activities and on profits from extraordinary items should be shown separately.

14.   *Unusual and Non-Recurring Items*
Any unusual and non-recurring item must be shown separately. Statement of Standard Accounting Practice (SSAP) No. 6 makes a distinction between 'Extraordinary' items and 'Abnormal' items. Extraordinary items are defined as those which occur outside of the normal activities of the business and which therefore tend to be unusual and non-recurring. An example would be the profit (or loss) on the sale of an investment which had not been purchased with the intention of resale. Abnormal items are defined as those which, though *abnormal in size,* do in fact occur as part of the ordinary activities of the business (i.e. the nature of the item is not unusual to the business). Examples could be excessively large bad debts (or 'bad' stock) being written off in a period.

The Profit and Loss Account should show the profit for the year (*including* abnormal items - detailed) *before* taxation and extraordinary items (detailed). Any tax on an extraordinary profit should be shown separately from taxation on normal profits. Pre-tax profit must be shown for each class of business.

15. *Transfers to and from Reserves*
    Must be shown

16. *Dividends paid and proposed*
    Must be shown

17. *Change of Procedures*
    A note must be made of any item which has been affected by a change in accounting procedures in the year (e.g. a change in method of valuing stock or calculating depreciation, etc.)

Other Requirements
The 1985 Act requires all accounts to be prepared in a standard format, and the profit and loss account can be presented by any one of two different approaches, Whichever approach is chosen can then be presented either vertically or horizontally. So in fact there are four different possibilities of presentation referred to as :

Format 1	(first approach - vertical)
Format 3	(first approach - horizontal)
Format 2	(second approach - vertical)
Format 4	(second approach - horizontal)

It is important to note that a company, having chosen a particular format, must use that format consistently in future years, unless there are special reasons for changing.

The current syllabus states that 'questions requiring the use of specimen formats will not be asked, but candidates will be expected to present their answers in good form'.

I propose therefore to show the information required by the Companies Act 1985 in Format 1. Whatever other 'good form' you want to present is up to you!

Profit and Loss Account (Format 1)

The previous pages of this lesson have listed the kind of information which *must* be disclosed in the profit and loss account. *In addition* to these requirements the Format 1 presentation requires *Cost of Sales* (i.e. cost of goods sold), *Gross Profit, Distribution Costs* and *Administrative Expenses* to be shown.

Now that you have read through the disclosure requirements for the profit and loss account, I should like you to read through them again whilst comparing each statement I have made with the following specimen profit and loss account. Repeat this exercise until you have a thorough understanding of *what* has to be shown and *how* it is to be shown.

The following account is presented according to **Format 1** :

249

Robinson P.L.C.
Profit and Loss Account for year ended 31 March, 19-3

	Notes	£ 000	£ 000
Turnover	1		18,000
Cost of Sales			(13,000)
Gross Profit			5,000
Distribution Costs			(1,100)
Administrative Expenses			(1,900)
Other Operating Income			60
Income from Investments	2		20
Other Interest Receivable	3		12
Amounts written off Investments			(10)
Interest Payable	4		(23)
Profit on Ordinary Activities Before Tax	5		2,059
Tax on Profit on Ordinary Activities	6		(850)
Profit on Ordinary Activities After Tax			1,209
Extraordinary Income	7	18	
Less Tax		(5)	13
Extraordinary Charges	8		(24)
Profit for the Financial Year			1,198
Dividends Paid and Proposed	9		(700)
			498
Balance of Retained Profits at 31 March,19-2			1,214
Balance of Retained Profits at 31 March, 19-3			1,712

Notes to the accounts

Note 1 - *Turnover*

Class of Business	£ 000
Foodstuffs	11,000
Hardware	3,000
Electrical	4000
	18,000

Geographical Market	
UK	10,000
Europe	4,000
Africa	4000
	18,000

Note 2 - *Income from Investments*

	£ 000
Quoted Investments	15
Unquoted Investments	5
	20

Note 3 - *Other Interest Receivable*

	£ 000
Bank Deposit	12

Note 4 - *Interest Payable*

	£ 000
Interest payable on loans repayable within 5 years	23

Note 5 - *Profit on Ordinary Activities Before Tax*
Details of charges in arriving at this profit :

(a) (i) <u>Staff Costs</u>   **£ 000**
         Wages and Salaries   1,260
         Social Security Costs   65
         Other Pension Costs   <u>75</u>
                                        <u>1,500</u>

    (ii) The average number of persons employed
          during the year as follows :

          <u>Class of Business</u>   <u>No. of Employees</u>
          Foodstuffs   1,200
          Hardware   120
          Electrical   <u>90</u>
                                     <u>1,410</u>

    (iii) Number of employees with emoluments   **Number.**
          between £30,001 - £35,000   1

(b)   <u>Directors' Emoluments</u>   **£ 000**
          Total emoluments   <u><u>145</u></u>

          Total pensions paid to directors   <u>22</u>
          Chairman's emoluments   <u>16</u>
          Emoluments of highest paid director <u>38</u>

          Number of directors (not including above)   **Number**
          receiving: £5,001 - £10,000   1
                              £10,001 - £15,000   2
                              £25,001 - £30,000   1

(c)   **£ 000**
          Hire of Plant and Machinery   160
          Auditors' fees   28
          Provisions for Depreciation   320
          (Also would be shown profit on each of the 3 classes of business)

Note 6 - *Tax on Profit on Ordinary Activities*
                                        £ 000
          UK Corporation Tax based on
          the years' profit at x%   815
          Tax credit on dividends received 20
          Overseas taxation   <u>15</u>
                                         <u><u>850</u></u>

Note 7 - *Extraordinary Income*
                                        £ 000
          Profit on sale of XYZ Investment
          not purchased with intention to sell   18
                              Less tax of   5

Note 8 - *Extraordinary Charges*
                                        £ 000
          Redundancy payments made in year   24

251

Note 9 - *Dividends Paid and Proposed*

	£ 000
Preference dividend $7^1/_2$% paid	110
Ordinary dividends :	
Interim of 0.45p per share paid	112
Final of 1.72p per share proposed	<u>468</u>
	<u>700</u>

NOTE - to student.

The above specimen account contains far more information than you would ever have to give in an examination question but you need to be familiar with all of his information as you don't know which 'bits' you will be called upon to deal with!

You will note in the above example that Distribution Costs and Administrative Costs, totalling £3,000,000 are *not* wholly accounted for in the notes. **Note 5** for example, *Profit on Ordinary Activities Before Tax,* shows details of many of the items making up the £3,000,000 but these items do not make up the whole amount. The 'missing' items which would make up the total of £3,000,000 are those profit and loss account charges which do *not* have to be disclosed - e.g. advertising, insurance, discounts allowed, general expenses etc., etc. **Note 5** only shows the items which *have* to be disclosed per the Act and of course the other items shown in the profit and loss account are demanded by the Act.

If, therefore, you had to construct a profit and loss account from given information, say a trial balance, you would simply add up the distribution costs and administrative expenses and show the total of *each* in the account, and then disclose the compulsory information regarding the make up of these items in 'notes to the account', (as per my note 5). Any charge or income falling into any of the other categories shown in the above profit and loss account would of course take its proper place (e.g. Income from Investments, interest payable etc.).

The item 'other operating income', £60,000 is not specified as to nature because it represents income (credits) which does *not* have to be disclosed - if, say, £20,000 of this was for rents received (which *does* have to be disclosed) then the item would need a note to the accounts saying that 'this item includes £20,000 in respect of rents received'.

The Balance Sheet

Whereas the profit and loss account has two acceptable forms of presentation (each either vertical or horizontal) the balance sheet has only *one* form which can be presented either vertically or horizontally, so making two possible formats. As with the profit and loss account I propose to deal with the vertical presentation (which can easily be switched to assets on the left, liabilities on the right if you wish to present it horizontally).

The following notes indicate what must be shown and how much detail is required.

Assets

Fixed Assets
Under the above heading there must be shown, under respective sub-headings :

(i)   *Intangible Assets* - e.g. goodwill, patents, trade marks, development costs.

    The period over which the goodwill is to be written off, must also be shown by way of note, also the reason for choosing such period. Whilst expense of research must be charged to profit and loss account in the year in which it is incurred, development costs may in certain circumstances be capitalised (i.e. included in the balance sheet as an asset). Where this has happened there must be a note stating the reasons for so treating the development costs and the period over which they are to be written off.

(ii) *Tangible Assets* - e.g. land and buildings, plant and machinery, fixtures and fittings. Freehold and leasehold land should be shown separately and there must be a distinction between long leases (over 50 years) and short leases (less than 50 years).

(iii) *Investments* - e.g. shares in and loans to associated companies, loans to employees, other loans, own shares held (nominal value shown). A distinction must be made between quoted and unquoted investments. Also, for quoted investments there must be a note of current market value where this is different to that amount shown in the balance sheet.

All Fixed Assets

All of the above fixed assets should be shown at cost, or revaluation where this has taken place, less depreciation to date (note that the provision for depreciation at the start of the year must be shown with the current year's depreciation added). All acquisitions and disposals of fixed assets during the year must be shown.

Where depreciation has taken place, Statement of Standard Accounting Practice No. 12 (SSAP 12) states that the *method* of depreciation used must be shown, also the effect on depreciation as a result of a change of method or revaluation.

Where revaluation of a fixed asset has taken place in the past, the *year* of the revaluation must be stated in notes. Where the revaluation has taken place in the current financial year the names of the valuers *or* their qualifications must also be stated together with a note as to the method of valuation used. Any tax liability which would arise following the revaluation must be stated.

Current Assets

STOCKS - amounts of each kind of stock - i.e. materials, work-in-progress, finished goods must be shown. Valuation may be by use of FIFO, LIFO, or weighted average method. (Note that LIFO would not be acceptable as a method of valuation by Statement of Standard Accounting Practice 9). Valuation may also be at current cost - i.e. what it would cost to replace the stocks now. SSAP 9 demands that the *basis* of valuation should be stated in notes - e.g. 'at lower of cost and net realisable value'. The *1985 Act* demands that if the replacement cost, or most recent purchase price (or production cost) of the stock in question is materially different from the value shown in the balance sheet then the amount of the *difference* should be shown in the notes.

Long term contracts should be shown at cost plus attributable profit or less foreseeable losses - this is a requirement of SSAP 9.

Debtors

Trade debtors (due within one year) should be shown. Amounts owed by related companies (due within one year) should be shown.

Prepayments should be shown.

Other debtors (due within one year) should be shown.

Quite separately should be shown :

Any amounts due after *more* than one year - e.g. amounts owed by related companies, loans to directors (in this case with full details of reason, interest, security and repayment) etc.

Amounts falling due 'within one year' and 'after one year' should be shown under these respective headings of *debtors*.

Other Investments

Certain investments may be treated as current liabilities - e.g. temporary investment of surplus funds. These should be shown as quoted or unquoted investments with a note as to current market value if materially different from the amount shown in the balance sheet.

Liabilities

Creditors - Amounts Falling Due within One Year

All amounts falling due to be repaid within the next year should be shown under the above heading. These would include trade creditors, bank loans and overdrafts, bills of exchange payable, dividends payable, accruals, taxation and *anything* else which is due to be repaid within one year.

The total of such liabilities would, in the balance sheet, be deducted from the total of current assets to give a figure of 'net current assets' (see example below).

Creditors - Amounts Falling Due after More Than One Year

This section would include such things as debenture loans, medium and long-term bank loans, amounts due to associated companies, taxation, other creditors, etc. Terms of repayment (i.e. earliest and latest dates or repayment) and interest rates must be shown for each item. Details of payments by instalments should also be given - i.e. when, and how much. Where any of the liabilities are secured this fact, and the nature of the security, must be shown in the notes.

If any debentures have been issued during the year the reason for making the issue should be stated.

Provisions for Liabilities and Charges

Any *provisions* made for pensions, tax (including deferred tax), or anything else should be shown.

Called Up Share Capital

Full details of the issued share capital must be shown, and where redeemable shares have been issued the earliest and latest dates of redemption must be given with details of any premium payable on redemption.

Any arrears of cumulative dividends must be shown by note together with the period over which the arrears have built up. Where an issue of shares has taken place during the year the reason for making the issue should be stated by way of notes.

Full details of the Authorised Share Capital must be shown.

Reserves

Share premium, revaluation reserves, capital redemption reserve and all other reserves including profit and loss account balance should be shown together with details of movements on those reserves.

Guarantees, Commitments and Contingencies

If there are any of the above liabilities (i.e. amounts which may possibly have to be paid out in the near future, but which do not, as yet, form part of the accounts) full details must be given.

For example, there may be plans to build additional plants, factories, etc. and even though contracts have not yet been formulated, if there is a distinct possibility of future expense on such projects, details of this contingent liability must be shown. Another example would be a possible payment for damages regarding a court action. Full details of such contingent (possible) liabilities must be shown by way of notes.

Details of any guarantees given by the company should be shown under this heading.

Specimen Balance Sheet

The following example should be studied carefully in conjunction with the above notes :

Todd P.L.C.
Balance Sheet as at 31 March, 19-3

	Notes	£ 000	£ 000
Fixed Assets			
Intangible Assets	1		30
Tangible Assets	2		297
Investments	3		50
			377
Current Assets			
Stocks	4	94	
Debtors	5	56	
Investments	6	14	
Cash at Bank and in Hand		20	
		184	
Creditors			
(Amounts falling due within one year)	7	87	
Net Current Assets			97
Total Assets less Current Liabilities			474
Creditors (amounts falling due after more than one year)	8		80
Provisions for Liabilities and Charges	9		23
Capital and Reserves			
Called up Share Capital	10	300	
Share Premium Account		12	
Revaluation Reserve		19	
Profit and Loss Account	11	40	371
			474

Notes to the Accounts

Note 1 - *Intangible Assets*

		Dev. Exp £ 000	Goodwill £ 000	Total £ 000	
(a)	Cost	120	200	320	
	Additions during year	–	–	–	
			120	200	320
	Written off to 31.3.82	80	160	240	
	Written off this year	28	22	50	
		108	182	290	
	Balance at 31.3.83	12	18	30	

(b)   Details of reasons and writing off periods (note what detail is required from lesson notes).

Note 2 - *Tangible Fixed Assets*

(a)

	Land and Buildings £ 000	Plant and Machinery £ 000	Total £ 000
Cost at Valuation at 31.3.82	200	120	320
Additions at cost	–	30	30
Revaluation	50	–	50
Disposals at cost	–	(10)	(10)
	250	140	390
Total Depreciation at 31.3.82	40	33	73
Provisions this year	10	14	24
Disposals	–	(4)	(4)
Total at 31.3.83	50	43	93
Net book value at 31.3.83	200	97	297
Net book value at 31.3.82	160	87	247

(b)	Land and Buildings at 31 March,1983 :	£ 000
	Freehold	200
	Long Leaseholds	–
	Short Leaseholds	–
		200

(c)   The freehold property was revalued on 20 January, 1983 by F. Jones, F.A.I. on the basis of current market prices of similar property in the area. It is considered that no tax liability will arise following this revaluation.

NOTE - to student - the set out of the above information can be in any form provided the necessary information is disclosed. It is accepted that buildings *do* depreciate whilst the land on which they stand usually appreciates in value - hence depreciation *and* revaluation of land and buildings!

Note 3 - *Investments (Fixed Assets)*	£ 000
Quoted Investments at cost	40
Unquoted Investments at cost	10
	50

The Quoted Investments have a stock exchange value on 31 March, 1983 of £45,000.

NOTE - to student.

Where the company holds more than one-tenth of the ordinary shares in another company then the name of that company must be stated together with the description of the shares and the proportion held.

Note 4 - *Stocks*

	£ 000
Raw Materials	60
Work-in-Progress	20
Finished Goods	14
	94

Current replacement cost exceeds the above total by £8,000

Note 5 - *Debtors*

	£ 000
Falling Due within one year :	
Trade debtors	49
Prepayments	4
	53
Falling Due after one year :	
Directors' Loans	3
	56

The director's loan was granted in November 1982 to Mr J. Simms to enable him to carry out his duties to the company in a proper manner. It is unsecured and interest free and is repayable on demand.

Note 6 - *Investments (Current Assets)*

	£ 000
Short term bank deposit	14

Note 7 - *Creditors - Amounts Falling Due within one year*

	£ 000
Trade Creditors	40
Bills of Exchange Payable	20
Corporation Tax payable 1.1.84	10
Social Security payable	7
Bank Loans and Overdrafts	10
	87

The bank loans and overdrafts are secured by a first legal mortgage over freehold land and buildings.

Note 8 - *Creditors - Amounts Falling Due after more than one year*

	£ 000
(i) 10% Mortgage Debenture Stock 1993/97	50
(ii) Bank Loans and Overdrafts	30
	80

Re: (i)   The Debenture Stock is secured by a floating charge over assets other than freehold land and buildings.

Re: (ii)   12% Bank Loan repayable by annual instalments of £15,000. Secured by first legal mortgage over freehold land and buildings.

Note 9 - *Provisions for Liabilities and Charges*

	£ 000
Pensions	17
Deferred Taxation	6
	23

(show any investments on Deferred Taxation)

Note 10 - *Called Up Share Capital*
           Authorised Share Capital - give full details
           Issued Share Capital - give full details (see lesson notes)

Note 11 - *Profit and Loss Account*

	£ 000
Balance at 31.3.82	18
Retained Profit for year	22
Balance at 31.3.83	40

NOTE - to student.   In illustrating the requirement of the companies Act the emphasis has been on showing the *MINIMUM* detail required (believe it or not!) by law. In practice more information may be revealed than the law insists on but in the examination you are usually asked to show the *minimum* information required by the Act and you would be penalised for showing anything which need not be shown. Often, information is given in the question which does *not* need to be shown so you must be very conversant with what exactly is required by the Act. This topic, more than any other in the syllabus demands a good memory!

Finally, you must know what items of information would appear in the Directors' Report.

Directors' Report

The following detail must appear within this report :

1.   A review of the development of the business during the year, and its position at the end of the year. This would include details of the main activities of the company and any significant changes in fixed assets during the year.

2.   Future developments likely in the business.

3.   Directors' names.

4.   Directors' interests in shares or debentures issued by the company.

5.   Market value of land where substantially different from the amount shown in the balance sheet.

6.   Recommended dividends, and proposed transfers to reserves.

7.   Details of any important happenings since the date of the balance sheet.

8.   Details of activities in the field of research and development.

9.   Where contributions made by the company for political *and* charitable purposes *together* exceed £200, the separate contributions (i.e. for political and charitable) must be disclosed. In addition, if an individual *political* contribution exceeds £200 the name of the recipient must be given.

      The above does not apply to payments to parties outside the UK.

10.   Where the average number of UK employees exceeds 250, the company must make a statement as to their policy for employment, training and promotion of disabled people.

11.   Details of company's purchase of own shares.

Once again, these are the *MINIMUM* requirements. Make yourself familiar with them.

S.S.A.P. 6

EXTRAORDINARY ITEMS AND PRIOR YEAR ADJUSTMENTS

Extraordinary Items

Any unusual and non-recurring item should be shown separately in the profit and loss account. A distinction is made between 'Extraordinary' items and 'Exceptional' items.

Extraordinary items are defined as those which occur outside of the normal activities of the business and therefore tend to be unusual and non-recurring. An example would be the profit or loss on the sale of an investment which had not been purchased with the intention of resale.

Exceptional items - these are items of abnormal size but which do occur as part of the ordinary activities of the business - i.e. the *nature* of the item is not unusual to the business. Examples are excessively large bad debts or bad stock being written off in that period, abnormal provisions for losses on long-term contracts, profits or losses on sale of fixed assets etc.

The profit and loss account should show the profit or loss for the year (including abnormal items clearly defined) *before* tax and extraordinary items (clearly defined), and profit and loss after extraordinary items. Tax on an extraordinary profit should be shown separately from tax on normal profits.

Prior Year Adjustments

These are adjustments to *previous* years' profits and losses as a result of the discovery of fundamental errors made in previous years or as a result of a change in accounting policies such as, for example, a change in the method of valuing stock. The adjustments necessary to correct previous years' profits or losses are nothing to do with the current year's profit and should *not* therefore be included within the current year's profit and loss account. Instead the total adjustment should be made to the opening balance of retained profits (i.e. the credit balance brought down from the previous year in the profit and loss appropriation account) which represents of course, prior-year profits retained.

Corrections of the type referred to above should rarely have to be made and should be distinguished from corrections of *estimates* made in previous years. For example, a company may set aside in Year 1 £200,000 of profits to cover future *estimated* redundancy payments - if in Year 2 it becomes apparent that the estimate was too optimistic and that redundancy payments will amount to £300,000 then the extra £100,000 will have to be charged to Year 2's profits. Such corrections of estimates made in previous years are *not* prior year items and do *not* therefore affect the opening balance of retained profits - instead they are shown in the current year's profit and loss account as a separate item.

Full disclosure of all extraordinary items, prior year adjustments and amendment of previous estimates must be made in the accounts.

EXERCISE 15.1

The accounts of Magnet P.L.C. are being prepared. The directors wish to adopt the following treatment for certain items in the company's published accounts for the year ended 30 June, 1982.

(Underlining indicates wording in the accounts).

1. <u>Interest</u>   <u>£16,850</u>

    No other information on interest payments is provided in the accounts. The amount was made up of :

	£
Overdraft interest	3,450
Interest on 9% mortgage loan (repayable 1984)	5,400
Interest on 8% debentures (redeemable 1990)	8,000

2. <u>Hire payments for plant and equipment</u>   <u>£7,000</u>

    The company also paid £18,000 for rent of premises during the year, but this amount is not separately disclosed in the accounts. (It has been deducted in the calculation of trading profit).

3   <u>Trade debtors</u>   <u>£134,000</u>

    The accounts do not disclose that a bad debts provision of £8,000 has been deducted from the gross debts of £142,000.

4. <u>Directors' emoluments</u>   <u>£69,950</u>

    No other information on payments to directors appears in the accounts. The above amount was in fact shared (unequally) by the company's four directors.

5. <u>Freehold land (at valuation 1974)</u>   <u>£35,000</u>

    No other information on this item appears in the accounts. The land is undeveloped and partly used as a rubbish tip. It was purchased in 1960 for £13,000, and was valued at £35,000 realisable value by X. Howitt on 20 May, 1974. The revaluation to £35,000 was made in the accounts to 30 June, 1974.

6. <u>Stocks and work-in-progress at lowest of cost,</u>
    <u>net realisable value and replacement price</u>   <u>£201,000</u>

    The accounts do not disclose that the amount of £201,000 was made up of :

	£
Stocks of raw materials	43,000
Stocks of finished goods	139,000
Work-in-progress	19,000

7. No mention is made in the accounts of a new method being adopted in valuing the above stocks.

8. <u>General Reserve</u>   <u>£90,000</u>

    The comparative figure for General Reserve last year shows an amount of £62,590, but the accounts do not disclose how the change in the reserve occurred.

Required

(a) A list of those treatments which are permissible within the 1985 Companies Act. Simply state the appropriate number for each treatment (i.e. permissible : numbers ......). Marks can be lost for treatments incorrectly listed.

(b) A list of those treatments which are not permissible within the 1985 Companies Act, (i.e. those which contravene the requirements of the Acts) and a brief explanation of why each treatment is not permissible. Give the appropriate number against each explanation. To gain marks, you must give the correct explanation.

NOTE   You are asked to consider the Companies Act requirements only. You are *not* asked to consider whether the treatments satisfy the usual accounting conventions.

EXERCISE 15.2

The following is a trial balance prepared from the accounting records of Melody Ltd at 31 March, 19-2.

	£	£
Authorised and issued share capital (£1 ordinary shares fully paid)		25,000
Bank overdraft		3,620
Bank and loan interest	1,270	
Cost of goods sold	105,800	
Trade creditors		14,790
Trade debtors	12,920	
Disposal of fixtures and fittings		2,600
Fixtures and fittings at cost	23,170	
Freehold property at valuation	36,000	
Mortgage loan		10,000
Profit and Loss account at 31 March, 19-1		20,860
Provision for depreciation of fixtures and fittings		9,530
Sales		146,000
Stock-in-trade at 31 March, 19-2*	20,760	
Sundry expenses	32,480	
	232,400	232,400

*Current replacement value - £25,000
Some of the following information is relevant :

1. Sundry expenses consisted of :	£	£
Directors' salaries -		
Chairman	3,000	
Director A	5,000	
Director B	2,000	10,000
Depreciation of fixtures and fittings		
for year to 31 March, 19-2		2,050
Entertainment expenses		430
Travel expenses		1,270
Other expenses - Distribution	13,000	
Administrative	5,730	
(includes £4,000 wages)		18,730
		32,480

All directors perform their duties within the United Kingdom.

2.   The mortgage loan is secured by mortgage over the company's freehold property; the company entered into the loan 3 years ago and the loan is redeemable by 10 annual instalments of £1,000 commencing 1 January, 19-4. The loan carries an interest rate of 9% per annum and £900 interest paid for the current year has been included in bank and loan interest.

3.   The company's bank overdraft is secured in two ways : by a debenture giving a floating charge over the company's assets, and by the personal guarantee of the company's chairman.

4.   The greater part of stock-in-trade is recorded at cost but certain specific items have been reduced to net realisable value.

5.   The directors have authorised an extension to the company's premises at an estimated cost of £13,000 but contracts are still being negotiated.

6.   The freehold property cost £26,000 in 1960. Three years ago the property was valued at a realisable value of £36,000 by I. Price, professional valuer; the asset was revalued in the company's accounts and the surplus on revaluation was immediately converted into a bonus issue of shares to shareholders.

261

7.	Fixtures and fittings at cost £23,170 include :

(i)	The items sold during the year for £2,600 which are still recorded at cost £5,000, with corresponding provision for depreciation £3,800.

(ii)	Items purchased during year. Recorded at cost £4,950, with corresponding provision for depreciation £495.

8.	Corporation tax at 40% on chargeable profits of £6,000 for the year to 31 March, 19-2 will be payable on 1 January, 19-3.

9.	Provision is to be made for a proposed dividend of 10% on share capital.

Required

The profit and loss account, for the year ended 31 March, 19-2 and the balance sheet at 31 March, 19-2, set out in good style to provide the *minimum* information required by the 1985 Companies Act, so far as the above information permits. Disclosure by notes to the accounts may be adopted where appropriate. Ignore comparative figures for previous year, directors' and auditors' reports.

NOTE	Marks will be deducted for disclosing information which is not specifically required by the Act.

EXERCISE 15.3

The following is a trial balance prepared from the accounting records of Phantom P.L.C. at 30 June, 19-5.

	£	£
Authorised and issued share capital (£1 shares fully paid)		50,000
Bank		8,100
Cost of goods sold	361,000	
Creditors		39,700
Debtors	43,800	
Deferred taxation		7,200
Interest received from temporary bank deposit		500
Equipment at cost	55,100	
Expenses	133,000	
Freehold property at valuation	75,000	
Investment (3,000 £1 shares in Wraith Ltd)	4,400	
Loss on sale of equipment	800	
Profit and loss account 30 June, 19-4		28,200
Provision for depreciation on equipment		26,400
Rents received		6,000
Revaluation reserve		16,000
Sales : For cash		164,000
On credit		336,000
Share premium account		10,000
Stock-in-trade at cost 30 June, 19-5	19,000	
	692,100	692,100

You are given the following information, some of which is relevant :

1.	The item 'cost of goods sold £361,000' in the trial balance was calculated after taking into consideration purchases of £149,000 and the current year's depreciation on equipment of £5,900.

2.	The item 'expenses £133,000' in the trial balance was made up as follows :

		£
Administration costs	(A)	64,300
Advertising	(D)	9,600
Directors' remuneration	(A)	20,300
Interest on bank borrowing		11,100
Rent of warehouse	(D)	3,500
Research and development	(A)	24,200
		133,000

262

(A) = Administrative cost.   (D) = Distribution cost.

3.   The company's bank account is maintained at Spectral Bank Ltd. The overdraft is unsecured.

4.   A provision is to be made for bad debts of £1,500.

5.   The loss on sale of equipment arose from the sale of equipment which cost £6,000; accumulated depreciation thereon was £4,000. No equipment was purchased during the year.

6.   The shares held in Wraith Ltd are unquoted; the directors of Phantom Ltd are of the opinion that the value of the shares is equal to the amount at which they appear in the trial balance.

7.   The revaluation reserve in the trial balance arose from revaluation of freehold property at £75,000 on 4 June, 19-1. The valuation was by J. Freeman based on current values of similar properties.

8.   The share premium account in the trial balance arose from the issue of 10,000 £1 shares at a price of £2 three years ago.

9.   Corporation tax (payable 1 April, 19-6) amounts to £4,800.

10.   No dividends are proposed; the last dividend was for £5,000 gross in September, 19-0.

Required :

The profit and loss account, for the year ended 30 June, 19-5 and the balance sheet at 30 June, 19-5 set out in good style to provide the *minimum* information required by the 1985 Companies Act, so far as the above information permits.

NOTES

(1)   Ignore comparative figures for previous year, directors' and auditors' reports.

(2)   Assume that all amounts are 'substantial' or 'material' for the purposes of disclosure.

(3)   Disclosure by way of notes may be adopted where appropriate.

(4)   Marks will be deducted for disclosing information which is not specifically required by the Act.

EXERCISE 15.4

The accounts of Pendant P.L.C. for the year ended 30 June, 19-7 are being prepared for publication. The following items appear in the draft accounts :

(Underlining indicates the actual words and figures appearing in the accounts).

Balance Sheet Items

		£
A.	Leasehold property at cost	150,000
	Less: accumulated depreciation	39,000
		111,000

The accounts do not reveal that the leasehold property consists of two leases. One has 91 years unexpired (cost £99,000, depreciation £8,000); the other has 10 years unexpired (cost £51,000, depreciation £31,000).

		£
B.	Plant and equipment at cost	200,000
	Less: accumulated depreciation	70,000
		130,000

The accounts do not reveal that the £200,000 includes £12,000 expenditure incurred on new plant and equipment during the year.

		£
C.	<u>Unquoted shares at directors' valuation</u>	<u>13,000</u>

The accounts do not reveal that the shares involved are 4,000 ordinary shares in Crumble Ltd, representing 4% of that company's voting capital. Nor is there any reference to the fact that some shareholders in Crumble Ltd have recently been selling the shares for £2 each.

		£
D.	<u>Contracts-in-progress at cost plus attributable profit, less foreseeable losses. (Cost included a relevant proportion of operating overheads).</u>	<u>78,000</u>

The accounts show comparative figures for the previous year, in which contracts-in-progress were shown at cost (i.e. without attributable profit, less foreseeable losses). There is no explicit mention of this change in the accounts, nor is there any disclosure of the effect of the change in accounting basis on the current year's profit.

		£
E.	<u>Trade Debtors</u>	<u>176,000</u>

The accounts do not reveal that this figure was devised by deducting a bad and doubtful debts provision of £10,000 from gross debtors of £186,000.

		£
F.	<u>Contracts placed for future capital expenditure on fixed assets</u>	<u>49,000</u>

This item does not appear in the balance sheet proper, but in a note to the accounts. The note does not mention a further £30,000 intended capital expenditure which the directors have sanctioned, but for which the company has not yet entered any contractual obligations.

Profit and Loss Account

		£
G.	<u>Operating profit (see note 4)</u>	<u>38,000</u>

Note 4 to the accounts shows certain items deducted in the calculation of operating profit, but no mention is made of the following cost items :

	£
Audit fees	1,000
Entertainment expenses	4,000
Rents paid	6,800

		£
H.	<u>Interest</u>	<u>18,600</u>

The accounts do not reveal that this figure was made up of £14,000 interest on 14% debentures (redeemable 1996) and £4,600 interest on an overdraft carrying an interest rate of 13% at the end of the year.

Required :
(a) A list of those treatments which are permissible within the 1985 Companies Act. Simply state the appropriate letters for each treatment (i.e. Permissible : letters ....). Marks may be lost for treatments incorrectly listed.

(b) A list of those treatments which are not permissible within the 1985 Companies Act. (i.e. those which contravene the requirements of the Acts), and a brief explanation of why each treatment is not permissible. To gain marks you must give the correct explanations.

NOTE You are asked to consider the Companies Act's requirements only. You are not asked to consider whether the treatments satisfy accounting conventions.

EXERCISE 15.5 EX

The following trial balance was extracted from the books of Annery Limited at 31 December, 19-9.

	£	£
Issued ordinary share capital (£1 shares)		600,000
Reserves at 1 January 19-9		372,500
Deferred Taxation		65,900
Taxation due 1 January 19-0		206,000
Creditors and accruals		317,500
Bank overdraft		97,700
Stock and work-in-progress valued at total cost of production	626,800	
Debtors and prepayments	495,200	
Turnover		3,160,200
Cost of goods sold	2,475,600	
Research and development expenditure	73,500	
Salaries and staff bonuses	316,800	
Directors' emoluments	53,400	
Rent and Rates	32,000	
Telephone, postage and stationery	17,100	
Lighting and heating	32,000	
Travel and entertainment expenses	5,900	
Audit fee	20,000	
Bad debts	2,600	
Hire charges	5,400	
Subscriptions and donations	1,500	
Dividends received		7,000
Investments		16,000
Plant and machinery at cost	960,000	
Provision for depreciation, 1 January 19-9		275,000
	5,117,800	5,117,800

You are provided with the following additional information :

(1)   The company began to undertake research and development of new products on 1 January, 19-9. The balance sheet on the research and development account is made up as follows :

	£
Pure research	57,000
Development expenditure	16,500
	73,500

The development expenditure relates to a new product which will come on to the market in January 19-0. Management is confident that the new product will earn a substantial profit for the company.

(2)   The figure for directors' emoluments includes directors' fees of £2,000 paid to each of the company's five directors.

(3)   Plant and machinery at cost £960,000 includes purchases of £60,000 made on 1 July, 19-9.

(4)   Depreciation is to be provided at the rate of 10% per annum on the cost of plant and machinery.

(5)   On 30 November, 19-9 Annery Limited sold its investments, which had cost £29,000 many years ago, for £45,000. The cash received from the sale was credited to the investments account. The directors estimate a tax liability of £4,800 on the gain arising.

(6)   A provision for tax on the current year's trading profits of £10,000 is to be made. In addition, £8,000 is to be transferred to the deferred taxation account as representing the estimated increase in tax liability which may arise on timing differences in the foreseeable future.

Required :

The profit and loss account, using Format 1 of Annery Limited for the year to 31 December, 19-9, the balance sheet at 31 December, 19-9 and notes attached thereto. The accounts should comply with the minimum requirements of the 1985 Companies Act and best accounting practice, so far as the information permits.

The notes to the accounts should contain a detailed statement of the accounting policies followed by Annery Limited, as required by Statement of Standard Accounting Practice 2 entitled 'Disclosure of Accounting Policies'.

NOTES

(i)   Advance corporation tax of $^3/_7$ may be assumed for the dividends received.

(ii)   A director's report, auditor's report and comparative figures for 19-8 are not required.

EXERCISE 15.6 EX

The financial director of Portland Ltd has prepared the following information with a view to drawing up the company's profit and loss account for the year to 30 June, 19-3.

	£ 000
Retained profit at 1 July 19-2	7,200
Turnover	17,500
Cost of sales (Note 1)	10,800
Loss on closure of factory in Scotland	760
Administration expenses (Note 2)	3,660
Distribution costs	1,200
Taxation (Note 3)	635
Dividends paid and proposed	100

NOTES

1.   The calculation of cost of sales includes opening stock of £1,000,000 and closing stock of £1,200,000, each valued on the marginal cost basis. The directors have since decided that the total cost basis gives a fairer presentation of the company's results and financial position, and the auditors agree with this assessment. Using the total cost basis, opening stock should be valued at £1,425,000 and closing stock at £1,840,000. You may ignore the effect on tax payable of this change in the method of stock valuation.

2.   Administration expenses include bad debts of £850,000. Bad debts are normally in the region of £100,000 per annum, whereas the figure for the current year includes a loss of £750,000 incurred when a major customer went into liquidation.

3.   The figure for taxation is made up of the following items :

	£ 000	£ 000
Tax payable on 'normal' trading profit		1,180
Less: Tax relief on bad debt arising from liquidation		
of major customer	375	
Tax relief arising from loss on closure of factory in Scotland	170	
		545
		635

Required :

(a)   Define exceptional items and extraordinary items in accordance with the provisions of Statement of Standard Accounting Practice 6. Give two examples of each.

(b)   Prepare the profit and loss account and statement of retained earnings of Portland Ltd, not necessarily in a form suitable for publication but in accordance with good accounting practice and complying with the provisions of Statement of Standard Accounting Practice 6.

The following balances have been extracted from the books of Newton Ltd as at 31 March 1987 :

	£000
Issued share capital	950
12% debentures repayable 2010	600
Bank loan	200
Plant and machinery at cost	1,800
Accumulated depreciation to 31 March 1986	900
Creditors	375
Debtors	719
Stock at cost	584
Cash at bank and in hand	35
Research and development expenditure	84
Goodwill at cost	72
Debenture redemption reserve at 31 March 1986	120
200,000 ordinary shares in Norfolk Ltd	430
Retained profit at 1 April 1986	108
Balance of profit for year to 31 March 1987	471

The following additional information is provided :

(i)   The balance of issued share capital is made up of the proceeds from 500,000 ordinary shares issued at par (£1) on incorporation, and a further 300,000 ordinary shares issued in January 1987.

(ii)   The bank loan is repayable by five equal annual instalments commencing 31 December 1987. Interest due on the bank loan has been paid up to date.

(iii) Debenture interest due for the year to 31 March 1987 has not yet been paid or provided for. It is the directors' policy to make an annual transfer of £20,000 to the debenture redemption reserve.

(iv)   The plant and machinery were purchased on 1 April 1980 and have been depreciated on the straight-line basis assuming a twelve-year life and zero residual value at the end of that period. The condition of fixed assets was reviewed in April 1986 and it is now estimated that they have a remaining useful life of four years from that date. The depreciation for the year to 31 March 1987 has not yet been provided for.

(v)   The cost and net realizable value of the company's stock, analysed in groups of similar items, are as follows :

Group	Cost	Net Realizable Value
	£000	£000
X	107	90
Y	326	502
Z	151	206

(vi)   The balance of research and development expenditure, all incurred during the year ended 31 March 1987, is made up as follows :

	£000
Research expenditure	25
Development expenditure	59

The expenditure has been incurred in respect of a new product which, it is hoped, will be marketed for the first time in 1990. The majority of the directors have substantial reservations concerning the prospects for the new product, but the Managing Director says, "it is a great idea and we need to give it a try".

(vii) The goodwill arose on the purchase of the trading assets of a small firm on 2 April 1986. The goodwill is believed to have a useful economic life of four years.

(viii) The shares in Norfolk Ltd were purchased some years ago. Norfolk, which supplies Newton with essential raw materials, has a total issued share capital of 250,000 ordinary shares of £1 each.

Required :

(a) A calculation of the balance of retained profit of Newton Ltd at 31 March 1987.

(b) The balance sheet of Newton Ltd at 31 March 1987 together with relevant notes, so as to comply, as far as the information permits, with the Companies Act 1985 and relevant Statements of Standard Accounting Practice.

(c) An explanation of your accounting treatment of goodwill and research and development expenditure in (a) and (b) above.

NOTES : Ignore dividends and taxation   (Spring 1987)

EXERCISE 15.8 EX

The following information is provided for Garner Ltd in respect of the year to 30 June 1987 :

	£000
Turnover	37,200
Cost of sales (Note 1)	24,600
Loss on closure of manufacturing division (Note 2)	7,300
Distribution costs	3,600
Administrative expenses	6,200
Bad debts write off arising from fundamental error (Note 3)	2,140
Retained profit at 1 July 1986	12,600

NOTES:

1. The cost of sales figure includes closing stock of finished goods valued at £2,370,000. The company's auditors have drawn attention to the fact that £520,000 of this stock is obsolete and should be written off.

2. In the past the company's activities consisted of a manufacturing division and a service division. The service division has been making healthy profits in recent years but the manufacturing division has been making losses. The manufacturing division was closed down during the year to 30 June 1987.

3. It has been discovered that last year's accounts were wrongly prepared. Owing to a clerical error, a debt due to Garner of £2,140,000, which was known to be bad, was wrongly classified as cash at bank.

Required :

(a) Define exceptional items and extraordinary items in accordance with the provisions of SSAP 6.

(b) Prepare the profit and loss account and statement of retained earnings of Garner Ltd in accordance with good accounting practice and complying with the provisions of SSAP 6. You are not required to produce statements in a form suitable for publication.

NOTES :
   (i) Ignore taxation
   (ii) No dividends were paid or proposed for the year to 30 June 1987.   (Autumn 1987)

EXERCISE 15.9 EX

The published accounts of Guyon Ltd for the year ended 31 March 1988 are being prepared. The following information is provided :

(a) The company purchased the business assets of T. Rayner, a trader, on 1 January 1988. The assets acquired included goodwill valued at £52,000.

(b) Guyon Ltd purchased 40,000 ordinary shares in Tours Ltd for £110,000 on 1 April 1987. The issued share capital of Tours then, and now, consisted of 100,000 ordinary shares of £1 each. Tours reported profits totalling £36,000 for the year to 31 March 1988, but paid no dividends. Guyon plays a full part in the financial and operating policies of Tours through representation on its board of directors.

(c)   The company manufactures five different types of goods. The following information is provided in respect of closing stocks of each of them :

Type	Prime cost £	Total cost £	Net realisable value £
V	35,000	61,000	92,000
W	12,500	16,000	5,000
X	21,100	23,200	36,500
Y	13,300	22,200	15,600
Z	30,500	41,200	63,800

(d)   Guyon's issued share capital consists of 1,000,000 ordinary shares of 25p each. The directors propose to pay a final dividend of 5p per share subject to the approval of the annual general meeting. The current rate of advance corporation tax may be taken as $^{27}/_{73}$.

(e)   The company sold a freehold property, surplus to requirements, for £300,000 on 1 March 1988. The amount received was credited to a fixed asset disposal account. The book value of the property is £140,000. The company is subject to mainstream corporation tax at 30%.

Required : Explain fully how each of the items, listed under (a) - (e), should be treated in the accounts to comply with the Companies Act 1985 and relevant SSAPs. Where appropriate you should calculate, as far as the information permits, the balances to be disclosed.   (Spring 1988)

EXERCISE 15.10 EX

Shepparton Ltd was incorporated on 1 October 1987. The books were balanced as at 30 September 1988 and a trial balance was extracted. A profit and loss account was then prepared and the remaining balances, together with the balance from the profit and loss account, are listed below.

		£
Share capital		280,000
Freehold property at cost		305,000
Retained profit at 30 September 1988		26,500
Plant and machinery at cost		100,000
Bank loan		80,000
Shares in Megon Ltd		6,200
Accumulated depreciation :	Freehold property	10,100
	Plant and machinery	20,000
Balance at bank		1,300
Stocks		153,400
Debtors		78,500
Trade creditors		32,100
12% debentures repayable 1999		150,000
Interest payable accrued due		21,300
National Insurance payments outstanding		4,800
Corporation tax due 30 June 1989		7,700
Prepaid expenses		3,100
Proposed dividend		15,000

The following additional information is provided :

(i)   The balance of share capital consists of the proceeds arising from the issue of 200,000 ordinary £1 shares on 1 October 1987.

(ii)   The bank loan was raised on 31 December 1987 and is repayable in four equal annual instalments commencing 31 December 1988.

(iii)   The shares in Megon Ltd were acquired as a temporary investment on 5 September 1988, using cash surplus to immediate operating requirements.

(iv)   Advance Corporation Tax may be taken as $^{25}/_{75}$ for the purpose of your calculations.

Required : (a) The balance sheet of Shepparton Ltd at 30 September 1988 together with relevant notes complying with the requirements of the Companies Act 1985 so far as the information permits.
(b) A general discussion of the limitations of published accounts from the viewpoint of 'external' users of accounting information.
                    (Autumn 1988)

EXERCISE 15.11 EX

The accountant of Chapman Ltd has prepared the draft accounts for the year to 31 March 1989. The accounts are prepared in accordance with Format 1 of The Companies Act 1985.

Profit and Loss Account : Year ended 31 March 1989

	£	£
Turnover		2,150,000
Less : Cost of sales		1,200,000
Gross profit		950,000
Less: Distribution costs	36,000	
Administrative expenses	527,000	563,000
Operating profit		387,000
Less: Taxation		112,000
		275,000
Dividends proposed		75,000
Retained profit for the year		200,000
Retained profit at 1 April 1988		736,000
		936,000

Balance Sheet as at 31 March 1989

Fixed Assets		£	£
Intangible assets:	Goodwill		36,000
	Research and development		64,000
Tangible assets :	Freehold property		500,000
	Plant and machinery		1,194,000
			1,794,000
Current Assets			
Stocks		321,000	
Debtors		197,000	
Cash at bank and in hand		3,000	
		521,000	
Creditors : amounts falling due within one year			
Taxation		95,000	
Dividends		75,000	
Trade Creditors		104,000	
		274,000	
Net current assets			247,000
Total assets less current liabilities			2,041,000
Provisions for liabilities and charges			
Deferred taxation			105,000
			1,936,000
Capital and Reserves			
Called up share capital			1,000,000
Retained profit			936,000
			£1,936,000

The following *additional information* is provided :

1. Advance corporation tax is to be provided in respect of the proposed dividend at the rate of $^{25}/_{75}$
2. The goodwill arose on the acquisition of the business assets of a supplier on 1 October 1988. It is estimated that the goodwill has a useful economic life of three years from the date of acquisition.
3. The balance of research and development expenditure consists of research expenditure, £50,000, and development expenditure, £14,000. The expenditure was incurred developing a new product which was launched on 1 May 1989 and is proving a great success.
4. The freehold property is stated at cost less depreciation. The property was professionally revalued at £900,000 on 1 April 1988 and it has now been decided to use this figure for the purpose of the accounts. The depreciation charge for the year must be increased from £12,000 to £22,000 to take account of this change.

5. On 30 April 1989 the company was informed that one of its major customers, Mansfield Ltd, had gone into liquidation. It is not expected that the £50,000 owed by Mansfield Ltd, at 31 March 1989, will be recoverable.

6. The company issued a £100,000 12% debenture on 6 May 1989.

7. The company has guaranteed repayment of a loan of £90,000 made to one of its suppliers, Groves Ltd. A receiver was called in during March 1989 to manage the affairs of Groves Ltd, and it is not expected that the company's assets will enable more than £32,000 of the loan to be repaid.

8. Chapman is suing Bridge Ltd for supplying defective goods which have been written off as valueless. The directors and their advisers are confident that Bridge will soon agree to a settlement of £36,500.

Required :

The profit and loss account of Chapman Ltd for the year ended 31 March 1989 and the balance sheet at that date redrafted to take account, where necessary, of the *additional information*. The accounting statements should comply, as far as possible, with the Companies Act 1985 and relevant SSAPs. You should, where necessary, explain the adjustment, indicate permissible alternatives and refer to the relevant SSAP.

NOTES:

(i) Notes to the accounts are *not* required.

(ii) The tax implications of adjustment to take account of *additional information* 2-8 should be ignored.

(Spring 1989)

SOLUTIONS

SOLUTION 15.1

(a)   Permissible numbers - 2, 3 and 5.

(b)   Not permissible :

No. 1 -
Separate amounts must be shown for interest on bank loans and overdrafts and other loans repayable within 5 years, and all other loans.

No. 4 -
Directors' emoluments must always be shown, and where the total exceeds £60,000 there must be shown Chairman's emoluments, and the amount paid to the highest paid director (if receiving more than the Chairman) and how many directors receive £0-£5,000; £5,001-£10,000, and so on.

No. 6 -
A full breakdown of stock must be shown.

No. 7 -
Any material change in methods of accounting must be stated.

No. 8 -
All movements in reserves must be shown.

SOLUTION 15.2

Melody Ltd
Profit and Loss Account for year ending 31 March, 19-2

	Notes	£
Turnover	1	146,000
Cost of Sales		(105,800)
Gross Profit		40,200
Distribution Costs		(13,000)
Administrative Expenses		(19,480)
		7,720
Interest Payable	2	(1,270)
Profit on Ordinary Activities Before Tax	3	6,450
Tax on Ordinary Activities	4	(2,400)
Profit on Ordinary Activities After Tax		4,050
Extraordinary Income	5	1,400
Profit for the Financial Year		5,450
Dividends Proposed	6	(2,500)
		2,950
Balance of Retained Profits at 31 March, 19-1		20,860
Balance of Retained Profits at 31 March, 19-2		23,810

NOTE - to student
In allocating expenses under the heading of 'Distribution' or 'Administrative' it should be fairly obvious for most items where to place them. However, salaries might appear under both headings (i.e. salaries in connection with distribution and those in connection with general administration - also depreciation of delivery vehicles and packing machinery, and other depreciation - i.e. office machinery). If an examination question does not give a breakdown of types of expense then read the items *literally,* and regard wages, salaries and depreciation as administrative expenses.

In the above profit and loss account there is no heading of 'Other Operating Income', 'Income from Investments' and others (because there are no amounts for them). In practice these headings with a 'nil' amount would only be displayed if there was a corresponding amount to compare with in the *previous* year. Without previous year's figures therefore, we assume that there were no figures for the previous year.

Notes to the Accounts

Note 1 - *Turnover*
Give analysis of 'Classes of Business' and 'Geographical Markets' (no information in question).

Note 2 - *Interest Payable*	£
On Bank loans and overdrafts repayable within 5 years	370
On Mortgage loan repayable by 10 instalments of £1,000 commencing 1 January, 19-4	900
	1,270

Note 3 - *Profit on Ordinary Activities Before Tax*   £
Details of charges in arriving at this profit :

	£
Staff Costs	
Wages and Salaries	4,000
Average number of persons employed (not given)	
Directors' emoluments	10,000
Provision for depreciation	2,050

Note 4 - *Tax on Ordinary Activities*
Based on 40% of chargeable profits of £6,000.

Note 5 - *Extraordinary Income*
Profit on sale of fixtures not bought with intention to re-sell.

Note 6 - *Dividends Proposed*
Ordinary Dividend - 10% proposed   £2,500

Melody Ltd
Balance Sheet as at 31 March, 19-2

	Notes	£	£
FIXED ASSETS			
Intangible Assets			−
Tangible Assets	1		48,440
Investments			=
			48,440
CURRENT ASSETS			
Stocks	2	20,760	
Debtors	3	12,920	
		33,680	
Creditors - Amounts falling due within one year	4	23,310	
NET CURRENT ASSETS			10,370
TOTAL ASSETS LESS CURRENT LIABILITIES			58,810
Creditors - Amounts falling due after more than one year	5		10,000
Provision for Liabilities and Charges			−
Capital and Reserves			
Called up Share Capital	6	25,000	
Profit and Loss account	7	23,810	48,810
			58,810

Notes to the Balance Sheet

Note 1 - *Tangible Fixed Assets*

(a)	Freehold Property £	Fixtures & Fittings £	Total £
Cost or Valuation at 31.3.-1	36,000	18,220	54,220
Additions at cost	–	4,950	4,950
Disposals at cost	–	(5,000)	(5,000)
	36,000	18,170	54,170
Total Depreciation at 31.3.-1	–	7,480	7,480
Provision this year	–	2,050	2,050
Disposals	–	(3,800)	(3,800)
Total Depreciation at 31.3.-2	–	5,730	5,730
Net Book Value at 31.3.-2	36,000	12,440	48,440
Net Book Value at 31.3.-1	36,000	10,740	46,740

(b) The Freehold Property was revalued in 1979.

Note 2 - *Stocks*
(a) Finished Goods £20,760

(b) The current replacement cost exceeds the above total by £4,240.

Note 3 - *Debtors*
Falling Due within one year : Trade Debtors £12,920

Note 4 - *Creditors - Amounts Falling Due within One Year*

		£
(a)	Trade Creditors	14,790
	Corporation Tax payable 1.1.-3	2,400
	Bank Loans and Overdrafts	3,620
	Proposed Ordinary Dividend	2,500
		23,310

(b) The bank overdraft is secured by a floating charge over the company's assets and by guarantee.

Note 5 - *Creditors - Amounts Falling Due after More than One Year*

9% Mortgage Loan £10,000

Repayable by 10 instalments commencing 1 January, 19-4.
Secured by mortgage over freehold property.

Note 6 - *Called Up Share Capital*

	£
Authorised and Issued Share Capital	
25,000 Ordinary Shares of £1 each fully paid	25,000

Note 7 - *Profit and Loss Account*

	£
Balance at 31.3.-1	20,860
Retained Profit for year	2,950
Balance at 31.3.-2	23,810

SOLUTION 15.3
Profit and Loss Account for year ending 30 June, 19-5

	Notes	£
Turnover	1	500,000
Cost of Sales		(355,100)
Gross Profit		144,900
Distribution Costs		(13,100)
Administrative Expenses		(116,200)
Other Operating Income	2	6,000
Interest Payable	3	(11,100)
Interest Receivable	4	500
Profit on Ordinary Activities Before Tax	5	11,000
Tax on Profit on Ordinary Activities	6	(4,800)
Profit on Ordinary Activities After Tax		6,200
Extraordinary Charges	7	(800)
Profit for the Financial Year		5,400
Balance of Retained Profits at 30.6. -4		28,200
Balance of Retained Profits at 30.6. -5		33,600

NOTE TO STUDENT : Depreciation has been included in Admin. Expenses, but could well be Distribution Costs

Notes to the Accounts

Note 1 - Breakdown of turnover if given

Note 2 - Rents Received   £6,000

Note 3 - Interest on Bank Loans and Overdrafts   £11,100

Note 4 - Interest on temporary bank deposit   £500

Note 5 - Details of charges in arriving at profit :

	£
Directors' Emoluments	20,300
Deprn. of equipment	5,900

Note 6 - Details of computation, if given

Note 7 - Loss on sale of equipment not purchased for re-sale   £800

Balance Sheet as at 30 June, 19-5

	Notes	£	£
FIXED ASSETS			
Tangible Assets	1		103,700
Investments	2		4,400
			108,100
CURRENT ASSETS			
Stocks of Finished Goods*		19,000	
Debtors	3	42,300	
		61,300	
Creditors - Amounts falling due within one year	4	52,600	
NET CURRENT ASSETS			8,700
TOTAL ASSETS LESS CURRENT LIABILITIES			116,800

Provisions for Liabilities and Charges	5		7,200
Capital and Reserves			
Called up Share Capital	6	50,000	
Share Premium Account		10,000	
Revaluation Reserve		16,000	
Profit and Loss Account		33,600	109,600
			116,800

* How valued, would be stated in notes.

Notes to Balance Sheet

Note 1 - *Tangible Fixed Assets*
(a)

	Freehold Land & Buildings £	Equipment £	Total £
Cost or Valuation at 30.6.-4	75,000	61,100	136,100
Additions at cost	–		
Disposals at cost	--	(6,000)	(6,000)
	75,000	55,100	130,100
Total Depreciation at 30.6.-4	–	24,500	24,500
Provision this year		5,900	5,900
Disposals	–	(4,000)	(4,000)
Total Depreciation at 30.6.-5	--	26,400	26,400
Net Book Value at 30.6.-5	75,000	28,700	103,700
Net Book Value at 30.6.-4	75,000	36,600	111,600

Note (b) The freehold property was revalued on 4 June, 19-1

Note 2 - *Investments*
Unquoted Investments £4,400
(No mention of Wraith Ltd on the assumption that Phantom holds less than 10% of the ordinary shares of Wraith).

Note 3 - *Debtors*

	£
Falling due within one year : Trade debtors	42,300

Note 4 - *Creditors - Amounts Falling Due Within One year*

	£
Trade Creditors	39,700
Bank loans and overdrafts	8,100
Corporation Tax due 1.4.-6	4,800
	52,600

Note 5 - *Provisions for Liabilities and Charges*

	£
Deferred Taxation	7,200

There has been no change during the year

Note 6 - *Called up Share Capital*

	£
Authorised and Issued :	
50,000 Ordinary Shares of £1 each, fully paid	50,000

276

SOLUTION 15.4

Permissible :   C and E

Not Permissible :

A -   Leases with less than 50 years to run must be shown separate to leases with more than 50 years to run.

B -   *All* movements (acquisitions and disposals of fixed assets) must be shown.

D -   Any change in the method or basis of valuation must be stated.

F -   Even though no contracts have been entered into, the £30,000 *is* a contingent liability and as such must be shown.

G -   Audit fees (only) must be shown

H -   Interest on the long term loan and on the bank overdraft must be shown separately.

LESSON 16

CONSOLIDATED BALANCE SHEETS

In an earlier lesson we saw how a company could purchase enough shares in another company so as to give the first company a controlling interest in the second company. We noted particularly that the second company (the subsidiary company) continued to operate as before, the only difference being that it now had *one* major shareholder (the holding company) to whom appropriate dividends would have to be paid out of the profits.

A holding company may have many subsidiaries (i.e. companies in which the holding company has a controlling interest, by virtue of the number of shares it holds in those companies), and at the end of the financial year all the companies will prepare their own individual balance sheets. In addition, the holding company will prepare a balance sheet of the *Group* - i.e. a balance sheet showing the position of the holding company *and* its subsidiaries collectively. If anyone wished to know the financial standing of the Group *as a whole,* then this Group balance sheet would be referred to. Such a balance sheet is called a Consolidated Balance Sheet. It shows the total assets of the Group *as a whole* and the total liabilities of the Group.

How do we set about preparing one? Well, to start with we simply lump together all the assets of all the companies in the group then do the same with liabilities.

EXAMPLE

Balance Sheet of Holding Co.

	£		£
Share Capital	80,000	Fixed Assets	50,000
Current Liabilities	5,000	Investment - being 20,000 shares in	
		subsidiary company at cost	20,000
		Current Assets	15,000
	85,000		85,000

Balance Sheet of Subsidiary Co.

	£		£
Share Capital - 20,000 shares of £1	20,000	Fixed Assets	16,000
Current Liabilities	3,000	Current Assets	7,000
	23,000		23,000

Now, if we merge *all* the items in the balance sheets, we have the semblance of a Consolidated Balance Sheet (C.B.S.) i.e. :

	£		£
Share Capital (H.Co.)	80,000	Fixed Assets	66,000
Share Capital (S.Co.)	20,000	Investment (shares in S. Co.)	20,000
	100,000	Current Assets	22,000
Current Liabilities	8,000		
	108,000		108,000

However, one rule which we must observe in preparing a C.B.S. is that we must not show any inter-company debts. For example, if the holding company is owed £1,000 by a Subsidiary Co., then the Holding Co's balance sheet will show an *asset* of £1,000 whilst the Subsidiary Co's balance sheet will show a *liability* of £1,000. This is an inter-company debt and the asset and the liability cancel each other out for the purpose of showing the Group balance sheet (the C.B.S.). Think about the reason for this - any 'outsider' (say a prospective investor) wants to see from the C.B.S. how the *Group* stands as a whole - any debts *within* the group are not of interest to him. An asset in the balance sheet of one company in the group which has a corresponding liability in the balance sheet of another company in the group *does not affect the over-all position of the group as a whole* and such items should not appear in the C.B.S.

With this in mind, look at the above C.B.S. What is wrong with it? There is an inter-company debt shown, this being the asset 'Investment' and the liability 'Share Capital of S. Co.'. In other words the Subsidiary Company has a liability to the Holding Company of £20,000, the Holding Company regarding this as its own asset.

These items cancel each other out and the C.B.S. *should* appear thus :

	£		£
Share Capital	80,000	Fixed Assets	66,000
Current Liabilities	8,000	Current Assets	22,000
	88,000		88,000

You may be wondering how we can say that this is the position of the Group, when the Subsidiary Company's share capital does not appear! But it *does* - it appears as part of the assets, less part of the liabilities (£16,000 + £7,000 – £3,000) in the above balance sheet, It is the assets less liabilities which *are* capital. All I am saying is that there is no need to then show that, of the 'capital' represented in the above balance sheet, £20,000 is owing by S.Co. to H.Co. and to H.Co. by S.Co.! This inter-company debt is cancelled out for the purpose of our C.B.S. The figure shown for Share Capital £80,000 is the H. Co's share capital representing its own Fixed and Current assets and liabilities (£60,000) plus the Subsidiary Company's assets and liabilities (£20,000).

For the above reasons, the share capital (and this includes reserves such as P & L account) of a subsidiary company will *never* appear in a C.B.S. because this liability will always be cancelled out against the corresponding asset 'Investment' in the holding company's balance sheet.

EXAMPLE 1.

Balance Sheet of H. Co. Ltd

	£		£
Share Capital	100,000	Fixed Assets	76,000
Reserves	20,000	Investment 30,000 shares in S.Co	
	120,000	at cost	34,000
Current Liabilities	8,000	Current Assets	18,000
	128,000		128,000

Balance Sheet of S. Co. Ltd

	£		£
Share Capital (£1)	30,000	Fixed Assets	30,000
Reserves	4,000		
	34,000	Current Assets	6,000
Current Liabilities	2,000		
	36,000		36,000

Consolidated Balance Sheet of H. Co. Ltd and its Subsidiary Co

	£		£
Share Capital	100,000	Fixed Assets	106,000
Reserves	20,000	Current Assets	24,000
	120,000		
Current Liabilities	10,000		
	130,000		130,000

Goodwill

Suppose that the 'Investment' item does not exactly cancel out against the 'Share Capital' item of the subsidiary company! In other words suppose that the cost of the shares in the subsidiary company is more that their balance sheet values. Then the item 'Investment at *cost*' in the holding company's balance sheet will be *more* than the item 'Share Capital' in the subsidiary company's balance sheet. In this case the difference will represent 'Goodwill' and this will have to appear in the C.B.S. to balance it.

To see this, turn to example 1, and read the item of 'Investment at Cost' in the holding company's balance sheet as £44,000 (not £34,000). If we assume that this extra £10,000 was paid by H. Co. in cash, then the current assets will now read as '£8,000' and the balance sheet will still balance.

In this case, the C.B.S. would now look like this :

	£		£
Share Capital	100,000	Goodwill	10,000
Reserves	20,000	Fixed Assets	106,000
	120,000	Current Assets	14,000
Current Liabilities	10,000		
	130,000		130,000

Goodwill, then in a C.B.S. represents the amount paid for a subsidiary company's capital which is over and above the balance sheet value of the capital acquired.

If the Holding Company acquires the shares in the subsidiary company for *less* than their balance sheet value, then the two items 'Investment' (in H. Co's balance sheet) and 'share capital' (in S. Co's balance sheet) again will not cancel each other out exactly - e.g. Investment at cost = £16,000 - Share Capital acquired = £20,000 - here we have £4,000 more liabilities than assets and this £4,000 will have to appear on the liabilities side of the C.B.S. as a 'Capital Reserve'.

EXAMPLE 2.

From the following balance sheets we are going to calculate the amount to be shown in the C.B.S. as 'Goodwill'.

Balance Sheet of H. Co. Ltd

	£		£
Share Capital	100,000	Assets	77,000
Reserves	10,000	Investments in Sub. Co's :	
		10,000 shares in S1 Co. at cost	15,000
		7,500 shares in S2 Co. at cost	8,000
		6,000 shares in S3 Co. at cost	10,000
	110,000		110,000

Balance Sheet of S1 Co. Ltd

	£		£
Share Capital (£1 shares)	10,000	Assets	13,000
Reserves	3,000		
	13,000		13,000

Balance Sheet of S2 Co. Ltd

	£		£
Share Capital (£1 shares)	7,500	Assets	9,000
Reserves	1,500		
	9,000		9,000

Balance Sheet of S3 Co. Ltd

	£		£
Share Capital	9,000	Assets	12,000
Reserves	3,000		
	12,000		12,000

Re: S1 Co. Ltd

H. Co. owns *all* the shares and these have a value of £13,000. H. Co. has had to pay a figure of £15,000 for these shares, and £2,000 has been paid for goodwill. For the purpose of the C.B.S. *GOODWILL = £2,000*.

Re: S2 Co. Ltd

H. Co. owns *all* shares, these having a value of £9,000. As only £8,000 has been paid for them, a capital reserve of £1,000 has been created. For the purpose of the C.B.S. *CAPITAL RESERVE = £1,000*.

Re: S3 Co. Ltd

H. Co. only owns two-thirds of the share capital of S3 Co. - H.Co. is, therefore, only acquiring two-thirds of the total value (i.e. $^2/_3$ of £12,000) which is £8,000. For this £8,000 of value H. Co. has had to pay £10,000 - i.e. Goodwill of £2,000. For the purpose of the C.B.S. *GOODWILL = £2,000*.

In the C.B.S. we can now show *one* figure representing Goodwill, viz :

		£
Goodwill re S1 Co.	=	2,000
Goodwill re S3 Co.	=	2,000
		4,000
Less: Capital Reserve re S2 Co.	=	1,000
Net Goodwill		3,000

To find Goodwill for the purpose of the C.B.S. we need to know two things -

1) *How much value is being acquired -*
   i.e. the value of the total share capital and reserves of the subsidiary company or, the value of the proportion of shares being bought (in the case of S3 Co. above, only 6,000 of a total of 9,000 shares were bought by H. Co. and as the *total* value of the shares was £12,000, the value being acquired by H. Co. was $^2/_3$ of this - £8,000, for which it paid £10,000).

2) *How much is being paid for that value -*
   The difference represents either Goodwill or Capital Reserve and this amount will show in the C.B.S. *every* year.

Minority Interests

Let us now finish off this example by preparing a C.B.S. :

C.B.S. of H. Co. and its subsidiaries S1, S2 and S3

	£		£
Share Capital	100,000	Goodwill	3,000
Reserves	10,000	Assets	111,000
	110,000		114,000

It does not balance! Why?

This is the balance sheet of the Group and it tells us that the *Group* owns assets of £111,000. Is this true? No! Some of these assets belong to people *outside* the Group - i.e. the people who own the other 3,000 shares in S3 company (above); as these people own one-third of the value of S3 company they therefore own £4,000 ($^{1}/_{3}$ of £12,000) of the value of S3 company. These people have a *MINORITY* share in S3 company and are referred to as *Minority Shareholders*.

We could therefore reduce the item assets £111,000 to a figure of £107,000 and all would be well, but although it is true that the Group does not *own* £111,000 of assets, it has got *CONTROL* of £111,000 of assets so we will leave this figure in the C.B.S. and show on the liabilities side of the C.B.S. an item 'Minority interests £4,000'. (If you insert this in the C.B.S. it will then balance).

The C.B.S. now 'says' - that the Group has assets of £111,000 of which £4,000 is owed to people outside the group (remember that a liability is something *OWED*).

SUMMARY

(1)   The capital of the Holding Co. (i.e. share capital + reserves) always appear in the C.B.S.

(2)   The share capital and reserves of the Subsidiary Co. are not shown in the C.B.S. (this value is already there in the form of assets less liabilities) nor is the Holding Company's asset 'Investment in Sub. Co. at cost', the liability and the asset being cancelled out by each other. If they will not exactly cancel out this means that the 'cost of investment' is either greater or less than the value acquired and this difference is treated as either Goodwill or Capital Reserve respectively and is shown in the C.B.S. every year thereafter *at the same figure*.

(3)   If the Holding Company only owns a proportion of the number of shares issued by the subsidiary company then it has only purchased *that proportion* of the total value of the shares. (Total value of shares being share capital plus all reserves).

(4)   If, say, $^{1}/_{4}$ of the shares issued by the subsidiary company do not belong to the holding company then $^{1}/_{4}$ of the value of the subsidiary company represents a *MINORITY INTEREST* and is shown as a liability in the C.B.S. (i.e. the group is 'claiming' *all* of the assets of the subsidiary company in the C.B.S. whereas some of these are owing to 'outsiders'). If all subsidiaries are 100% owned by the holding company then there obviously cannot be any minority interests.

Two very important observations must now be made.

1.   Goodwill is the excess paid by the holding company for the subsidiary's shares or proportion of shares *AT THE DATE OF TAKING CONTROL*. In calculating Goodwill we want to know how much was paid and how much value was acquired *when the holding company took control*. It is no use looking at the value of the subsidiary's shares as per its 1980 balance sheet if these shares were acquired in 1977, when the value was probably quite different. The goodwill as calculated appears in the C.B.S. at the same figure every year thereafter.

2. Minority Interest is that part of the total value of the subsidiary company which belongs to 'outsiders'. If the C.B.S. at 19-1 includes £x of assets which belong to 'outsiders' then the minority interest (liability) at 19-1 is £x. If the value of the minority interest has changed to £y by 19-2 then it is shown as £y in the 19-2 C.B.S. In other words minority interest is calculated by looking at the value of the subsidiary company *AS AT THE DATE OF THE C.B.S.* - the date that the holding company took control is irrelevant.

Briefly then :

1) In calculating Goodwill : First Basic Question is 'What was the value of the subsidiary company *when it was acquired?*'

2) In calculating Minority Interest : First Basic Question is 'What is the value of the subsidiary company *now* ?'

(If at this point you are a little bothered by my statement that 'Goodwill is calculated on the basis of values at 'take over' date and that once calculated it appears in every future C.B.S. *at the same figure* ', then please be patient for a little while.

What I have said *is* true and I am not going to change it - but it does want further explanation, which I will give you after you have done the following question).

QUESTION
The balance sheet of S. Ltd, a subsidiary of H. Ltd, as at 31 December 19-4 was :

	£		£
Share Capital (£1 shares)	60,000	Total Assets	85,000
Profit and Loss account	25,000		
	85,000		85,000

	£		£
Summary of Profit and Loss account			
Balance at 31 December, 19-1	17,000		
Plus profits for 19-2	4,000		
Balance at 31 December, 19-2	21,000		
Less loss for 19-3	2,000		
Balance at 31 December, 19-3	19,000		
Plus profits for 19-4	6,000		
	25,000		

Show the amounts *that would appear in the C.B.S. as at 31 December, 19-4* in respect of (a) goodwill and (b) Minority Interests, on the basis of each of the following assumptions :

(a) On the assumption that H. Ltd acquired 60,000 shares in S. Ltd on 31 December, 19-2 for £85,000.

(b) On the assumption that H. Ltd acquired 45,000 shares in S. Ltd on 31 December, 19-1 for £62,000.

(c) On the assumption that H. Ltd acquired 48,000 shares in S. Ltd on 31 December, 19-3 for £64,000.

N.B. (a), (b) and (c) are 3 *separate* exercises.

Show your answer in this form :

	Goodwill	Minority Interests
	£	£
Assumption -		
(a)		
(b)		
(c)		

I should like you to work this question and then turn to page 289 to check your work. Do not proceed further until you can happily produce a 100% correct answer.

Treatment of changes in Subsidiary Company's value

You know that goodwill is calculated by comparing the purchase price of the subsidiary's shares with the value of those shares *at the date they are acquired*. Once determined, this figure for Goodwill appears in all subsequent consolidated balance sheets and would only change its amount if further subsidiary companies were acquired.

But surely, Goodwill *must* change as the value of the subsidiary's shares changes from year to year? For example, if H.Co. acquires all the shares in S.Co. in Year 1, when the shares have a value of £ 10,000 and £12,000 is paid for those shares - then the following things happen :

EXAMPLE 3.

Section of H. Co's Balance Sheet, Year 1

Liabilities	£	Assets	£
		(1) Investment at cost	12,000

Section of S. Co's Balance Sheet, Year 1

	£		£
(2) Share Capital (£ shares)	8,000		
Reserves	2,000		
	10,000		

Section of Consolidated Balance Sheet, Year 1

	£		£
		(3) Goodwill	2,000

i.e. (1) cancels out against (2) and the 'odd' £2,000 of asset which does *not* cancel out is shown on the C.B.S. (3)

Now, as the years go by, the value of S. Co. is going to change as it makes profits and losses and whilst the item (1) above will remain 'at cost', item (2) *is* going to change and by Year 2 the position could be as follows :

Section of H. Co's Balance Sheet, Year 2

Liabilities	£	Assets	£
		(1) Investment at cost	12,000

Section of S. Co's Balance Sheet, Year 2

		£		£
(2)	Share Capital	8,000		
	Reserves	3,500		
		11,500		

To keep the C.B.S. in balance we can either show Goodwill at Year 2 as £500 (now that the value of the shares has come more into line with the purchase price) or we can leave Goodwill at its original figure of £2,000 and show on the *other* side of the C.B.S. the increase in value which has taken place in the capital of S. Co. i.e. £1,500 *since the shares were acquired* - i.e. since Year 1, viz :

Section of Consolidated Balance Sheet, Year 2

		£			£
(4)	Increase in Reserves of S. Co.	1,500	(3)	Goodwill	2,000

The practice is to do this rather than alter Goodwill year by year. It is very important to note that the increase shown in the C.B.S. (4) is the increase (or decrease) since the date the shares were acquired - (i.e. since the date Goodwill was calculated).

If the holding company owns only a proportion (say $^3/_4$) of the subsidiary's shares, then only *that* proportion ($^3/_4$) of the increase or decrease in reserves will be shown in the C.B.S. This should be obvious in that the *Group* can only take credit for an increase in reserves which *belongs* to the Group - (i.e. $^3/_4$).

SUMMARY

Let us look at a detailed C.B.S. and see what it tells us.

Consolidated Balance Sheet of H. Co. Ltd and its Sub. Co., S. Ltd.

	£		£
Authorised and Issued Share Capital		Goodwill	7,000
200,000 Ordinary Shares of £1 each	200,000	Fixed Assets	311,000
		Current Assets	35,000
Reserves			
H. Ltd	70,000		
S. Ltd (increase since acquisition)	5,000		
	275,000		
6% Debentures	50,000		
Minority Interests	8,000		
Current Liabilities	20,000		
	353,000		353,000

From this we can see that :

(1)   The *HOLDING* company has an issued share capital of £200,000 and total reserves of £70,000.

(2)   The value of the shares in S. Ltd acquired by H. Ltd was £7,000 less than the amount paid for them by H. Ltd.

(3)   That part of the subsidiary's reserves which belongs to the holding company (i.e. the proportion according to the number of shares held by the holding company) has increased by £5,000 *since the shares were acquired.*

(4)   Assets and Liabilities of H. Ltd and S. Ltd *combined* are as follows :

	£
Fixed Assets	311,000
Current Assets	35,000
Current Liabilities	20,000
Debentures	50,000

(5)   Of the net assets of S. Ltd which are incorporated into the C.B.S. (as part of the amounts in note (4), £8,000 worth belongs to minority shareholders of S. Ltd.

It should be clear by now that the main 'difficulties in preparing a C.B.S. are in the calculation of :

(a)   Goodwill (capital reserve)
(b)   Increase/decrease in the subsidiary companies' reserves
(c)   Minority interests

and in tackling a C.B.S. question you should set about working out these amounts immediately. The preparation of the rest of the C.B.S. is more or less a matter of addition.

So let me now remind you for the last time, that in calculating

(a)   *GOODWILL* - you are concerned with the value of the subsidiary (or a proportion of the value if the subsidiary is not wholly owned) *at the date the subsidiary was 'taken over'.*

(b)   *RESERVES OF SUBSIDIARY* - you are concerned with the increases/decreases in the reserves (or a proportion of these increases/decreases if the subsidiary is not wholly owned) which have taken place *since the date the subsidiary was 'taken over'.*

(c)   *MINORITY INTERESTS* - you are concerned with the appropriate proportions of the total value of the subsidiary *at the date of the C.B.S. - i.e. now.*

Let us now look at an amended past examination question.

The following are summarised balance sheets of Aire Ltd, Beal Ltd and Calder Ltd at 31 December, 19-4.

	Aire Ltd	Beal Ltd	Calder Ltd
	£	£	£
Issued Share Capital (£1 Ordinary shares)	200,000	50,000	20,000
Profit and Loss account at 31 December 19-2	68,000	39,000	8,000
Net Profit (LOSS) 19-3	18,300	(3,200)	3,000
Net Profit 19-4	21,700	7,300	4,000
Current liabilities	72,000	16,900	5,000
	380,000	110,000	40,000
Fixed and current assets	286,200	110,000	40,000
40,000 Ordinary shares in Beal Ltd at cost	70,000	–	-
15,000 Ordinary shares in Calder Ltd at cost	23,800	–	–
	380,000	110,000	40,000

On 31 December, 19-2 Aire Ltd acquired its shares in Calder Ltd. On 31 December, 19-3 Aire Ltd acquired its shares in Beal Ltd. No dividends were paid or proposed by any of the companies in the relevant years.

Required :

> The consolidated balance sheet of the group at 31 December, 19-4.
> It is important that you submit your calculations of the items in the consolidated balance sheet.
> Ignore taxation.

WORKING of Answer :

Goodwill

(i)   Aire Ltd owns $^4/_5$ of Beal Ltd (i.e. 40,000 of the total of 50,000 shares issued by Beal) - the shares were acquired on 31 December, 19-3 when Beal Ltd was worth a total of £85,800 (£50,000 share capital plus £39,000 Profit and Loss account less £3,200 loss).
Value acquired = $^4/_5$ of £85,800 = £68,640.
This was acquired for £70,000 - therefore *£1,360* was paid for Goodwill.

(ii)   Aire Ltd owns $^3/_4$ of Calder Ltd.
Shares were acquired on 31 December, 19-2 when Calder was worth £28,000.

Value acquired therefore = $^3/_4$ of £28,000	=	£21,000
	=	23,800
Goodwill paid for	=	2,800
(iii) Total Goodwill = £13,60 + £2,800	=	4,160

Reserves of Beal and Calder for the C.B.S.

(i)   Since acquisition by Aire on 31 December, 19-3 Beal's reserves (Profit and Loss account) have increased by £7,300. Aire can take credit for $^4/_5$ of this increase - i.e. £5,840.

(ii)   Since acquisition by Aire on 31 December, 19-2 Calder's reserves have increased by £7,000. $^3/_4$ of £7,000 = £5,250.

(iii)   Total increase in reserves of subsidiaries = £11,090.

Minority Interests

At 31 December, 19-4 (date of C.B.S.) :

(i)   Beal is worth £93,100 (capital and reserve) $^1/_5$ of this belongs to minority shareholders - i.e. *£18,620*.

(ii)   Calder is worth £35,000. $^1/_4$ of this = minority interest = £8,750.

(iii)   Total minority interest = £27,370.

> All we need to now do is to amalgamate the fixed and current assets and the liabilities on our C.B.S. looks thus :

Consolidated Balance Sheet as at 31 December, 19-4

	£	£		£
Share Capital		200,000	Goodwill	4,160
Profit & Loss account				
Aire	108,000		Fixed and Current Assets	436,200
Increase in Subs.	11,090	119,090		
		319,090		
Minority Interests		27,370		
Current Liabilities		93,900		
		440,360		440,360

Pre-Acquisition Profits

You will recall that we only show in the C.B.S. the increases that have taken place in the Reserves (i.e. retained profits) of the subsidiary companies *since they were acquired* - the subsidiaries' reserves already in existence at the 'take-over' date are *not* shown in the C.B.S. because they represent profits which were earned by the subsidiary *prior* to being 'taken over'. In other words they are pre-acquisition profits and from our past studies we know that the holding company cannot take credit for any pre-acquisition profits. For this reason we must never show in the C.B.S. *any* profits (reserves) which were earned by the subsidiary *before* it was acquired by the holding company. As you will remember, any dividends received by the holding company which come out of the pre-acquisition profits of the subsidiary are regarded as being a 'refund' of part of the cost of the shares.

Cancelling Out of other Inter-Company Debts for the C.B.S.

You are already aware of the need to cancel out inter-company debts when preparing the balance sheet of the group (i.e. the C.B.S.) and you have seen that the *main* inter-company debt is that which is represented by the item *Investments in Subsidiary Co.* in the holding company's balance sheet and the item *Share Capital and Reserves* in the subsidiary company's balance sheet. The difference between these two amounts at the date the shares are acquired by the holding company is of course *GOODWILL*.

Other inter-company debts which need to be cancelled out against each other when drawing up the C.B.S. are :

1) Ordinary debts - e.g. A. Ltd owes B. Ltd (both A. and B. being part of the group).

2) Bills of exchange which are payable to, and receivable from, companies within the group - A. Ltd draws a bill which is accepted by B. Ltd - the item 'Bills Receivable' in A's balance sheet is cancelled out against the item 'Bills Payable' in B's balance sheet. If A. Ltd has *discounted* the bill (i.e. sold it) then it is no longer an inter-company debt.

3) Dividends proposed shown as a current liability in the subsidiary company's accounts will appear as a current asset in the holding company's accounts and as this is a form of inter-company debt these amounts will cancel each other out for the purpose of the C.B.S. If, however, the subsidiary company is only partly owned then the proportion of the proposed dividend which does not belong to the group will show as a minority interest (or a current liability) in the C.B.S.

Inter-Company Profits

If a company in the group (A) has sold goods to another company in the group (B) and the goods are still in the stock of (B) at the date of the C.B.S., then the *whole* of the profit made by (A) on the sale of the stock should be cancelled out against the *whole* of the profit included in the cost price of the stock in (B's) books, e.g. -

288

(A) sells £ 1,000 of goods to (B) for £1,200. A C.B.S. is drawn up before (B) sells any of the stock. The £200 profit is now in (A's) Profit and Loss account and is included as part of (B's) stock. For the purpose of the C.B.S. the Profit and Loss account of (A) is reduced by £200 and the stock of (B) is reduced similarly.

The reason for this is that the £200 profit is *unrealised* as it has not yet been sold to someone *outside* the group and we know that it is wrong to include unrealised profits either in the Profit and Loss account or in the stock.

ANSWERS - to Questions on page 284

Assumption (a)

			£
Value of S. Ltd as at 31 December, 19-2	= Share Capital		60,000
	P & L account		21,000
			81,000
	Cost of acquiring shares		85,000
	GOODWILL =		4,000

			£
Value of S. Ltd as at 31 December, 19-4 =	Share capital		60,000
	P & L account		25,000
			85,000

None of this value belongs to outsiders as S. Ltd is wholly owned by H. Ltd.

Assumption (b)

	£	£
Value of S. Ltd as at 31 December, 19-1 =		77,000
$3/4$ of the value of S. Ltd as at 31 December, 19-1	57,750	
Cost of acquiring $3/4$ of shares	62,000	
GOODWILL paid for	4,250	
Value of S. Ltd as at 31 December, 19-4 =		85,000
$1/4$ of the value of S. Ltd as at 31 December, 19-4 =		21,250 (Min. Int.)

Assumption (c)

	£	£
Value of S. Ltd as at 31 December, 19-3 =		79,000
$4/5$ of the value of S. Ltd as at 31 December, 19-3 =	63,200	
Cost of acquiring $4/5$ of shares	64,000	
GOODWILL paid for	800	
Value of S. Ltd as at 31 December, 19-4 =		85,000
$1/5$ of the value of S. Ltd as at 31 December, 19-4 =		17,000 (Min. Int.)

Solutions -

	Goodwill *	Minority Interest
ASSUMPTION	£	£
(a)	4,000	–
(b)	4,250	21,250
(c)	800	17,000

NOTE :

GROUP ACCOUNTS (S.S.A.P.14)

A holding company is one which either

(i)   is a member of another company and controls the composition of that other company's board of directors,

or

(ii)   where it holds more than half of the nominal value of the ordinary share capital of the other company.

The 'other company' referred to above becomes the subsidiary company of the holding company.

The 'group' is the holding company and all its subsidiaries.

Consolidated accounts present the information shown in the separate accounts of all companies in the Group as if they were the accounts of one single company, i.e. consolidated accounts show the position of the Group as a whole.

All companies within the Group are expected to adopt the same accounting policies and to have identical financial year ends. Where this is not the case appropriate adjustments and disclosure of this fact should be shown in the consolidated accounts together with the reasons for the different treatment.

Most of the procedures in preparing C.B.S.s, which you have followed in the preceding pages are those required by SSAP 14.

We know, for example, that only post-acquisition profits of a *subsidiary* company appear in the Consolidated Balance Sheet. It is therefore, in practice, important to know the exact date of acquisition, as only profits made subsequent to this will be made available (as distributable profits) to the group as a whole. SSAP 14 defines the exact date of acquisition as the *earlier* of :

a)   the date on which consideration passes
        or
b)   the date on which an offer becomes unconditional.

To date we have used in all examples the net asset values shown in the balance sheet of the newly acquired subsidiary in order to determine goodwill or capital reserve on acquisition.

By now, the principles of this procedure should be firmly established and you should thoroughly understand what 'is happening' when you do your calculations.

Now we must introduce a requirement of SSAP 14 that the net assets of the subsidiary company being acquired *must* be valued at their 'fair market value' at the date of acquisition (rather than at their balance sheet values). This is obviously going to affect the calculation of Goodwill or Capital Reserve on acquisition. Obviously, the *new* values of the assets of the subsidiary will be incorporated into the C.B.S. and will therefore affect 'minority interests'.

When the examination question gives the 'fair market value' of the assets of the subsidiary company, then all you need do is to substitute these 'fair market values' for the relevant items on the subsidiary's balance sheet, and calculate goodwill and minority interests based on these *changed* net assets. Simply substitute 'new figures for old' and calculate as normal!

ACQUISITIONS AND MERGERS (S.S.A.P 23)

At this stage you should be very familiar with the preparation of Consolidated Balance Sheets and in doing so you are using the *Acquisition Method of Accounting*. You should notice that on acquisition of a subsidiary the consolidated balance sheet shows only the distributable profits of the holding company - the distributable profits of the subsidiary are, in effect, 'frozen'. From thereon, only the increases or decreases in the distributable profits of the subsidiary are reflected in the C.B.S. - i.e. the original balance of the subsidiary's distributable profits are 'ignored'. In other words, the pre-acquisition profits of the subsidiary company are no longer available for distribution by the Group.

Is this fair? Exactly the same members are still interested in the combination of companies yet the profits of one company (the holding company) are available for distribution whilst the profits of the company 'taken over' are not! They are treated as pre-acquisition profits and are therefore not available for distribution as dividends.

The *Merger Method* takes heed of this argument - it is referred to in the U.S.A. as 'pooling of interests'. The main features of the merger method are as follows :

(i)   Shares issued by the holding company in exchange for shares in the subsidiary company are valued at nominal value - not at market value.

(ii)   The C.B.S. includes the retained profits of *both* companies and treats them as *distributable* profits - i.e. the distributable profits of the subsidiary company at the time of take over are merged with the distributable profits of the holding company. Pre-acquisition profits cease to have any meaning.

Let us look at two companies who are going to join together using the *MERGER* method.

Balance Sheets at 31 December 19-4 (before combination)

	A Ltd	B Ltd		A Ltd	B Ltd
	£	£		£	£
Share Capital (£1 shares)	1,300	800	Net Assets	1,900	1,300
Reserves	600	500			
	1,900	1,300		1,900	1,300

On 1st January 19-5 A Ltd purchases all of the shares in B Ltd by issuing 800 £1 shares in A Ltd, each share having a market value of £2.00.

Using the *MERGER* method, the shares issued by A Ltd will be valued at £800 (nominal value) and to produce a consolidated balance sheet we need to literally *merge* the two companies, viz :

Consolidated Balance Sheet

		£			£	£
Share Capital (£1 shares)		2,100	Net Assets :	A Ltd	1,900	
Reserves : A Ltd	600			B Ltd	1,300	3,200
B Ltd	500	1,100				
		3,200				3,200

Note that the reserves of both companies are now available for all shareholders in the group. No question of pre-acquisition profits! To quote one excellent author - 'the effect of the merger method is to treat the two companies as having been joined together 'since the cradle'.

The above is a straight-forward example where the nominal value of shares issued for purchase was the same as the nominal value of the shares being purchased.

291

Let us now look at some different situations :

(a) *Where the number of shares issued exceeds the nominal value of the shares being purchased.* Under the acquisition method this excess 'amount' paid would be treated as goodwill. Under the merger method this excess is not shown as goodwill but is deducted from the reserves of the two companies in the C.B.S.

(b) *Where the number of shares issued is less than the nominal value of the shares being purchased.* Like the acquisition method this difference is shown as a capital reserve in the C.B.S.

(c) *Where the holding company purchases less than 100% of shares in the subsidiary.* In this case there will be a minority interest but under the requirements of SSAP 23 this minority must not be more than 10%.

To illustrate the above situations let us study the following examples :

Balance Sheets (before combination)

	A Ltd £	B Ltd £		A Ltd £	B Ltd £
£1 Ordinary Shares	6,000	3,000	Net Assets	8,000	4,000
Reserves	2,000	1,000			
	8,000	4,000		8,000	4,000

The following three different situations should be dealt with *separately* in producing C.B.S.s :

a) A Ltd issues 4,000 £1 ordinary shares to acquire the whole share capital of B Ltd.

b) A Ltd issues £2,500 £1 ordinary shares to acquire the whole share capital of B Ltd.

c) A Ltd issues 3,000 £1 ordinary shares to acquire 2,700 shares in B Ltd.

ANSWERS
(a)

Consolidated Balance Sheet

	£	£			£
£1 Ordinary Shares		10,000	Net Assets :	A Ltd	8,000
Reserves : A Ltd	2,000			B Ltd	4,000
B Ltd	1,000				
	3,000				
Less: excess paid	1,000	2,000			
		12,000			12,000

(b)

Consolidated Balance Sheet

	£	£			£
£1 Ordinary Shares		8,500	Net Assets :	A Ltd	8,000
				B Ltd	4,000
Reserves : A Ltd	2,000				
B Ltd	1,000	3,000			
Capital Reserve		500			
		12,000			12,000

292

(c)

Consolidated Balance Sheet

	£	£	Net Assets :		£
£1 Ordinary Shares		9,000		A Ltd	8,000
				B Ltd	4,000
Reserves: A Ltd	2,000				
B Ltd (90% only)	900				
	2,900				
Less excess paid	300 *	2,600			
Minority Interest		400			
		12,000			12,000

*Remember that in merger accounting we are only concerned with the nominal values of the shares being acquired.

COMMENT

It is sometimes argued that merging companies in this way, instantly creates reserves capable of distribution to shareholders as dividends, whereas the acquisition method, with which we are so familiar, denies the group access to the profits already earned by the subsidiary before 'takeover'.

Surely the *combined* shareholders should, when the merger takes place, have access to the same profits which were already available to them as shareholders of separate concerns! The requirement of SSAP 14 that the net assets acquired should be treated at 'fair values' (so affecting goodwill calculations) does *not* apply to *merger methods*.

The acquisition and merger accounting methods both have their respective merits. A real merger, in the truest sense, where the companies concerned have genuinely *merged* with prospects of long continuity, should probably adopt the merger method.

For many years the legality of merger accounting was in doubt but the 1985 Companies Act makes it quite legal. One of the main requirements is that the acquiring company must purchase at least 90% of the shares of the acquired company.

To date, the use of this method is not on a large scale but it is interesting to note that Trust House Forte Ltd used the method in a combination some years ago when the method's legality was certainly in question!

ACCOUNTING FOR ASSOCIATED COMPANIES (S.S.A.P.1)

When a company acquires more than 50% of another company's issued share (voting) capital the investing company is referred to as the *Holding Company* of the other - i.e. of the Subsidiary Company (see SSAP 14). The Holding Company and its subsidiaries are referred to collectively as *The Group*.

Where, however, a company or group of companies have a less than 50% 'interest' in another company but do have a *significant influence* over that other company, then that other company is referred to as an *Associated Company* (*not* a subsidiary company).

Such influence in the associated company could be generated through a close relationship in a joint venture or through the investing company (or group of companies) acquiring at least 20% of the other company's equity voting rights.

Accounting Procedures for Associated Companies

The investing company or group of companies must show in their financial statements (consolidated statements in the case of an investing Group) the following details :

(i)   The total amount paid for shares in the associated company, distinguishing between:

        (a)   the share of net assets acquired,
        (b)   the share of the goodwill acquired,
        (c)   the premium paid (or discount) on acquisition.

(ii)   Dividends received and receivable from the associated company.

(iii)   The share of the associated company's *retained* profits (less losses). For example, if the investing company or group held 30% of the voting shares in the associated company and the latter made £120,000 profit and paid dividends of £90,000, then the investing company would own 30% of the retained profit of £30,000 - i.e. £10,000. This £10,000 would be shown by the investing company as a Reserve *and* as an increase in the item 'Investment in Associated Company (i.e. Debit Investment, Credit Reserves).

(iv)   Loans to and from associated Companies.

EXERCISE 16.1

The following are summarised balance sheets of Snap Ltd, Crackle Ltd, and Pop Ltd at 31 December, 19-8.

	Snap Ltd £	Crackle Ltd £	Pop Ltd £
Issued Share Capital (£1 shares)	100,000	40,000	40,000
Profit & Loss account at 31 December, 19-6	93,330	19,100	36,000
Net profit 19-7	12,400	10,300	7,200
Net profit 19-8	5,200	3,100	9,400
Current liabilities	19,670	22,600	33,700
	230,600	95,100	126,300
Shares in Crackle Ltd at cost	50,000	–	–
Shares in Pop Ltd at cost	70,000	–	–
Sundry assets	110,600	95,100	126,300
	230,600	95,100	126,300

Snap Ltd acquired the shares in its subsidiaries as follows :

31 December, 19-6	30,000 shares in Crackle Ltd.
31 December, 19-7	32,000 shares in Pop Ltd

No dividends were paid or proposed by any of the companies in the relevant years
Ignore taxation.

Required : The consolidated balance sheet for Snap Ltd at 31 December, 19-8.

Summarised balance sheets of Frank Ltd, George Ltd, and Harry Ltd at 31 December, 19-5 are shown below:

	Frank Ltd	George Ltd	Harry Ltd
	£	£	£
Issued share capital (£1 ordinary shares)	50,000	100,000	15,000
Revenue reserves	73,200	46,000	12,600
Debentures	50,000	80,000	15,000
Current liabilities	96,800	64,000	27,400
	270,000	290,000	70,000
75,000 shares in George Ltd at cost	130,000	–	–
Sundry assets	140,000	290,000	70,000
	270,000	290,000	70,000

Frank Ltd purchased its shares in George Ltd on 31 December, 19-3 when the revenue reserves of George Ltd were £60,000. Since that time George Ltd has not declared any dividends.

On 31 December, 19-5 the following transactions took place :

(1) Frank Ltd acquired two-thirds of the share capital of Harry Ltd by purchasing 10,000 shares in that company at £2 per share. The purchase price was entirely satisfied by the issue of 15,000 new ordinary shares in Frank Ltd to former shareholders in Harry Ltd.

(2) Frank Ltd made a loan of £12,000 to George Ltd.

(3) George Ltd acquired all the debentures of Harry Ltd for £15,000 cash from the existing debenture holders.

None of the three transactions above have yet been entered in the accounts of the companies concerned.

Included in the current assets of George Ltd at 31 December, 19-5 were goods which were purchased from Frank Ltd for £6,300. These goods had cost Frank Ltd £4,200.

Required : The consolidated balance sheet of the group at 31 December, 19-5.

EXERCISE 16.3

The following are summarised balance sheets of Harrison Ltd and Robinson Ltd before combination :

Balance Sheets

	Harrison Ltd	Robinson Ltd		Harrison Ltd	Robinson Ltd
	£	£		£	£
£1 Ordinary shares	40,000	20,000	Net Assets	65,000	30,000
Reserves	25,000	10,000			
	65,000	30,000		65,000	30,000

Treat the following as *separate* exercises; Note that the 'fair market value' of Robinson's net assets is considered to be £35,000.

(a) Harrison Ltd issues 12,000 £1 ordinary shares, with a market value of £3.00 per share to acquire the whole share capital of Robinson Ltd.

You are required - to show the consolidated balance sheet using (i) the acquisition method *and* (ii) the merger method.

(b) Harrison Ltd issues 22,000 £1 ordinary shares with a market value of £1.25 each to acquire 18,000 shares in Robinson Ltd.

You are required - to show the consolidated balance sheet using (i) the acquisition method *and* (ii) the merger method.

EXERCISE 16.4

The following are summarised balance sheets of Delta Ltd, Easy Ltd and Fox Ltd at 30 June, 19-3.

	Delta Ltd	Easy Ltd	Fox Ltd
	£	£	£
Issued share capital (£1 shares)	150,000	50,000	30,000
Profit and Loss account at 30 June, 19-2	41,200	27,000	15,300
Net profit 19-3	17,000	4,800	3,300
Current liabilities	69,300	30,200	22,400
	277,500	112,000	71,000
40,000 shares in Easy Ltd at cost	59,000	–	–
Sundry assets	218,500	112,000	71,000
	277,500	112,000	71,000

Delta Ltd acquired its shares in Easy Ltd on 30 June, 19-2.

On 30 June, 19-3 Delta Ltd acquired 20,000 shares in Fox Ltd, at a price of £2 per share. The purchase price was entirely satisfied by the issue of 25,000 shares in Delta Ltd to former shareholders of Fox Ltd. The effect of the transaction has not yet been recorded in the relevant accounts.

No dividends were paid or proposed by any of the companies in the relevant years.

Required : The consolidated balance sheet for the group at 30 June, 19-3 after the acquisition of Fox Ltd.
NOTE   Ignore taxation.

EXERCISE 16.5 EX

The following are the summarised balance sheets of Ashton Ltd, Batley Ltd and Corby Ltd at 31 December, 19-5.

	Ashton Ltd	Batley Ltd	Corby Ltd
	£	£	£
Issued share capital (£1 shares)	200,000	100,000	150,000
Profit and Loss account :			
Credit (Debit) balance at 31 December, 19-3	99,000	(10,800)	64,300
Net profit (LOSS) 19-4	26,000	(3,200)	28,000
Net profit (LOSS) 19-5	14,400	5,000	(6,000)
Sundry liabilities	160,600	109,000	113,700
	500,000	200,000	350,000
80,000 shares in Batley Ltd at cost	60,000	–	–
90,000 shares in Corby Ltd at cost	150,000	–	–
Sundry assets	290,000	200,000	350,000
	500,000	200,000	350,000

Ashton Ltd acquired the shares in its subsidiaries as follows :

31 December, 19-3	80,000 shares in Batley Ltd
31 December, 19-4	90,000 shares in Corby Ltd

No dividends were paid or proposed by any of the companies in the relevant years.

Required : The consolidated balance sheet for the group at 31 December, 19-5.

NOTE   Ignore taxation.

EXERCISE 16.6 EX

The summarised balance sheets of Nine Ltd, Ten Ltd and Jack Ltd at 31 December, 19-8 were as follows :

	Nine Ltd	Ten Ltd	Jack Ltd
	£	£	£
Share capital (£1 shares)	100,000	120,000	80,000
Profit and Loss account at 31 December, 19-7	72,100	37,600	57,200
Net profit 19-8	14,000	9,200	17,500
	186,100	166,800	154,700
12% debentures	80,000	120,000	–
Trade creditors	51,000	46,200	32,100
	317,100	333,000	186,800
Fixed assets at book value	111,900	212,000	121,300
90,000 ordinary shares in Ten Ltd at cost	130,000	–	–
Current assets	75,200	121,000	65,500
	317,100	333,000	186,800

The shares in Ten Ltd were purchased on 31 December, 19-7. On 31 December, 19-8 Nine Ltd acquired the entire share capital of Jack Ltd. The shareholders of Jack Ltd exchanged their existing shareholdings for shares in Nine Ltd. Each share in Nine Ltd and Jack Ltd was valued at £2.00 and £2.50 respectively for the purpose of this exchange. You may assume that all the legal and other necessary formalities were completed on 31 December, 19-8 although no entry was made in the books of account to record this event, before the above balance sheets were prepared.

At 31 December, 19-8 the stocks of Nine Ltd include goods purchased from Ten Ltd at a cost of £8,000. The cost of these goods to Ten Ltd had been £6,000.

Required :
(a)   A consolidated balance sheet for the group at 31 December, 19-8.

(b)   A brief discussion of the effect of acquiring the shares in Jack Ltd on the 'gearing' within the Nine Ltd group of companies.

NOTE   Ignore taxation. No dividends were paid or proposed by the companies in any of the relevant years.

EXERCISE 16.7 EX

The summarised balance sheets of Hide Ltd and its subsidiaries Watkin Ltd and Davey Ltd at 31 December, 19-9 were as follows :

	Hide Ltd	Watkin Ltd	Davey Ltd
	£	£	£
Ordinary share capital (£1 shares)	800,000	240,000	160,000
Reserves at 31 December, 19-8	180,000	67,200	18,000
Net profit (LOSS) for 19-9	80,000	60,000	(12,400)
Less: preference dividend for 19-9	–	(5,000)	–
	1,060,000	362,200	165,600
10% Preference shares	–	50,000	–
Loan from Watkin Ltd	10,000	–	–
Trade creditors	365,100	103,100	76,200
Preference dividend payable	–	5,000	–
	1,435,100	520,300	241,800
Fixed assets at book value	671,800	151,700	140,000
180,000 ordinary shares in Watkin Ltd at cost (purchased 31 December, 19-6)	272,000	–	–
160,000 ordinary shares in Davey Ltd at cost (purchased 1 January, 19-9)	–	205,100	–

Loan to Hide Ltd		–	12,000	–
Current assets		491,300	151,500	101,800
		1,435,100	520,300	241,800

The following additional information is provided:

1. The balance on Watkin Ltd's reserve account was £52,000 at 31 December, 19-6.

2. During 19-9 a cheque made out for £2,000 was received by Watkin Ltd from Hide Ltd and wrongly credited to a customer's account.

3. No ordinary dividends have been paid by Watkin Ltd and Davey Ltd since 19-5.

Required:
(a) The consolidated balance sheet for the Hide Ltd group of companies as at 31 December 19-9.

(b) A discussion of the uses and limitations of group accounts from the viewpoint of :

    (i)   the shareholders of the holding company;
    and
    (ii) the creditors of the holding company.

NOTE   Ignore taxation.

EXERCISE 16.8 EX

The summarised balance sheets of Dingle Ltd, Eagle Ltd and Fender Ltd are as follows :

Balance Sheets as at 31 December 1988

	Dingle	Eagle	Fender
	£000	£000	£000
Fixed assets	100	260	720
Current assets	85	170	555
	185	430	1,275
Ordinary Share capital (£1 shares)	80	200	500
Retained Profit 1 January 1988	70	100	360
Profit for 1988	20	80	200
Proposed dividend	--	(60)	(150)
	170	320	910
Trade Creditors	15	50	215
Proposed dividend	--	60	150
	185	430	1,275

Grimshaw Ltd made the following investments on 1 January 1988 :

Company	Shares acquired	Price Paid
Dingle	64,000	£178,000
Eagle	80,000	£151,000
Fender	50,000	£116,000

Required :
Calculate separately for each company the amounts (if any) to be included in the group accounts of Grimshaw Ltd in respect of each of the following items :

    (i)   Share of profit reported for 1988
    (ii) Goodwill/premium paid on acquisition
    (iii) Minority interest at 31 December 1988

You should explain, briefly, the principles followed when making your calculations.

The result of your calculations under (i) - (iii) should be presented in the following format :

	Dingle £000	Eagle £000	Fender £000
Share of profit			
Goodwill/premium			
Minority interest			

NOTE :

There were no significant differences, on 1 January 1988, between the book values and market values of the assets of any of the companies.

(Spring 1989)

SOLUTIONS

SOLUTION 16.1

WORKINGS

			£
Goodwill :	Value of Crackle at 31 December,19-6	=	59,100
	$3/4$ of this	=	44,325
	Cost of acquisition		50,000
	GOODWILL		5,675

			£
	Value of Pop at 31 December, 19-7	=	83,200
	$4/5$ of this	=	66,560
	Cost of acquisition	=	70,000
	GOODWILL		3,440

NET GOODWILL = £9,115

Changes in Reserves since acquisition

		£	
Crackle's reserves at 31 December, 19-6	=	19,100	
Crackle's reserves at 31 December, 19-8		32,500	
Increase		13,400	x $3/4$ = £10,050

		£	
Pop's reserves at 31 December, 19-7	=	43,200	
Pop's reserves at 31 December, 19-8		52,600	
Increase		9,400	x $4/5$ = £ 7,520
Total Increase			£17,570

Minority Interests

Value of Crackle at 31 December, 19-8	=	£72,500	
$1/4$ (minority interest) of this	=		£18,125
Value of Pop at 31 December, 19-8	=	£92,600	
$1/5$ of this	=		£18,520
TOTAL			£36,645

Consolidated Balance Sheet at 31 December, 19-8

	£	£		£
Issued Share Capital (£1) shares		100,000	Goodwill	9,115
Profit and Loss account	110,930		Sundry Assets	332,000
Increase in Subsidiary'				
Reserves	17,570	128,500		
		228,500		
Minority Interests		36,645		
Current Liabilities		75,970		
		341,115		341,115

300

SOLUTION 16.2

Consolidated Balance Sheet as at 31 December, 19-5

	£	£		£
Issued Share Capital		65,000	Goodwill	11,600
Share Premium		5,000	Sundry assets	482,900
Revenue Reserves	71,100			
Less losses of George Ltd	10,500			
		60,600		
		130,600		
Minority Interests		45,700		
Debentures		130,000		
Current liabilities		188,200		
		494,500		494,500

NOTE

Goodwill -	George Ltd £10,000; Harry Ltd £1,600.
Reserves -	As Harry Ltd was only acquired on the day of the C.B.S., there is as yet no change.
Minority Interests -	George Ltd £36,500; Harry Ltd £ 9,200
Debentures -	Of Harry Ltd are ignored as they are now wholly an inter-company debt - George's sundry assets would be reduced by the £15,000 cash outlay for these debentures.
Unrealised Profit -	Frank Ltd has made a profit on stock of £2,100 at the expense of George Ltd. This inter-company profit must be eliminated by reducing Frank's revenue reserves, and reducing George's current assets by £2,100.
Loan -	The £12,000 loan when *entered in the accounts* will show as an asset for Frank Ltd and a liability for George Ltd. Ignore this inter-company debt completely.
New Issue -	Frank Ltd issues only 15,000 shares of £1 to satisfy a payment of £20,000 - i.e. the shares are issued at a premium of £5,000.
In the examination -	Show your calculations of goodwill, etc. as in the previous exercise.

SOLUTION 16.3
(a) (i)

Consolidated Balance Sheet

	£		£
£1 Ordinary Shares	52,000	Goodwill	1,000
Share premium	24,000	Net assets	100,000
Reserves	25,000		
	101,000		101,000

NOTE - that SSAP 14 insists, when using the acquisition method, that the 'fair values' of the assets acquired should be used.

Consolidated Balance Sheet

(ii)

	£		£
£1 Ordinary Shares	52,000	Net assets	95,000
Capital Reserve *	8,000		
Reserves	35,000		
	95,000		95,000

* 12,000 £1 shares were issued by Harrison Ltd to acquire 2,000 £1 shares of Robinson Ltd.

Consolidated Balance Sheet

(b) (i)

	£		£
£1 Ordinary Shares	62,000	Net assets	100,000
Share premium	5,500		
Capital Reserve on acquisition	4,000		
Reserves	25,000		
Minority Interest	3,500		
	100,000		100,000

Consolidated Balance Sheet

(ii)

	£		£
£1 Ordinary Shares	62,000	Net Assets	95,000
Reserves *	30,000		
Minority Interest	3,000		
	95,000		95,000

* Harrison Ltd	£25,000
Robinson Ltd (90%)	9,000
	£34,000

£34,000 - LESS £4,000 excess paid -
(22,000 £1 shares issued to acquire 18,000 £1 shares) = £30,000

SOLUTION 16.4

Goodwill

Easy Ltd.	£2,600 Capital Reserve
Fox Ltd.	£7,600 Goodwill
Net Goodwill =	£5,000

Reserves

		£
Profit & Loss account of Delta Ltd at 30 June 19-3		58,200
Add 4/5 of increase in Easy Ltd = 4/5 of £4,800		3,840
		62,040

Minority Interests

		£
Value of Easy at 19-3	= £81,800 x 1/5	16,360
Value of Fox at 19-3	= £48,600 x 1/3	16,200
		32,560

Consolidated Balance Sheet at 30 June 19-3

	£		£
Share Capital (1£ shares)	175,000	Goodwill	5,000
Share Premium	15,000		
Profit and Loss account	62,040	Sundry Assets	401,500
	252,040		
Minority Interests	32,560		
Current Liabilities	121,900		
	406,500		406,500

NOTE TO STUDENT :

Delta issued 25,000 shares of £1 to satisfy a purchase price of £40,000. Therefore, credit share capital with *nominal* value issued (£25,000) and remaining 'profit' goes to share premium account.

LESSON 17

CURRENT COST ACCOUNTING

Most items in the Profit and Loss account and balance sheet of a business are shown at, or are based on, actual cost ('historic cost'). Changes in the value of money and its purchasing power, and consideration of what it would cost to replace items or get the same services are generally ignored.

Since the mid 1930s, there have been attempts to introduce some kind of system which would make allowances in accounts for inflation which is taking place and therefore, hopefully, make the accounts more meaningful than they are under an 'historic cost' system only.

Statement of Standard Accounting Practice (SSAP) No. 16 was published in April 1980 and applies to companies with shares or loan stock listed on the stock exchange, and to other (non-listed) companies who satisfy at least two of three qualifications, namely -

    (i)   annual turnover of more than £5 million,
    (ii)   opening balance sheet total of more than £2.5 million, and
    (iii)   250 or more employees.

This Standard is no longer mandatory but remains as a useful reference to Current Cost Accounting. The accountancy profession are still very unsure of what would be a suitable treatment of inflation in connection with a company's accounts and balance sheet.

However the examination syllabus still requires an appreciation of the drawbacks to conventional historical cost accounting and for you to have some appreciation of the possible methods to overcome these drawbacks.

Over the years there have been numerous suggestions, but the best available resulted in the publication of SSAP 16 which was obviously not an ideal solution in view of the withdrawal of its mandatory status!

You should therefore be familiar with the requirements of this historic SSAP which required the above companies to produce, in addition to historic cost accounts (i.e. the accounts we are already familiar with - they do make *some* sense!) a set of current cost accounts (i.e. the Profit and Loss Account and Balance Sheet we are familiar with, but adjusted to account for price changes in the period).

Before looking at the make-up of current cost accounts, let us examine one of the basic concepts behind the idea of inflation accounting. This is best done by looking at balance sheets of A Co. Ltd for 1985 and 1990 :

	1985 £	1990 £		1985 £	1990 £
Shareholders Funds			Fixed Assets		
Total assets less liabilities	22,600	54,300	1 Factory	15,000	40,000
			30 Machines	4,000	8,000
Current Liabilities			Current Assets		
Creditors - materials for					
60 'Whatsits'	900	1,200	Stock of 100 'Whatsits'	1,500	3,500
			Debtors -		
			sale of 50 'Whatsits'	1,200	2,200
			Bank	1,800	1,800
	23,500	55,500		23,500	55,500

Note that the company holds *exactly the same assets* in 1990 as in 1985 - the only thing that has changed is the monetary value given to them (because of price changes - i.e. inflation). In *real* terms the company is not worth any more than it was in 1985, but the danger is that we look at the 'increased' shareholders' funds and decide to pay a dividend out of the increase, in which case we would be paying away original permanent capital. All the increases shown are due purely to price changes - to inflation! But how can an 'outsider' tell from normal accounts (without the detail as above) that the increases are not real? Only by creating a separate capital maintenance reserve into which increases due to price changes are channelled whilst real increases from profits are kept in the normal reserves.

The top left section of our balance sheets would then appear (assuming no profits) :

	1980
	£
Shareholders Funds at 1985	22,600
Capital Maintenance Reserve -	
(Current Cost reserve per SSAP 16)	31,700
Shareholders Funds at 1990	54,300

Now we can see clearly that there is no real progress between 1985 and 1990, and consequently there should be no obligation to pay dividends. The idea then is to keep capital intact by adjusting the profit shown in our historic profit and loss account so that the adjusted figure represents real profits (rather than artificial profits, which will be held in the current cost reserve) which are available for distribution.

Our supplementary current cost profit and loss account will therefore start off by showing the historic cost profit (taken from the normal Profit and Loss account) which will then be adjusted in order to arrive at a figure representing current cost operating profit.

The adjustments to be made to the historic cost profit (before interest and tax) are :

1. Depreciation adjustment
2. Cost of sales adjustment (COSA)
3. Monetary working capital adjustment (MWCA)
4. Gearing adjustment

Let us look at each in turn with a view to understanding the purpose of each adjustment. I have tried to be as basic as possible so that the concepts will come over to you. Armed with these basic concepts you are then in a position to delve deeper, should you want to, into the complexities and variations which may arise in practice.

1. Depreciation adjustment

The depreciation charge in our historic profit and loss account will have been based on a percentage of the *cost* of that particular fixed asset. However, the *current replacement cost* of that asset will be higher (assuming rising prices) than the original cost, and the charge for depreciation should be based on what the asset would cost *now* rather than what it cost years ago. In this way, we will be looking at a figure for depreciation which reflects the truer value of that part which has been consumed through wear and tear. If, therefore, we take a percentage of current replacement cost (rather than historic cost) the charge for depreciation will obviously be more than that charged in the historic profit and loss account (the one we are all familiar with) : the more depreciation we charge, the less the profit becomes; so having worked out the *difference* in the deprecation charge this difference is deducted from the profit figure in the supplementary 'current cost Profit and Loss account' (see page 309). What could be easier?

But - how do we know the current replacement cost of, say, plant and machinery? The easiest way is to look at suppliers' price lists at the end of the financial year. However, it is considered that, unless there have been special circumstances to which the asset has been subjected to in the period (e.g. a sudden change in technology) then current replacement cost should be calculated by applying special index numbers, prepared for that type of asset, taken from Central Statistical Office publications.

The formula used is as follows (memorise this) :

$$\frac{\text{Index at Current Rate}}{\text{Index at Date Asset was Purchased}} \quad \text{x} \quad \frac{\text{Amount of Depreciation shown in historic P \& L account}}{1}$$

The resulting figure represent depreciation based on *current* cost and the difference between this figure and the figure for depreciation in the historic profit and loss account is the depreciation adjustment - i.e. the extra depreciation which should have been charged, and which will now be deducted from the historic profit in the 'supplementary Current Cost Profit and Loss Account' (see example on page 309)

If indices are not given in a question you *will* be given the current replacement cost on which to calculate the adjustment. Should you be told the current replacement cost at the beginning *and* end of the year then you should take the *average* of these figures.

2.   Cost of Sales adjustment (COSA)

When sales take place they are obviously at current value but the *cost* of those sales will not necessarily be shown in the historic trading account at what they were worth - i.e. current value - at the time the sales took place. for example, we could buy goods in May for £10,000 and sell them in August for £15,000, in which case we show a gross profit of £5,000 in the historic accounts - but if those same goods would cost £11,000 to replace in August (when they are sold) then in current terms we have only made £4,000 profit.

Think about this - the goods we have sold *have* to be replaced and it is going to cost us £1,000 more to replace them which effectively reduces the profit we are showing.

In the situation just described we would need to make a *cost of sales adjustment* by deducting £1,000 from our historic profit figure (this would be shown in the supplementary current cost Profit and Loss account - see page 309

However, it is not so easy to arrive at the current replacement cost - £11,000 in the above example - of all the stocks sold in a period so again it will be necessary to apply index numbers to the stock figures (to convert from historic cost to current cost), using a different index for each type of stock. If goods are turning over *very* quickly it may not be necessary to adjust anything. Think about this - if stock is selling before the suppliers have time to increase their prices then the cost value of the stock will also be current value at the time the stock is sold.

Opening and closing stocks are adjusted by applying the following formula (memorise) :

(i) $\dfrac{\text{Average Index for year}}{\text{Index at \textit{start} of year}}$ x $\dfrac{\text{Opening Stock}}{1}$ (as shown in historic accounts)

(ii) $\dfrac{\text{Average Index for year}}{\text{Index at \textit{end} of year}}$ x $\dfrac{\text{Closing Stock}}{1}$ (per historic accounts)

This converts the opening and closing stock figures to current cost and alters historic Cost of Sales (Cost of Goods Sold). The difference is the cost of sales adjustment (COSA).

For example :

Historic Trading Account for year ended 31 December, 1980

	£		£
Opening Stock	4,000	Sales	40,000
Purchases	26,000		
	30,000		
Less closing stock	2,000		
Cost of Sales	28,000		
Gross Profit	12,000		
	40,000		40,000

Stock Price Index = 120 (1st January 1980); 140 (31 December 1980); 134 (average for year).

Applying the above formula :

(i) $\quad \dfrac{134}{120} \quad$ x $\quad \dfrac{£4,000}{1} \quad = £4,466$

(i) $\quad \dfrac{134}{140} \quad$ x $\quad \dfrac{£2,000}{1} \quad = \quad £1,914$

If we now imagine these converted figures (to current cost) in the above Trading Account we have the following picture :

Trading Account

	£		£
Opening Stock	4,466	Sales	40,000
Purchases	26,000		
	30,466		
Less closing stock	1,914		
Cost of Sales	28,552		
Gross profit	11,448		
	40,000		40,000

The difference (reduction in profit) is £552 and this COSA will be deducted from the historic profit in the Supplementary Current Cost Profit and Loss Account (see example on page 309).

NOTE:
Because of the withdrawal of SSAP 16, candidates will *not* be required to have knowledge of the following additional adjustments (3 and 4). they are left in the text for your interest only.

3.   **Monetary Working Capital Adjustment (MWCA)**

The reason for making the adjustments above - for depreciation and cost of sales - is to reduce the profit available to shareholders to avoid paying away (dividends) *apparent* profits (as shown in the historic Profit and Loss Account) by 'keeping back' sums which are needed to finance the company's operations in times of rising prices, e.g. more money is needed to buy the same fixed assets and stock.

With regard to stock - should we be providing extra funds (through the cost of sales adjustment) to buy stock with, when our creditors are allowing us credit? If prices of stock rise, our creditors allow us that much more credit! Why should we make provision for extra funds (by reducing the available profit figure by use of the cost of sales adjustment) to cover increases in the cost of stocks when our creditors are giving credit to cover this? Price changes are being financed by the supplier during the credit period, therefore extra funds do not have to be found by the business, and this reduces the need for the cost of sales adjustment dealt with above. In other words, some of the profit 'taken from' the shareholders in the supplementary current cost Profit and Loss Account can be 'given back' (see page 302).

However, whilst we are 'gaining funds' from our creditors we are in effect 'giving away' part of those funds to our debtors in that we are allowing them to buy goods from us without asking for immediate payment, thereby tying up some of our funds.

We should not therefore just look at creditors when doing our monetary working capital adjustment, but rather at *creditors less debtors* (i.e. net creditors). If the debtors are more than the creditors then we are in effect 'giving away' - to debtors - more than we are 'receiving' - from creditors - and the difference needs to be recouped by *adding* to the cost of sales adjustment (therefore reducing the historic profit even more, so 'keeping back' more from the shareholders to help our financing of stocks which are increasing in price).

In dealing with COSA and MWCA we have in fact looked at most of the working capital items, the main exception being the bank balances. The suggestion is that this should be included in the MWCA only if it would have a material effect on the current cost profit. It is therefore probably safe to think of MWC as being simply the difference between debtors and creditors.

The way to fine the MWCA is as follows :

Assume the following :	31 Dec. 1980	31 Dec 1981	
Debtors	£40,000	£60,000	
Creditors	£30,000	£35,000	
Index Numbers	<u>120</u>	<u>140</u>	Average <u>130</u>

First of all find the Monetary Working Capital (MWC) - i.e. debtors less creditors or vice-versa - at the start of the year (opening MWC) and at the end of the year (closing MWC). Then find the difference between these two figures and note this.

Then work the following formula (memorise) :

$$\frac{\text{Closing MWC}}{\text{Closing Index No.}} \quad x \quad \frac{\text{Average Index No.}}{1}$$

MINUS

$$\frac{\text{Opening MWC}}{\text{Opening Index No.}} \quad x \quad \frac{\text{Average Index No.}}{1}$$

Finally, deduct the result of this from the first figure noted above to give the MWCA.

Using the above information -

(i)	MWC at start	=	£10,000	MWC at end	=	£25,000		
	Difference	=	£15,000	(NOTE this)				

(ii) $\dfrac{25,000}{140} \times \dfrac{130}{1}$ MINUS $\dfrac{10,000}{120} \times \dfrac{130}{1}$ = £12,381

(iii) £15,000 – £12,381 = £2,619 MWCA

In this example we have been dealing with a net debtors situation and the resultant MWCA of £2,619 is *deducted* from historic profit in the supplementary profit and loss account, by adding it to the COSA. If a net creditor situation then the MWCA would be *added* to historic profit - by reducing COSA. The reasons have been given earlier in this lesson.

4.   Gearing Adjustment

The three adjustments we have just looked at have been entered into our supplementary statement **(see page302) ?** and the net effect has been to reduce the historic profit figure and therefore has reduced the shareholders' claim on funds - all this to provide the company with the extra finance needed to buy stock and assets at increased prices, i.e. to, at least maintain capital intact in real terms.

These adjustments may reduce the profit figure so much that dividends are not paid. Now, although we have taken account of funds being supplied by creditors (allowing for debtors) we have not allowed for the fact that there may be funds being supplied by persons other than creditors - e.g. preference shares, debentures and other loans, bank overdrafts, etc. - i.e. the liabilities other than creditors. Even when prices are rising the liability to repay these borrowings remains the same, which is a benefit for the ordinary shareholders (equity) and this benefit is recognised by a 'gearing adjustment' - i.e. a percentage which is used to reduce the total of the three adjustments we have already dealt with (depreciation, cost of sales and monetary working capital) which leads to more profit being made available to the ordinary shareholders **(see page 302)?**

The percentage used is determined by seeing what proportion the assets which have been financed by borrowing (other than from creditors, which we have already allowed for), bear to the total assets at their current cost values provided by this borrowing, plus the ordinary shareholders' funds (share capital plus reserves). *Proposed dividends are to be treated as part of shareholders' funds.*

EXAMPLE

Current Cost Balance Sheet (Average Figures)

	£ 000		£ 000
Ordinary Share Capital	3,000	Fixed Assets	4,000
Share Premium	300	Stock *	800
Current Cost Reserve	500	Debtors *	500
Other Reserves and Retained Profit	200	Cash/Bank <>	
			(where not included in MWCA)
	300		
	4,000		
Debentures <>	500		
Trade Creditors *	600		
H.P. Creditors <>	300		
Taxation <>	100		
Proposed Dividends	100		
	5,600		5,600

* Already dealt with in the first three adjustments.

Therefore :

$$\frac{\text{Assets financed by borrowing } (<>) \ £600}{\text{Assets finance by borrowing } (<>) \ £4,700} = 12.8\% \ (\text{approx.})$$
plus Ordinary Shareholders' Funds

(NOTE - that the £600 is after deducting the asset cash, and that *the £4,700 includes the proposed dividend*).

Therefore, 12.8% of the adjustments already made (i.e.taken off historic profit) will be added back *less* the interest on the borrowings, to give Current Cost Profit before tax (see below).

Example of Supplementary Current Cost Profit and Loss Account

	£	£	£
Profit before Tax as per Historic Profit &			
Loss Account (say)			20,000
Less Current Cost Adjustments:			
Depreciation (say)		4,000	
Cost of sales	552		
Monetary Working Capital	2,619 *		
		3,171	
			7,171
Current Cost Operating Profit			12,829
Plus Gearing adjustment (12.8% of £7,171)		918	
Less Interest		100	818
Current Cost Profit Before Taxation			13,647
Less Taxation			6,400
Current Cost Profit Attributable to Shareholders			7,247
Less Proposed Dividends			2,000
Retained Current Cost Profit			5,247

* This figure assumes debtors exceed creditors - otherwise it would be deducted from cost of sales.

Current Cost Reserve

The concept of maintaining capital was outlined at the beginning of this lesson and you must therefore understand that the amounts which are being taken from historic profit, through the various adjustments, are being diverted into the Current Cost Reserve Account (i.e. DR. Historic Profit and Loss Account; CR. Current Cost Reserve Account). Any additions to historic profit (e.g. Gearing adjustment, and possibly MWCA), will be taken out of Current Cost Reserve (i.e. DR. Reserve; CR Historic Profit and Loss account).

Current Cost Balance Sheet

SSAP 16 states that in addition to the supplementary current cost profit and loss account there should also be shown a supplementary current cost balance sheet. This can be in summarised form. All liabilities are to be included at the same amounts as shown in the historical cost balance sheet.

Current assets, other than those subject to the cost of sales adjustment (i.e. Stocks) are to be shown at the same amounts as in the historical cost balance sheet. Other assets (i.e. fixed assets and stock) should be shown at their 'value to the business', which would normally be net current replacement cost.

The balance sheet should also include a *Current Cost Reserve*. this is a reserve which caters for revaluation surpluses or deficits as a result of price changes of fixed assets and stock; also the monetary working capital and gearing adjustments. In effect the amounts of profit being 'held back', by the adjustments we made to the historic profit, are being placed to this reserve in order to maintain capital. The gearing adjustment however would be a debit entry to this reserve account.

Finally

SSAP 16 required the supplementary accounts to show the 'current cost earnings per share' for the current period. This would be the 'current cost profit attributable to shareholders' before extraordinary items (see page 309), divided by the number of issued shares.

At the present time there are strong feelings within the accountancy profession regarding the validity of current cost accounting concepts. Whilst 'historic' accounts ignore inflation, the readers of such accounts do in fact temper their ultimate decisions by mentally acknowledging the effect of current inflation, and they have many years' experience of doing this.

I am convinced that this situation cannot be bettered! I feel that the readers of 'current cost accounts' are placing themselves in the hands of compilers of indices for a wide variety of items and looking at idealistic ideas. I do not think that the chief examiner would agree with my sentiments - therefore, ignore what I have said but bear it in mind!

EXERCISE 17.1

The summarised profit and loss account and balance sheet of Rociety Ltd, a trading company, prepared under the historical cost convention, were as follows :

Profit and Loss Account for 1980

		£ 000	£ 000
Sales			1,400
Less:	Opening Stock	156	
	Purchases	1,024	
	Closing Stock	(196)	
	Cost of goods sold		984
Gross Profit			416
Less:	Depreciation	50	
	Other running costs	300	350
Net Profit			66

Balance Sheet at 31 December, 1980

	£ 000	£ 000
Fixed assets purchased 1 January 1979		500
Less: depreciation (10% straight line)		100
		400
Stock	196	
Debtors	160	
Bank	20	
	376	
Less creditors	136	240
		640
Share capital		300
Reserves at 1 January 1980	274	
Profit for 1980	66	340
		640

The following price indices are provided for the company's stocks and fixed assets :

	Stock	Fixed Assets
1 January 1979	*	80
Average for November/December 1979	120	*
31 December 1979	*	90
Average for 1980	130	96
Average for November/December 1980	140	*
31 December 1980	142	104

Stock turn over, on average, once every two months.

* indices not provided

Required :

A summarised profit and loss account for 1980 and balance sheet at 31 December 1980, prepared on the *current cost basis*. The profit and loss account should contain a cost of sales adjustment and a depreciation adjustment, whilst the balance sheet should contain a current cost reserve.

NOTES :

Ignore

     (i)   the monetary working capital adjustment,
     (ii)   the gearing adjustment,
     (iii) taxation,
     (iv) dividends.

Calculations to nearest £ 000.

EXERCISE 17.2

The following information related to Appleby Ltd.

Summarised Balance Sheets as on 30 June, 1979 and 30 June, 1980

	30 June 1979		30 June 1980	
	£ 000	£ 000	£ 000	£ 000
Fixed asset at cost		600		600
Less: depreciation		270		360
		330		240
Current Assets				
Stocks	150		235	
Debtors	120		160	
Cash	70		120	
	340		515	
Less: Current Liabilities				
Creditors	90		80	
		250		435
		580		675
Financed by :				
Ordinary shares		100		100
Reserves		200		295
10% Loan stock		280		280
		580		675

311

Summarised Trading and Profit and Loss account for the year ended 30 June, 1980.

	£ 000	£ 000
Sales		1,300
Cost of Sales :		
Opening stock	150	
Purchases	1,040	
	1,190	
Less: Closing stock	235	955
Gross Profit		345
Expenses (excluding interest)	132	
Interest	28	
Depreciation	90	250
Net profit (all retained)		95

NOTES

1.   There was only one fixed asset which was purchased on 1 July, 1976; to purchase the same asset new on 30 June, 1980 would cost £987,500 while its replacement cost of 30 June, 1979 was £812,500.

2.   Transactions occur evenly throughout the year.

3.   On average stock was acquired three months before the year end.

4.   The price index for the stock at the end of each month was as follows :

March 1979	115
April 1979	120
June 1979	126
December 1979	138
March 1980	141
April 1980	145
June 1980	147
Average for the year ended 30 June, 1980	138

You are required to :

(a)   Prepare a current cost profit and loss account for the year ended 30 June, 1980 making the adjustments recommended by SSAP 16.

(b)   Prepare current cost balance sheets as at 30 June, 1979 and 1980.

EXERCISE 17.3 EX

The following information has been extracted from the accounts of Norwich Plc prepared under the historical cost convention for 1986 :

Profit and Loss Account Extracts 1986

	£m
Turnover	200
Operating profit	15
Less : Interest payable	3
Net profit	12

Summarised Balance Sheet at 31 December 1986

	£m	£m
Fixed assets at cost less depreciation		60
Current assets: Stocks	20	
Debtors	30	
Bank	2	
	52	
Less : Current liabilities	30	
Net Current Assets		22
Total assets less current liabilities		82
Less : 15% debentures		20
		62
Capital and reserves		62

The company's accountant has prepared the following current cost data :

Current cost adjustments for 1986	£m
Depreciation adjustment	3
Cost of sales adjustment	5

Replacement cost at 31 December 1986	
Fixed assets, net of depreciation	85
Stocks	21

Required :

(a)   A calculation of the current cost operating profit of Norwich Plc for 1986 and the summarised current cost balance sheet of the company at 31 December 1986, so far as the information permits.

(b)   Calculations of the following ratios from both the historical cost accounts and current cost accounts :
       (i) interest cover;
       (ii) rate of return on shareholders' equity;
       (iii) debt/equity ratio.

(c)   A discussion of the significance of the ratios calculated under (b) and of the reasons for differences between them.

NOTE : Ignore taxation.

(Spring 1987)

313

SOLUTIONS

SOLUTION 17.1

ROCIETY LTD.
Current Cost Profit and Loss account for the year ended 31 December, 1980

	£ 000	£ 000
Historical cost trading profit		66
Less: current cost operation adjustments:		
Cost of sales adjustment	27	
Depreciation adjustment	<u>15</u>	<u>42</u>
Retained current cost profit for the year		<u>24</u>

Current Cost Balance Sheet as at 31 December, 1980

Fixed assets		650
Less: depreciation to date		<u>130</u>
		520
Stock	199	
Debtors	160	
Bank	<u>20</u>	
	379	
Less: creditors	<u>136</u>	<u>243</u>
		<u>763</u>
Share capital		300
Current cost reserve		165
Reserves at 1 January 1980	274	
Retained current cost profit	<u>24</u>	<u>298</u>
		<u>763</u>

WORKING NOTES

(i) <u>Cost of sales adjustment</u> £

Opening stock £156,000 x	$\frac{130}{120}$	=	169,000
Purchases			<u>1,024,000</u>
			1,193,000
Less closing stock £196,000 x	$\frac{130}{140}$		<u>182,000</u>
			1,011,000
Less historical cost of goods sold			<u>984,000</u>
Cost of sales adjustment credited to current cost reserve			<u>27,000</u>

(ii) <u>Depreciation adjustment</u> £

£50,000 x	$\frac{104}{80}$	=	65,000
Less historical cost depreciation for year		=	<u>50,000</u>
Depreciation adjustment credited to current cost reserve			<u>15,000</u>

314

Current cost reserve

(iii)

	£ 000		£ 000
Provision for depreciation	30	Fixed assets (revaluation)	150
		Profit and Loss account (cost of sales adjustment)	27
		Profit and Loss account (depreciation adjustment)	15
Balance c/d	165	Stock (revaluation)	3
	195		195
		Balance b/d	165

(iv) <u>Fixed assets revaluation</u>

				£
£500,000 x	$\dfrac{104}{80}$		=	650,000
Less: historical cost			=	500,000
Credited to current cost reserve				150,000

(v) <u>Provision for depreciation</u>

		£
£650,000 at 10% straight line for two years	=	130,000
Less: historical cost depreciation for two years	=	100,000
Debited to current cost reserve		30,000

(vi) <u>Closing stock revaluation</u>

For the purposes of the balance sheet the closing stock needs to be revalued at current cost :

£196,000 x	$\dfrac{142}{140}$	= (to nearest £ 000)	=	£199,000

The £3,000 increase is credited to current cost reserve.

SOLUTION 17.2

APPLEBY LTD
Current Cost Profit and Loss account for the year ended 30 June, 1980

(a)

	£ 000	£ 000
Turnover		1,300
Profit before tax and interest on the historical cost basis		123
Current cost operating adjustments :		
Depreciation adjustment	(45)	
Cost of sales adjustment	(35)	
Monetary working capital adjustment	(8)	(88)
Current Cost Operating Profit		35
Gearing adjustment	24	
Interest on net borrowing	(28)	
		(4)
Retained Current Cost Profit for the year		31

Current Cost Balance Sheets

	as at 30 June 1979		as at 30 June 1980	
	£ 000	£000	£ 000	£ 000
Fixed assets at valuation		447		395
Current assets:				
Stocks	164		245	
Debtors	120		160	
Cash	70		120	
	354		525	
Less: Current Liabilities				
Creditors	90		80	
		264		445
		711		840
Financed by:				
Ordinary shares		100		100
Reserves		200		295
Revaluation surpluses:				
Fixed Assets		117		155
Stock		14		10
		431		560
10% Loan Stock		280		280
		711		840

WORKING NOTES

(i) Depreciation adjustment

$$\text{Average replacement cost} = \frac{£812,500 + £987,500}{2} = £900,000$$

$$\text{Therefore current cost depreciation} = \frac{£900,000 \times £90,000}{£600,000 \text{ (historical cost)}} = £135,000$$

Less historical cost depreciation charge	=	£90,000
Depreciation adjustment to current cost Profit & Loss account	=	£ 45,000

(ii) Cost of sales adjustment

Opening stock £150,000 x $\frac{135 \; 138}{115}$	=	£180,000
Purchases	=	£1,040,000
		£1,220,000
Less closing stock £235,000 x $\frac{138}{141}$	=	£230,000
Current cost of sales	=	£990,000
Less historical cost of sales	=	£955,000
Cost of sales adjustment to current Profit & Loss account	=	£35,000

NOTE

Indices for March 1979 and March 1980 are used for the opening and closing stocks respectively because, on average, stock was acquired three months before the year end.

(iii) Monetary working capital adjustment

Opening MWC is £120,000 − £90,000	=	£30,000
Closing MWC is £160,000 − £80,000	=	£80,000

The increase in MWC is, therefore, £50,000.

To apply the indices:

$$\left(£80{,}000 \times \frac{138}{147}\right) - \left(£30{,}000 \times \frac{138}{126}\right)$$

$$= £75{,}102 - £32{,}857 = \text{(To nearest £ 000)} \qquad = \quad \underline{\underline{£42{,}000}}$$

The monetary working capital adjustment is £50,000 − £42,000 = $\underline{\underline{£8{,}000}}$

This amount is deducted from the historical cost profit.

(iv)	Gearing adjustment	30 June 1979	30 June 1980
		£	£
	Net borrowing		
	10% Loan stock	280,000	280,000
	Cash	(70,000)	(120,000)
		210,000	160,000

Therefore average net borrowing (L) = $\underline{£185{,}000}$

		30 June 1979	30 June 1980
	Shareholders' interest		
	Ordinary shares	100,000	100,000
	Reserves	200,000	295,000
	Revaluation surpluses (see below):		
	Fixed assets	117,000	155,000
	Stock	14,000	10,000
		431,000	560,000

Therefore average shareholders' interest (S) = $\underline{£495{,}500}$

Gearing adjustment is : $\dfrac{L}{L + S} = \dfrac{£185{,}000}{£185{,}000 + £495{,}500} \times \dfrac{100}{1} = 27.2\%$

This is applied to the total of current cost adjustments already made :

(£45,000 + £35,000 + £8,000) x 27.2% = $\underline{£24{,}000}$

(v) **Fixed asset revaluation**   £

At 30 June 1979	£330,000 x	$\dfrac{£812{,}500}{£600{,}000}$	=	447,000	(current cost)
Less historical cost				330,000	
Revaluation surplus				117,000	
At 30 June 1980	£240,000 x	$\dfrac{£987{,}500}{600{,}000}$	=	395,000	(current cost)
Less historical cost				240,000	
Revaluation surplus				155,000	

(vi) **Stock revaluation**   £

At 30 June 1979	£50,000 x	$\dfrac{126}{115}$	=	164,000	(current cost)
Less historical cost				150,000	
Revaluation surplus				14,000	
At 30 June 1980	£235,000 x	$\dfrac{147}{141}$	=	245,000	(current cost)
Less historical cost				235,000	
Revaluation surplus				10,000	

LESSON 18

INTERPRETATION OF ACCOUNTS

I need hardly stress the importance of this topic. Banks are constantly lending money to businesses of all sizes and every time a bank grants a loan or allows an overdraft facility it takes a risk - the risk of not getting all its money back or, at least, the risk of having difficulty in recovering the money. The main difficulty for the bank is in assessing the *degree* of risk it is taking.

How does the banker set about assessing this risk? Well, to start with, the manager has his own impressions of his customer as to reputation, financial standing, business ability, prospects, etc, these impressions having been acquired through past dealings with his customer. In addition to these impressions the manager will want to study the accounts of his customer - i.e. to interpret them and draw out of them some conclusions which will aid him in assessing the risk.

What will the accounts tell him? They may tell a lot or only a little but they will certainly provide him with a good basis on which he can make some reasonable assumptions

Interpretation of accounts is not difficult in itself. What the student might find difficult is in deciding how to tackle the problem, particularly 'where to start'. In an examination (or in practice) you are going to be faced with a mass of figures and information and you must have some *method* in the way you set about extracting your information from the accounts before you.

I am going to suggest a method of approach which you may want to follow or you may devise your own method, in which case I can guide you by indicating what you should look for in the accounts. Before I do this however, I want to stress the things you should *not* do when answering a question on interpretation.

The question itself will probably give you a balance sheet or balance sheets to work from together with extracts of information relating to Trading and Profit and Loss items.

Do Not:

(a) Spend time in calculating ratios, returns, etc. unless you can derive some useful information from your answers. For example, to state that the 'net profit is $12^1/_2\%$ of sales' without any further comment is just a waste of time - you are not being tested on arithmetic!. If however, you can show the significance of this percentage, then do so.

(b) Recite obvious things (e.g. 'stocks have increased by £x') unless you can say what the *relevance* of your statement is (e.g. 'stocks have increased by £x which indicates that......
and therefore........).

(c) Make bold statements unless you can support them by 'evidence', e.g. the statement that 'the company is overtrading' must be accompanied by the reasons on which you have founded this impression.

(d) Be afraid to say that you would require more information. This is fine provided you can say *why* you want this information and how you would use it.

(e) Think that there is *one* right answer to the question - provided you can show that you understand the information given to you and provided you can 'argue' on the facts in a coherent manner then you will obtain good marks.

Tackling the question

The interpretation question usually asks you to discuss the financial position and the prospects of the company in question, and I am going to suggest that you use a method of approach which will bring out and highlight a lot of the required information. By using this method you know 'where you are going' right from the word go and the length of the question is not going to cause you to panic!

My method involves looking at six major areas of information, in order. It is unlikely that you will have time to cover all six areas but you should certainly aim to deal with the first four out of which you can pick up more than enough marks.

These are the six areas:

(1) Shareholders Stake (i.e. share capital and reserves).

(2) Long term loans.

(3) Working capital.

(4) Liquidity.

(5) Trading figures (i.e. stock, debtors, creditors).

(6) Other items (according to question).

This then is the order of approach - we can start immediately to construct our answer by looking at everything connected with :

(1) Shareholders Stake

We will assume that the question shows the following:

	Year 1 £	Year 2 £
Share Capital	50,000	60,500
Capital Reserves	4,000	5,000
Revenue Reserves	9,000	14,500
	63,000	80,000

Questions arising out of this information:

(a) Was the increase in share capital due to a bonus issue or an issue of shares for cash? If the latter, this could be an important point if later we come to the conclusion that the company is in need of more long term funds for it would be unlikely that another issue could be made so soon.

(b) What caused the increase in capital reserves?

(c) From the information above, it is obvious that profits are being retained in the business which is an indication of good policy. What were the profits this year? Are they good? How do they compare with previous years? If they are down, why is this? The question may state the reason (a fire, strikes, etc.) but an inspection of the expenses (if given - if not, you want a breakdown of expenses from the directors) may show that the reduction in profit is due to a large increase in a particular type of expense. If you find that sales have increased by 60 per cent and general expenses have increased by 60 per cent then something is wrong, because although some expenses increase as sales increase (variable expenses), few will increase exactly in proportion (e.g. to double sales does not involve doubling wages) and many expenses will remain the same - i.e. *fixed costs* which do not, in the short term, vary with turnover (sales).

You should now look at the 'return on long term capital'. If for example there are long term loans of £20,000 in Year 2, in addition to the shareholders' funds of £80,000, and there is an operating profit (i.e. before payment of interest) in the same year, then the 'Return' is 25%, which indicates that the company is utilising the long term funds at its disposal in an effective way. Always look at this ratio, *Return on long term capital* viz.:

$$\frac{\text{Net Profit before Interest and Tax}}{\text{Shareholders Stake + Long term Loans (if any)}} \times \frac{100}{1}$$

and compare with previous years to see the trend.

Another thing you should always look at in this section is to what extent the shareholders are supporting the company's total assets. For example, if total assets amount to £1,000, then total liabilities amount to £1,000, and these various liabilities represent various *claims* against the assets - if share capital plus reserves (shareholders stake) amount to 50% of the total claims then this is the bank's cushion of security against things going wrong (remember that in a liquidation the shareholders are the very last people to be repaid - the lenders come earlier, depending on what security is held). As a 'going concern' the company may make losses which will be absorbed by the cushion. A stake of 50% in the assets is reasonably substantial; 30% would be bordering on the unsatisfactory.

The above should give you an idea of what to look for - there are no 'rules of thumb', just the need to apply common sense and judgement.

(2) Long Term Loans

You want to know when they are due to be repaid, whether they are secured on assets of the company (i.e. is there any security left for the bank?) and to confirm that they really are *long* term. In the case of directors' loans a Letter of Postponement from the directors, whereby they postpone their own repayment in favour of the bank's repayment, may be needed. (Be careful here - you would not gain any marks for suggesting a Letter of Postponement where the amount is small and the directors are good customers! This is a *real* situation, not an academic exercise).

(3) Working Capital

(i)   What is the amount of working capital?

(ii)   Is this enough? You know already that the current ratio is our guide here.

Question shows balance sheet:

	Year 1 £	Year 2 £		Year 1 £	Year 2 £
Share capital	150,000	150,000	Fixed assets (cost)	220,000	284,000
General Reserve		10,000	Less depreciation	20,000	25,000
P & L a/c	40,000	70,000		200,000	259,000
Debentures	30,000	30,000			
Bank	10,000	5,000	Current assets:		
Creditors	25,000	50,000	Stock	30,000	40,000
			Debtors	25,000	16,000
	255,000	315,000		255,000	315,000

Net profit for year   = £40,000
Working capital Year 1   = £20,000
Working capital Year 2   = £1,000

In year 1 the company's current assets therefore are being 'carried' or 'supported' as follows:

Current assets	£55,000
'Support' for these:	£
Working capital	20,000
Bank overdraft	10,000
Creditors	25,000
Total	55,000

This is quite good - the company is doing its share of supporting stocks and debtors and is not relying too much on credit to do this.

If however, the company starts carrying larger stocks or more debtors then the additional support needed should ideally come from an increase in working capital rather than from an increase in creditors.

Assuming stock and debtors to be at their normal levels, then we could say that working capital of £20,000 is adequate in Year 1 - i.e. it forms a good proportion of the total support (about 36%). What about year 2?

Current assets	£56,000
'Support' for these:	£
Working capital	1,000
Bank overdraft	5,000
Creditors	50,000
Total	56,000

The company is *not* doing its share of supporting its current assets - it is relying fairly heavily on credit. Working capital forms a low proportion of the total support (less than $2^1/_2\%$). Working capital at year 2 - inadequate!

(iii)   Why has working capital changed?

Continuing the above example, why has working capital been depleted after a year of good profits? A 'mini' source and applications of funds statement will answer this, viz.:

		£
Source		
Profits (+ depreciation)		45,000
Applications		
New fixed assets		64,000

Decrease in Working Capital   =   £19,000

This now leads on to another question:-

(iv)   *Why* has the company purchased more fixed assets? - to replace worn out assets or to prepare for increased production? If for the latter reason (the question will probably indicate this - if not, you want to know!), then the company may have to carry considerably more stocks and debtors to meet the increased sales. Where is the increased support for the current assets to come from? - more reliance on creditors? Is that what the requested bank lending is for? Let us suppose that it is planned to double sales (turnover) and that (using a new example) the *present* position is thus:

Total current assets	£10,000

Support for these:	£
Working Capital	6,000
Bank overdraft	2,000
Creditors	2,000
	10,000

The request is for an increased overdraft facility of £5,000. In that case we want to know:

(v)   What will be the position in x months from now?

Total current assets (double)	£20,000

Support:	£
Existing Working Capital	6,000
New bank overdraft (if granted)	5,000
Creditors (double)	4,000
	15,000
?	5,000
Total support	20,000

Where is the additional £5,000 to come from? Will profits increase the existing working capital (£6,000) enough to provide the extra support needed, or will the company try to extend the credit it is allowed by suppliers (and we know the danger associated with this), or will they be asking the bank for more increased overdraft facilities?

Remember too that should the company make losses or buy *more* fixed assets or have to repay any long term loans in the near future then this will have the effect of reducing its working capital even more, resulting in a need for even more credit.

(Many of these questions may of course be answered from the examination question itself - e.g. you may be told what future profits are likely to be and you will therefore have an idea of how the 'gap' we have just seen may be filled).

With my last example in mind it may be relevant to say that in view of the heavy reliance on credit foreseen by our projected figures, it would be preferable for the company to have access to long term capital rather than to bank lending - e.g. by mortgaging the premises or by issuing more debentures or by issuing more shares(the latter producing permanent capital). *Do not* suggest that the company issues more shares or debentures if the company is obviously a private limited company whose access to share/debenture holders is very limited.

It should be obvious from the above that the consideration of working capital resources has quite a prominent place in any interpretation question. Naturally you will come across a variety of situations according to which particular question you are dealing with and I have only used in my examples some suggested situations, but you can usually apply the basic questions I have outlined to any situation.

(4) Liquidity

When referring to the liquidity of an asset we are referring to the ease and speed at which it could be converted in to cash. Balance at bank or cash in hand are of course perfectly liquid, whereas debtors are 'near' liquid and stock is not quite as liquid as debtors (because it has to go through the process of being converted into debtors before it becomes cash).

Certain liabilities of the company in question will have to be paid off in the very near future and part of our interpretation procedure must be in seeing that payments which are due, can in fact be met. For this purpose we are interested in the liquidity of the assets. It may be that the bulk of the current assets are in the form of stock which may mean that cash will not be forthcoming for some time (especially if the stock is turning over slowly or it consists of some bad stock).

It should not be difficult for you to determine whether the assets are sufficient and liquid enough to meet pressing debts and you will also be concerned as to future liquidity in deciding whether the repayments to the bank will be maintained as promised by the customer or in deciding how repayments are likely to be made, For example, you may find that *with* the requested overdraft facility the company will just about be able to meet the corporation tax liability which is due, whereas the overdraft was requested for an entirely different purpose than this!

Apart from these specific types of observation, a general impression of the liquidity position can be got by seeing how far total current assets, *less stocks*, go towards repaying current liabilities. Such ratio is referred to as the *Liquid Ratio* or *Quick Ratio* - e.g. Current Assets (less stocks) = £1,000; Current Liabilities = £800 - Liquid (or Quick) Ratio = 1.25 to 1.

A liquidity ratio of 1 to 1 is quite reasonable - it means that the company, without selling its stock (an extreme situation) could cover its liabilities in full. A ratio of 1.5 to 1 is even better but a ratio any higher than this could indicate that too much is tied up in debtors and bank - *idle money* which is not working for the company. Perhaps there are many bad debts within debtors? As with the current ratio, much depends on the *type* of business in question.

(5) Trading Figures

In comparing two years' figures,

(i)   Are there any large fluctuations in creditors, debtors or stocks? If so, why?

(ii)   Creditors:
Are there many small debts or one or two very large ones? If one large creditor exerts pressure for repayment this could cause trouble for the company.

What is the period of credit being taken by the company? Compare creditors with purchases (if given) e.g. Creditors = £4,000; purchases for the year = £40,000 - therefore, period of credit taken = 1/10 of a year (about 5 weeks).

Does this seem reasonable considering the type of business? Compare with last year if possible to see whether the period of credit is being extended.

(iii)   Debtors:
How many are there? It is better to spread the risk of bad debts over many rather than have a few large debtors.

What period of credit is being allowed by the company? Compare debtors with sales (if given) - e.g. Debtors = £6,000; Sales = (for year) £36,000 - therefore period of credit = 1/6 of a year (2 months).

If we found that the period for creditors was increasing whilst the period for debtors was decreasing, then this would be significant in deciding that the company's resources were being strained.

A comparison of bad debts with the sales figure could give an idea of the reliability of the debtors.

If the accounts you are interpreting are those of a contractor, it could be that the figure for debtors includes retaining fees (which will only be paid if the contract is completed satisfactorily). This would raise the question - 'How good a worker is the contractor?

(iv)   Stock:
Relevant questions might be;

(a)   what does it include? (any 'dead' stock?)

(b)   how is it valued? (this, remember, affects the profit shown in the accounts)

(c)   how fast is it being turned over - i.e. how many times does the average amount of stock held get sold and replaced in a year? To find this:

$$\frac{\text{Cost of Goods Sold}}{\text{Average Stock}} = \text{(say) } 6$$

This means that the average stock is sold (turned over) 6 times in a year - i.e. stock remains in the stores, on average, for 1/6 of a year before being sold and replaced. Is this a good turnover? It is for a furniture dealer but not for a fishmonger! In other words, it depends on the type of business. As stock 'turns over' profits are made, so obviously a quick turnover is very desirable.

Sometimes 'Cost of goods sold' is not given in which case you could use 'sales' instead. This would not give you an accurate figure (i.e. 4 = 3 months storage) but it would allow you to observe the 'trend' by comparing with previous years' figures.

(6)   Other items

For example:

(i)   Are there any Investments? Are they quoted? Should they be sold to provide funds? Could they be used as security, etc?

(ii)   Inspect and consider every *large* item in the accounts and pay particular attention to any major changes that have taken place.

(iii) Consider the significance (if any) of items in the accounts and information in the question which has up to now been ignored.

Finally.

You must study this lesson with the previous lessons on Accounting Ratios, Cash Budgets and Statements of Source and Application of Funds very much in your mind! These areas are very relevant to the final interpretation and should be used in answering the compulsory question on interpretation. Therefore, do please study this lesson with constant reference to these previous lessons.

Your Answer

Do not put all your points into report or essay form. Instead, tabulate your points as you go along so that they are easy to 'pick up' by the examiner - i.e. fairly short sentences or short paragraphs wherever possible - do not 'ramble on' but *do* bring out the significance of your points.

EXERCISE 18.1

Mercury Ltd is a private company which operates a garage. The garage deals in new and second-hand motor vehicles, petrol, oil and motor accessories, and undertakes repairs and servicing.

Early in January 19-9 a fire destroyed equipment in the garage's lubrication bay. The equipment was a few years old, and although the insurers agreed to pay its current worth of £1,000, replacement with new equipment would cost £2,300. Alterations to the lubrication bay for speedier servicing had been planned for the future and the directors decided it would be sensible to make these improvements immediately at the cost of a further £1,500. The directors approached the company's bank for an overdraft of £5,000 to provide the necessary funds and to meet the corporation tax payment due in January 19-9.

Summarised balance sheets of Mercury Ltd at 31 December 19-7 and 31 December 19-8, and appropriation accounts for the years 19-7 and 19-8 are shown below:

Balance Sheets

	19-7 £	19-8 £		19-7 £	19-8 £
Issued Share Capital	10,000	10,000	Freehold Property		
General reserve	25,000	25,000	(at valuation made		
Retained earnings	4,150	7,550	31 December 19-5	27,500	27,500
6% Mortgage Loan	5,000	5,000	Equipment at cost		
Corporation tax on			less depreciation	9,250	9,850
profits of:			Stocks	12,500	15,500
19-6	2,800		Debtors:		
19-7	2,300	2,300	Trade	6,000	7,000
19-8		2,600	Finance Company	1,800	1,000
Trade creditors	8,000	9,000	Bank	200	600
	57,250	61,450		57,250	61,450

Appropriation Accounts

	19-7 £	19-8 £
Net profit before corporation tax	5,500	6,000
Less provision for corporation tax on profit of the year	2,300	2,600
Retained profit	3,200	3,400

Among the company's transactions during 19-7 and 19-8 were:

325

	19-7	19-8
	£	£
Cash sales	54,000	58,000
Sales of cars through finance company	36,000	48,000
Credit sales	54,000	56,000
Total sales	144,000	162,000
Purchases	100,000	108,000
Directors' emoluments	8,500	9,000
Depreciation for the year	1,600	1,900
Additions to equipment	–	2,500
(No disposals of equipment in either year)		

The mortgage loan was made by a major oil company which is a supplier to Mercury Ltd : repayment is due in 20 years time.

Mercury Ltd does not conduct hire purchase transactions. Customers requiring hire purchase are accommodated by a reputable finance company. Mercury Ltd acts as an intermediary for the finance company, and receives full payment in exchange for customers' completed agreements.

Required:
A discussion of the company's financial position using relevant ratios.

EXERCISE 18.2

The following are summarised balance sheets of Swiftvend Ltd at 31 December 19-3 and 31 December 19-4:

	19-3	19-4		19-3	19-4
	£	£		£	£
Issued share capital	10,000	10,000	Warehouse equipment	5,500	4,800
Profit & Loss account	17,400	25,300	Vending machines	23,200	33,200
Corporation tax (due			Stocks:		
within 12 months)	4,200	5,280	supplies	3,620	4,800
Creditors	3,000	4,000	repair components	2,100	2,600
Bank	–	820	Bank	180	–
	34,600	45,400		34,600	45,400

Details of fixed assets are shown below:

	Cost	Depreciation	Net
	£	£	£
Warehouse equipment at 31 December 19-3	7,000	1,500	5,500
Depreciation 19-4	–	700	(700)
Warehouse equipment at 31 December 19-4	7,000	2,200	4,800
Vending machines at 31 December 19-3	38,000	14,800	23,200
Less disposals 19-4	4,000	4,000	–
	34,000	10,800	23,200
Acquisitions 19-4	21,000		21,000
Depreciation 19-4	–	11,000	(11,000)
	55,000	21,800	33,200

You are given the following information derived from the company's profit statements:

	£	Years ended 31 December 19-3 Per cent of sales (approximate)	£	19-4 Per cent of sales (approximate)
Supplies for vending machines	30,480	34.2	42,100	35.0
Wages (servicing, etc)	17,150	19.1	23,800	19.8
Depreciation	7,600	8.4	11,700	9.8
Components for repairs	2,940	3.3	4,300	3.6
Administration	5,500	6.1	6,100	5.1
Travelling	4,410	4.9	6,000	5.0
Rent of warehouse	5,000	5.6	5,000	4.2
Rental payments for sites	2,090	2.3	2,120	1.8
Directors' remuneration	5,200	5.8	5,700	4.8
Corporation tax on profit of year	4,200	4.7	5,280	4.4
Retained profit	5,070	5.6	7,900	6.6
Sales	90,000		120,000	

Swiftvend Ltd, which was established 5 years ago, owns and services vending machines which dispense drinks and certain items of food. The machines are installed in a variety of buildings in an urban area. George, who is executive director of the company and owns most of the shares, approached the company's bankers early in 19-5 to arrange overdraft facilities of £5,000 for the succeeding 12 months. He explained:

'We are continuing with our programme of controlled expansion of vending machines in well-chosen locations. We plan to purchase another 50 machines during 19-5, of which 20 will be replacements for existing machines. We made a similar expansion last year, but rather fewer replacements. In any case, prices have risen, so that at £500 per machine the total cost will be about £25,000.

We reckon that the physical volume of sales will increase by almost as much as last year, but, in order to keep up with inflation, we will have to increase our prices, so sales for the year are likely to be about £160,000.

Our major costs for supplies, wages, repairs and travelling should be about the same proportion of sales as in the past two years. Our warehouse rent is fixed at £5,000 for a couple of years yet, and we are now concentrating on providing machines as a service in offices so that we should not be paying any extra for site rentals. Administration and directors' remuneration are unlikely to rise by much more than last year.

All this indicates that we should be able to meet the vending machine costs from our funds generated during the year (as we did last year) but we need borrowing facilities to cover fluctuations in our financing needs, particularly in relation to working capital.'

Required: A full discussion of the financial position and prospects of Swiftvend Ltd with reference to the proposed overdraft facility.

EXERCISE 18.3

Summarised accounts of Toothbrush Ltd for the year ended 31 December 19-6 and 31 December 19-7 are shown below:

Balance Sheets

	19-6 £	19-7 £		19-6 £	19-7 £
Issued share capital	35,000	35,000	Equipment at cost	75,000	75,000
Retained profits	11,550	15,100	Less accumulated		
10% debentures			depreciation	37,500	45,000
(redeemable in 25 years secured				37,500	30,000
by mortgage on freehold property)		30,000	Freehold factory	–	48,000
Corporation tax payable:			Stock-in-trade:		
January 19-8	2,500	2,500	Materials	2,000	2,850
January 19-9	–	2,800	Finished goods	2,500	6,750
Creditors	5,600	8,300	Debtors	8,000	9,900
Bank overdraft	–	3,800	Bank	4,650	–
	54,650	97,500		54,650	97,500

Revenue Accounts

	19-6 Units (000s omitted)	£	19-7 Units (000s omitted)	£
Prime cost (direct materials and labour)		20,000		22,000
Factory overheads		30,000		27,500
Production at cost	1,000	50,000	1,100	49,500
Add stock of finished goods 1 January	50	2,500	50	2,500
	1,050	52,500	1,150	52,000
Less stock of finished goods 31 December	50	2,500	150	6,750
	1,000	50,000	1,000	45,250
Administration expenses		5,000		5,800
Debenture interest				3,000
Directors' emoluments		4,000		4,600
Net profit		6,000		6,350
Sales	1,000	65,000	1,000	65,000

Appropriation Accounts

	19-6 £	19-7 £
Retained profits brought forward	8,050	11,550
Net profit	6,000	6,350
	14,050	17,900
Corporation tax on profit of year	2,500	2,800
Retained profits 31 December	11,550	15,100

The items 'factory overheads' in the Revenue accounts were made up as follows:

	19-6 £	19-7 £
Factory rent	4,500	
Depreciation of equipment	7,500	7,500
Maintenance and repairs	4,000	4,700
Indirect labour (supervisors, etc.)	8,000	8,800
Sundry indirect materials, etc.	6,000	6,500
	30,000	27,500

Throughout 19-6 and 19-7 the company had an overdraft limit of £5,000 which has been exceeded occasionally. In March 19-8, the overdraft was £6,100 and the company requested an increase in the limit to £12,000 for one year in order to give time for the liquidation of stocks and the purchase of some urgently needed equipment. The company proposes that the limit should revert to £5,000 in March 19-9.

The company manufactures a single type of toothbrush in a range of colours. The managing director explains that a change in the popularity of certain colours caused the stock build-up; the excess stocks of the old colours will take about a year to liquidate at the present rate.

Required:

A report on the financial implications of this information. You are not required to reach a decision regarding the granting of the overdraft.

EXERCISE 18.4 EX

You are considering the possibility of acquiring shares in Cotford Plc., which brews beer, manufactures a range of spirits and soft drinks and is the owner of public houses and hotels. The information given below has been extracted from the company's published accounts.

Profit and Loss Account Extracts, Year to 30 June

	1988 £000s	1987 £000s
Turnover	21,200	17,200
Operating profit	2,750	2,085
Interest payable	(800)	(550)
Profit before tax	1,950	1,535
Taxation	(590)	(395)
Profit after tax	1,360	1,140
Dividend paid and proposed	(500)	(315)
Retained profit	860	825

Summarised Balance Sheet at 30 June

	1988 £000s	1987 £000s
Tangible assets at cost or valuation	28,900	16,300
Investments	880	700
	29,780	17,000
Current Assets	3,850	3,150
Current Liabilities	4,500	4,000
Net current liabilities	(650)	(850)
Total assets less current liabilities	29,130	16,150
Less: borrowing repayable after more than one year	7,520	5,100
	21,610	11,050
Financed by :		
Share capital : ordinary shares of £1 each fully paid	2,400	1,700
Revaluation reserve	9,000	—
Profit and loss account	10,210	9,350
	21,610	11,050

The company revalued its non-industrial freehold and leasehold properties on 30 June 1988. No depreciation is provided on these assets, as it is the company's policy to maintain them, out of expenditure charged to revenue, to a standard which ensures that their estimated aggregate residual values exceed net book amounts.

The present market value of each Cotford share is £6.20. The typical price/earnings ratio of companies in Cotford's line of business is 10.

Required :

(a)   Calculate the ratios, listed below, for 1987 and 1988. Base your calculations on the information provided in the accounts above. You should present the ratios in the following form :

	1988	1987
Working capital ratio		
Interest cover		
Debt/equity ratio		
Total asset turnover		
Operating profit percentage		
Return on total assets		
Return on equity		

(b)   A report on the financial performance and position of Cotford in each of the following broad areas:

    (i)   solvency and gearing;

    (ii)   asset utilisation;

and   (iii)   profitability.

You should base your analysis on the information provided, the ratios calculated under (a), and any other relevant calculations.   (Autumn 1988)

EXERCISE 18.5 EX

Notley Ltd was incorporated in May 1989 to purchase and sell a single product, and it plans to commence business operations on 1 July 1989. The business is to be managed by two directors who, in June 1989, will together subscribe equally for the entire issued share capital consisting of 60,000 ordinary shares of £1 each, at par. Fixed assets costing £54,000 and stocks costing £30,000 will be acquired in June 1989 and paid for in July.

The directors have made arrangements for venture capital to be provided, if required, in the form of a five year loan carrying interest at 12% per annum. The amount of the loan will be equal to the estimated cash deficiency, if any, at 30 September 1989, and will be advanced on 1 October 1989. The bank has agreed to provide overdraft facilities to meet any cash deficiencies not covered by this arrangement. Interest on venture capital will be payable, annually, on 30 September (*ignore interest on any bank overdraft*).

The estimated revenue account for the year to 30 June 1990 (which does not take account of interest on venture loan capital) is as follows :

Estimated Revenue Account   **Comment**

	£000	
Sales	500	Credit period: $1^1/_2$ months
Less Cost of stock sold	300	Credit period on purchases : one month
Direct labour costs (variable with turnover)	50	Payable on the last day of each week
Variable expenses	60	Payable one month after the date incurred
Fixed expenses	24	Payable quarterly in advance : first payment 1 July 1989
Directors' remuneration	48	£2,000 (each) payable on last day of each month
Depreciation	9	Fixed assets' estimated life : six years
Net Profit	9	

The following additional information is provided :

(i)   Sales will accrue at an even rate during the six months to 31 December 1989 and are estimated at £200,000. Thereafter, and for the foreseeable future, sales are estimated at £50,000 per month.

(ii)   Purchases each month will be sufficient to replace items sold.

(iii)   The market rate for the services provided by each of the two directors is estimated at £1,600 per person per month.

(iv)   The entire profit is to be distributed as dividends.

Required :

(a)   A cash forecast for each of the four quarters to 30 June 1990 showing the estimated accumulated cash surplus or deficit at the end of each quarter.

(b)   An explanation for the difference between the forecast trading profit for the year to 30 June 1990 and the expected change in the cash balance over the same twelve-month period. You should support your explanation with an appropriate numerical calculation.

(c)   Your assessment of the prospects of Notley Ltd from the viewpoint of the two directors. You should include in your assessment an estimate of profit for the year to 30 June 1991.

NOTES :
(i)   Assume that a year consists of 48 weeks, a quarter of 12 weeks and a month of 4 weeks.
(ii)   Ignore taxation.   (Spring 1989)

EXERCISE 18.6 EX

Ashbury Industrial Appliances Ltd has banked with you for many years and has always been a first class customer. The directors' report describes the company as 'merchants of industrial products'. It is run by three brothers - Jim Toil, Peter Toil and Jeff Toil - who own all the shares. The published accounts for 1988 reported profits of £14,000 after charging depreciation of £40,000 and directors' remuneration of £90,000. The balance on the company's current account with your bank on 30 September 1989 is £75,000.

Newton Engineering Ltd is located nearby and manufactures a number of the products merchanted by Ashbury Industrial Appliances. The entire share capital of Newton Engineering is held by Bill Whatley and his wife. Bill, who is also managing director, plans to retire, and the Toil brothers wish to purchase the business. Newton Engineering's accountants have supplied the information below based on last year's published accounts.

Bill Whatley and his wife are asking £75,000 for the entire share capital of Newton Engineering. Bill claims that this is a bargain in view of the fact that: 'turnover is increasing; profit is going up; my company has a couple of highly skilled employees who have worked for me for years; the balance sheet shows the business is worth £84,000; and the machinery runs like a dream'.

The brothers have approached your bank to finance the acquisition. Jim and Peter are very keen to make the purchase, but Jeff is a little less enthusiastic. A friend of Jeff's, who works at the Government's Business Statistics Office, has told him that a firm in Newton Engineering's line of business should have a current (working capital) ratio of 2 : 1 and should collect its debts, on average, within 30 days.

The brothers approach you for advice.

Required :

A full analysis of the proposal to acquire the shares of Newton Engineering Ltd, based on an examination of the past performance and future viability of the business.

In your answer you should show the relevant accounting ratios and a statement of funds for the year to 30 September 1989. Your answer should also include an evaluation of the claims made by Bill Whatley and a *brief* assessment of the likely willingness of the bank to provide financial support for the proposed acquisition.

NOTE: Assume that you are making the analysis on 30 September 1989.

Newton Engineering Ltd
Profit and Loss Account Extracts Year to 30 September

		1988	1989
		£	£
Turnover		360,000	365,000
Net profit before tax		8,000	11,000
After charging: Depreciation :	premises	1,000	1,000
	machinery	8,000	8,000
Directors' remuneration		16,000	11,000
Interest		1,600	1,600
Hire charge		1,500	1,700

331

Balance Sheet at 30 September

Fixed Assets	1988 £	1988 £	1989 £	1989 £
Leasehold premises at cost 1970	25,000		25,000	
Less: Accumulated depreciation	18,000	7,000	19,000	6,000
Machinery at cost	85,000		85,000	
Less: Accumulated depreciation	42,000	43,000	50,000	35,000
		50,000		41,000
Current Assets				
Stock: materials	14,000		7,000	
work in progress	1,000		1,000	
finished goods	16,000		45,000	
Debtors	35,000		24,000	
	66,000		77,000	
Current Liabilities				
Creditors	21,000		23,000	
Corporation tax	2,000		3,000	
Income tax and social security paymts.	5,000		6,000	
Bank overdraft	12,000		2,000	
	40,000		34,000	
Net current assets		26,000		43,000
		76,000		84,000
Financed by:				
Shareholders' equity		56,000		64,000
Loan repayable 31 December 1990		20,000		20,000
		76,000		84,000

(Autumn 1989)

EXERCISE 18.7 EX

The following information is provided for Turquand Ltd, a trading company, in respect of 1988:

1.

Balance Sheet at 1 January 1988

	£000	£000
Fixed Assets		
Tangible fixed assets at cost		200
Less : Accumulated depreciation		35
		165
Intangible asset: Development expenditure		12
Current Assets		
Stock	63	
Debtors	51	
Cash at bank	13	
	127	
Current Liabilities		
Trade creditors	35	
Net current assets		92
Total assets less current liabilities		269
15% loan repayable 31 December 1990		60
		209
Capital and Reserves		
Called-up share capital		100
Retained profit		109
		209

2.   **Transactions during 1988 include :**   £000

	£000
Receipts from customers	362
Payments to suppliers	214
Bad debts written off	5
Administration and distribution expenses	62
Development expenditure - amount paid	11
Tangible fixed assets owned on 1 January 1988, revalued at	375
Purchase of fixed assets	39
Loan repaid (early) on 31 December 1988, including interest due	69

3.   **Details at 31 December 1988**   £000

	£000
Stock in hand	75
Debtors	52
Trade Creditors	42

4.   **Accounting Policies**

Tangible fixed assets, which were revalued on 1 January 1988, are written off on the straight-line basis over their estimated useful life. On this basis, a charge of £42,000 must be made for the year.
Development expenditure is carried forward to the extent its recovery out of related revenues is reasonably assured. It has been decided that, of the expenditure to date, £15,000 is recoverable at 31 December 1988.

Required :
(a)   The trading and profit and loss account for 1988
(b)   The statement of sources and applications of *working capital* for 1988 showing the net increase or decrease in working capital.
(c)   The balance sheet at 31 December 1988.
(d)   An assessment of the financial progress of Turquand Ltd during 1988. This assessment should include a comparison of the respective merits of the statements prepared under (a) and (b) as indicators of performance during the year.

NOTE : Ignore taxation and dividends.

                                                         (Autumn 1989)

SOLUTIONS

SOLUTION 18.1

Shareholders Stake and Profits - The shareholders' stake in the company is very adequate at 69% in 19-8 indicating a soundly based company.

Revenue reserves are out of proportion to issued share capital as a result of a policy of retaining profits over the years which is prudent policy. I suggest that some of these profits are capitalised by way of a bonus issue, subject to the limits of Authorised Share Capital. This will remove any obligation to pay dividends from this reserve.

The return on long term capital is about $12^1/2\%$ in each year - i.e. the company is consistently making quite reasonable use of the long term funds at its disposal. The return on shareholders' capital is about 14% which is quite reasonable.

The increase in profit is consistent with the increase in sales. Management's control over expenses appears good.

Long Term Loans - Presumably the loan is secured by the property but in view of the small loan there would be sufficient equity in the property should the bank require security.

Working Capital - This shows an increase in 19-8 of £2,600 and the present position is :

Current Assets	£24,100
Supported by :	£
Working Capital	10,200
Tax Due	4,900
Creditors	9,000
	£24,100
Current Ratio = 1.7 to 1	

This is a very healthy position - no heavy reliance on credit; even though the working capital will be reduced by £1,500 for improvements, and £1,300 for equipment, the position is sound, as future profits will 'top up' the working capital.

Liquidity - The liquid ratio is about 0.62 to 1 in 19-8 which is on the low side. What are the chances of reducing holdings of stocks to help the situation?

The £5,000 being requested, plus the present balance of £600 will be used :

	£
New equipment	2,300
Less insurance claim	1,000
	1,300
Corporation Tax due	2,300
Improvements	1,500
	5,100

This leaves a margin of £500 which is low - probably more than £5,000 is required for comfort. A cash budget showing flows of cash over the next few months would be useful.

Future profits should quickly repay the required overdraft if 19-8's position is maintained where the cash flow was :

	£	
Net Profit	6,000	
Add back depreciation	1,900	
	7,900	less tax commitment

Trading Figures - Stock turnover is just over 7 in both years - i.e. stock is held for about 7 weeks before being sold. Stock is not high in relation to sales. A satisfactory position.

The company is taking 4 - 5 weeks credit from suppliers and allowing 5 - 6 weeks to its debtors. These periods are very reasonable and are consistent in both years. The finance company is making payments to the garage very promptly.

Other Items - Adequate provisions are being made for corporation tax and depreciation. This is consistent with the general impression of a conservative, but sound well-managed concern.

One way to rectify the somewhat strained liquidity position would be for Mercury to increase the present Mortgage Loan to provide more 'permanent' funds.

SOLUTION 18.2
Swiftvend Limited

Shareholders Stake and Profits - Shareholders' stake in the company, at 78/79% is excellent, providing a substantial 'cushion' of safety for lenders.

The increase in profit is encouraging and substantiates the idea of 'controlled expansion'. Costs which one would expect to be relatively 'fixed' have increased together with sales in the right proportions, particularly administration, rent of warehouse, and rent of sites. A modest increase in directors' remuneration is good.

Return on capital employed is excellent at 34/37% - a very attractive 'use of funds'. Part of retained profits, the size of which indicates a good profit retention policy, could be capitalised to remove any obligation to pay dividends from these reserves.

Working Capital - the company has no working capital - current ratio in 19-4 being 0.73 to 1, but this does not seem to be causing many problems in that creditors appear to be being paid in good time although the tax liabilities are probably proving burdensome to the company as all profits generated are being immediately ploughed back into the purchase of more machines.

Working capital is too low and this is why the bank is being asked to help. The question is : Can the company 'weather' this period of rapid expansion without ready capital (some of the best companies have gone through this period at some time)? The facts in the question indicate the elements to instil confidence of their ability to do this.

Liquidity - Is non-existent in 19-4! Funds are being generated on a 'day to day' basis and being used in the same way. The comments regarding working capital are again relevant here.

According to George's estimates the position in 19-5 should be as follows :

		£	£
Sales			160,000
Less	supplies, wages, repairs and		
	travelling - i.e. 63.4% of sales	101,500	
	Administration (+ approx 10%)	6,710	
	Directors fees (+ approx 10%)	6,270	
	Warehouse rent	5,000	
	Site Rentals	2,120	121,600
Incoming Flow of Funds			38,400

Even allowing for corporation tax payment on profit, after allowances for depreciation, these funds should be sufficient to cover purchase of new vending machines and to reduce the bank lending substantially.

Trading Figures - Stocks are obviously turning over at a satisfactory rate which would be expected in these circumstances.

Creditors would seem to be being paid in about 5 weeks which is reasonable.

Other Items - the accounts give an impression of good ambitious management and as the type of business is not speculative, the prospects would seem to be good.

SOLUTION 18.3

Shareholders Stake and Profits - The shareholders claim to the assets of the company is a hefty 85% in 19-6, falling to 51% in 19-7, due to the issue of debentures in 19-7. However, 51% provides a very satisfactory 'cushion' of security for the bank.

Retained profits suggest a prudent policy in the past.

The increase in profit of £350 is very modest but it is interesting to note that the large stock of finished goods in 19-7 (valued at factory cost) has distorted the 19-7 profit figure, so causing a large increase in the factory overheads carried forward at the end of 19-7 compared with the amount carried forward in 19-6. If stock had been valued at *prime* cost, the profit in 19-7 would have been only £4,100 - a reduction of £1,900!

Return on long term capital employed is poor at 13% in 19-6 and only 8% in 19-7. The position is even worse in view of the above comments regarding stock.

Long Term Loans - By issuing debentures in 19-7 the company has been able to acquire its own premises, so saving the yearly rent, but at the same time committing itself to debenture interest of £3,000 - a net saving of £1,500. However, to offset this is the interest on the bank overdraft.

Working Capital - A current ratio of just over 2 to 1 in 19-6 has fallen to just over 1 to 1 in 19-7, despite the injection of £30,000 from the debenture issue. The cause is of course the purchase of the factory. The position will worsen with the purchase of more equipment as suggested.

There is an urgent need for more permanent capital.

Liquidity - Liquid ratio = 0.51 to 1 in 19-7 which is hopelessly inadequate with imminent commitments for debenture interest, corporation tax and purchase of more equipment, together with difficulties in selling present stock.

Has the corporation tax due on 1 January, 19-8 been paid yet? How much will the new equipment cost? Will the limit of £12,000 be enough? A cash budget should be asked for to indicate 'true' requirements.

Trading Figures - Debtors are 'paying up' in about 8 weeks (6 weeks in 19-6) which is a long time in normal trade. Why is this? How many debtors are there? Is there one main debtor? Ask for a list of main debtors.

Although purchases are not given, the periods of credit from suppliers (using 'sales') in 19-7 are nearly double the periods in 19-6 which confirms the liquidity crisis referred to above.

Stock turnover has reduced by about 50% in 19-7, obviously due to the difficulties in selling off the old colours. Will these eventually sell?

Other Items - The company is obviously not in a position to expand in any way and badly needs more permanent capital, which a bank loan cannot provide.

336

APPENDIX A

Tables of Factors for Use with Discounted Cash Flow Questions
Table of Factors for r = 10%

Year	Future Value of £1	Present Value of £1	Present Value of £1 received per year	Annual Value of £1 received now
n	$(1 + r)^n$	$(1 + r)^{-n}$	$\dfrac{1 - (1+r)^{-n}}{r}$	$\dfrac{r}{1 - (1+r)^n}$
1	1.100	0.909	0.909	1.100
2	1.210	.826	1.736	0.576
3	1.331	.751	2.487	.402
4	1.464	.683	3.170	.315
5	1.611	.621	3.791	.264
6	1.772	.564	4.355	.230
7	1.949	.513	4.868	.205
8	2.144	.467	5.335	.187
9	2.358	.424	5.759	.174
10	2.594	.386	6.145	.163

Table of Factors for r = 14%

Year (n)	Future Value of £1	Present Value of £1	Present Value of £1 received per year	Annual Value of £1 received now
1	1.140	0.877	0.877	1.140
2	1.300	.769	1.647	.607
3	1.482	.675	2.322	.431
4	1.689	.592	2.914	.343
5	1.925	.519	3.433	.291
6	2.195	.456	3.889	.257
7	2.502	.400	4.288	.233
8	2.853	.351	4.639	.216
9	3.252	.308	4.946	.202
10	3.707	.270	5.216	.192

Table of factors for r = 15%

Year (n)	Future Value of £1	Present Value of £1	Present Value of £1 received per year	Annual Value of £1 received now
1	1.150	0.870	0.870	1.150
2	1.322	.756	1.626	0.615
3	1.521	.658	2.283	.438
4	1.749	.572	2.855	.350
5	2.011	.497	3.352	.298
6	2.313	.432	3.785	.264
7	2.660	.376	4.160	.240
8	3.059	.327	4.487	.223
9	3.518	.284	4.772	.210
10	4.046	.247	5.019	.199

APPENDIX B

Table of Factors for use with Discounted Cash Flow Questions

Table of factors for n = 6 years

Interest Rate % r	Present Value of £1 $(1 + r)^n$	Present Value of £1 received per year $\dfrac{1 - (1+r)^n}{r}$	Annual Value of £1 received now $\dfrac{r}{1 - (1 + r)^n}$
2	0.89	5.60	0.18
4	.79	5.24	.19
6	.70	4.92	.20
8	.63	4.62	.22
10	.56	4.36	.23
12	.51	4.11	.24
14	.46	3.89	.26
16	.41	3.68	.27
18	.37	3.50	.29
20	.34	3.33	.30
22	.30	3.17	.32

Table of factors for n = 8 years

Interest Rate %	Present Value of £1	Present Value of £1 received per year	Annual Value of £1 received now
2	0.85	7.33	0.14
4	.73	6.73	.15
6	.63	6.21	.16
8	.54	5.75	.17
10	.47	5.33	.19
12	.40	4.97	.20
14	.35	4.64	.22
16	.31	4.34	.23
18	.27	4.08	.25
20	.23	3.84	.26
22	.20	3.62	.28
24	.18	3.42	.29
26	.16	3.24	.31
28	.14	3.08	.33
30	.12	2.92	.34

L

Last In, First Out (LIFO), 93-94
Liquidation Basis of Valuation, 51-52
Liquidity, 323
Liquidity Ratio, 182
Long Term Contract Valuation 98-101

M

Mainstream Corporation Tax, 202-204
Maintainable Earnings Basis, 54
Manufacturing Accounts, 9-13
Marginal Cost, 69-70
Margin of Safety, 72-73
Merger Method, 291-293
Monetary Working Capital Adjustment, 304, 306-308
Money Cost of Capital, 229

N

Net Present Value (NPV), 216-219, 229
Net Profit Margin, 179-180
Net Realisable Value (NRV), 94,95,98

P

Patents, 88, 89
Payback Method, 230
Pre-Acquisition Profits, 38
Price Earnings Ratio, 54-55
Prime Cost, 10
Prior Year Adjustments, 259
Profit and Loss Account (Format 1), 249-252
Prudence Concept, 13

Q

Quick Ratio, 182

R

Ratio Analysis, 178-189
Redemption of Debentures, 45-46
Reducing Balance Depreciation, 85
Reduction of Share Values, 25,26
Replacement Cost Basis, 54
Research and Development Expenditure, 87-88
Reserves, 3-7
Return on Capital Employed, 230-231
Return on Equity, 180
Return on Gross Assets, 180-181
Return on Long Term Capital Employed, 180
Revenue Reserves, 6
Revision, 1-13

Rights Issues, 24

S

Sales to Long Term Capital Ratio, 181
Shareholders' Stake Ratio, 181, 319-320
Sinking Fund, 8
Straight Line Depreciation, 85
SSAPs :
    No. 1, 293-294
          2, 13
          6, 259
          8, 209
          9, 92-99
          9, (Revised) 99-101
         10, 144-146
         12, 84-87
         13, 88
         14, 290
         15, (Revised) 206-209
         22, 89-90
         23, 291-293
Stock Turnover, 183
Stock Valuation, 92-98

T

Tangible Fixed Assets, 84
Tax Shield, 188
Total Asset Turnover Ratio, 186
Trade Marks, 88
Trading Figures, 323-324

U

Unfranked Investment Income, 205-206
Unit Cost Stock Valuation, 93
Usage Basis of Depreciation, 85

V

Valuation of Assets, 84-92
Valuation of Contracts, 98-101
Valuation of Stocks, 92-98
Variable Costs, 69

W

Weighted Average Cost of Capital, 227-228
Working Capital, 125-131, 320-323
Working Capital Ratio, 131
Work-In-Progress (WIP), 10-13

Typeset in 12pt Times by Prima Typesetting, Bexhill-on-Sea, East Sussex for Northwick Publishers.

NOTES

NOTES

NOTES

NOTES

NOTES

NOTES